A Quick
and Dirty
Guide to
War

A Quick and Dirty Guide to War

Briefings on Present and Potential Wars

JAMES F. DUNNIGAN and AUSTIN BAY

WILLIAM MORROW AND COMPANY, INC.
New York

Library of Congress Cataloging in Publication Data

Dunnigan, James F.
   A quick and dirty guide to war.

   Bibliography: p.
   Includes index.
   1. War.   2. World politics—1975–1985.   I. Bay,
Austin.   II. Title.
U21.2.D83   1984   355′.033′0048   84-22797
ISBN 0-688-04199-X

Printed in the United States of America

2 3 4 5 6 7 8 9 10

BOOK DESIGN BY BERNARD SCHLEIFER

To peace

Preface

Wars don't just happen. Organized violence, like the weather, is never a complete surprise. There are signs and long-term trends. You cannot predict the exact outcome of a war or battle anymore than you can predict exactly what the weather will be at noon tomorrow. You can, however, analyze past and ongoing conflicts and use the results to determine the major trends shaping similar current and future events.

No one can predict an outbreak of war by psychic magic or mathematical hocus-pocus. Intelligence analysts, however, can estimate the likelihood of war or armed conflict in the same way meteorologists predict a hurricane. Weather forecasters collect current weather data, compare the most reliable information with evidence gained from past experience, add a large dose of intuition and probability, then stick their necks out and put a storm track on the weather map.

The daily press tends to play down the predictability of wars. This is understandable as sameness does not sell newspapers or induce one to view the TV news. Wars are easier to sort out than the news suggests. This does not imply that all journalists indulge in sensationalism, that is simply not the case, though TV reporting has yet to resolve successfully the conflict between the camera's need for drama and the journalist's commitment to factual reporting. Actually, the problem with the daily press is often that it does its job too well in recording and reporting the events of the last twenty-four hours. Such reports tend to be nearsighted. A sound historical and contextual focus is lost in the magnification of immediate headlines.

While newspapers come to conclusions too quickly, the prediction professionals in think tanks have the opposite problem: They seem never to come to a conclusion. This puts military leaders and citizens in a predicament. The press screams out often sensational predictions and conclusions while government officials are served by think-tank advisers who essentially say that definitive conclusions are impossible to reach.

It's true that no one can predict the future with any precision. At the same time, government leaders, and the citizens who elect them, must plan for and make decisions about the probable future. Military and diplomatic analyses must be made, defense and state department budgets must be planned. Even deciding to do nothing is a decision, and often the least favorable one. How then, do decisions usually get made?

The two primary sources of decision-influencing information, the press and the experts, are used quite differently. The press, while often suspect because of the political leanings of reporters and editors, is highly regarded for its immediacy and the wide range of conclusions it provides. Moreover, press conclusions are in the open and subject to useful criticism and debate. At least this gives the government decision maker and the citizen a variety of analyses from which to choose.

Then we have the experts. There exists within the government a multibillion-dollar-per-year intelligence and analysis community. These are the experts who, with a worldwide network of agents, analysts, and electronic wizardry, are charged with creating an official analysis of present events and future prospects.

This group is responsible only to the decision makers they support, and this creates a curious relationship. These experts, given their enormous resources and professional pride, strive for an academic perfectionism. This often leads to an extensive, expensive, and complex analysis of every topic under study, whether the subject is Russian wheat production, bee excrement, or toenail growth rates of nineteen-year-old corporals. The employers of the experts usually have neither the time nor the experience to grasp all the data they are given. The usual result is unfortunate. The decision makers reach their conclusions based on press information, gossip, and very brief summaries of the massive research done for them: 2,532 pages of analysis and research shrink to a single three-by-five-inch briefing card. Expert information often becomes an after-the-act justification for conclusions the decision makers have already reached. Thus the tail (decision makers' conclusions) wags the dog (research done by the appointed experts).

This absurd situation is caused in part by the security requirements under which the experts operate. One must have a security clearance to work on or review all of the research. Much of this work thus is subject to very little criticism and informed debate. In addition, massive amounts of raw information often tend to blur the situation rather than illuminate it. Common sense gets lost in the metric shuffle of increasingly arcane forms of analysis.

Bureaucratic analyses also suffer from the committee problem. As in any large organization, there are more chiefs than Indians in the intelligence community. All these chiefs must justify their existence and often do so during uninformed debates on the validity of the research done and preliminary conclusions reached.

The research gatherers and analysts (the Indians) are often quite competent and dedicated. So are their superiors (the chiefs). But many potential futures are created with no easy way of choosing the "official" one.

Remember that we are attempting to predict the outcome of wars that have not yet been fought or, if they are in progress, not yet concluded. The potential outcomes have varying implications for the size and compositions of defense budgets and armed forces. The size of these budgets also has serious effects on the economies that produce the funds through taxation. Thus the decision makers' most immediate problem is not how correct their experts are but how well any decisions can be "sold" to other interest groups within the government. Accurate analysis and prediction become secondary to the more immediate problem of getting enough people to agree on a course of action and move forward to a conclusion. The defense intelligence and analysis community fails so often not because of a lack of skill or resources, but because there are so few people with the ability, power, or sheer nerve to choose from the often unpleasant conclusions presented them. Ugly realities are often swept aside in favor of more palatable political pictures. The official version is generally the more expedient, not the most accurate, product of billions of dollars of research and analysis.

Our approach in presenting a lot of data is to be open, straightforward, even simple. We try to explain, but we leave a lot of the interpretation to you. Most of you are citizens, taxpayers (probably), and voters (we hope). What you have here is often no more than many military and political decision makers have available when crucial decisions must be made. As several early readers have pointed out, we have given a complex body of knowledge a manageable form. Observe all, and reach your own conclusions.

This book covers current major wars and violent political conflicts, ongoing and potential. It explores the geographical factors and historical trends affecting these conflicts, takes a look at the human beings involved, then focuses on the present and possible future conflicts.

The key to understanding current wars, and their likely outcomes, is knowledge of the fundamentals. We look at the political, ethnic, and economic makeups of the participating societies, the local geography, the societies' essential history, and the capabilities of their armed forces. This is the foundation for a conflict assessment.

If you can "predict" the past with such tools (and historians have been "predicting" the past and present for centuries), you can expect to have a better understanding of the present and future. Afghanistan, for example, is the world's longest-running, most ancient insurgency. When not fighting foreign invaders, the Afghans fight whichever group is foolish enough to declare itself the government. This has been going on for 2,500 years. The Russians are as unlikely to buck the trend as were Alexander the Great's hoplite infantry.

While this book is nonfiction, it makes many potentially, and one hopes ultimately, fictitious predictions. Portraying the future is a popular spectator sport, but the spectators' wrath will fall on those who fail too often to divine events that have not yet happened.

Our primary technique in predicting the future is first to predict the past, with the idea that the future is an extension of the past. Details may differ, but patterns remain remarkably consistent.

World Wars I and II could be seen incubating in the Balkans, central Europe, and North China. Today the Middle East is the primary source of potential world conflict. How do we know this? We compile data, turn the data into lists employing commonly used geopolitical factors like population and gross domestic product (GDP, or the total value of domestic goods and services produced yearly by a country), sort through the lists, then take a qualitative and a quantitative look at the new arrangements of information. In some cases we applied simple statistical mathematical analyses to the information to create the conflict models that lie behind this book. The war chart at the end of the book, which was prepared through this method, clearly shows that the Middle East in general and the Persian Gulf in particular are steady producers of little wars. Out of such conflicts, world wars grow.

There is nothing mysterious about this technique. Common sense and intuition might tell you that the Middle East is the world's most dangerous trouble spot. However, when all the trends are laid out in a comparative manner, you can begin to get a better picture of why this is true, and where the trouble might lead.

Data about armed conflict are relatively easy to find. Enterprising journalists and opposition politicians spend a great deal of energy collecting and reporting this information. An armed confrontation's causes, however, are often more obscure. History and geography give the best clues. Geopolitical interests rarely change, though sometimes the actors do. People have to eat and find shelter. Nations have to feed their people and maintain some degree of order. Our analysis of the available evidence relies on such primary human concerns. When one gets fancy and tries to guess the reasons for specific actions or policies, one generally walks where the ground is not. Experience teaches the analyst to guess where the ground might be.

There may be a large number of tactical options, but there are relatively few strategies. Strategy usually takes place on such a grand scale that one can guess with reasonable accuracy what strategic path a group has chosen to take. We assume that survival is the basic human strategy. A group of people can become a community of farmers; that's one strategic option for survival. Another group can become a gang of thieves. Although a couple of bad crops may turn the farmers into thieves, trends begin to emerge. The thieves, if they are to survive as thieves, must sharpen their wilier skills. Farmers forced to become thieves have to learn the trade from point zero, or hire some thieves to do their dirty work, another strategy. Farmers harassed by thieves can buy them off, which may work if the thieves are just hungry, or they can fight the crooks. Or perhaps the farmers can hire a few samurai to protect them. (The movie *Seven Samurai* is a detailed look at this strategy.) One can substitute oil for crops, nations for farmers and thieves, fighter-bombers for samurai.

This book focuses on basic strategies. Just as opposing armies keep track of each other by building up data over time, we kept track of a number of conflicts. Patterns begin to emerge. An analyst would call it a picture of the situation. A few good guesses about "state secrets" enhance the picture. Governments attempt to keep military secrets, but over time most of the details leak out. People can't keep their mouths shut.

As we mentioned earlier, weather prediction is a good analogy for this method of forecasting. A computer powerful enough to model all the essential elements of a weather system has not yet been developed. However, we can generate useful weather predictions. Most of them rely on analyses of past weather events. Farming has long been dependent on such crude but useful predictions. It would be helpful but not essential for a farmer to know exactly how much rain there would be in a given growing season. Knowledge of when the first and last frosts will occur would also be useful but isn't absolutely essential. Farmers get by with a weather almanac of past events and an ability to judge the present situation.

Judging contemporary warfare and the potential for future wars is somewhat more complex than judging weather patterns. Herein we provide you with an almanac of past and current events. Add your judgment, and you have as good a means as any for predicting the course of present and future wars.

Acknowledgments

We wish to thank the following people for their help and advice in the research and preparation of this book: Kathleen Ford Bay, Margaret Boeth, Alison Brown Cerier, Jack Dunnigan, Diane Goon, Sonia Greenbaum, James M. Hardesty, Sterling H. Hart, Ken Hoffman, Bonnie Hoskins, John Kohan, Joseph Jacobson, Jim Llamas, Lionel Leventhal, Doug MacCaskill, Ray Macedonia, Jay Maloney, Bill Martel, Steven Patrick, Christina Pogoloff, Allen Rehm, Jim Simon, John Stewart, Dick Weary, and Bob Wood.

The maps were prepared by Marie Frederick of Washington, D.C., with the assistance of Marcia Scott.

We would like especially to thank A. A. Nofi for his invaluable research assistance, counsel, constructive criticism, energy, sense of humor, professionalism, erudition, and particularly his advice on the charts.

Contents

How to Use This Book

Each "intelligence briefing" or chapter consists of ten or eleven complementary sections, plus appropriate appendices. The authors designed this book so that the reader, usually a taxpayer putting up the bucks for the departments of state and defense, has a chance to play the role of highfalutin politico or military officer. In a very real sense the book is an adult role-playing game, with the reader as decision maker and the authors as briefers.

These briefings are not designed to be exhaustive. A briefing without some brevity isn't very functional. The challenge to both authors and reader is to do justice to the complexities of the issues—which entails including a certain amount of detail—while making the information readily available to someone who has to be at work on time. Most people don't have the time to become "experts." The book takes that into account.

Reading each chapter from start to finish will provide a more thorough description of each conflict. We know, however, that many of you will require only certain kinds of information, such as superpower interest in a region. If that's what you want to know, then go straight to the Superpower Interest section in the chapter. If you understand the organization of each chapter and its sections you can then locate the information you want.

INTRODUCTION

Gives a summary of what is covered in the chapter. It also includes a brief description of who is fighting over what.

SOURCE OF CONFLICT

Contains a brief description of how the situation became a conflict. It outlines the major causes of the conflict. We attempt to give a general outline of the situation.

WHO'S INVOLVED

Describes the most important players in the conflict.

GEOGRAPHY

Analyzes the fundamental geographic considerations involved.

HISTORY

Describes some of the more important historical events still affecting the region and takes the situation up to summer 1984. In some chapters (Lebanon and Afghanistan especially) in which there is a lot of history, this portion will be more expansive.

LOCAL POLITICS

Gives an in-depth look at some of the area's more peculiar political participants.

The section deals with personalities and the organizations they inspire. Americans in general lose sight of just how divided a population can be politically. A multiplicity of political parties is the norm in non-Communist countries. In Communist countries, the lack of means of expression often leads to a high potential for violent outbursts from the opposition (Communist or otherwise).

PARTICIPANT STRATEGIES AND GOALS

Takes a practical view of the political-military strategies and options of the players. Draws on information in the entire chapter to synthesize participant aims.

This section tears away the volumes of superfluous detail that usually surround a current conflict. The fundamental issues are usually quite straightforward. While not slighting the numerous undertones of a situation, a clear description of who wants what from whom goes a long way toward putting each conflict into better perspective.

SUPERPOWER INTEREST

Since the superpowers are the most crucial, and dangerous, of the saber rattlers, this section summarizes Russian and American interests and, in some chapters, China's.

A chart compares each superpower's political, military, historical, and economic interests. Each superpower's interest is rated Low, Medium, or High. A glance at the chart quickly shows you how involved a superpower might become in a particular area. When there is conflict in a region in which both superpowers have several High interest ratings, you can be sure serious trouble is not far behind.

POTENTIAL OUTCOMES

Gives the reader a look at possible futures, depending on certain events. Consider this to be the authors' betting line.

COST OF WAR

Estimates the fiscal and human cost of the conflict.

The cost of any war is expressed in two currencies: lives and material wealth. Wealthy nations generally fight a war of matériel. Life is precious, so they can afford to throw wealth into the battle instead of lives. Poor nations have nothing to commit but lives. Wars between nations with material resources are more likely to escalate. Warfare between less wealthy nations tends to be bloodier, assuming the combatants can afford sufficient weapons to fight more than one or two battles.

Even without a lot of weaponry, warfare in poor nations can cause numerous nonbattle deaths. Civilians flee the areas where fighting occurs. Deprived of their normal shelter and sources of food and other support, the refugees are more prone to disease and death. War is hardest on the youngest and the oldest refugees.

When large populations are forced to flee for extended periods, ugly situations often arise in the areas they flee to. Their new neighbors are rarely pleased with the descending horde of strangers. Frictions usually develop which frequently lead to still another war.

The purely wealth-destroying aspects of warfare often have a curious effect. If the population is not seriously depleted and is given some means to rebuild, the result will often be a reconstruction superior to prewar conditions. Losing a war, however, is a very expensive way to revive one's industrial infrastructure.

Still, few people really consider what the differences might be if the destruction of war had not taken place. The afflicted populations usually move forward, carrying their hatred with them. They are guided not by visions of what the future might have been without the war, but by a primordial urge for revenge. Turning that urge into a reality is, over time, the highest cost of any war, for it provides the psychological framework for the next bloodletting.

APPENDICES

For the reader who is interested in more specific information and the sidelights involved in each conflict, "special appendices" are attached to most chapters. The "information packages" in the appendices usually provide more background information or additional analyses. In some cases, exotic items are tossed in so the reader can spice up a dragging cocktail party conversation.

QUICK LOOKS

Short descriptions are given of particularly interesting local situations that we felt should be especially highlighted.

A DATA BANK ON WARS PRESENT AND POTENTIAL

This final part combines all the conflicts discussed in the preceding chapters, plus several dozen other wars, into several truly "quick and dirty" charts. The introductions to these chapters tells how they can enhance the information found in the other chapters.

PART 1

The Middle East

A ring of fire circles the Middle East, from the partisan war for the Afghan highlands to the drizzle of rockets and sniper bullets in downtown Beirut. These ancient lands have become the major battlegrounds of the late twentieth century. The fanaticism, local governmental instabilities, the armaments, and the oil produce a volatile political mixture reminiscent of the Balkans in 1912. The Middle East is the most likely spot for the spark igniting the Third World War. All the elements are there: unresolvable antagonisms, heavily armed adversaries, open fighting on many fronts, and keen superpower presence and interest. The ring of fire could quickly engulf us all.

A long, sad series of ongoing and potential conflicts plagues the region. This section analyzes the seemingly endemic civil war in Lebanon, and the closely related, ongoing armed dispute between Israel and most of its neighbors. The two other major regional conflicts have little to do with Israel. The bloody Iran-Iraq War has caused more death and destruction than all the Arab-Israeli wars combined. The seeds of this ugly war, with its human-wave attacks and chemical weapons, lie in a number of historical Arab-Persian animosities. Meanwhile, to the east and north rages yet another episode in the three-hundred-year-old conflict between Russia and its Central Asian neighbors. This time, the Russians seek to subdue the one Asian tribal group no one has been able to conquer in all recorded history, the mountaineers of Afghanistan.

1. *Lebanon: The Crusaders' Children*

INTRODUCTION

Since 1975 civil war has raged in Lebanon. Israel and Syria have taken sides, sometimes with the same factions.

For a thousand years Lebanon has been an uneasy collection of Christians and outcast Moslem sects. The influx of a million Palestinian refugees since the creation of Israel in 1948 has upset the fragile balance between Christian and Moslem. A dozen or so local religious warlords, with cross or scimitar supplemented by explosives, defend their fiefs' millennium of ethnic and religious identity against (a) an imperial vision of a "Greater Syria," (b) displaced Palestinians, (c) Israeli intrigue, (d) the warlord next door. Involved are armed religious factions, Syria backed by Moscow, Israel, a down-but-not-out PLO, Iranian agents, come-and-go peacekeepers, and the innocent and not-so-innocent caught in between. The chaos and conflict in Lebanon refuse to abate.

SOURCE OF CONFLICT

Lebanon is filled with simplistic historical visions. It is also filled with armed men who believe in them. The U.S. Marines who bivouacked around Beirut International Airport from 1982–1984 were pacifiers and liberators to some, another form of Crusader to others, this time wearing camouflage fatigues instead of armor.

Lebanon in the 1940s, 1950s, and 1960s seemed like an oasis of tolerance where Maronites, Greek Orthodox, Sunni Moslems, and Shiites lived together in a Middle Eastern Switzerland. Arab princes and businessmen from orthodox Moslem countries ogled the girls,

drank, and did their banking. The underground trade with Israel flour-
ished—after all, many Lebanese said, this is Phoenicia, we'll sell to
anybody. But displaced Palestinians living in camps weren't part of the
consensus, nor were the Syrians who envisioned Lebanon as an integral
part of their country. Those who saw Lebanon in the late 1970s got a
glimpse of the eleventh and twelfth centuries; with no outside power in
total control, the uneasy consensus returned to its armed fragments.
Now armies from the east and west meet in on-again-off-again battles.

The current conflict in Lebanon is technologically and politically
complex. Combat ranges from sniping and unorganized street fights to
sophisticated electronic warfare and the use of surface-to-surface missiles. The weapons and tactics reflect the spectrum of battle from neighborhood versus neighborhood to superpower against superpower; in
some cases, however, the local neighborhoods have weapons almost as
sophisticated as those of the superpower troops, and the local soldiers
do have more opportunity and a greater willingness to use them.

The various Lebanese factions have displayed a political savvy
Washington and Moscow have not matched. But then the constant
struggle for political survival has honed their skills. Jerusalem and
Damascus understand them somewhat better. Two problems lie at the
core of the conflict:

(1) What should be done with the Arab Christians, including a
substantial minority of the Palestinian Christians?

(2) Where should the Palestinians go since the creation of Israel?

The agreement of 1932 that gave the then majority of Christian
Lebanese guaranteed control of the major governmental functions has
since been outdated by demographics: Because of birthrates and immigration, the Moslems now outnumber the Christians three to two. The
Palestinian problem is code-named "the overall Middle East settlement." Diplomatic rhetoric, Arab-Israeli wars, and the Israeli invasion
of 1982 have not resolved it. Arabs who openly settle with the Israelis
get killed; Anwar Sadat was shot and Bashir Gemayel blown to bits.

The role of outside peacekeepers in Lebanon is not news. When
Turkish invaders took control in 1517, the local fighting diminished.
Turkish political control in Lebanon was not absolute, and the area still
experienced the occasional factional dispute, one in 1860 being particularly bloody. After the Turkish empire collapsed in 1918, the British
and French, under a League of Nations mandate, kept an imperial
pressure on the local instability. In 1957 American Marines intervened
and took the role of the strong outsider ready to keep the peace.
Vietnam changed the Middle East's perception of the Marines and

produced a United States that was politically reluctant to take unilateral military action.

Today, Syrian ambitions include the reconstruction of Greater Syria. The French and Americans hope for a stable eastern Mediterranean. The Russian demand "for a say in the Middle East" affects Lebanon, both through Russia's support for Syria and the PLO and through covert aid to terrorist organizations. On the political fringe are Iran and Ayatollah Ruhollah Khomeini, who sees himself as Saladin returned to throw the West back across the Bosporus, or perhaps the English Channel.

WHO'S INVOLVED

Syria—President Hafez al-Assad must keep his state militarized to maintain control of the populace. But almost all the Syrian internal political factions have visions of Greater Syria, an idealized state that encompasses Lebanon, Jordan, and Israel. Since the late 1970s, Syria has stationed approximately 30,000 troops in the Bekaa Valley. Of these, 25,000 were officially mandated by the Arab League to keep the peace.

Israel—1982's Operation Peace in Galilee brought the Israel Defense Forces (IDF) to Beirut; consolidation and withdrawal effectively partitioned the country. Troop strength varies, perhaps 12,000 as of summer 1984. Can be rapidly reinforced or rapidly withdrawn (to reappear rapidly).

Arab allies of Israel—Christian and Shiite militias near the border. This pro-Israeli militia has 3,000 men under arms.

Shiites—1,000,000 people, the largest single group in Lebanon. Most Iranian Moslems are also Shiites, giving this group a sectarian connection to Tehran's radical regime. Lebanese Shiites live in Beirut's southern suburbs, South Lebanon, and the Baalbek region.

Iranian-controlled Shiites—Small but most explosive group. The sect takes credit for blowing up the United States Embassy and attacking the French and American peacekeepers. May number as few as 300.

Maronite Christians—600,000 strong, they control a large portion of Lebanon's wealth. Inhabit East Beirut and north-central Lebanon. They are the most powerful of all Christian groups in the Arab world, though by no means are they the most numerous. (According to the best reports, the Greek Orthodox are the most numerous.) At first a schismatic sect named for fifth-century hermit Saint Maron, the Maronites trace their origin to the Orontes River-valley area in Syria (near Hama, one of the sites of anti-Assad Syrian rebellions and massacre of civilians by Syrian government troops). They fled from the Orontes region to escape the seventh-century Moslem onslaught and settled near isolated Mount Lebanon. Some of the Maronites claim ancestors among original first-century Christian converts in Lebanon.

Druze—Islamic sect, 300,000 of whom live in Lebanon. Inhabit the Shuf Mountains, Aley, and Hasbeya. (Over 50,000 Druze live in Israel, 100,000 in Syria, 13,000 in the occupied Golan Heights.) The Druze have served with distinction in the Israel Defense Forces (IDF), and the Israeli Druze have provided support for the Lebanese Druze.

The Druze sect dates from the tenth century. Founded in Egypt by Caliph Hakim of the Shia dynasty of the Fatimids, the sect came to the Lebanese mountains to escape persecution. "Main-line" Moslems consider them to be heretical. The Druze, like the Christians, have been severely persecuted by larger and more powerful Moslem groups. The Druze have a mystical tradition and believe in emanations of Allah and the transmigration of the soul. They also believe Caliph Hakim isn't dead and that he will reappear to lead them to victory and salvation. Only a small minority are ever initiated into the deeper mysteries of the sect. They conceal their beliefs from outside groups, a practice called *taqiyya,* which gives them a strong internal identity and an extreme distrust of outside interference. Nevertheless, they have a long tradition of tolerance for other religious faiths, provided the others leave them alone.

Sunnis—Main-line Moslems, 600,000 strong. They live in West Beirut, Sidon, Tripoli, and Akkar.

PLO—the Palestinian Liberation Organization, the largest Palestinian resistance group. The PLO chairman, Yasir Arafat, has been expelled, several times, but is still a political force. As of summer 1984, may still have 4,000 loyalist troops in Lebanon.

PLO factions—Various groups, most controlled by Syria. Perhaps 20,000 troops.

Palestinians—Either left Israel on their own initiative or were expelled, depending on whose story you hear. Victimized by fellow Arabs, by the Israelis, by the PLO, they wait, hunger, and die in the refugee camps. Approximately 450,000 in Lebanon.

Greek Orthodox—400,000 strong. Christian but not always allied with the Maronites. Live in Al Koura, East and West Beirut. Many claim, with perhaps more legitimacy than the Maronites, to be the descendants of first-century Christian converts.

Armenians—Both Orthodox and Catholic. There are 250,000 living in East and West Beirut and Anjar.

Melchites—Christian sect. 250,000 strong. Live in Christian districts.

Protestants—100,000 (including other Christian minorities). Live in West Beirut (near the American University) and Tripoli.

United Nations and various multinational peacekeeping forces—Italians and Americans, Fijians, Senegalese, Irish, the UN Secretary General, all come and go. The thrust of the mission is to avoid superpower confrontation (no kidding).

France—Deserves a special recognition as a result of long French historical interest and political involvement. In 1536 the Turks recognized the French as protectors of all European and Asian Christians in the Turkish empire. The Maronites have a phrase, which translates as "Truly France is our benevolent mother." In a surprisingly consistent manner, though under a different political guise, France continues to fulfill this historical role.

United States—Strong support for a political settlement and a strong Sixth Fleet (see Participant Strategies and Goals).

Russia—5,000 to 7,000 troops in Syria, manning SA-5 long-range antiaircraft sites (with possibly two battalions of airborne troops for local security). Support for radical groups (see Participant Strategies and Goals).

GEOGRAPHY

Mountains provide safety for their inhabitants by isolating them from outside aggressors. Isolation can also lead to factionalization. Foreigners usually fail to appreciate the mountainous character of Lebanon.

Still, the country's 10,450 square kilometers are remarkably diverse. There are sandy beaches along the coast, fertile valleys, and 3,000-meter snowcapped peaks. Tourist brochures focus on the ancient Phoenician ports of Sidon and Tyre or downtown Beirut, not on the two mountain ranges that enclose the Bekaa Valley. In fact, the narrow coastal strip is rarely more than three kilometers wide.

The Lebanon Mountains rise from the rocky Mediterranean coast. The Anti-Lebanon Mountains in the east, with snowcapped Mount Hermon by the Israeli border, range from the Bekaa to Syria. The Bekaa Valley between them is barely more than ten kilometers wide.

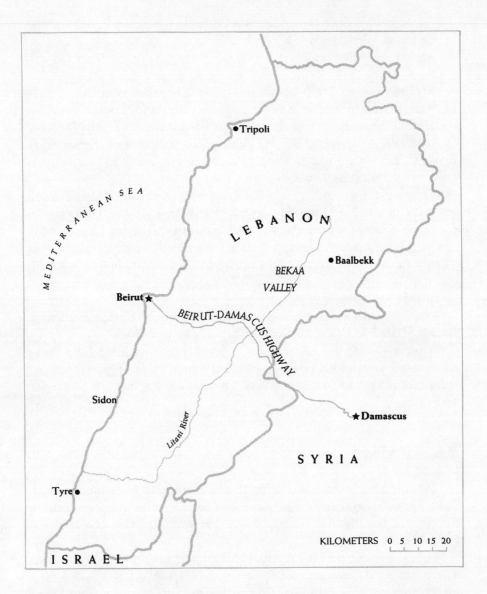

Lebanon at its broadest part is almost 60 kilometers. Its length is approximately 225 kilometers. South and east of Beirut lie the Shuf Mountains, part of the first rugged coastal range; many Druze inhabit this region. North, between Beirut and Tripoli in the Lebanon Mountains, runs a series of rugged east-west valleys (Marounistan), the traditional home of the Maronites. Between the northern port of Tripoli and the Syrian border lies the Akkar, a fertile agricultural plain. The Litani

River drains both the Lebanon and the Anti-Lebanon Mountains via the Bekaa Valley, then bends west to empty into the Mediterranean; the Litani draws a significant political and tactical line across southern Lebanon just north of Tyre. The major east-west route is the Beirut-Damascus highway, a traffic artery easily severed in either mountain range.

The isolation that made the Lebanese mountains attractive to dissidents has been somewhat overcome by civil engineers. Although the road network is primitive by European standards, armored forces backed by infantry can move rapidly through the region. Roadnets are extensive enough that truck-borne terrorist attacks, like that on the U.S. Marine compound at the Beirut International Airport in October 1983, are relatively easy to execute. Finally, strongpoints and fortifications that could slow down or resist Crusader or Moslem sieges cannot stand up to intense air strikes.

HISTORY

Lebanon's once numerous cedars provided the resins required for Egyptian mummification. They also provided the planks for Phoenician ships. Their backs protected by the mountains, the early Phoenicians, from about 1500 B.C. on, used the sea for communication and trade. Carthage, Rome's ancient North African enemy, was a Phoenician colony.

The mountain backlanders were very similar to their Canaanite neighbors to the south; shepherds and subsistence farmers, they worshiped Baal, one of the Old Testament's false gods. For centuries to come, no matter who was the current imperial ruler (Hittite, Assyrian, Roman, Byzantine, Arab, and, later, French and British), the mountaineers were generally left alone as long as they paid taxes and didn't interfere with trade and communications.

The collapse of Byzantine control in the face of the seventh-century Arab Moslem invasion framed the present-day set of affairs. Initially the Moslems were tolerant of Christians and of Jews, whom Mohammed called "people of the book." But this attitude changed. How it changed depends on the religion and ethnic identity of who tells the story, but conflicts erupted, exacerbated by Byzantium's attempts to retake the region.

Though by no means the only Christian sect in the area, the Maronites began to rise in prominence. They saw the Greek Orthodox as direct beneficiaries of Constantinople and the Moslems as the imperialist masters. In the eleventh century the Druze began to enter Lebanon in significant numbers. When the Crusaders arrived in the eleventh and twelfth centuries, the Maronites viewed the westerners as their protectors. The West at that time meant the Western church. In 1180 the Maronites recognized the pope in Rome as the leader of all Christendom. It was a purely political recognition—the Maronite liturgy remained written in Syriac. Later papal decisions were ignored as irrelevant, since communication with Rome often lapsed for years. But the Maronites didn't find bliss with the Crusaders and their subsequent Latin states. The Maronites, along with the Druze, engaged in several rebellions against Crusader knights and mercenary forces.

In 1289 the Sunni Moslem Mamluks of Egypt took Tripoli. After years of fighting the Byzantines and Crusaders, the Mamluks began persecuting the Greek Orthodox; they also went after the Druze. The Maronites seemed to have cut a deal—leave us alone in the mountains and we will pay your taxes. Whether the Mamluks played divide and conquer or the Maronites survived by guile is unclear.

In 1517 the Turks toppled the Mamluks. The Druze became the nominal lords of Lebanon with the Christians as vassals—nominal since the Maronites maintained a strong political and theocratic ministate. Lebanon prospered.

In 1860, responding to a Druze massacre of Christians, the European powers moved to establish a Christian ruler in Lebanon, though one still under nominal Turkish control. Years of relative calm resulted. After World War I, the French were given Syria under a League of Nations mandate and they immediately made Lebanon a separate state. In 1920 the French added several Syrian countries to Lebanon in the Bekaa Valley.

In 1932 a census showed the Christians were in the majority. Based on this census, a system of allocating parliamentary seats and executive positions was established.

In World War II, Lebanon rejected the Vichy government of France and chose to support the Free French and the Allies. As a result, Lebanon became independent in 1943.

In 1957, with the threat of outside intervention from Syria and the then extant United Arab Republic, U.S. Marines entered the country. *Life* magazine published pictures of Marines being greeted on the beaches by bikini-clad sunbathers.

In the early 1970s, after being kicked out of Jordan by King Hussein's Bedouin forces during the Black September War, the PLO entered Lebanon en masse. The fragile political situation once again tipped toward sectarian violence. In several Lebanese villages, the PLO became a de facto government.

Since that PLO *Völkerwanderung,* Lebanon has become a mosaic of religious and political fiefdoms bristling with weapons. The region looks more like a Roman arena than a country. Factional gladiators slay one another for survival. Regional and superpower Caesars sit in the stands—Jewish, Syrian, French, American, Russian, and Iranian, Caesars who put thumbs up or thumbs down. Vague alliances are made, then broken with the thrust of a knife in the back. The American Caesar and the Saudi banker temporarily succor the wounded PLO gladiator, removing him from the arena floor. He slips back from behind the (Iron) curtain. The Syrians' armor-clad Goliath stakes out one end of the arena. An Israeli David controls the other end. This late-twentieth-century David is about five times as big as Goliath and has a better press agent.

Too much tongue in cheek? Perhaps, but the arena analogy conjures up an image that recounting 4,000 years of savagery, intrigue, and manipulation could only begin to suggest.

Here's a look at the arena in summer 1984, two years after the 1982 Israeli invasion: The Israelis occupy the southern quarter of Lebanon, skirting the UNIFIL (UN troops) lines west of Beaufort Castle, crossing the Litani River, and reaching into the lower Shuf region.

The Syrians occupy the Bekaa Valley and the Baalbek region, areas they believe belong to Greater Syria. Since pulling back from around Beirut, the Syrians have rarely left their "old provinces." Fighting outside the Bekaa is conducted by Palestinian groups under Syrian control.

Multinational occupation in and around Beirut has proved to be ineffective, but then international peacekeeping efforts in the Middle East have always been a failure.

The Druze have largely emptied the Shuf of Christian villages. What few remain serve more as bins for hostages than as towns. The Maronites in 1976 purged large numbers of Moslems from East Beirut and the suburbs.

Yasir Arafat may have left Beirut and Tripoli, but the PLO remnants and the various splinter groups remain powerful both in the north and in the Bekaa. They are, however, no longer a de facto government.

Local and international political discussions continue despite endemic cease-fire violations. Governments, alliances, friendships, troop deployments, and phone service are subject to change without notice. Human hope and hate remain the only constants.

LOCAL POLITICS

National Liberal Party (NLP)—Camille Chamoun's Christian-dominated party. Controls the Tiger Militia.

Popular Front for the Liberation of Palestine (PFLP)—Ahmad Jibril's radical Palestinian group.

Phalange Party—Controls the Lebanese Forces militia. May number as many as 20,000 troops. Run by the Gemayel clan.

National Salvation Council—Group set up by Bashir Gemayel to form a national government (under his leadership, of course).

National Unity Government—A collection of warlords who talk and bicker while their militias shoot at one another. It is, however, the best hope for Lebanese who want to end a peace enforced solely by foreigners, i.e., Israel or Syria. As of summer 1984, the NUG was led by Prime Minister Rashid Karami.

Islamic Togetherness—A North Lebanese Sunni Moslem fundamentalist group that advocates public floggings, etc. It seems to be opposed to the Syrians, which is logical since the Syrian Alawites oppress Syria's Sunni majority.

Druze factions—Major group is the National Movement (formerly run by the now dead Kamal Jumblatt). Other splinter and left-oriented groups exist, among them the Progressive Socialist Party. Total of perhaps 15,000 troops. Presently the Druze are backed by Syria.

Lebanese Arab Army—Moslem breakaway faction of the Lebanese Army. At one time numbered 2,000.

Saiqa—Pro-Syrian Palestinian commando group. Strength estimates vary radically from 1,100 to 5,000.

Patriotic Christians—Group of Christians (many Greek Orthodox) from Moslem West Beirut who see themselves as a political alternative to the Maronites.

Moslem Brothers—Also known as the Moslem Brotherhood. Radical Sunni group active in Syria, Jordan, and Lebanon. Ten thousand supporters were slaughtered by President Assad in the Syrian town of Hama in 1981.

Marxist Democratic Front for the Liberation of Palestine (DF)—Marxist Palestinian faction, founded by George Habash, with intimate Russian connections.

Palestine Liberation Front (PLF)—Splinter Palestinian group, neutral during Syrian-PLO rift.

Socialist Arab Labor Party—Lebanese group allied with Habash. Suspected of several assassinations of foreign diplomats.

Guardians of the Cedars—Radical Christian sect, recognized as gifted terrorists.

Amal—Shiite militia group. May have 15,000 troops. Well organized and well armed.

Al-Murabitoun—Sunni Moslem militia unit allegedly supported by Libya. Group was originally formed by Nasserite Arab nationalists. During 1982 unit was largely dismantled by the Israelis, but after the Israeli withdrawal, Al-Murabitoun returned. It has fought street battles with its former allies, the Druze. Al-Murabitoun lost to the Druze.

Arab Red Knights—Radical splinter group of Islamic terrorists with a great name.

Marada—Also called the "Giants' Brigade." Run by the Franjiehs, and located in Zghorta area.

Squad 16—Lebanese security police. Supposedly under governmental control—but then, who's the government?

Hizbullah (also Hazbullah)—The "Party of God" terrorist group, allied with Iraq's Al-Dawa (see chapter on the Gulf War). One of several amorphous but dangerous Iranian-backed terrorist groups capable of dramatic and suicidal action. Others include Islamic Jihad (Islamic Holy War), Islamic Unity, and a half dozen more. Many of them are temporary organizations and alliances of convenience. Their names change from terrorist operation to operation. Islamic Jihad claims responsibility for the attacks on the French and U.S. Marine compounds, on the U.S. Embassy, and on the U.S. Embassy annex. (See appendix The Suitcase from Allah in the Persian Gulf chapter.)

Armenians—Armed, neutral, and left alone.

Red Line Agreements—United States proposals once tacitly accepted by Syria and Israel; date from 1975–1976. Syria could maintain forces in Lebanon but not install ground-to-air missiles or use aircraft to support troops. This attempt to stop factional fighting effectively divided Lebanon into Israeli and Syrian zones prior to war in 1982.

Green Line—Line dividing East and West Beirut into essentially Christian and Moslem zones.

Walid Jumblatt—Son of Kamal Jumblatt, who was allegedly assassinated by the Syrians. Had a reputation as a sophisticated Lebanese playboy, but on his father's death assumed leadership of the Druze.

The Gemayels—Maronite Christian family-clan. Amin Gemayel—

Became president of Lebanon, replacing his assassinated brother, Bashir. Broke Israeli withdrawal agreement under pressure from Syria and factional opponents. Bashir Gemayel—Younger brother of Amin. Bright, articulate, and utterly ruthless warlord. Made chief executive of Lebanon and assassinated by terrorist bombing on September 14, 1982.

The Franjiehs—Major northern Maronite family. Maintain their family names comes from "Franks," as in French Crusaders. Often rival the Gemayel and Douaihis clans. Alleged to have excellent contacts with the Syrian regime.

Mufti Hassan Khaled—Lebanese Sunni Moslem religious leader.

Saeb Salam—Former Lebanese prime minister, Sunni Moslem leader, opposed to Al-Murabitoun.

Nabih Berri—Shiite Moslem leader. Western-educated lawyer with strong American connections. Viewed as a moderate acceptable to Christians and middle-of-the-road Moslems.

Major Saad Haddad—Commander of militia in "The Republic of Free Lebanon," i.e., the border strip north of Israel. Militia is composed of perhaps 3,000 Shiites and Christians. Haddad died in 1984. Some of the pro-Israeli militias have merged into a loose organization called the Army of South Lebanon.

UNIFIL—United Nations Interim Force in Lebanon.

Hamra Street—Beirut drag, lined with lots of pricy French boutiques.

Voice of Hope—Radio station WORD, set up in southern Lebanon border strip. Operated by born-again Christians from California under the aegis of Israel.

Voice of Free Lebanon—Pirate radio station of the Phalange.

Voice of Arab Lebanon—Pirate radio station of Al-Murabitoun.

Philip Habib—United States special envoy and negotiator. As an American of Lebanese Arab extraction, he allowed the United States to play Arab ethnic politics in the Middle East. A skilled, resourceful, and courageous diplomat.

PARTICIPANT STRATEGIES AND GOALS

Maronite Christians—Rely on a tough and brutal private army to exert local control while maintaining strong Western ties, to France in particular. The Maronites want a return to the situation prior to 1975 when they controlled the parliament, the army, and the major government executive posts. This is not likely to happen. Even the United States-sponsored security plans require the Maronites to share power. To the Maronite extremists, sharing means losing. With strong economic backing, they might outlast their neighbors should the factional fighting continue. The Maronites know this, and so do their Swiss bankers. An Israeli attack that drove the Syrians out of Lebanon would boost Maronite fortunes.

Druze—Maintenance of autonomy, which means remaining armed no matter what a political settlement may say. The Druze at one time or another have fought against or cooperated with everyone in the Middle East. They have shown they can survive alongside the Israelis and the Syrians as long as they are allowed to maintain their own communities and religion. They will not submit to a political solution that denies them either. Strange as it may seem, given their intense fighting against the Maronites, the Druze still have more in common politically with the Christians than with either the Israelis or the Syrians.

Lebanese Sunnis—Avoid coming under the yoke of Syria's Alawite-ruled government. The Sunnis have a major stake in a stable self-governing Lebanon, but they have been torn between the demands of the PLO and the Israeli invasion. They have tried to stay out of the cross fire and, with Saudi help, might try to pick up the pieces.

Syria—Maintaining an active presence in Lebanon does several things:

(1) It keeps Syria militarized and makes it easier for Assad's Alawite Moslem minority to stay in control (dictators need external enemies). (See in next chapter, Local Politics, Syria.)

(2) It perpetuates Syria's image as the key front-line state in the confrontation with Israel, and deflects extremists' criticism from the unofficial Syrian-Israeli agreement that has made the Golan border with Israel as quiet as the border between Vermont and New Hampshire.

(3) It keeps alive the possibility of absorbing the Bekaa and Baalbek regions into the Greater Syria that Assad believes is his imperial right.

(4) It provides as a side benefit the opportunity to make the PLO into an arm of the Syrian Army. Arafat was his own man. His retreat from Tripoli made Syria the master of the armed Palestinian cause.

Iran—Lebanon's a wonderful place to throw bombs at the Great Satan's, the United States', Embassy and Marines.

Israel—Security is the name of the game, which means keeping the northern border out of 130-mm artillery range (about 40 kilometers).

Ben Gurion dreamed of having a Christian state as an Israeli neighbor, but the Israelis are painfully aware that a Christian state would be small and not economically viable.

The Israelis want:

(1) Recognition by the Lebanese government (something Bashir Gemayel was prepared to do).

(2) A comprehensive security arrangement that will destroy the PLO. Occupation of southern Lebanon costs lives and shekels; Israel can waste neither. Israeli-backed Arab militias, such as the late Major Haddad's, may be the next best bet.

Russia—Needs a demonstration of the effectiveness of its arms, something to compensate for the 85-to-1 aircraft-loss rate sustained during the 1982 Israeli invasion of Lebanon. Eighty-five MiGs biting the dust was terrible PR for Russia's most important export, weapons. Still, retaining some control over Syria is the most important political aim. If Syria kicks out the Russians (as Egypt did), then their only clients in the Middle East are South Yemen and Libya, and even the Russians don't consider Qaddafi reliable. The mutual defense pact between Syria and Moscow, from the Russian perspective, must be supported with arms and, if necessary, troops. But the Syrians may want the treaty to serve primarily as a deterrent to outright Israeli or United States invasion. From the Syrian government's cynical perspective, 7,000 Russians in Syria can be handled, if necessary, by the Syrian Army; 70,000 cannot. Thus the Russians are left supporting directly, indirectly, and often very indirectly, small radical groups whose capabilities are limited to terrorist action and some street fighting. Supporting such groups, however, does keep the pot boiling and keeps America off-balance.

United States—Ultimately the United States wants the Arabs to recognize Israel's existence as a state. This means solving the Palestinian problem. Reagan's plan involving Jordan had a great deal of merit. The Jordanians would have assumed a central negotiating role for the Palestinians, with the aim of turning the West Bank into an autonomous Palestinian region administered by Jordan. An Israeli monitoring "presence" (euphemism for troops) might have been somewhere in the deal. But diplomatic and economic leverage do not work on fanatics. Nor does one Marine amphibious unit dug in around the airport—as the United States learned painfully. Marines became terrorist targets. The United States strategy of arming Israel to the teeth, arming Jordan and Egypt, promising protection to the Persian Gulf states, then jawboning Arab moderates is about the best that can be managed, but there are policy enhancements that entail possible benefits and certain risks.

Any United States economic and political tilt toward Iraq, vis-à-vis the Iran-Iraq War, plays on deep Syrian fears of Baghdad. The traditional rivalry between Syria and Iraq involves border disputes, relative military power, and the prestige of leadership in the Arab world. Iraq is at Syria's back door, geographically and politically. And there is also the lingering possibility of American intervention in Lebanon. No matter how bitter the partisan rhetoric in the United States regarding whether or not to use American troops or how committed the current United States government may be to not using combat forces, no responsible political Middle Eastern leader—especially a calculating leader like Assad—can ever rule out their use. The U.S. Navy makes a big impression. Libya's Colonel Qaddafi calls the U.S. Navy the world's number one terrorist force. It frightens him. It reminds others that the American giant, though often fumbling and frequently kicked, has, in the final analysis, a very long and powerful arm. The United States won't allow a radical anti-American government in Lebanon. And in a game like Lebanon, the threat of military trump is a valuable political card.

SUPERPOWER INTEREST

	Political	Military	Historical	Economic
Russia	High	High	Low	Low
US	High	Medium	Medium	Medium to High

Political—The Russians' last strong client in the Middle East is Syria. United States prestige and past guarantees of Lebanese sovereignty make the region a priority.

Military—Israeli destruction of Russian arms carries great political clout since Russia's trump is its willingness to send guns and ammo. The U.S. Sixth Fleet and Israel (as well as Egypt and Jordan) are the preponderant military forces in the eastern Med.

Historical—Russia is more interested in Turkey than in Lebanon. American historical interests lie farther south (in Israel) and began in 1947. But support for Lebanese stability has a track record in Washington.

Economic—Lebanon is of little consequence to the Russians. American interests vacillate with the situation in the Persian Gulf.

Willingness to exercise power is important in the Middle East, and the Arab oil states require lots of reassurance that the United States is willing to either apply power itself or do it through surrogates.

POTENTIAL OUTCOMES

1. 40 percent chance: Lebanon is partitioned. Southern Lebanon below the Litani becomes a quasi-military state run by Israeli-backed Christians and Shiites. The Bekaa, Baalbek, and northern Lebanon, including Tripoli, become a province of Syria. Sidon, the Shuf, and West Beirut become a Moslem state with an autonomous Druze region. The area from East Beirut to Tripoli becomes a Maronite Christian state. Diplomatic terms for this include "cantonization into confessor states."

2. 15 percent chance: Factional fighting continues and after more bloodletting, a political accommodation is reached. The Maronites lose parliamentary power. If Israel alone withdraws, chance drops to 10 percent; if Syria withdraws, goes to 25 percent. If both Syria and Israel withdraw, goes to 40 percent.

3. 15 percent chance: Same situation as outcome 1 vis-à-vis Israel and Syria, but the remaining Lebanese state does not become fractured.

4. 10 percent chance: United States peace plan is accepted by the Lebanese and mutual withdrawal of Israeli and Syrian troops arranged. Goes to 15 percent when Khomeini dies; to 40 percent if United States tilts to Iraq; to 60 percent if Sunnis in Syria rebel against the Alawites or if threat of rebellion is very serious.

5. 10 percent chance: Syria attacks and absorbs all of Lebanon. Stops Israeli counterattack (politically more than militarily) and gives Israel assurances it will close border to terrorists as it has along the Golan. If this happens, there will be a long guerrilla war waged by Lebanese factions.

6. 5 percent chance: a Maronite victory: 5 percent chance: a Druze victory. Bloodbath occurs with either Maronite-Phalange or Druze-Moslem victory.

COST OF WAR

Since late 1975, approximately 50,000 have been killed, several hundred thousand injured, and over $50 billion in expenses and losses, just for the Lebanese. Since 1976–1977 the Syrians have committed nearly 30,000 troops to occupying portions of Lebanon. This has cost them over $100 million a year, much of this subsidized by Russia. After the 1982 Israeli invasion, another $300 million a year in Israeli expenses must be added. Add several more hundred million in expenses and the losses of the other foreign peacekeepers and helpers, and you have a $100 billion war. You could have paid each Lebanese family $50,000 not to fight.

WARLORDS AMONG THE CEDARS

Lebanon has existed in a state of war since 1975. It is a civil war in which the nominal Lebanese government plays a minor role. The current Lebanese War is very much a private, even free-enterprise affair. Numerous private armies, led by charismatic warlords, settle their differences with firepower rather than reason. Given the long-standing conditions in Lebanon, this is not an unreasonable state of affairs.

Throughout its long history, Lebanon has rarely governed itself. The foreign powers that traditionally controlled Lebanon, just as Syria and Israel are attempting to do today, did so loosely. Internal government was left to whichever groups were capable of maintaining order and collecting taxes.

Each of the many ethnic groups rallied around its own leader. These local lords provided protection from all kinds of dangers, economic and military, that foreign and other Lebanese ethnic entities could project.

The peace was maintained by private militias. The majority of their members were part-time soldiers. The combat strength of these militias was and is largely defensive. Against a superior enemy, they use terrorist tactics.

The current situation is more violent because both sides are well financed, particularly by outside powers, and thus are able to maintain more full-time fighters equipped with more firepower.

Because the war has eliminated many jobs, the opportunity to be a full-time, well-paid militiaman is appealing. There are also psychological incentives like serving one's people, obtaining revenge, or having a little adventure.

The presence of so many armed partisans of one cause or another usually created a balance of terror that was quite effective in keeping the peace. Most grievances were literally not worth going to war over.

Long periods of peaceful, but armed, coexistence were thus interrupted by short, vicious periods of conflict. During these civil disorders, imbalances caused by major shifts in population and/or wealth were confirmed. The current unpleasantness is another of these adjustment periods.

The warlord culture in Lebanon arose from the antagonistic relationships that have long existed between the various ethnic groups. Most of these groups originally fled to Lebanon to escape persecution. They usually distrust central governments, and most of them believe that the Lebanese government won't look out for their welfare. Hardened by constant struggle to survive, these groups generally choose effective leaders and form efficient fighting forces.

Warlords in Lebanon are not an alien presence, nor are they a particularly odd social development. Armed factions with warlord leadership usually are a natural outgrowth of people seeking security in an insecure environment.

2. Israel and the Middle East: Babies, Shekels, and Bullets

INTRODUCTION

Israel's many wars with its Arab neighbors have not brought about a permanent peace. The military situation remains unsettled, with a potential for large-scale conventional, and even nuclear, war.

The participants in this situation read like a *Who's Who in the Middle East*, plus the superpowers and every nation dependent on Middle Eastern oil. In 1947 Israel fought Saudis, Jordanians, Egyptians, Syrians, Palestinians, and a few Iraqis. In 1956 Israel once again fought the Egyptians, who deployed Palestinian units in their army. In 1967 Israel fought Egypt, Jordan, Syria, and a host of Arab combat contingents supplied by Iraq, Libya, and Algeria. In 1973 the Israelis took on the Egyptians and the Syrians, both once again supported by a scattering of Arab contingents. The terror war against Israel involves the Palestinians and contingents of guerrillas from across the globe, including Japanese Red Army fanatics and German terrorists. In the 1982 Lebanon War, Israel tangled with the Palestinians, the Syrians, and practically every armed faction in the entire Middle East.

Put simply, Israel is growing stronger militarily and weaker economically. An internal Israeli economic war is being waged between fiscal needs and the demands of defense. The Arab population grows faster than the Jewish. Long-standing differences among different Jewish ethnic and religious groups cause more divisions within Israel. In terms of producing a wider war, like World War III, any full-scale combat involving Israel remains the most dangerous in the Middle East.

SOURCE OF CONFLICT

The basic source of conflict is the very existence of Israel and the dispersal of its former Palestinian inhabitants. The Middle East is an area of long memories and tenaciously held grudges. Three major (and several minor) wars have been fought over this issue since 1945. Israel has been victorious every time. Yet the antagonisms remain, and new ones have arisen.

Any Middle Eastern war involving the State of Israel has the potential of escalating into a worldwide conflict. United States commitment to Israel's survival and Russian support for Israel's most militant opponents mean that any local war could become a superpower confrontation. So far Israel has more than held its own in the political arena and mastered its opponents on the battlefield.

But there are subtler kinds of combat, the demographic and economic wars that Israel and dozens of other countries have yet to master. Ultimately, motherhood is mightier than either the pen or the sword. Demographic combat—the battle of human population statistics—can beget several problems. Here are a few examples.

A population boom brings more mouths to feed, as in India. There can be more workers or more dissidents, as with Russia and its Moslems. If a nation is being built out of struggle, population growth can bring either more soldiers or more guerrillas. South Africa faces this prospect, as does Zimbabwe with the Matabele. A slowdown in population growth can mean having not enough soldiers, as is expected for West Germany in the 1990s. In democracies a population increase can result in more voters to appease—and these new potential voters may be culturally or ethnically different from the groups currently in power. The problem isn't unique to democracies. Totalitarian societies fear rapid increases in nondominant ethnic groups (for example, Russia and its majority of non-Russian groups). Either traditions change or revolutions erupt.

Israel, with a Jewish population of 3.5 million, faces two kinds of potential problems. The most obvious is Arab population increase. Arabs number 15 percent (approximately 500,000) of the population in the State of Israel proper. Some of these Arabs are pro-Israeli Druze. But in the occupied West Bank, 30,000 Israeli settlers mix with at least 800,000 and perhaps as many as 1.15 million Arabs. Extreme Zionists talk of annexing the West Bank, calling it biblical Samaria and Judea.

To do so would create a huge demographic shift unless the Israelis completely displace the Palestinians. NOTE: In 1981 the total Arab population of the occupied zones of Gaza and the West Bank was 1.15 million.

Palestinians average 5 children per family; the Israeli average is 2.7.

Some Israelis dispute the notion of the demographic time bomb, citing figures of Arab emigration from the West Bank of some 20,000 per year, but these people seem to have been the wealthier Palestinians, and the number appears to be dropping.

The other political population problem Israel faces is even more subtle. The Ashkenazim, the Jews of Europe, who are currently in political and cultural power are slowly being outnumbered by the Asiatic and African Sephardim. Finally, immigration into Israel, the staple of Israel's huge Jewish population increase, has begun to level off.

Then there's the economic war. The horrendous inflation rate in Israel shows that this is one fight Israel is losing.

Overwhelming military superiority vis-à-vis one's neighbors, such as that enjoyed by Israel, can be an expensive kind of staying ahead of the Joneses. Tanks exact not only a huge initial capital cost, but also high fuel and maintenance bills. Do you buy tanks, build roads, buy butter, or support a government bureaucracy? War costs money. You can continue to print shekels, but unless the amount of "work and value" in the country reflects the number of shekels circulating, inflation results. Losing an economic war may be slower and less dramatic than losing a shooting war, but the effect can be just as devastating.

And finally there is that shooting war. At present Israel has an overwhelming military advantage. But new and more sophisticated weapons are coming into Arab hands. Examples are SA-5s in Syria, SS-22s in Syria, AWACS in Saudi Arabia, and 7,000 Russian troops presently billeted in Syria.

What Does This Mean?

Josiah, King of Judah, fought the forces of Necho, King of Egypt, on the plain of Megiddo. Josiah took a couple of arrows and died. This story is covered in the Old Testament (II Chronicles). Megiddo is better known by its New Testament name, Armageddon. The battle of Armageddon, according to some interpretations of the prophecy, will lead to the destruction of the earth.

Various "plains of Megiddo" have been identified in the nexus region of Israel, Lebanon, and Syria. Identification of the specific piece of dirt doesn't matter; what does matter is that this is one of those regional conflicts (like central Europe) that could lead to World War III. World War III means nuclear-armed opponents will be squaring off. It doesn't take a revelation to realize how dangerous that is.

WHO'S INVOLVED

Israel—Is Israel a democracy under siege by PLO terrorists and intransigent Arab neighbors, or a European colony of Jewish Crusaders?

Egypt—The most populous Arab country. Cairo signed a peace treaty with Israel, then the peace went "cold."

Jordan—King Hussein is caught between Arab radicals, Arab money, and Israeli military might.

Syria—Visions of Greater Syria (see chapter on Lebanon), a threatened dictatorship, and militant pan-Arabism lead Syria into constant struggle with Israel. But the Golan border remains quiet and free of terrorists.

United States—The United States moral commitment to Israel is real. American arms and dollars support Jerusalem. Or is it Tel Aviv? The American Embassy remains in Tel Aviv because the United States doesn't want to offend the Saudis. The United States wants to have Israel and it wants to have peace. The United States wants to buy Arab oil. The United States wants Arab allies. The United States wants a lot.

Russia—Moscow supported the creation of Israel, but Arab disenchantment gave Russia the opportunity to win friends by supplying arms. Then the Arabs started paying for the arms, which was even better for the cash-strapped Kremlin. And the Middle East is such fecund ground for upsetting United States diplomacy.

Palestinians—Dispersed around the Middle East, some throw bombs, most just suffer. They suffer at the hands of Israelis and at the feet of other Arabs.

Wild Cards

Iraq—A less militant Iraq (perhaps bled by the Gulf War) could open the door to a "moderate Arab settlement."

Saudi Arabia—Money can't buy happiness or peace, but it can act as a prod. The Saudis have been paying off everybody because they're scared of everybody.

Lebanese factions—Lebanese conflict could topple everyone's house of cards (see chapter on Lebanon).

Super Wild Cards

Iran—Successful spread of the Islamic Revolution could topple moderate regimes.

Libya—Arab atomic weapons could bring out the nukes Israel has stashed.

GEOGRAPHY

Israel is surrounded. That's the Israeli point of view.
Israel is (choose any or all):

(1) A Zionist dagger in the side of Arab political unity.
(2) A European-Zionist-Crusader dagger in the side of Arab unity.
(3) An American-Zionist dagger in the side of Arab unity.
(4) A necessary enemy; otherwise Arabs would only be fighting each other.
(5) A disheartening reality that could be ignored except for those obnoxious Palestinians.
(6) A tough Zionist bunch that, like it or not, must be lived with.
(7) All of the above. (the Arab point of view)

The map shows that Israel *is* shaped something like a dagger, 20,000 square kilometers' worth—the Red Sea port of Elath at the point, the Negev Desert as a double-edged wasteland, Jordan to the east, and the Sinai to the west.

Up north it begins to get complicated.

The Jordan Rift Valley, with the Dead Sea to the south, and the Jordan River and Lake Tiberias (the Sea of Galilee) to the north, not only separates the West Bank from Jordan but provides a militarily significant division. Operations in the valley are hindered by extremely broken terrain, a veritable badlands. The Dead Sea, at a −396 meters below sea level, is the lowest point on the planet.

The central hills of Israel and the West Bank are also broken and

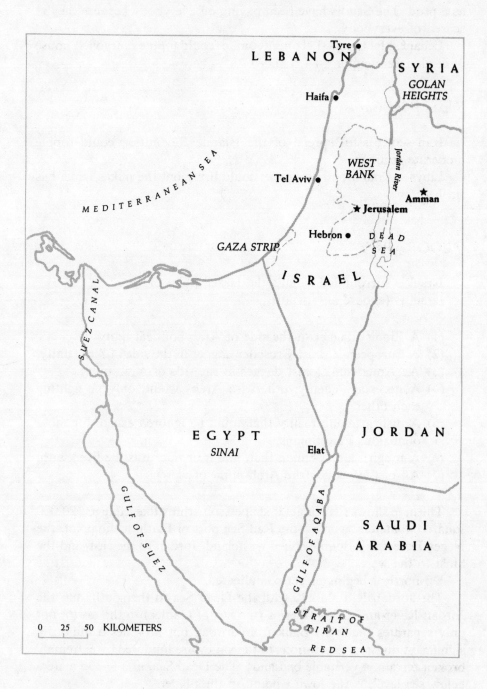

rugged. Agriculture is an iffy proposition, given the scarcity of water and the area's rockiness. On the coastal plain, north to south on the Mediterranean, are the major transportation arteries, the Tel Aviv metropolitan area—and the occupied Gaza Strip. The coastal plain, like the Negev, is agriculturally productive if sufficient water is available for irrigation.

Jordan, on the other side of the river, lies on the Arabian Plateau. Most of its present territory, 91,000 square kilometers, not including the West Bank, is open desert. In fact, 88 percent of the country is desert waste. Bedouin nomads inhabit the desert. Amman, however, is a large, modern, urban area. The western area of Jordan has a large number of Palestinians and a substantial Arab Christian community. Over 90 percent of Jordan's 2.3 million inhabitants are Sunni Moslems.

Jordan has few natural resources. Several oil companies have explored the eastern provinces, but unlike Iraq to the east and Saudi Arabia to the south, Jordan has yet to show any significant petroleum reserves. In 1984 Jordan made two new oil strikes in the Mafraq region near the Iraqi border. The field may contain enough oil to meet Jordan's domestic needs, but will take several years to develop.

The Golan Heights border region is characterized by difficult, buckling mountains that rise from Israel and meet the Damascus plain. Syrian guns on the Golan Heights shelled Israeli farms for twenty years; 130-mm guns sited in the hills can almost reach the seacoast. This is why the Israelis are very reluctant to withdraw from the Golan even if Syria were interested in negotiating.

The Israeli-Egyptian border (from the Negev to the Sinai) is characterized by large sand plains and broken, rocky terrain. The interior of the Sinai Peninsula is broken by mountains and a number of rocky mesas. The southern tip of the Sinai juts into the Red Sea. The Strait of Tiran, between Sinai and Saudi Arabia, controls sea traffic into the Gulf of Aqaba. Egyptian threats to close the straits to Israeli shipping or actually to close down the strait entirely, as in 1967, have figured in all three major Arab-Israeli wars.

HISTORY

Contemporary Zionism, the political movement dedicated to the creation of a Jewish state in the old biblical homelands, was given its framework in the nineteenth century by Theodor Herzl. Jews settled the Ottoman-controlled Palestinian region, always with the ultimate

intention of establishing their own state. The Palestinians didn't like the
Ottomans either, but they wanted a Palestinian state as well as a Bedouin state (somewhere across the Jordan River and then south into the
Arabian Peninsula) free of Turkish control. World War I, the British
and French defeat of the Turks, Lawrence of Arabia, and the conquest
of Syria by Arab tribes allied to the West created a political situation
characterized by several mutually exclusive goals. Britain's 1917 Balfour Declaration promised the Jews a "Jewish home." But the Brits had
also promised the Arabs their own states. The way Britain's League of
Nations mandate was drawn created further problems. The Turks made
the East and West banks of the Jordan part of the same administrative
district. Under the mandate, the west zone came under a British admin-
istrator while the east became the semiautonomous state of Transjordan, an emirate that included large portions of present-day Syria.

Essentially, the defeat of the Ottomans left the Arabian Peninsula
and the Holy Land vulnerable to any politician with an itch to draw
new maps. Significant numbers of Palestinians ended up in Jordan,
Israel, Lebanon, and Syria. Several riots and armed exchanges between
Jews and Arabs occurred during the 1920s. Jewish leaders demanded
that the Balfour Declaration be carried out, asserting that the Emirate
of Transjordan was effectively an Arab state, so where was the land for
the Jews? The British and French put off a response to that demand
until Hitler's Holocaust made Western opposition to a Zionist state
impossible. Jewish rebel activities, like Irgun terrorism, also had an
effect. But the Arab League didn't agree. Palestine had been Arab since
the Prophet's imperialist forces overran the Jordan Valley; except for
the period when Latin Crusader states hung around for a couple of
centuries. Israel looked like the work of Jewish Crusaders backed by
the West.

With postwar Britain and France retreating from colonies, "backed
by the West" came to mean "backed by the United States." America
gave Israel weapons, money, and strong moral support. Arabs needed
weapons and Russia was ready. Russian willingness to send weapons
has proved to be the basis of a working relationship, though almost all
Arab countries have no love, and less trust, for Moscow.

These armed client states, Jewish and Arab, cannot be controlled
by their superpower supporters. The presence of radicals willing to
engage in worldwide terror campaigns further complicates the situation. Russian troops in Syria and American troops in the eastern Mediterranean (whether currently on ship or shore) raise the political and
military antes.

As for more recent events, the 1982 Israeli invasion of Lebanon left everybody in disarray, including Israel. The PLO is divided into several factions, with the strong anti-Arafat rebel sect effectively controlled by Syria's Assad regime (terror now has an address, at least according to the Israelis and the Americans). Arafat has become the "Wandering Jew" of Middle Eastern diplomacy, but he's a waif with an international reputation and a strong influence among West Bank Palestinians.

Jordan looks at the Syrian arms buildup and winces. The country's large Palestinian population creates a dangerous situation. Moderate factions press King Hussein for help in setting up the West Bank as an autonomous region, but radicals could turn any agreement Hussein makes into a call for his assassination and a civil war in Jordan.

Syria and Israel are at loggerheads in Lebanon. Lebanon is at loggerheads with Lebanon (see chapter on Lebanon). The Golan Heights border is as quiet as the Swiss border—real stability and respect exist there; no terrorists cross that zone.

Egyptian criticism of the 1982 Israeli invasion of Lebanon finally provided a diplomatic opening to the Islamic Conference, but Egyptian readmission was inevitable. Egypt's size, power, and prestige could not be ignored. And Egypt did not deny the Camp David accords. Egypt is using the peace to improve its agriculture, to modernize its army, and to sidestep Islamic fundamentalists.

The Gulf War has sapped Iraq (see chapter on Iran-Iraq War).

Inflation in Israel vacillates between 120 percent and 200 percent. Some estimates go as high as 400 percent yearly inflation. Any government in democratic Israel that imposes too much austerity could be toppled by a no-confidence vote in the Knesset.

Defense is gobbling up from 30 percent to 35 percent of the Israeli GNP (gross national product). The Labor-Likud coalition government faces economic strains and internal ideological and political frictions. It is likely to be a short-lived, rocky marriage

Significant Dates

May 14, 1948—Israel declares its independence; the simmering conflict with its neighbors breaks into total war—the Palestine War. Four armistice agreements are reached between Israel and Egypt, Jordan, Lebanon, and Syria. But no general peace agreement, or recognition of the Jewish state, is made.

October 1956—Israel invades the Sinai and occupies the Gaza Strip as Britain and France invade the Suez region—the 1956 Sinai War.

June 1967—Egyptian President Gamal Abdel Nasser sends nearly 100,000 troops and 200+ tanks into the Sinai; he asks the UN to withdraw its UNEF peacekeepers and they depart. The Strait of Tiran is closed to Israeli shipping. Israel launches an "anticipatory counter-offensive" against Egypt and its war-ready allies, Jordan and Syria. Israel takes the Sinai, the Golan Heights, and the West Bank—the Six-Day War.

November 22, 1967—UN Security Council Resolution 242 calls for an end to warfare by all states in region, territorial integrity, and political independence; sets guidelines for Israeli withdrawal from areas seized in 1967 War.

October 1973—Egypt and Syria attack Israel during Yom Kippur. Egyptians cross the Suez Canal and inflict a surprise defeat on Israeli counterattackers. Light Israeli forces on the Golan are almost overrun by Syrian armor. Israelis counterattack and cross the canal into Africa. Israeli counterattacks punish Syrian forces. War ends with Egyptian Army in Sinai surrounded. Russia threatens to intervene and the United States responds with a worldwide general alert, including nuclear retaliatory forces—the October War.

November 1973—UN Resolution 338 calls for a lasting peace based on negotiations; followed October War.

November 1977—Sadat visits Jerusalem. Camp David agreement ends the state of war between Egypt and Israel.

May–June 1982—Israel launches Operation Peace in Galilee into Lebanon; at first a small series of moves on the northern border, it eventually breaks out into a full-scale two-day war between Israel and Syria. Israelis shoot down 85+ Syrian aircraft with the loss of one Israeli plane.

LOCAL POLITICS

Israel

Likud Party—The right-of-center Israeli party. Composed of Liberal, Herut, and La'am factions. Never held power until 1977 when Likud's Begin became prime minister. Militant policies have a broad appeal among Sephardic Jews who have been oppressed under Arab or pro-Arab regimes.

Labor Alignment—Left-of-center party. Contains Labor and Mapam factions. Regarded as party most likely to achieve a settlement based on granting a Palestinian homeland. Composed primarily of Ashkenazim.

Religious splinter parties—Extreme Orthodox parties support Likud.

Other splinter parties—Include Communist Party, socialist factions.

Ashkenazim—Jews of European origin.

Sephardim—Jews of Asian and African origin.

Histadrut—General Federation of Labor, Israel's all-encompassing labor, economic, and industrial organization. Over 65 percent of Israel's workers belong to Histadrut.

Mossad—Israeli intelligence service.

The Irgun—Underground Jewish resistance and terrorist group. Fought against the British and Arabs from 1945 to 1948.

The IDF—Israel Defense Forces (the army), now the holy of holies. Soldier for soldier the best tactical army in the world. Only Jews and Druze Arabs are subject to the Israeli draft; the Druze have decided to submit willingly to conscription (see chapter on Lebanon), since the Druze are considered heretics by the other Moslems anyway.

Syria

Arab Ba'ath Party (Socialist Resurrection Party)—Dominant Syrian party. Upper echelons controlled by Alawites (see chapter on Lebanon). Colonel Rifaat al-Assad's relationship with his brother, President Hafez al-Assad, remains murky, though he may still be his brother's choice as heir to Syrian power. Rifaat seems to spend a lot of his time in Switzerland. Rifaat commands the elite Special Defense companies. His rival, General Ali Haidar, commands the Special Forces. The Special Defense companies and the Special Forces spend a lot of time warily watching one another. The situation gets even more intense. Ten percent of the Syrian population, the Alawites, dominate the remaining 90 percent (85 percent Sunni Moslem, 5 percent Armenians and others). Several reports maintain that President Assad is ill. Syria, for all its might, could experience a bloody power struggle. Israel is a necessary enemy that focuses would-be rivals on an external threat.

Other parties—Syrian Arab Socialist Party, Arab Socialist Union, Unionist Socialist Party, Communist Party.

Moslem Brotherhood—Has actively opposed the Alawites, especially President Assad. Has instigated at least three armed rebellions in Syria which the Syrian Army crushed.

Jordan

Arab National Union—Sole party allowed in Jordan's constitutional monarchy.

The Arab Legion—Jordanian Army. The best in Arab world, largely Bedouin, personally loyal to Jordan's king. Can be regarded as the real army of Saudi Arabia, since the Jordanians have been the Arabs' best soldiers and they have close ties to the Saudi throne. This is one reason the Saudis heavily subsidize their brethren to the north.

September 1970—"Black September," when Palestinian radicals tried to take over Jordan. A Syrian unit participated, disguised as a Palestinian force. The Jordanians defeated the Palestinians and later expelled all PLO guerrillas. Both the PLO and the Jordanians remember this date.

Iraq-Iran War—Jordan has been a solid Iraqi ally, supplying Iraq through its port at Aqaba and allowing Iraqi warplanes to use Jordanian air bases.

Egypt

New Wafd Party—Center-right opposition.

Arab Socialist Union—Official government party.

National Democrats—Majority party in power.

Socialist Labor Party—Center-left opposition.

National Unionist Progressive Party—Pro-Russian opposition.

Liberal Party—Right-wing opposition.

Communist Party—Party of Communist labor.

Moslem Brotherhood—Egyptian branch. Armed, dangerous and devout. No sense of humor when it comes to religion.

Palestinians—Most visible representative is the PLO (Palestinian Liberation Organization), which is wracked by factionalism and fratricide. Some West Bank mayors have tried to carve out a separate, non-PLO international position.

PARTICIPANT STRATEGIES AND GOALS

Israel—Hang tough against Arab terrorist groups by continuing reprisal tactics. The Israelis seek to extend political ties to Egypt, including increasing trade and technical assistance for agriculture and industry). Punish Syria when it gets too militant in Lebanon. Goals are primarily recognition by Arabs of its right to exist as a state; consolidation of West Bank frontier; destruction of radical terrorist factions who launch attacks upon Israelis.

Egypt—Try to end its theoretical isolation in the Arab world (knowing that because of its size and power it was never truly isolated because of Camp David); develop a stronger moderate base that might include Jordan and some PLO faction (and end the "unanimous vote" policies that prevail in the Arab League and Islamic Conference meetings that only play into the hands of intransigent radicals). Primary goals are recovery of position as dominant Arab country; control and suppression of Islamic fundamentalist groups within Egypt; development of Sinai oil fields; development of Egyptian economy; protection of Egyptian Western Desert and Sudan from Libya (see chapter on Libya, appendix Desert Fever).

Jordan—Continue to pursue a moderate line that fends off attacks by Arab radicals and Israeli annexation of the West Bank. Primary goals are resolution of Palestinian question that does not entail dismemberment of Jordan; control and suppression of Islamic fundamentalist groups within Jordan; protection from potential Syrian aggression.

Syria—Continue to walk the militant line against Israel, which ensures all radical Arab support and keeps Syria militarized (see chapter on Lebanon). Primary goals are resolution of situation in Lebanon with incorporation of the Bekaa Valley into Greater Syria (again see chapter on Lebanon); return to Syria of the Golan Heights; recognition of Syrian leadership of the Arab world. The ultimate goal is annexation of Jordan and Palestine into a "complete" Greater Syria.

Palestinians—Try to use world opinion to improve conditions under Israeli occupation. Radicals will continue their terror war and try to recover from their defeat in Lebanon by the Israelis and by Syrian-backed Palestinians. Their goals are more divergent. Moderates seek a Palestinian state independent of Israel. Radicals seek a Palestinian state and the destruction of Israel.

SUPERPOWER INTEREST

	Political	Military	Historical	Economic
Russia	High	High	Medium	Medium to Low
US	Very High	Very High	Medium	Medium

Political—Russia has lost so many times in the Middle East (Egypt, etc.), and recovered without any long-term damage, that Moscow is still interested. But this isn't Poland. United States domestic political commitment to Israel makes the area a hot issue.

Military—Great testing ground for Russian weapons, which are prestige exports for Moscow. Expanded Russian use of Syrian naval bases is a secondary military consideration. Unbalancing the West and adding problems to overall Persian Gulf defense raise the stakes. The United States wants stability in the region, enforced by the Sixth Fleet. Israel, and possibly Egypt; and the United States commitments are long-term.

Historical—Russia would like to get to the Mediterranean, but Turkey or the Balkans are historically preferred routes. United States interest begins in 1947; prior to 1947 the area was the concern of Britain, France, the Crusaders, et al.

Economic—Political prestige is tied to economic effectiveness and weapons sales, but the Russians are already in a position to acquire Arab oil via Afghanistan and Iran. The United States can live without the region, even without Saudi oil, but Western Europe and Japan cannot—this could be a High rating if one concludes the United States cannot live without Western Europe and Japan.

POTENTIAL OUTCOMES

Note: a 90 percent sure thing—Israel will withdraw from Lebanon; only the day of departure is undetermined. The West Bank is a different story. Israel cannot stay, occupy, and incorporate the West Bank and keep an Israeli demographic superiority. To incorporate the West Bank would mean to abandon democracy. But with Arab refusal to recognize Israel's right to exist, there appears to be small hope for a long-term solution. For future-watchers we offer these possibilities. However, the Middle East is a difficult subject for probability equations. A radical with a weapon and the will to use it is an ultimate variable.

1. 38 percent chance: Status quo with Israeli withdrawal from Lebanon (perhaps a few forces left along the border with Lebanese allies). Israeli economy suffers further; perhaps border areas of West Bank are incorporateed into Israel.

2. 17 percent chance: Israeli-Syrian War. If this occurs, there is a 15 percent chance of escalation into a major all-front war. 95 percent chance of an Israeli victory; 65 percent likelihood that Assad's Alawite minority is toppled from power as a result of a loss; and a likely replacement government is a Syrian Sunni-majority government. The result: an increase in Jordanian ability to negotiate a West Bank settlement. If there's a Syrian "victory" and Israel is not destroyed, look for no negotiations of any kind. The Israelis would give up nothing and the Arabs wouldn't budge, since they could anticipate Israel's defeat in the next round of fighting.

3. 15 percent chance: Jordan, Egypt, and some PLO moderates form a negotiating team. Jumps to 55 percent if outcome 2 leads to toppling of Assad regime and Assad is replaced by a Syrian Sunni (and secular) government. If this happens, there's a 50-50 chance that a Palestinian entity is created on the West Bank. Israel retains "defensive settlements," there's no Arab militarization, Jordan is in charge of Palestinian foreign affairs.

4. 12 percent chance: Jordan and Syria go to war. If this occurs, there's a 60 percent chance that Israel will intervene on Jordan's side with air power.

5. 8 percent chance: Egypt renounces Camp David. Results in a 20 percent chance of a major war. All Israeli-held land becomes "non-negotiable"; probably no significant negotiations on anything for over a decade.

6. 8 percent chance: There's an armed Palestinian revolt on the West Bank. If this occurs, a 25 percent chance exists of an internal settlement between Palestinians and Israelis, giving Palestinians autonomy with security guarantees to Israel; a 70 percent chance of a bloodbath; a 5 percent chance of mass Palestinian expulsions into Syria by the Israelis.

7. 2 percent chance: Israeli economy comes to a halt and United States demands a West Bank Palestinian state as the price for aid; 6 percent chance this happens if there's a Labor government in Jerusalem.

The Mushroom Beyond the 100th Percentile: We're not into predicting the millennium or Armageddon (that's for theologians, prophets, and religious salesmen); however, the existence of nuclear weapons in the region creates two dangerous possibilities. Case one is an Arab-versus-Israel nuclear war. The initial warheads could fly from either direction. These would be small-yield, aircraft-delivered A-bombs or small warheads on SCUD-type battlefield missiles. This rates a 5 percent chance if a major war occurs. Case two is a general nuclear war between the United States and Russia as a result of an Arab-Israeli war. As long as the Arab-Israeli conflict stays conventional, there's less than a 1 percent chance of a superpower conflict. If the Arab-Israeli war goes nuclear, the chance of superpower participation jumps to 85 percent. If the superpowers fight in the Middle East, there's a 10 percent chance of superpower nuclear warfare. There's also a chance of the terrorist-delivered nuke. This would be the suitcase from Allah; see the appendix by that title in the chapter on the Persian Gulf-Arabian Peninsula. We offer no percentage on this event. Suffice it to say that there are many people in the Middle East who would use a nuclear weapon if they could get one. If these people did get hold of one, it's a sure thing they would try to use it. Mossad, the CIA, et al., are on the watch for this eventuality.

COST OF WAR

The human toll of over 100,000 dead and injured is dreadful. The economic toll could be considered equally grim. Most nations can get away with spending only 5 percent of their GNPs on defense. Israel, and its fractious neighbors, spend at more than twice that rate. Since the 1948 creation of Israel, the Israelis have spent over $200 billion in war-related defense expenditures. Total Arab military expenditures have been in the $350–$400 billion range. The damage to crippled economies may double the actual economic costs.

If Peace Came, What Would Be Fought Over?: Many commentators focus on the Arab-Israeli conflict in the Middle East without realizing that this dispute is only one of many in the region. What would be the patterns of conflict should the Arab-Israeli dispute be solved?

The first thing to consider are those differences that divide peoples in the Middle East: ethnicity, politics, religion, history, and wealth.

(1) The major ethnic groups are Arabs, Egyptians, Europeans, Africans, and Aryans.

(2) Political differences range from orthodox Marxism to unfettered capitalism.

(3) The major religious groups are Moslems (of various kinds), Catholics (Orthodox and Roman), and Jewish (Orthodox and non-Orthodox).

(4) A plethora of ancient territorial claims exists in the region, claims driven by ideas like Greater Syria, the Persian empire, the "leader" of the Arabs, and Greater Egypt.

(5) Then there is the division between the very wealthy and the poor.

Each of these divisions has in recent memory been the cause of armed conflict. The Arab-Israeli differences stem from a combination of many of them. The primary elements are ethnic (European Jews moving in on Palestinian Arabs), political (socialist Jewish settlers displacing basically capitalist Palestinians), religious (Jews dominating Moslem and Christian Arabs), and wealth (the rich Arabs generally fled Palestine in 1948, leaving the poor Arabs and Middle Eastern Jews to envy the wealthier European and American Jews).

Even while the Arab-Israeli conflict continues, all these other conflicts increase in intensity. Internally, Israel has increasingly visible antagonisms between poor Middle Eastern Jews and wealthier European Jews.

The wealthier Palestinians have dispersed throughout the Middle East where they have become unpopular with the economically less successful locals. These Palestinians are also politically suspect in the wealthy Persian Gulf kingdoms, which have become dependent on their skills.

The disparities of wealth are a fundamental cause of disputes throughout the Middle East. When combined with religious and ethnic differences, a volatile mixture is created. The Iran-Iraq conflict springs from this combination. The presence of oil wealth in Iran created class, religious, and political differences which destroyed the shah's government and produced the radical religious government of Ayatollah Khomeini. Similar differences produce potential conflicts in the Arabian Peninsula, between Libya and Egypt, and elsewhere.

When two parties have a dispute, they will go to war only if one feels that it has a chance of success. No one feels they have a reasonable chance of success against the Israelis. This was a significant factor in producing peace between Egypt and Israel. Warfare, then, is much more likely in disputes that do not involve the Israelis.

The Israelis themselves are most threatened by internal conflicts, particularly those created by the fiscal havoc military spending is causing the economy and internal societal relationships.

Why Israel's Relative Military Power Increases: Many Israeli soldiers, particularly the younger ones, consider themselves the professional heirs of Heinz Guderian and the *Panzertruppen* of World War II. This appears to be more than a bit ironic, but perhaps only superficially so, since the troops hold Guderian's military professionalism in high regard, not Nazi politics. The proud and successful Israeli armor troops note two critical differences between themselves and their German models: They will not persecute Jews and they will not ultimately lose their war.

Religion and ethnic heritage have much less to do with military competence than do education, technical skill, and leadership. The Israelis have all three. As individual fighters, the Arabs are not outclassed by the Israelis. However, when it comes to creating technically competent, well-led, and resourceful combat units, the Israelis have the edge.

Events like those in the 1973 October War have honed the Israeli edge. The Egyptians trained hard, planned carefully, and, at least in the early stages of the war, were well led. After the 1967 War, many Israelis thought that they had an innate military superiority over the Arabs. In 1973 this overconfidence and contempt cost them many lives. Nowadays, any Israeli soldier who attempts to rest on past accomplishments is brought up sharply with a reminder about 1973.

It is difficult to maintain a superior military capability during peacetime. This is true for the Arabs as well as the Israelis. A large pool of highly educated, technically skilled manpower gives Israel an advantage. The Arab nations are torn between training scarce technicians to prepare for war or training them to build the peacetime economy. The usual solution is to attempt both and accomplish neither. As the weapons become more complex, the Israeli advantage widens.

The leadership gap also continues to widen. The Israeli armed forces, while not entirely neutral politically, are not nearly as involved with running the government as their Arab counterparts are with theirs. The battlefield performance of political soldiers is usually dismal compared with that of purely military officers.

The Arabs are catching up in one area. They are piling up more equipment. This is the least significant aspect of battlefield power. New Arab military equipment just gives the superb Israeli Army something new to capture.

3. The Persian Gulf and the Arabian Peninsula: Ring of Fire Around Arabia

INTRODUCTION

The Persian Gulf is surrounded by oil fields and battlegrounds. Ancient antagonisms between Arabs and Persians (Iranians) and more recent disputes between conservative religious groups and socialist reformers ignite several conflicts, such as the big war up north between Arab Iraq and Persian Iran. Little wars down south, between radical groups and conservative religious governments, are sparked by the same hot passions. And the oil, the lubricant for the industrial economies of Western Europe and Japan, adds fuel to the fire. The various antagonists read like a membership list of OPEC (Organization of Petroleum Exporting Countries). This situation is the *raison d'être* for the RDF (Rapid Deployment Force, now called the Central Command), the United States's fire brigade, which, if used, may get there in time to stir the ashes. All the combat, historical tensions, strategic interests, and intrigue combine to create the potential for World War I-level casualties and Great Depression-style economic dislocations.

SOURCE OF CONFLICT

The Persian Gulf is the site of global and regional conflicts. First and foremost, there is the strategic tug-of-war between the West (the United States, Japan, and Western Europe) and Russia over control of oil-supply lines. Second, there are a number of petty but lethal inter-tribal and ethnic squabbles that have existed for centuries. In the past these squabbles weren't so deadly. Now, however, everyone is armed with automatic weapons and tanks. Some of the participants have first-rate jet fighter-bombers and tactical missiles capable of carrying chemical and nuclear warheads. And some of the participants have used chemical weapons and reserve the right to use them again.

The Gulf War between Iran and Iraq is the latest manifestation of an old conflict between the Persians and their neighbors over control of the mouths of the Tigris and Euphrates rivers—the Shatt al-Arab. This fight has reoccurred with some regularity since at least 500 B.C. In the current conflict, supersonic aircraft, Exocet antiship missiles, and modern tanks mix with human-wave infantry attacks led by religious zealots. These high- and low-tech forces, tied to inadequate logistics systems that are incapable of supporting sustained offensives, produce high-casualty attrition combat along a static front. Call it World War I in the salt marsh and sand.

The Gulf War, however, is just one of several ongoing or quiescent wars in the nations that circle the Persian Gulf and the Arabian Peninsula. Energy and geography make political conflict and subterfuge between these countries worldwide concerns. The tiny nation of Oman sits at Saudi Arabia's back door. It also covers the south side of the Strait of Hormuz, that delicate neck of the Persian Gulf. Just west of Oman lies the People's Democratic Republic of South Yemen, a Marxist client state of Russia. Oman and South Yemen waged a quiet little "camel war" for almost ten years (roughly 1972 to 1982). South Yemen received boatloads of Russian equipment and a large number of East European combat advisers. The Omani Army got a better deal. They received a brigade of the late Shah of Iran's imperial army and a small but very effective group of British Army instructors.

North of South Yemen lies Yemen. Twice in the last decade South Yemen has invaded Yemen, once allegedly accompanied by Cuban advisers. But invading Yemen is nothing new. During the 1960s, the Egyptian Army, at Nasser's direction, waged a bitter war in Yemen. Egyptian aircraft dropped Russian chemical bombs on Yemeni royalist tribesmen and inflicted huge casualties. The guerrilla resistance, under the spiritual leadership of their imam, forced an Egyptian withdrawal. (See Afghanistan chapter for what seems to be a similar situation.)

Then there's the big prize, Saudi Arabia, with its cousins, the United Arab Emirates (UAE), little brother Kuwait, a couple of oil-soaked sandpits named Bahrain and Qatar, and a Saudi offspring named Aramco. Theology was kind to Saudi Arabia, for it was the original home of Allah's Prophet, Mohammed. Geology was kind to Saudi Arabia, leaving it with 150+ billion barrels of crude. Saudi Arabia is also the temporary home of nearly one million Yemeni workers who are treated as very second-class citizens. This makes the Yemenis, along with a restive Shiite minority in Saudi Arabia and Bahrain, receptive to the Islamic revolutionary gospel being spread by the ayatollah's followers.

The revolutionary appeal of Islam exacerbates these local conflicts. As of fall 1984, a Shiite revival, led by the Iranians, has been sending religious shock waves throughout the region. Twenty years from now, Sunni purists could stage an uprising. Iraq, whose leadership is predominantly Sunni Moslem, has a population that is Shiite by a narrow majority. The Iranians have tried to co-opt the Iraqi Shiite community. (See appendix to African chapter on the revolutionary appeal of Islam.)

WHO'S INVOLVED

The Gulf War

Iran—Supported by Syria and Israel. The latter has sold Tehran spare parts for United States weapons. Tehran is also buying weapons from North Korea.

Iraq—Supported by Jordan, Saudi Arabia, and France.

Wild Cards

The Kurds—This central Asian tribal group has been waging a war against both Baghdad and Tehran. Iraq may offer the Kurds an "autonomous province" in exchange for their support.

Saudi Arabia—The Saudi support for Iraq so far has been solid. During one six-month period they were giving Iraq $1 billion a month.

Russia—Moscow has tried to sit on the fence. Russian arms have been sent to both Iran and Iraq, but the alleged Russian shipment of mycotoxins to Iraq, for the chemical munitions used by Baghdad, sent an ominous signal to Tehran.

The Arabian Peninsula

Oman—Supported by the UAE, Saudi Arabia, and Great Britain.
South Yemen—Supported by Russia and Eastern Europe.
Yemen (also called North Yemen)—South Yemen's other target.

Saudi Arabia—Had two armed clashes with the South Yemenis in 1969 and 1973.

Russia—Has maintained an increasing naval force in the Indian Ocean. Has treaties with a number of countries in the area.

United States—Has stated intention of intervening militarily should the need arise. Exact nature of this need has never been defined.

Wild Cards

Cuba—Has been helping train terrorists in South Yemen. In 1984 there were 20,000+ Cuban troops across the Red Sea in Ethiopia, engaged in killing Eritreans and Somalis in support of the Ethiopian dictatorship run by Russian ally Colonel Mengistu.

Iran—The shah sent troops to help Oman. The Islamic revolutionary regime wants to have complete control over the Strait of Hormuz; the Iranians could attack Oman.

Pakistan—The Pakistani government has sent a large number of technicians and soldiers to serve as mercenaries throughout the Arabian Peninsula.

Jordan and Egypt—If the United States equips a Jordanian strike brigade to support weak gulf states, Jordan becomes an even more significant player. Egypt, as the largest Arab nation, could see the need to act should Saudi Arabia be threatened.

GEOGRAPHY

Let's start below the ground with a little oil geography. On the Arabian Peninsula, immense structural traps of Mesozoic Age carbonates like limestone hold the world's biggest deposits of oil. Saudi Arabia's Gawahr field (also spelled Khawahr) holds over 80 billion barrels of crude. (A fraction less than ten billion barrels were found in Alaska's Prudhoe Bay oil field.) Down south in the Oman mountains, the fields are in the comparatively puny 1.5-billion range, in other words, huge by any standard.

In Iraq, Iran, and Kuwait, the subsurface is a little different. Kuwait's oil is held in sandstone deposits instead of carbonates; and in Iran, faulting makes locating new oil fields more difficult. But in an era of fossil-fuel-powered economies, the presence of lots of oil increases the

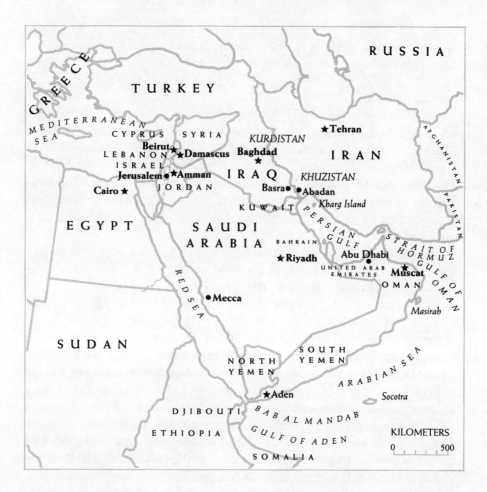

strategic significance of the sand and mountains aboveground, where the oil pump sits.

Key terrain includes the Shatt al-Arab, the combined delta area of the Tigris and Euphrates rivers, which divides Iraq and Iran. Also important are the Strait of Hormuz and Bahrain Island.

Control of the Shatt al-Arab has been one of the most basic reasons for Arab-Persian conflicts.

Bahrain Island lies near Saudi Arabia midway between the Strait of Hormuz and the Shatt al-Arab. Any government in Bahrain unfriendly to the Saudi monarchy would seriously threaten Saudi Arabia and the UAE.

The terrain around the mouth of the Shatt al-Arab, in the Basra-

Abadan-Khorramshahr area, consists of mud flats, marsh, salt flats, and salt marsh. Upriver the country becomes increasingly rugged and dry. The northern border area of Iran and Iraq is cut with rugged mountains and hills. The Kurdistan region also has this kind of mountainous terrain.

Iraq has an area of 438,000 square kilometers and a population estimated at 13 million, slightly more than half of whom are Shiite Moslems. Iran has an area of almost 1.65 million square kilometers and a population of 40 million, well over 75 percent of whom are Shiites. The Baluchis in eastern Iran make up a large and potentially anti-Tehran minority. Prior to the revolution, the capital city of Tehran had a population of about four million. Accurate current population estimates are unavailable.

Kuwait, tucked between Iraq and Saudi Arabia, is 18,000 square kilometers of desert. Tiny Bahrain (680 square kilometers) consists of six islands, the main one called Bahrain. The terrain is sandy with a low interior plateau. Qatar (11,000 square kilometers) is flat, barren desert. Slightly less than half of the 250,000 people living in Qatar are Arab, 20 percent are Pakistani, 20 percent Indian, and 10 percent Iranian. The United Arab Emirates (formerly called the Trucial States or the Trucial Coast) are a federation of seven Arab states: Abu Dhabi, Dubai (where the federal city, Dubai, is located), Sharjah, Ajman, Umm al-Qaiwan, Ras al-Khaimah, and Fujairah. Less than 20 percent of the 1.2 million people living in the UAE are citizens of the emirates; the rest are guest workers or immigrants without citizenship status. The terrain is desert. The southern boundary of the UAE runs into the Rub al-Khali (Empty Quarter) of Saudi Arabia. The boundary is undefined. In fact, almost all the borders on the southern end of the Arabian Peninsula are undefined. The Rub al-Khali borders of Oman, South Yemen, and Yemen are not drawn. Oman and South Yemen are separated by an administrative line. Yemen and South Yemen share an indefinite desert boundary.

Oman, the elbow of the peninsula, is approximately 300,000 square kilometers—the size approximate since no one is sure of the borders. This is a legacy of the desert nomads who moved through the backcountry at will and encountered arbitrary notions like borders only when they entered the coastal cities. Part of Oman is separated from the rest of the country—the Musandam Peninsula, which juts into the Strait of Hormuz. A third of the world's daily oil production sails through this passage. The Strait of Hormuz, the narrow channel between the tips of

Oman and Iran, is the throat of the Persian Gulf. The deepest part of the channel lies on the Omani side, and is traversed by outgoing oil tankers. The strait narrows to 50 kilometers, or even less if various Iranian and Omani islands are taken into account. Antiship-missile batteries, firing Exocet-type missiles, or long-range guns sited on these islands can easily close the gulf to merchant shipping, but mines are the weapon of choice, as they don't expose people or aircraft. A long coastal plain stretches northwest of Muscat. Mountains lie in the interior. Foothills and dry desert extend to the south and west. Oman, bordering the Arabian Sea, benefits from the summer monsoons. Of the 850,000+ people living in Oman, almost half are of the Ibadhi Moslem sect, the rest are either Sunnis or Shiites. Sizable Indian and Baluchi Pakistani communities live in Muscat and Matrah.

South Yemen has a population of almost 1.8 million. Covering 290,000 square kilometers, the terrain consists of a flat and sandy coastal zone with a mountainous interior. The administrative line dividing South Yemen and Oman moves from the low coastal zone, through rocky, dry country, into the mountains and desert. Aden is the capital of South Yemen and its major city. The city of Aden is unusual compared with the rest of the Arabian Peninsula and the South Yemeni hinterland in that it has a large foreign (African, Indian) population and a strong labor union movement.

Yemen has a population of nearly six million. Twenty-five percent of the Yemenis work outside the country as emigrant labor, most in Saudi Arabia. Most of the country's 195,000+ square kilometers are very mountainous. There is a 64-kilometer-wide coastal strip along the Red Sea. The mountainous interior is well watered and supports intensive agriculture. The tallest mountains are over 3,600 meters high. Sana, at an altitude of 2,130 meters, is the capital. Yemen was once the largest part of the ancient Kingdom of Sheba.

Saudi Arabia is approximately one third the size of the continental United States (2,330,000+ square kilometers). Exact population figures are hard to find, but there are approximately 8.7 million people. About seven million are Saudis. Riyadh, with a population of 1.8+ million, is the capital. Desert of some form or other—sand, plain, rocky waste—covers the land. The country has no permanent rivers. There are five principal areas: the northern region near Jordan, which is desert populated by Bedouin nomads; the al-Hasa (Eastern Province), which borders the Persian Gulf; the Najd region, where Riyadh is situated; the Asir, a mountainous area on the southern Red Sea coastline; and the al-Hijaz (Western Province) region, bordering the Red Sea. Mecca, Islam's most holy city, is located in the Hijaz.

HISTORY

The Gulf War

Persia has occupied Iraq three times since 1500: 1508–1514, 1529–1543, and 1623–1638. Boundary disputes, specifically over the Shatt al-Arab, and old enmities (see appendix on Arab Versus Persian) caused the wars. In 1639 both parties signed the Treaty of Peace and Frontiers, a peace ensured by tribute money paid by Baghdad to the Persian shah.

But that failed to resolve the border problem.

In 1818 war broke out again, also over the Shatt al-Arab. The first Treaty of Erzerum (1823) failed to resolve the dispute again. In 1847 Britain and Russia tried to stop an impending Persian-Ottoman war (the Ottomans took the part of their Arab vassals) over the river mouth and imposed the second Treaty of Erzerum. Abadan, Khorramshahr, and the eastern bank of the Shatt became Persian. The Ottomans received sole control of Zuhab Province, an area that for almost two centuries had been under Persian military occupation.

But these efforts failed to resolve the border problem.

The failure of the 1911 Tehran Protocols, the collapse of the Ottoman Empire after World War I, Iraqi independence, and the Persian refusal to acknowledge the new Arab state produced a chaotic boundary situation. The Kurds exacerbated things by conducting guerrilla actions against both Arabs and Persians. The Kurds didn't acknowledge any border anyway. In 1936 the Iraqis made several concessions that set the boundary in midchannel on the thalweg line. The Persians guaranteed the Shatt would be open to Iraqi shipping.

This agreement held until Iraqi nationalists came to power in 1958. They regarded the agreement, with some justification, as a sellout of Arab interests. When the radical Ba'ath Party took control in 1968, its nationalist program included a demand for the "return to Iraq" of the Arab-populated areas of Khuzistan. The Ba'athists called for Arab resistance to Iranian authority in Khuzistan.

The Iranians returned the favor by sponsoring anti-Iraqi activity by the Kurds. By 1976 a full-scale Kurdish rebellion against Baghdad was under way. The Kurds received the backing of the United States.

Iraq harbored a fugitive the Shah of Iran didn't like—Ayatollah Khomeini, an influential Shiite priest turned revolutionary leader. The Iraqis wanted the Iranian border to be closed to Kurdish rebels and the shah wanted the ayatollah out of the region to keep him from stirring up Shiite activists. A deal was cut, but events proved that sending Khomeini into exile in France wasn't going to solve the shah's internal problems.

The regime of Saddam Hussein in Baghdad saw the chaos that followed the fall of the shah and the establishment of the extremist Islamic Revolution as an opportunity to settle the border problem in Iraq's favor. Successful flexing of Iraqi military might would also forestall any Iranian attempts to promote the Islamic Revolution among Iraq's Shiite community.

The Gulf War began in August 1980 with a direct assault into Arabistan by Iraqi tanks and motorized infantry. The very modern Iraqi offensive soon degenerated into static, 1915-style attrition warfare. The Iranians fell back, reinforced the line with student revolutionaries organized into Revolutionary Guard units, then counterattacked with armor and human-wave assaults. The war stalled. Iran refused various Iraqi peace overtures. From late 1983 through 1984 the war has remained stalled, with the Iranians holding salients inside Iraq. The Iranian strategy of pitting human-wave attacks (often including children armed with assault rifles) against the Iraqi defensive positions began slowly to weaken the Iraqi Army. Iraq responded to the World War I tactics with a World War I weapon—chemical agents. The Iraqis used liquid mustard (either HD- or HN-series chemicals), allegedly laced with mycotoxins similar to the chemical agents the Russians have used against the Afghans. The deadly genie of gas warfare was once again out of the bottle.

In summer 1984 this full-scale conventional war continued. Iran launched lurching, foot-infantry offensives. Iraq responded with carefully laid ambushes. Air and armor forces have been used piecemeal; as a result, they are very ineffective.

Oman and South Yemen

The South Arabian states have a history of antagonism between the nomads in the hinterland and the more worldly coastal dwellers. Religion was usually the nominal reason for their squabbles. These bandit-level affairs tended to flare suddenly, then die a negotiated death after a half dozen or so principals were beheaded. Negotiated settlements usually involved promises of obeisance to the sultan and some yearly tribute. Political sides didn't really exist with any more definition than borders drawn in blowing sand. The sand hasn't changed, but the situation has. South Arabia possesses a decidedly strategic position, with easy air-and-sea access to East Africa, the Indian Ocean, the Red Sea, and the Persian Gulf.

Fighting among leftist groups (1965–1968) left the British protectorate of Aden in chaos as Britain withdrew from the colony. The National Liberation Front (NLF), a coalition of socialists and Communists, won the street battles and established a new government in November 1967. In June 1969 the radical Communist wing of the NLF took control.

The Communist regime in South Yemen has tried several times "to open Saudi Arabia's back door." So far, the South Yemenis have failed miserably, though not for want of death and destruction. South Yemen served as the support agency for the Palestinian attack on an Israeli tanker in the nearby Mandeb Strait (Bab al-Mandeb) in 1971. The southerners have fought pitched battles against Saudi forces inside Saudi Arabia (1969 and 1973). In the early 1970s a number of guerrilla and terrorist training camps of the Palestinian Liberation Organization (PLO) and the more radical Popular Front for the Liberation of Palestine (PFLP) were set up in South Yemen.

South Yemen's longest sustained combat was with Oman. Beginning with political sponsorship of dissident residents of Dhofar, the South Yemenis began to supply arms and troops to the Dhofar Rebellion along with East German and Cuban military advice. They also set up an Omani "government in exile," indicating they had a bigger goal than Dhofar. The Dhofar War began in the early 1970s, with full-scale guerrilla battles in 1972 and 1973.

In 1973 the Shah of Iran offered his paratroops to the Sultan of Oman. In September 1973 nearly 1,000 of the 3,000 active Dhofari rebels defected to the Omani government, just as the Iranian-led offensive began to hit back. In December 1973 and early 1974 offensive operations by the shah's paratroopers laid the groundwork for the rebels' defeat, though the fighting dragged on into 1975. Omani units in the Dhofar also operated with British advisers. Jordan also sent military support units. Some Iranian Army advisers remained in Oman until the fall of the shah.

In 1979 South Yemen signed a treaty of friendship with Russia. Oman accused Russia of providing renewed support to the would-be rebels. In 1979 there were reportly 800 to 1,000 East Bloc military advisers in South Yemen.

Sporadic fighting erupted in Dhofar in 1979 and 1980. In late 1980 and early 1981, South Yemeni troops made several raids across the administrative line.

South Yemen also has an on-again-off-again border war going with Yemen. In February 1979 South Yemeni mechanized forces, allegedly accompanied by East German and Cuban advisers, attacked Yemen and took the villages of Qatabah and Harib. Fighting took place as deep as 60 kilometers inside Yemen. The United States responded by sending aid and equipment to the Yemeni government in Sana. Fighting renewed in October and December 1980.

Yemen and South Yemen, despite the fighting, have discussed unification on several occasions. The problem, according to most Yemenis, is South Yemen's professed communism. Moslems regard communism as incompatible with their religion. The urban Communist elites may be in trouble if they fail to stem the Islamic Revolution the Iranians plan on exporting to South Arabia.

Oman is currently receiving new United States and French equipment along with United States and European training groups. The British have been by far the most effective trainers. South Yemen continues to serve as a major terrorist training base. The old British naval base of Aden is increasingly used by Russian ships. The Russians are improving sea and air facilities in South Yemen.

Islamic revolution in Kuwait, Bahrain, and the UAE continues. Ayatollah-inspired assassinations and bombings have severely disrupted these rich Arab states. Propaganda directed at gulf-state Shiites has so far failed to ignite a revolution, probably because the Shiite Arabs don't care very much for the Persians, and the chaos in Tehran isn't as appealing as domestic peace.

LOCAL POLITICS

Iran

Islamic Republican Party—Ayatollah Khomeini's political front. Completely dominated by the priests (mullahs).

Revolutionary Guards—Iranian youths forming the Islamic revolutionary army. Were used to purge the remnants of the old imperial army. Now operate as political and military shock troops.

Tudeh Party—Iranian Communist Party.

National Front—Ill-defined anti-Islamic republic opposition group composed of a few remaining supporters of the shah, and some liberals who supported the interim Bakhtiar regime after the shah's fall. Operates out of France.

National Council of Resistance—Anti-Islamic republic group composed of liberals and leftists, a large number of whom once supported Khomeini. Former President Bani-Sadr, the only man in the entire 3,500-year history of Persia who was ever democratically elected to any national office, is involved with some individuals in the National Council of Resistance. Most members of any consequence are in exile in France.

Khuzistan—Iranian province, also called Arabistan, with a large Arab minority (30+ percent); the province also has enormous productive oil fields.

The Great Satan—The United States. The Lesser Satan is Russia. Other minor Satans have included France, Iraq's Saddam Hussein, Israel, etc. They are Satans because of their support for the shah, for the Tudeh Party, for Western values, and for pushing Russian atheistic domination, etc.

Iraq

Arab Ba'ath Party—Iraqi element of Arab Ba'ath socialist party. Bitterly at odds with Syrian Ba'athists.

Kurds—Border-area ethnic group between Iran and Iraq (see map); major political organization is Kurdish Democratic Party (KDP).

Al-Dawa—Iraqi Shiite opposition group, loyal to Iranian revolutionary regime. Full name is Al-Dawa Al-Islamiyah—Islamic Call. Involved in numerous terrorist incidents in the Persian Gulf area and in Lebanon.

The National Progressive and Democratic Front in Iraq—Coalition group of almost every kind of anti-Iraqi Ba'athist opposition. Includes Nasserites, the Shiite socialist party, Communists, etc. Based in Damascus, Syria.

Arabian Peninsula

Oman—An absolute monarchy, no political parties. Current ruler a benevolent, educated autocrat; last ruler a medieval (and rather murderous) autocrat.

Dhofar Province—Site of the low-grade war between Oman and South Yemen, sometime home of PFLOAG—Popular Front for the Liberation of Oman and the Arabian Gulf—which later became PFLO —Popular Front for the Liberation of Oman. PFLO was a Marxist group supported by South Yemen. As of summer 1984 the PFLO exists as a "dormant" opposition front.

South Yemen—A people's republic, dominated by ruthless Yemen Socialist (as in Communist) Party.

Yemen—A republic with no political parties and a suspended constitution. Politics are essentially tribal and the government rules by granting fiefs to local tribal rulers. Courts are basically Islamic or tribal. Outside Sana it's more or less the fourteenth century.

National Democratic Front—South Yemeni-sponsored leftist political organization opposed to Yemeni government. An organ of South Yemeni government.

General

Mecca—Most holy city in Islam. Regarded as a protectorate of Saudi monarchy.

The Mahdi—Literally "the Expected One," the restored leader of Islam who will lead Moslems to final worldly victory. There have been several dozen Mahdis in the last century.

PARTICIPANT STRATEGIES AND GOALS

Gulf War

Iran—Maintain war of attrition in hope that more numerous Iranian manpower will grind Iraq down. Radicalizing Shiites in Iraq, and in the Arabian Peninsula countries, will further weaken Iraqi and Arab power. Revolutionary Iran's goal is to spread the gospel of Islamic "Koranic" government (based on a xenophobic interpretation of the Koran) and drive Western influences out of the Islamic world. There is also no toleration of Communist atheism. Iran wants to be the dominant power in the gulf. The ayatollah and his mullahs see the creation of an Islamic republic in Iran as move number one in the establishment of a pan-Islamic federation. Iran will be one "holy province" in this Islamic mega-state. Iran also has another motive: The war is a populist diversion from the revolutionary excesses of the Islamic revolutionaries and the resulting failing economy.

Iraq—Hang on and hope that modern weapons and good defensive tactics will bleed Iran until it can no longer take offensive action. (And if that doesn't work, use more chemical weapons, the desperation weapon of a desperate regime.) The Iraqi regime also hopes that either by assassination or by aging, the principal Islamic revolutionary leaders in Tehran will die off. Iraq wants to be the dominant power in the gulf. Saudi Arabia, whose support is absolutely essential to Iraq, isn't sure it wants a too powerful Iraq, but it would rather have Iraq's Arabs than the Persians.

Russia—Despite Tehran's 1982–1983 purge of the Communist Tudeh Party, wherein all the party members the Islamic revolutionaries could catch were put to death, Russia maintains considerable influence in Iran. The Russians want to play both sides of Iranian politics as well as both sides of the Gulf War. Moscow has resupplied Iraq with weapons and parts, and has allegedly given the nod to Bulgaria and Czechoslovakia to join North Korea in resupplying Iran. Russia wants to keep Tehran from exporting Islamic revolution to Russia, and play for time to consolidate its move into Afghanistan. Russia wants Tehran to stop supporting the Afghans. The long-range Russian goal is to get the United States out of the Persian Gulf and possibly establish a permanent Russian military presence in Iran.

United States—Try to maintain some third-party contacts within Iran and hope that if moderates come to power, they will be pragmatic enough to see that the United States is the only adequate regional counterbalance to Russian influence. This means the United States must be wary of tilting to Iraq as the Saudis have asked Washington to do. (Iraqi-Syrian relations are strained, as are United States-Syrian relations.) Because Iraq needs weapons to continue to fight Iran, it would welcome United States weapons sales and covert political support as long as few strings were attached. The United States wants to ensure stable gulf governments so that the oil flow isn't interrupted, and knows this means that a military commitment must be made. The U.S. Central Command (the old RDF, Rapid Deployment Force) has trained in Egypt and begun to plan for critical logistical support by improving airstrips in Saudi Arabia and by storing supplies in Diego Garcia (see Quick Look at Diego Garcia). The United States is also talking about equipping an Arab "reaction force." The logical choice for this role would be the Jordanians, but the Israelis won't like it.

Kurds—Play both sides and get the best deal possible for the establishment of a new country called Kurdistan.

France—Iraq is a great market for French weapons systems, and is a longtime (though often unreliable) trading partner.

Arabian Peninsula

South Yemen—Continue to foster revolt in Yemen and Oman, at least until the Communist revolutionary zeal diminishes or is destroyed and replaced by Islamic revolutionary zeal.

Oman—Continue to improve armed forces and buy more modern weapons. But Oman may have a two-front war, with the Communists in South Yemen and with the Islamic revolutionaries around the Strait of Hormuz. Oman will rely increasingly on clandestine United States support. To embrace the United States openly would make Oman vulnerable to Islamic revolution—from within and without.

Yemen—Rely increasingly on the Saudis to keep out the South Yemenis. This is an indirect way of depending on the United States to counterbalance the Russians down in Aden.

Russia—Continue to develop the port of Aden as a naval and air base for intervention in the Persian Gulf, the Indian Ocean, the Red Sea, and the Strait of Hormuz, should the U.S. Central Command show up or a leftist putsch succeed in toppling a gulf state.

United States—Reconfigure the U.S. Central Command along the lines of hi-tech light infantry. Try to get Oman to agree to a permanent United States military presence, say, on the island of Masirah, an old British base. Masirah is off the coast and is not as likely to disturb the local population as a base on land might. The United States and the Saudi monarchy are in this together. The Saudis want to stay rich, which means being able to sell their oil, and the United States, for the sake of its own economy as well as its allies', must blunt both left-wing and Islamic revolutionary destabilizations as well as Russian and Russian-client penetration. This takes long-range planning, careful politics, domestic support, and a Central Command that can actually get to the Persian Gulf in time and in force. Selling AWACS aircraft to Saudi Arabia has limited the effectiveness that surprise air raids would have against Saudi oil fields and military installations, but that is only a beginning.

SUPERPOWER INTEREST

	Political	Military	Historical	Economic
Russia	High	Medium to High	High	Medium
US	Very High	Very High	Medium to High	Very High

Political—The United States' interest in the Saudi monarchy is very high, and American allies depend on United States protection. Russia's chief interests are its border and containing the Iranian Islamic Revolution.

Military—Russia's Middle Eastern SSRs are conquered provinces, and their populations cannot be called pro-Russian. Russia's neighbors in this area have not forgotten what happened to the formerly independent nations now occupied by Russian bureaucrats and soldiers. Russia feels safest when these neighboring countries are fighting each other. Occasional outbreaks of peace are seen as a threat to Russian security. Russian agents are usually involved in any agitation during periods of war or peace—in other words, all the time. As for the United States, the Carter administration gave the then RDF (later Central Command) a big job.

Historical—Russia has always coveted Persian ports as direct outlets to the Indian Ocean. Russia has also pursued a policy of trying to secure direct control of its neighboring nations. United States interests date from after World War II, when the British began to withdraw from "east of Suez," leaving a power vacuum.

Economic—Unless Russian oil reserve estimates are severely inflated, Russia can do without gulf-area oil. United States allies Japan and Western Europe are very vulnerable to an oil cutoff. The United States is less so.

POTENTIAL OUTCOMES

Gulf War

1. 65 percent chance: Attrition stalemate continues until war stops from mutual exhaustion, followed by a diplomatic cover that allows both sides to look like victors. Such a cover would be an agreement suggested by an Islamic third party (Pakistan? Saudi Arabia? even

Turkey?) that is so vaguely worded that everybody can claim victory. Look for all kinds of sideshows in this one, like Iranian closure of the Strait of Hormuz, which would divert domestic Iranian attention. Arabic, Russian, and French support of Iraq may well ultimately ensure a stalemate that would save Iraq, and in that sense Iraq would be a victor—but more a survivor than a victor.

2. 25 percent chance: Iranian victory, destruction of Iraqi regime, and control of the Shatt are achieved by Iranian superiority in manpower (the Iranians had more troops to lose). Goes to 55 percent if Iranian Shiites can foment a rebellion in Iraq. In a sense, Iran has already won an important victory in that it defeated the initial Iraqi offensive and pushed the invaders out of Iran.

3. 10 percent chance: Iraqi victory, control of the Shatt are won by consistently slaughtering Iranian zealots on the battleground. Goes to 50 percent if revolutionary regime in Tehran folds.

Oman and South Yemen

1. 75 percent chance: On-and-off guerrilla action continues, with occasional bouts of terror and border raids. Drops to 50 percent after 1986.

2. 10 percent chance: South Yemenis invade Oman. Goes to 20 percent if Western military advisory teams are withdrawn from Oman. Goes to 40 percent if Iran closes Strait of Hormuz and the United States fails to send troops to Oman. Goes to 60 percent if Iran invades Oman.

3. 10 percent chance: South Yemeni invasion of Yemen.

4. 5 percent chance: Marxist government in South Yemen falls. Not very likely, but the Islamic revolution game could affect every country on the peninsula.

COST OF WAR

In the case of the Iran-Iraq War, excesses of wealth and passion have produced a very expensive bloodbath. Based on reports published in Western newspapers and an analysis of casualty rates in comparable World War I attrition battles, it is estimated that casualties in the Iran-Iraq War reached more than 700,000 in 1984. This figure may be low. Neither Iraqi nor Iranian information is reliable. In addition, there have been over two million refugees. The direct cost of the war has been more than $20 billion. The economic destruction and losses have cost another $30 billion. This does not account for spillover effects, such as the increases in insurance and shipping costs incurred by neutral nations as a result of Iranian or Iraqi attacks on shipping. There are thus incremental economic costs spread to oil-dependent economies around the globe.

So much for the northern end of the Persian Gulf. Farther south, the injury rate decreases while the arms bill balloons. Each year for the past ten years, an average of $10 billion of excess military spending occurred, affecting the entire globe. This $100 billion, instead of being invested productively, produced armaments which, in Arab hands, have been put to ineffective use.

SOLDIERS OF THE QUEEN

Most nations are understandably nervous about trusting foreigners to run their armed forces. Yet mercenary troops have long been a logical way for rulers to control their subjects while avoiding revolution coming from the local military barracks. The only trick is to obtain reliable mercenaries. The ruler has to make sure he is buying troops who will stay bought once they sign their contracts.

The British are familiar and at ease with mercenary arrangements. The Gurkhas from northern India still serve in the British and Indian armies. In the "merc world," the British participate by supplying officers and NCOs to many nations. In the middle and late 1970s, this old tradition was very much alive in the Persian Gulf, particularly in Oman. In the 1980s the Soldiers of the Queen, though less overtly active, continue to press on.

The rulers of the Persian Gulf states are generally local strongmen whose power the population prefers to recognize rather than resist with arms. So, raising troops from among the locals is not a good way to sustain the strongman's power. An obvious solution is to use mercenaries. Troops are easy to obtain; many groups in the area have traditionally served as mercenaries for whomever could afford it. The Baluchi tribesmen of Iran, Afghanistan, and Pakistan soldier for the highest bidder. Other groups from that part of the world, particularly Pakistanis, are available (officially or otherwise) to serve foreign rulers. The Pakistani government has made several defense arrangements with Persian Gulf potentates, "lending" brigades and fighter-bomber squadrons for local defense. The deal is that the lendee pays for the maintenance and expenses, and Pakistan gets back the troops and equipment when it needs them (for example, prior to a war with India).

One problem with using locals is the danger of their being lured into local political intrigues. For this reason, gulf rulers have always looked favorably on obtaining British officers and NCOs to lead mercenary or even local troops.

As with any army, the officers and senior NCOs are the key to effectiveness and reliability. The British Army has had several hundred years' experience in leading mercenary forces, and has acquitted itself well in this capacity. While the British government has not been averse to interfering in the affairs of the gulf states, it has generally done so with diplomacy and tact. The United States, Russia, and Cuba rarely display such tact.

British officers and NCOs serving in foreign armies often "resign" from the home forces for the duration of their foreign service. They often rejoin the British Army afterward. What is most striking about this foreign service is that the British mercenaries actually command foreign troops in the service of a non-British ruler. This arrangement serves all concerned and demonstrates why mercenaries survive and will most likely continue to do so.

ARAB VERSUS PERSIAN: SUNNIS AND SHIITES

Iraqi and Iranian enmity can be traced back to local Arab-Persian ethnic confrontations as well as political conflicts over control of river valleys (the Tigris and Euphrates, for example) and trade routes. Some Iranian militants also resent Arabs because historically Arab elites have exercised an often very arbitrary political and economic hegemony in Persia. As the Persians saw it, the liberality of Islam—equality before God—didn't translate into political equality in the Arab empire. This is an old anger. Other angers also affect the current war, such as disputes between Sunni and Shiite Moslems and the lingering Persian, Arab, and Ottoman disputes over the Shatt al-Arab.

A quick history of the Sunni-Shiite schism provides some background. After Mohammed's death, his successors had difficulty consolidating the new Islamic political empire. Abu Bakr, the first caliph, died after only two years in office. A period of confrontation followed between the new Arab political and military elite and the tribes of their empire. Taxes imposed on tribesmen by the government in Medina were one issue, but the fundamental problem was political and judicial inequality. Abu Bakr's replacement, Umar, was killed by an angry Persian slave. The Islamic movement plunged into a political contest between Mohammed's followers, Ali and Uthman. Uthman was the choice of the secular Meccan power elite. Ali, Mohammed's son-in-law, was the favorite of the Arab tribes. Uthman was murdered. Another power struggle between Mu'awiya and Ali's followers erupted into an intra-Islamic war. Ali became caliph, was murdered, and Mu'awiya took control of the movement. Mu'awiya's followers centered Islam about a Meccan elite. The Shiites, "the followers of Ali," rejected this as secular. They also objected to the "citification" desired by Meccan merchants.

Among Arabs, Shiism still retains an antiestablishment appeal, both politically and religiously. It's a little different with the Iranians. In the 1500s the Safavid rulers of Persia adopted Shiism as one more way to distinguish their empire from that of the Ottomans and the Turks' Arab fiefs. An early Persian literary movement known as Shuubiya is regarded by some as a Persian reaction to Arab dominance. Iranian Shiism blends Shiism's resentment of the Meccan secularists with the old Persian monarchical tradition. Iranian Shiism became in part a way of drawing ethnic and cultural distinctions. It also made the Persian Shiites a bit more attractive to Arab Shiites, who often chafed under the rule of Arab Sunnis. Iran's Islamic revolutionaries have hoped to use this appeal to topple the governments in Bahrain and Iraq. So far Shiite Arab minorities still seem to prefer Sunni Arab leaders to a leadership controlled by Persians.

Shiism is also, according to some Sunnis, tainted with elements of animist religions, Manichaeism, and Persian astrological notions. In other words, modern Shiism is a heresy, a mixed-bag "people's religion." The Shiites in turn resent this Sunni snobbery.

THE SUITCASE FROM ALLAH: NUCLEAR KAMIKAZES

The Western world has been shocked by Arab and Iranian terrorists who willingly blow themselves to Paradise while taking a few infidels to glory. The 1983 attack on the U.S. Marine compound in Beirut may be the most famous suicide terrorist attack of recent times, but it is by no means unique.

There exists a tradition, especially among Shiite Moslems, of suicidal action in the cause of Allah. In the twentieth century, TNT has replaced daggers. A high-explosive blast, however, is an inconsequential firecracker compared with "the suitcase from Allah," a terrorist-borne nuclear weapon. United States security analysts pale at the thought of Islamic terrorists acquiring a nuclear weapon by theft or black-market purchase. A nuke acquired by theft, from a United States nuclear-weapons igloo in West Germany, for example, is actually the least worrisome prospect. While the terrorists could grab a small tactical nuclear warhead (say, from a 155-mm howitzer shell), they would be hard pressed to detonate the device unless they also stole the weapon's activation codes. These codes, which activate and control supersecret PALs (permissive action links) on the weapon, are held in United States command channels. Unless the terrorist can break into a half dozen United States headquarters simultaneously, then know which one of several million potential codes goes with the precise warhead stolen, the nuclear weapon is just a hunk of uranium and high explosive. But it's a hunk that's good for a lot of headlines.

A weapon acquired by purchase or codevelopment, with the Pakistanis or Iraqis, for example, presents another kind of problem. It is indeed possible to make a crude atomic weapon and carry it around in a steamer trunk. Even if it failed to make the big bang, the target area could still be contaminated with low-level radiation.

Where would Islamic terrorists use such a weapon? Getting one to the United States (to drop out of the Goodyear blimp, as suggested in the movie *Black Sunday*) would be quite a feat, but not impossible. Penetrating Israeli security takes work, but Mossad could slip up and nuclear terrorists could slip in. A major candidate for a terrorist-delivered nuke is Russia, at least Moscow's border Moslem republics. The Russians are well aware of this. The terrorists would detonate the nuke and hope the Russians would think the United States did the dirty deed. Then the two superpowers would eradicate themselves with a strategic nuclear exchange. This "maximum result" isn't very probable; the United States and Russia would most likely contain any further escalation. The terrorists' "point," however, would have been more than made.

There has been no shortage of volunteers for suicide missions in the past, and there won't be one for the job of nuclear triggerman. As one Shiite terrorist leader told *The Washington Post* (February 3, 1984), "In one week I can assemble 500 loyalists ready to throw themselves into suicide operations. No border can stop me. We are coming to the end of the world. Presidents and ministers are eating each other up. Military men are traitors. Society is corrupt. The privileged, the notables are not worried about the poor. Only Islam can give us hope." Such millenarian thinking justifies the use of any kind of weapon—and any degree of destruction.

POISON GAS, THE EVIL GENIE IN THE BOTTLE

World War I's huge trench systems and enormous attrition battles forced tacticians to look for ways to break the deadlock. In April 1915 at Ypres, Belgium, the Germans experimented with chlorine gas. A special engineer regiment dispersed along the front trenches. When the wind began to blow toward the British and French forces, the troops opened the chlorine cylinders. This experiment, with its resulting greenish-yellow cloud, opened a two-division-wide hole in the Allied lines. The Germans were as little prepared for their success as the Allies were to defend themselves against the gas. After-action reports speculated that if the Germans had followed up the gas attack with a prepared infantry assault, they could have broken through to the English Channel.

Poison gas offers the would-be user a cheap mass-casualty weapon. Chemical agents like liquid mustard are relatively easy to make. College chemistry students, if provided with a lab, can synthesize even more exotic weapons. Almost every Third World country can produce potential chemical agents and use them, either in aerial sprays (like crop dusting from aircraft), mines or firepots on the ground, or artillery shells.

Chemical weapons may be of dubious value when used against well-trained and equipped soldiers like those of central Europe. British and United States forces estimate that trained troops, with equipment available, would have fewer than 5 percent casualties even from a surprise attack by nerve gas. But Third World forces, like Afghan guerrillas or Iranian Revolutionary Guards, have no protection. And poison gas not only kills, but it terrifies.

Mustard gas (H, HD, or HN in chemical symbols) isn't a gas but a liquid. It is a delayed-action and persistent chemical agent. Mustard produces large and painful blisters eight to twelve hours after contact. Apparently, the Iraqis sprayed Iranian lines while the Iranian infantry was massing for its attacks. They may also have used GA, a nerve agent.

Chemical weapons, however, are dangerous to the user. Iraqi troops are little better prepared to face Iranian chemical attacks. And persistent chemical agents, like mustard gas, remain on the battlefield. Farmers in France, sixty-five years after World War I, still occasionally develop mustard blisters after plowing up old battlefields. Civilians continue to suffer long after the shooting, and spraying, stop.

QUICK LOOK AT DIEGO GARCIA:
THE STRATEGIC SPRINGBOARD

A quick look at the following map of the Indian Ocean is a lesson in strategic position. From Diego Garcia, United States and allied forces can respond to crises in the Persian Gulf, the Horn of Africa, or the Indian subcontinent, including Pakistan, or can direct naval forces to cover the Cape of Good Hope or the Indonesian and Malayan straits. (See chapter on the Falklands for a discussion of such island bases.)

Nominally a British possession, Diego Garcia is leased by the

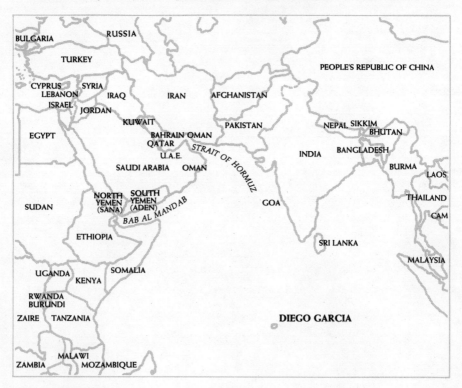

United States. U.S. Navy task forces require logistical and communications support. Long-range recon and antisubmarine air patrols are flown from the Diego Garcia air-base complex. The runways can handle B-52s. The United States is putting equipment aboard merchant ships that sit on call in Diego Garcia's harbor. This is called "prepositioning." The equipment is earmarked for use in the Persian Gulf should the Central Command be required to fight in the region. Plans call for enough equipment to support a 12,500-man, Marine amphibious brigade; some heavy equipment and trucks for the Central Command will also be stored. This puts United States heavy equipment at less than five days' sailing time from several potential trouble spots in the Indian Ocean region. But even with such support, the Central Command is on a long, delicate logistical tether. (See chapter on the Persian Gulf.)

4. Afghanistan:
The Ancient Insurgency

INTRODUCTION

An independent, warlike Afghan tribal population is fighting a Russian army that has taken over its country. It is a vicious guerrilla war in which both sides consider civilians to be fair game and little mercy is shown to prisoners.

This is the war "most likely to continue." It could continue for decades. The Russians can afford a long war, while the Pathans have never shown any interest in submitting to superior military power. Russia wants to prevent the existence of an unruly nation on its borders. Russia's enemies want to keep that country occupied and make it look bad.

It is a war of attrition for both sides. The Russians stand guard in their urban strongholds, sending elite troops, air power, and reluctant Afghan "allies" out on sweeps of guerrilla-held areas. The guerrillas hold most of the countryside and stage raids on cities and Russian convoys.

The tribes are controlled by local leaders. The cities are controlled by merchants and, recently, Communist bureaucrats. Afghans are normally at odds with each other and can unite only in a stronger hatred of outsiders, particularly non-Moslem invaders. An overwhelming majority of the Afghans want the Russians out.

Russia subdued its central Asian tribes through armed struggle and political subversion. The same approach seems to be under way in Afghanistan. The Afghans resist by accepting war as a way of life, and death in battle as a religious obligation. Russia wants the Afghans to behave like suitably respectful and docile neighbors of the Soviet Union.

(The Finns, who are also tenacious fighters, can be docile, so why not the Afghans?)

The war is causing a steady drain in numbers of dead and wounded soldiers and civilians, and it is destroying the Afghan economy.

SOURCE OF CONFLICT

Afghanistan is the war that after 2,500 years won't go away. Afghanistan's location makes it a permanent arena for geopolitical conflict. Its mountainous terrain and isolated, tribal societies are impossible to control.

This does not mean Afghanistan is never relatively calm. In the absence of imperial invaders, or feuds with the central government, the insurgency becomes low-level banditry and smuggling. These inevitable minor tribal squabbles are fought with shouts and a few rifles. But imperial invasions and external political interference have been the rule in Afghanistan, not the exception. At some point in history, nearly every significant Eurasian imperial power has tried to conquer and then contain Afghanistan's loose confederation of tribes, stratospheric heights, and fierce religious and ethnic passions. In the historical perspective, the score is imperialists zero, Afghans . . . well, it's tough to give them a number because they don't have sovereign control either. The cities belong to the cops and bureaucrats; everything else belongs to the tribes.

Enter another imperial invader and, for the fourth or fifth time, label it Russian.

The 1980s' version of the Afghan conflict is the result of a failed Russian "shock" invasion that sought to obtain power by a direct strike at the Afghan government in Kabul. The Russians made this move only after less direct means of persuasion failed (that is, KGB agents pulling strings within the Afghan government).

The invasion intensified the ongoing tribes-versus-state insurgency. As a result, the guerrilla war became more virulent and violent.

With the former India-based British imperial counterbalance to Russian expansion long gone, and its substitute, the Shah of Iran, replaced by the Khomeini regime, Moscow was presented with:

(1) An opportunity to forestall the spread of the Islamic Revolution to Russia's central Asian provinces.

(2) An opportunity to achieve a historic goal, extension of Russia's control to the Indian Ocean.

(3) A chance to prevent an unfriendly state from existing on Russia's tenuous borders.

The Afghan takeover was supposed to go quickly, with uncooperative leaders removed rapidly by coup and a cooperative head of state installed. In urbanized Western Europe, controlling cities means political control; this isn't true in many undeveloped countries, and particularly not in Afghanistan. The Russians gambled on a "city strike" and lost. The December 1979 invasion failed to shock the Afghans into surrender. The result was a much larger war.

There are two Afghanistans: the cities, with an educated elite and some industry; the rural, outback regions, with subsistence farmers, nomadic herders, and hill tribes with a long tradition of independence and violence.

As a result there are two wars. The city war pits an occupying army against an uncooperative populace laced with a few active terrorists. The Russians can handle this war; it simply requires waiting, propaganda, and effective brutality.

The war in the outback is a less certain thing. Eighty-five percent of the Afghans live in rural areas; these tribal people are, in the main, self-supportive and independent of the cities. Among the tribes, Islam is the chief philosophical and social force. They don't care much for infidels—in this case, the Communists, who are avowed atheists. The tribes also have a strong sense of their turf and bitterly resist any outside interference. These social factors have produced aggressive guerrilla conflict in the hills and countryside. The inadequately equipped but highly motivated and resilient tribal forces face first-line superpower troops supported by advanced combat aircraft, but heavy firepower isn't the whole story.

WHO'S INVOLVED

Mujahadeen—Afghan Islamic guerrillas opposed to the regime in Kabul and to the Russians. The mujahadeen are very loosely organized —this is a minus and a plus. While it is difficult for this informal resistance organization to coordinate its activities, there is also no central command for the Russians to go after. There are approximately 100,000 to 125,000 mujahadeen, with perhaps 20,000 active at any one time.

PDPA—People's Democratic Party Afghanistan (Afghan Communist Party). The 0.1 percent of the population currently controlling the government in Kabul. The party was led in 1984 by Babrak Karmal. The PDPA exists in two factions, the Khalq and the Parcham.

Russia—Russian combat forces, KGB, support and service personnel from Vietnam, Bulgaria, East Germany. The eight Russian divisions in Afghanistan in 1984 account for approximately 15 percent of Russia's effective operational forces (Category 1 [CAT 1] divisions).

Afghan Army—A conscripted force that numbered nearly 50,000 before the Russian invasion. Now may have as few as 8,000 effective soldiers. Riddled with PDPA political appointees as well as mujahadeen bullets. Referred to by mujahadeen as the "Karmali armed forces."

KHAD—Afghan secret police, in large part trained by the KGB. Now effectively the Afghan arm of the KGB.

Other participants—Pakistan, Iran, United States, China, and India.

Wild Card

Baluchis (pronounced Ba-loo-kees)—South-central Asian Aryan tribe whose traditional territory is split among Pakistan, Iran, and Afghanistan.

GEOGRAPHY

Afghanistan is the crossroads of the Eurasian land mass. Hairatan, the Afghan town where the new Russian-built railroad bridge crosses the Amu-Darya River, was once a major stopping point on one of the silk routes from China. Those routes ran east to west. Today the silk is oil and the camels are tankers. The route from the oil fields to Russia runs south to north, through Afghanistan. The orientation of the political compass may have shifted, but the pathway still runs through Afghanistan.

Afghanistan, like Chad in Africa, is one of those central nowheres on the way to everywhere. If you're in the middle of the map and bumping against everyone, then you're either the conductor or the conduit. Historically, Afghanistan has been a bit of both. The fact is, Afghanistan is like a mountainous Poland, a very mountainous Poland,

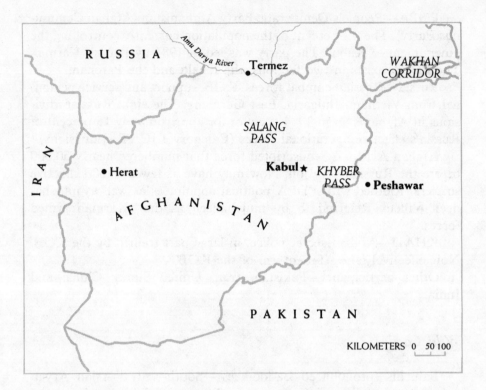

which makes it a very tribal, very backward, and very poor kind of
Poland. To go through Afghanistan takes spikes, not roller skates.
Poland is flat; Afghanistan has the Hindu Kush. Poland has no natural
borders, so an invader can move through it quickly. Afghanistan has
too many natural borders that must be chipped away tribe by tribe,
valley by valley.

Afghanistan-beyond-Kabul isn't in the twentieth century except for
the automatic rifles. Strong legs still move at an eleventh-century pace.
Lack of communication and transportation is a cause and an effect of
the lack of political cohesion outside the local valley. More than twenty
different languages are spoken, a function both of the linguistic isolation
in the hills and the ethnic mix created by the flux of human beings.
Language barriers hinder communication between people and create
misunderstanding between potential allies. They also frustrate centralized political control.

Being politically backward and, in geographic terms, being a peculiar kind of hillbilly do have their advantages, especially when you've

been invaded by a superpower geared to fighting a mechanized war in Europe. These characteristics have frustrated all kinds of past invaders.

The map provides further insight. Afghanistan is landlocked; it is also a land bridge. A narrow strip in the northeast, the Wakhan Corridor, touches China. Pakistan lies to the east and south, Iran to the west, and the Turkmen, Uzbek, and Tadzhik SSRs to the north. The average altitude is about 1,200 meters, with the tops of the Hindu Kush breaking 6,000. Central Afghanistan is a plateau with an average altitude of approximately 1,800 meters. This area supports small-scale subsistence farming and lots of goat and sheep grazing.

The drainage system is also landlocked. Most Afghan rivers disappear into interior basins and shallow desert lakes. A few of the streams in the east empty (via the Kabul River) into the Indus, but they are not navigable. Until 1978 there were no railroads. The Russians now are building one south from Termez. Major surfaced roads are few in number, tend to follow river valleys, and generally run through vulnerable transportation bottlenecks like the Salang and Zarmast passes.

The natural gas fields in the northwest (around Maimana and Shibarghan) have, according to Afghan sources, been occupied by Bulgarian "service personnel."

HISTORY

Afghanistan is a classic case of history repeating itself. The strong historical continuities make the present-day situation seem less puzzling.

2,400 Years Ago: The Persians

In the sixth century B.C., the Persians (Iranians) conquered the western and southern parts of what today is Afghanistan. The Persian empire was brutal, but when it came to hill tribesmen, the Persians knew to leave well enough alone. Their army stayed away as long as the taxes came in on time, and the tribes fought only one another and left the caravan routes relatively unscathed. This is one approach to controlling Afghanistan—ostensible control of the political top while the tribes control themselves.

2,200 Years Ago: The Greeks—Alexander the Great Didn't Do it Right Either

In the third century B.C., Alexander the Great marched through Afghanistan on his way to India. He tried to conquer the tribes, a second approach to controlling the country. Alexander thought he was destroying the old Persian empire; he failed to realize he was suddenly mixing in an ethno-nationalist war. The tribal kingdoms of the Hindu Kush, no longer allied with the Persians, waged a guerrilla conflict to maintain their traditional independence. Alexander's successors didn't try to continue the war. Instead they attempted to maintain control of the trade routes and key passes. The idea was to make money and live in a safe, secure fortress.

1,300 Years Ago: Religion as Politics

Despite an influx of Buddhism in the third century B.C., and the influence of Christianity from the first through the ninth centuries A.D., the driving social force in Afghanistan was a tribalism that after the latter part of the seventh century A.D. became firmly coupled to Islam. Islam gave Afghanistan its first real internal cohesion; the heterogeneous tribes finally shared something very essential.

300 Years Ago: The Persian Consolidation

Persia conquered most of what is present-day Afghanistan. This was the first true consolidation of the area. A Persian, Ahmad Shah, became Emir of Afghanistan and actually began to rule the area as a recognizable political unit. But the government was decidedly feudal.

150 Years Ago: Great Britain Takes Its Turn

The emir's heirs retained control until Dost Mohammed became emir in 1835. Dost was a wily politician; he had to be. Expanding British interests, this time coming from the south and heading north, put the Afghan tribes in a vise between the czar and the English king. The British defeated Dost in the First Afghan War (1838–1842), then reestablished him as a puppet governor.

Dost tried to pit the Russians against the British. A Russian political mission was established in Afghanistan. In 1878 the vise slipped in the form of the Second Afghan War, and Dost's son, Shere Ali, entered early retirement.

In 1880 the British placed Abdur Rahman Khan in power as emir, helped him establish a regular army and a centralized administration, ordered him to be a buffer against the Russians, and seemed to have complete control.

The British miscalculated. Tribal warfare and banditry by border tribes—the nineteenth-century moniker for guerrilla warfare—became endemic. The British bled and the tribesmen bled, even after the establishment of the Durand line, one of those mythical political creations that supposedly secured the proper division between Afghanistan and British India (now Pakistan). You can't make a nomad believe in borders drawn in Victorian parlors. And you don't split up cousins. One of the continuing sources of trouble was that the Baluchis ended up in three different countries: Afghanistan, Pakistan, and Iran.

As for the czar's involvement, after defeat in the Russo-Japanese War, the Russians needed to cut their foreign policy losses. In 1907 they agreed to a treaty which gave Afghanistan its independence under British influence. Influence meant that the Afghan government was supposed to control the tribesmen. An oft-tried tactic.

World War I to 1978: From the Third to the Fourth Afghan Wars

Afghanistan remained relatively quiet during World War I, but after the Bolshevik Revolution and the conclusion of the war, intrigue and violence once again became the norm. Habibullah, king during the war, was assassinated under mysterious circumstances. There is a strong case for Russian complicity; the new Bolshevik regime regarded itself as being practically at war with Great Britain, and Habibullah was viewed, perhaps incorrectly, as being pro-English.

In 1919, taking advantage of postwar unrest in India and the British preoccupation with postwar recovery, the Afghans invaded India. This was the Third Afghan War. The invasion and erstwhile British involvement prompted the Treaty of Rawalpindi (1919), which gave Afghanistan the right to conduct its own foreign affairs.

Though initially supported by the new Bolshevik regime, Amanullah, son of Habibullah, had a few surprises. While the Reds went about reconquering the old Czarist empire, Amanullah began supporting fellow central Asians in the rebellious Russian provinces of Turkestan and Uzbekistan. The Basmachi partisans openly resisted the Red Army from 1917 to 1932, and at one time they may have had 20,000 insurgents in the field. The Russians have not forgotten this.

Apparently Amanullah saw in the Red-White civil war a way to escape the Russian yoke and organize a "Central Asian Confederation." The Russians could fight and defeat the Basmachi inside Russia, but Afghanistan was too big a challenge for the new Red Army. Remnants of the Basmachi retreated to Afghanistan.

Amanullah encouraged development of the economy and brought Afghanistan to the edge of the industrial age; he also made some big mistakes and met strong religious and social opposition. The hill tribes perceived rapid change as a threat to their freedom. The opposition became a rebellion. In 1929 Amanullah abdicated, plunging the country into a short and bloody civil war.

In October 1929 a council of tribal elders and religious leaders (often there is no difference between tribal and religious leadership) elected Muhammad Nadir Shah, King of Afghanistan. A leader with tacit British support, Muhammad Nadir managed to calm tribal animosities while promoting education, modernization, and development of the cities. He kicked all Russian advisers out of the country. For more than thirty years, Afghanistan was relatively quiet.

The Russians did not cease conspiring. Also the explosive growth of the world economy after World War II had a side effect on Afghanistan—an educated middle class began to develop. This class did not embrace the old ways and agitated for a new order in Afghanistan.

In 1964 a new constitution was adopted. Officially Afghanistan was a constitutional monarchy, with elections (1965) and a legislature (the Shura). On July 17, 1973, Lieutenant General Sardar Muhammad Daud Khan staged a coup with limited bloodshed and abolished the monarchy. King Zahir was on vacation in Italy. The Republic of Afghanistan came into being, the 1964 constitution was abolished, and the royal family's vacation became permanent.

In this case "Republic" meant military rule. Daud Khan became president and prime minister, his position strongly supported by the Afghan Army. In January and February 1977, after convening a national assembly (Loya Jirgah) composed of notable elders selected by the provincial governors, Daud pushed through a new constitution that legalized his one-party state and provided for a presidential government. He was elected president, nominally ending military rule. Daud promptly dissolved the assembly. But by April 1978 the situation had changed. Pro-Moscow elements and members of the armed forces disillusioned with Daud staged the bloody Saur Revolution that toppled Daud. The president was killed. Nur Mohammed Taraki, leader of the banned People's Democratic Party of Afghanistan (PDPA), left prison and became prime minister and president of the Revolutionary Council. The PDPA, the Afghan Communist Party, banned all other political parties.

1979: The Fourth Afghan War

Taraki ruled over chaos and intrigue that was promoted from all sides; the KGB, disgruntled army commanders, slighted tribal elders, Afghan merchants, and Islamic fundamentalists. The fundamentalists didn't like the influence of "the atheists," meaning the Communists. The tribes in the hills and the city dwellers objected to the new government's social and economic reforms.

The day-to-day level of banditry in the countryside, particularly in the eastern provinces, rose in intensity, and the desertion rate in the army increased. In September 1979 Taraki fell in a factional putsch, a coup allegedly approved by Moscow.

Hafizullah Amin replaced Taraki. Amin spoke out for the need of national reconciliation, but sent the Afghan Army into the field with increasing frequency.

Though installed by pro-Moscow Communists, Amin never had the full trust of Moscow, nor did he walk and talk the Russian party line. In December 1979 Amin was assassinated during a Russian invasion of the country. A former deputy premier under Taraki, Babrak Karmal, an Afghan Communist kept on ice in Eastern Europe, replaced Amin. Karmal alleged that Amin was secretly pro-United States. His proof was the obvious fact that the traditionalist Islamic tribesmen were now in full rebellion against the Kabul government. Karmal's analysis avoided mentioning the biggest spur to rebel recruitment: the invasion of Afghanistan by the Russian Army. The Organization of the Islamic Conference has refused to recognize the legitimacy of Karmal's regime.

Russia's Fortieth Army, with 100,000+ troops, is engaged in active combat within Afghanistan. Including air and logistic support, the number of Russian military personnel deployed in Afghanistan approaches 135,000.

Given past Russian operations, the 135,000 military personnel figure is probably supported by 35,000 to 40,000 civilians and quasi-civilians, MVD internal security-type troops, KGB units, KGB agents in administrative, security, and economic-support sectors. If logistics and engineering personnel manning the northern road from Kabul and the Salang tunnel in the mountains north of Kabul, and if those building the "friendship" railroad bridge across the Amu River at Termez and Hairatan, are included, the military personnel figure of 135,000 is low. Armed construction workers, as the Cubans in the Grenada invasion demonstrated, can act as military forces.

The Russian Army's high command may also think the 135,000 count is low, for very different reasons. One report (from a Moscow military lecture attended by United States officers) maintains that some Russian officers think they can win a military victory if the Politburo lets the army have 305,000 combat personnel. The figure was probably generated by a computer tucked away in the Kremlin. This concept of a perfect force level smacks of Russian "derived norms" planning, based on identifying "scientific norms." Russian military planning proceeds with the same ponderous self-confidence as the central planning for the national economy. The United States political and military establishment fell into the same "we'll plan them into the ground" mentality during the Vietnam War. Russia will certainly repeat some of the mistakes of Vietnam.

But from strategic and tactical military perspectives, Afghanistan isn't a Red Vietnam. There are several reasons the analogy fails.

First, the Russians are not responsible to a democratic electorate or free press. The names of Berrigan, Ellsberg, and the Chicago Seven of Russia would be found, if at all, on gravestones, not in headlines.

Second, there is not as yet, and isn't likely to be, a single dominant leader of the Afghan resistance like Ho Chi Minh in Vietnam.

Third, the Russians are not dealing with governments and guerrilla combat units as organized as those in Vietnam, Laos, and Cambodia.

Finally, the entirely different terrain mandates a different kind of combat. Under the jungle canopy, the Viet Cong guerrillas could mount legitimate battalion-sized operations, and the North Vietnamese could operate divisions.

The mujahadeen don't deploy battalions, they deploy tribes. Individual Afghan guerrillas may have exceptionally high emotional and theological motivations, which ironically can sustain a long war, but to keep up a series of decisive operations like those managed by the North Vietnamese—short battles that move from objective to objective—requires unit integrity and organization.

Afghanistan is a genuine insurgency. Vietnam was a more conventional jungle war. To be a Vietnam in any military sense would require large main-force engagements between a politically organized Afghan resistance and the Russian Army, with the Afghan forces being supplied by a rapid, coordinated, and sophisticated logistics net. To be a Vietnam in the political sense would require open opposition to the war in Moscow.

In 1980 the Russians began a "limited" scorched-earth policy that continues. Known resistance centers (villages and certain valley areas) are bombed by aircraft, barraged by artillery, then swept by ground forces. As to how limited the policy truly is, if Pakistani figures of 2.5+ million refugees are accurate, that's scorching 3,000 of Afghanistan's 15,000 villages. The ground forces look for food caches and destroy any crops and livestock the high explosives missed. It's an ugly, brutal tactic, but ultimately might be effective.

Unlike the Viet Cong and the North Vietnamese, the mujahadeen have no outside logistical support. Scorched earth will either:

(1) Drive more mujahadeen into Pakistan, which is fine with the Russians.

(2) Fail miserably because the mujahadeen are tough enough to take it.

(3) Or kill so many people and starve the rest that the insurgency withers. This is called genocide.

In the long run the Russians' central question is: Can our soldiers kill Afghans faster than new Afghans are born and raised? With approximately 15 million Afghans still inside the country, and with a population growth of less than 1 percent, approximately 70,000 males a year become old enough to fight. If we accept the Russian figure of 120,000 Afghans killed over three years, the Russians would be more than 30,000 deaths a year short, even if many of the deaths had not been noncombatant women and children in the bombed villages.

The Russians want to reduce the population pool of the active guerrillas. Not all 15 million Afghans are involved in the war. The Pushtuns, who comprise more than two thirds of the population, are the most active fighters. By pushing millions of Pushtuns across the border into Pakistan and making deals with whichever tribes are willing, Russia hopes to chip away at guerrilla support.

This analysis, especially to a Western, humanist audience, seems cold, crude, and brutal, but such thinking has always had a home in Moscow. Stalin and his model ruler, Ivan the Terrible, made constant use of such savage mathematics. If they cannot break the spirit of the mujahadeen (and in all likelihood they cannot), the Russians believe the only way to win this Fourth Afghan War is to practice genocide.

The mujahadeen claim to control 95 percent of the country during the day and 99 percent at night. Resistance groups in Kabul and Herat regularly bomb and snipe at Russian personnel and the few remaining Afghan Army troops. Tribal groups badger Russian forces in the provinces. Significant large-scale actions have included an attack on the Salang tunnel, the overrunning of a supply depot in Kandahar, and the claimed destruction of a "nearly 200-vehicle column" in Kunar. A huge 200-vehicle ambush is unlikely, but it makes for good copy in the international press.

Mujahadeen propaganda has claimed raids have been made by insurgents and sympathizers into Soviet Tadzhikistan. These reports have also been discounted, but they do play strongly on Russian fears.

The mujahadeen remain factional and disorganized. This is their greatest weakness; it is also their greatest strength. In comparatively wealthy Europe the Russians can stymie opposition by taking over already established political systems and by occupying transportation nets and economic centers. In poor, rural, and divided Afghanistan such an approach cannot be engineered. You can't just walk in and take the grocery store if the grocery store consists of 1,000 half-wild goats. You have to go kill each goat, and that's a job.

This is the true land of the individual fighter. The most effective mujahadeen combat group is an old tribal raiding party of around twenty men. (See appendix on Mujahadeen Tactics, which contains further comments on shooting goats, Afghan-hill-tribe style.)

LOCAL POLITICS

Parcham (Flag or Banner) faction, PDPA—Babrak Karmal's faction of the Afghan Communist Party. View themselves as pragmatists. Maintain that the Khalq faction is too ideological to rule effectively. Pro-Russian with leadership all trained in Moscow. Though party claims many more as members, actual membership is less than 10,000. It could be as low as 4,000.

Khalq (Masses) faction, PDPA—Rival Afghan Communist faction. Personality conflicts and ideological disputes with the Parcham approach a blood feud. Many Afghan Army officers are (or were) members of Khalq. To say that the members of the Khalq faction are any less pro-Russian than the Parcham is misleading; they are pro-Khalq, meaning they want their directorate in power.

National Fatherland Front—A belated attempt by the divided PDPA to heal the breach between the Parcham and Khalq factions and incorporate the tribal councils into one political group.

Afghan Mettat—Small and bizarre allegedly right-wing faction. Stems from an old, virulently anti-British group. May have been involved in the toppling of Daud and the assassination of Taraki. One theory is that this politically ineffectual but violent faction may have always been a Muscovite tool of the Ali Agca, use-the-right-wing-radicals-to-shoot-the-pope kind. Only mentioned here as an example of the byzantine nature of Afghan politics.

Mujahadeen—This section describes the six basic insurgent groups of the mujahadeen, but the factions may actually be 100 times 6. There are 100,000 to 125,000 mujahadeen, with approximately 20,000 engaged in operations at any moment. Pushtuns seem to comprise the largest ethnic group among them (the Moslems in western Afghanistan seem to be less destructive).

Hizb-i Islami, two factions
Jamiat-i Islami
Harakat-i Inqilab-i
The National Islamic Front (NIFA)
The National Liberation Front

In 1981 the last three groups formed the Islamic Unity of Mujahadeen of Afghanistan. Some members are trying to create a Grand Alliance against the Russians and the PDPA. While such an alliance would greatly increase the effectiveness of the insurgency, these political activities tend to be engaged in by the educated and urbanized elite, whom the hill tribesmen have always found suspect. The focus of the factions is always on the single shared political element, Islam. They fight "for the preservation of Islam and their country." The mujahadeen all seem to agree, at gut level, that the insurgency is a war against not just infidel but atheist invaders, and Russians at that. The Russians have beaten central Asians in the past, but they've never conquered the Afghan tribes. One can almost hear a tribal elder saying something to the effect that "my granddaddy didn't let them flatlanders into these here hills. I ain't neither."

PARTICIPANT STRATEGIES AND GOALS

Russia—The Russians can pacify Afghanistan sufficiently if they can reconstitute a puppet army to carry out the day-to-day dirty business, strengthen the KHAD (Afghan secret police), and establish a strong centralized government. They have the will and the ability to do it. Chemical weapons and mass-terror bombings will work ultimately. If all else fails, they can just drive all the mujahadeen into Pakistan. A little cut won't become the Islamic infection that they fear.

The Russians haven't completely ruled out a troop withdrawal. Russia has maintained, ever since the December 1979 invasion, that its "limited contingents" would leave Afghanistan when all "outside interference" stopped. What constitutes outside interference is irrelevant; if Russia decides to pull out the troops, it can do so by declaring the mission accomplished. Moscow is saved from embarrassment; it can even declare the pullout to be a victory, along the lines of "we saved an underdeveloped country from Western intervention."

Russian goals are:

(1) Pacify the Islamic revolutionaries.

(2) Move Russia's bases closer to the Indian Ocean and the Persian Gulf.

(3) Incorporate Afghanistan as an SSR. This shores up the frontier by creating a new frontier.

Mujahadeen—The mujahadeen strategy is uncomplicated and straightforward—resist. Their simple and fragmented nature leaves them few options on how to go about it. In small bands the fighters cross the Pakistan border from the refugee camps, or from within Afghan population centers. They hit and run. Assassination of Russians and Afghan collaborators is often an individual act. Some tribal leaders arrange truces with the Russians. None of these have lasted long and generally favor the Afghans, as no tribal leader has the same degree of control over his tribal warriors as do Russian commanders over their troops.

Given these constraints, the mujahadeen goals are equally straightforward:

(1) Ideally, send the Russians and their lackeys packing and sufficiently bruised so that the Kremlin doesn't try this game for another century.

(2) Realistically, at least get the Russian Army out and let Afghan

Communists run the cities. (They may be atheists but they're our atheists.)

(3) Best Scenario: Spread Islamic revolution into Russia. This is not bloody likely but would be more than likely bloody for the Islamic revolutionaries inside Russia.

The Baluchis—With their land divided by artificial political borders, drawn by Britons, and acceded to by Russians, the Baluchis dislike and distrust the Pakistani government (though their men are, by tradition, mercenaries and many serve in Pakistani units). Their dislike for the Persians is even more intense historically. Like the Kurds caught between Iran and Iraq, the Baluchis want their own state. They have guns and they know how to use them: For hundreds of years Baluchi mercenaries soldiered for the British in India and for the Arab states ringing the Persian Gulf. The Russians can strike a deal so that the Baluchis get what they want and the Russians get an effective mercenary force that could be used to destabilize already unstable Pakistan, that could play an important role in post-Khomeini Iran, and that could police the other Afghan hill tribes (meaning Russians wouldn't have to risk their lives.)

The Russians may have 200 advisers in Iranian Baluchistan, backed up by about 30 East Germans. Russian personnel are involved in construction at the Chah Bahar naval base and the Konarak air base near the entrance to the Persian Gulf. The infrastructure of control in Baluchistan is beginning to take shape. A People's Republic of Baluchistan, or Baluchi SSR, whichever the propaganda cover, might well include Pakistan's Baluchi-populated Northwest frontier province.

Potential Afghan Allies

Pakistan—The Russians and the mujahadeen both perceive Pakistan as the key to the situation. With Iran in turmoil, all significant supplies must cross the border between Pakistan and Afghanistan. The Russians have tried politically and militarily to close the border; political pressure on the Pakistanis works to a degree, but the Pakistanis don't control the border, the tribes do. Russian efforts to cut off supply routes, including the liberal use of air-delivered mines (the small plastic variety that blow off feet) have worked somewhat, but the border remains virtually open.

Afghan-Pakistani relations are tense. The Pakistanis object to the flood of three million Afghan refugees. At the peak in 1981, the Pakistanis reported as many as 1,500 new refugees crossing the border each day. The Pakistanis have benefited from increased United States aid. Maybe Uncle Sam will foot the bill for the Afghan refugees.

While the Pakistani Army is one of the best in the Third World, it couldn't resist a determined Russian drive through the Khyber Pass. Current defense agreements between the United States and Pakistan, as well as the prospect of yet another guerrilla war, would make the Russians hesitate to cross that border, but overt Pakistani aid to Afghanistan could trigger such a response.

Finally, corruption in Pakistan limits the effectiveness of outside aid to the rebels. Several reports accuse Pakistan of skimming the cream from weapons shipments sent to the rebels by the Saudis, Egyptians, and Americans.

Iran—With the shah gone, Iran can no longer act as the counterweight to Soviet central Asian involvement. Besides, right now Iran is otherwise engaged in Islamic Revolution and in the Gulf War. However, the fact that there are Russian troops in Afghanistan attracts the attention of even the most fanatical fundamentalist. While Russians attacking Iran from Russia itself must cross the Zargos and Elburz Mountains, the terrain from Afghanistan is less formidable, and the attackers would not be canalized through three or four passes.

Russian influence in a neighboring Islamic state also increases the political threat to the nascent Islamic government in Tehran. The political threat, however, cuts both ways. The Russians are edgy because the ayatollah has succeeded in throwing over a dictator (the shah) under the auspices of the Islamic Revolution. The Russians are nervous about their own Moslems, for the Iranians have an ideological interest in promoting their brand of revolution and religion. The mujahadeen are the ayatollah's kind of folks.

United States—There is an opportunity here to make the Russians bleed a little, but it's very hard to take advantage of. Supply is a political and geographical nightmare. Also, the United States was caught off guard by the Russian invasion (the norm, you might say). The United States lacks sufficient central Asian specialists, including linguists, to take full political advantage of the situation. The U.S. State Department has tried to prove the Russians have used chemical weapons in Afghanistan. The employment of Russian chemical weapons, though in our opinion adequately documented by evidence coming out of Afghanistan (especially given Russian chemical warfare doctrine, and offensive and defensive capabilities) is still questioned by some legitimate news organizations. The U.S. State Department is paying its dues for lack of forthrightness in the past.

Finally, United States involvement is inhibited by Afghanistan's being on the Russian border and away from the sea-lanes. The only real lines of communication to Afghanistan run through Iran (off limits to the United States), through politically insecure Pakistan, and through Russia. The Wakhan Corridor to China has been incorporated into Russia, thus closing that limited point of contact.

The United States could supply certain types of weapons, like hand-held antiaircraft missiles. Egypt supposedly sent 300 of the Russian version (SA-7 Grails) in early 1980, but reports of their use are few and far between. The Redeye would be a strong political statement because it would significantly increase Russian aircraft losses. (See section on The Redeye for more information on its use.)

As for other United States responses, the Russian grain embargo, which was largely ineffective thanks to Argentina and Canada, has already been removed. As far as the Kremlin is concerned, the U.S. Senate's failure to ratify SALT II is a minor nuisance. The 1980 Olympics boycott may have stung the Russians, but the Olympics come and go. Two areas that the United States can influence may worry the Kremlin: (1) Poland, where Solidarity's anti-Communist resistance movement may be strengthened by the Afghans' example, and (2) China, whose relations with the United States were strengthened by the Russians' invasion of Afghanistan. The possible philosophical reinforcement for Solidarity is one of those brow-wrinkling maybes; the second consideration, the United States-Chinese rapprochement, is an on-again-off-again relationship, but it's one the Kremlin truly fears.

China—The Chinese regard the Russian invasion as a direct threat to their sometime ally, Pakistan. Outside of supplying a few assault rifles and political rhetoric, China has done very little. It could launch a spoiling attack along the Amur River, but starting World War III in Asia isn't worth 135,000 Russians in Afghanistan from the Chinese point of view. China can stir up trouble among Russian Moslems, but then its own Moslem minorities might catch the infection. China's policy of settling Han Chinese along the far western borders with Russia, to create a more Chinese ethnic mix, is still a couple of generations away from aborting an Uzbek-Turkoman revolution against Peking. China is in a position to portray itself as the true natural ally of the Third World, but that accolade has little impact beyond limited intellectual circles.

Another Potential Ally

India—From New Delhi's perspective, increased United States, Egyptian, and Western aid to Pakistan has refueled the Indo-Pakistani arms race. Once again, India is shopping for sophisticated weapons, but this time it doesn't seem to be MiG hunting. The de facto Russian-Indian alliance has begun to unravel. The invasion into Afghanistan contributed to the unraveling, as have Communist-exacerbated riots in the northeastern provinces. Some Indians feel the Russians are behaving like a new brand of British imperialists. One New Delhi newspaper reported that Russian officers have received manuals based on the old British officer guides for operations in India and Afghanistan. This kind of press doesn't bode well for relations with Moscow. It is a significant part of the Third World propaganda price the Russians have paid and continue to pay for their invasion.

SUPERPOWER INTEREST

	Political	Military	Historical	Economic
Russia	Very High	Very High	Very High	Medium to Low
US	High	Low	Very Low	Very Low
China	High	Medium to High	Medium to High	Low

Political—The Russians want to show their own Moslems that Islamic Revolution doesn't have a chance inside the empire. The United States wants to show the Third World that the Russians are the true twentieth-century imperialists. China wants to enhance its own prestige at the expense of Russia and show the rest of Asia that Russian domination isn't inevitable.

Military—The Russians have approximately 50 Category I (full strength) combat divisions, and eight or nine of them are in combat in Afghanistan. Afghanistan extends Russia's central position, provides air bases to threaten the Persian Gulf, and gets the Russians a step closer to the Indian Ocean. Geography inhibits the United States from providing significant arms and economic aid. China is interested in seeing Russia defeated, but its primary military concerns are Vietnam and the Russian-Chinese border.

Historical—The Kremlin has always been involved in central Asia. The czar continually redrew the northern Afghan borders (by reducing the northern khanates in 1865, 1868, 1869, and 1873). With the British counterweight to Russian expansion removed in 1947 and the fall of the Shah of Iran, 1979, Russian historical interests in expanding to the Indian Ocean have been unchecked. Historically, the United States has had little interest in Afghanistan; as far as the West was concerned, it was a British-Russian problem. The Chinese have always been concerned about the central Asians, either as potential invaders or as people to be dominated to ensure that the Chinese heartland is protected by buffer states. Afghanistan, however, isn't as strategic to the Chinese as Mongolia or Tibet.

Economic—The northwestern gas fields may be significant finds. The gas is ending up in Western Europe via the Russian pipelines. This means foreign exchange for the Russians, but the $100 million a year's worth of gas doesn't begin to offset the $20+ billion a year the war costs. Underdeveloped Afghanistan holds little economic interest to either superpower. Its strategic appeal is geographic position. China has no significant economic interest in Afghanistan.

POTENTIAL OUTCOMES

1. 55 percent chance through 1988: On-again-off-again insurgency. Russians control nominal power in Kabul, garrison the cities. The mujahadeen control the countryside.

2. 20 percent chance before 1987: The Russians decide to withdraw their armed forces. If this occurs, there's a 70 percent chance of a "Communist" regime being installed in Kabul as window dressing for Russia's withdrawal. It will be Communist in name only.

3. Fifteen percent chance before 1988: The Afghan rebels are totally defeated by means fair and foul. A devastated Afghanistan is incorporated into Russia as Afghanistan Soviet Socialist Republic, or is left "independent" in the Eastern European sense.

4. 10 percent chance before 1988: The Russians co-opt the Baluchis by promising to create a sovereign Baluchistan out of parts of Afghanistan and Pakistan. Baluchi support expands the conflict into western Pakistan. This becomes a bargaining chip with the Pakistanis: Either Pakistan's support for the Afghan insurgents fades (and the level of insurgent activity diminishes) or the Baluchi rebellion begins. The Russians might try this power play anyway; a Baluchi state would place

them on the Indian Ocean. The Afghan insurgency continues, but the Russians let the Baluchis do the dirty work.

COST OF WAR

Total losses to date have been several hundred thousand dead, over a million injured and wounded, and over $50 billion in property and GDP (gross domestic product) losses. More than a million civilians have been killed by direct and indirect military action. There have been over five million refugees (one third of the population), half of whom have fled across the border to Pakistan.

The Russians have kept their losses down by deploying ground forces sparingly and using the remnants of the Afghan Army. As of 1984, Russian military casualties have totaled 40,000, with 15,000 dead. Their dead and wounded are currently fewer than 10,000 a year. The Russians have kept casualties down by using their superior artillery and aircraft as much as possible. When they do have to send in ground forces, they try to use Afghan government troops (what's left of them) as much as possible. Most Russian casualties occur during guard duty for convoys, military bases, and government installations.

Afghan Army losses have been just as high. The troops tend to desert when the going gets tough.

Estimates on mujahadeen battle deaths vary widely. Since the resistance fighters don't get much medical assistance beyond prayer and first aid, a minor wound can lead to death. Perhaps 60,000 mujahadeen have been killed because of combat. Sixty thousand mujahadeen have survived their wounds.

The economy has always been subsistence agriculture and herding. The losses in these areas total several billion dollars a year. The loss of capital goods (housing, production tools, etc.) has been high, perhaps $3 billion worth, amounting to a large percentage of the national total.

Russia's costs have been significant. The normal peacetime expense involved in maintaining each active division is several hundred million dollars a year. In this limited war, each division (and its supporting air units) is costing half a billion dollars a year, and this includes the building of new support facilities. Thus the additional military cost is about $4 billion a year. The total cost for the Russians to maintain forces in Afghanistan is close to $20 billion a year. Much of this is used to build military bases and transportation networks (roads, airfields, and railways).

On purely military grounds, the Russians justify spending 10 percent of their military budget as follows:

(1) Their troops are getting their first real combat experience in over thirty years. Troops are being rotated in and out of Afghanistan every six months.

(2) New weapons and tactics are tested as they couldn't be otherwise.

(3) New military bases are being constructed, which will place Russian military forces in a better position should there ever be a war in the Persian Gulf area.

Several million refugees have fled over the border to Pakistan. They, plus several million more inhabitants whose economic activities have been disrupted by the fighting, account for the loss of a large portion of the prewar national income, estimated at $4 billion. Also the housing and farm equipment of many of the refugees and those still in the country have been destroyed.

RUSSIAN TACTICS AND WEAPONS IN THE FOURTH AFGHAN WAR: TOUGH AND BRUTAL, BUT EFFECTIVE?

The Russians have run a number of cordon-and-destroy operations in the valleys. These operations seek either to surround guerrilla-infested areas or, failing that, to establish blocking positions (anvils) against which maneuver forces try to flush the guerrillas. Initially, the motorized riflemen operated with familiar concepts like mixed tank-infantry columns. In open terrain, or even in a wide-bottomed valley, where mechanized units can spread out in lines and columns of tanks and armored personnel carriers, these conventional tactics work well; unfortunately for the Russians, in closed terrain such as foothills and high valleys, the units become road-bound, sitting ducks waiting for an ambush. A mine in front of the column and a mine in the rear can effectively immobilize the unit. The Russians are now using more air-mobile tactics; that is, moving airborne infantry or specially trained motorized rifle infantry in helicopters instead of on the easily ambushed roads. Armed helicopters, such as the Mi-24, provide convoy escort; they also patrol for moving mujahadeen bands like air cavalry.

The initial Russian invasion force included some Category II (what the United States would call reserve or National Guard) divisions drawn from the provinces near Afghanistan. These units were manned by central Asian reservists, mostly Uzbeks and Tadzhiks. A political problem developed: The Soviet central Asians found that they had more in common with the Afghans than with their Slavic officers and senior noncoms. They were replaced by Slav-manned divisions from western Russia, though Afghan observers say a "special operations commando" of politically pristine central Asians exists. Russian troops serve for six months at a time, and more than two thirds of the combat units rarely participate in active combat.

Against Third World opponents, the Russians use chemical weapons. They terrorize the populace and deny them territory by killing livestock and crops and generally contaminating the countryside. Reports from refugees in Pakistan attest to the effectiveness of the terror tactics. Area-denial use of chemical weapons is supposed to restrict mujahadeen infiltration and supply routes. As noted, we believe the evidence overwhelmingly indicates that chemical weapons have been utilized. The extent of this use can only be estimated, and its effectiveness remains to be seen. The Russians consider chemicals to be just another weapon. Their troops are taught this and equipped accordingly.

The Russians seem to have used a number of light, air-dropped plastic mines as area-denial weapons. About the size of a roll of Scotch tape, this type of mine packs just enough punch to blow off toes or maim a foot. Usually these mines are painted in camouflage colors or a sandy brown. The fuse system is such that cumulative pressure will cause them to go off; just handling them too much for too long will eventually set them off. Some observers report seeing "booby trap" versions of these plastic mines, often shaped like small toys or bottles. Dropped en masse among the hills and in border areas where legs are the chief means of transportation, the mines can be a major tactical obstacle. A wounded mujahadeen slows down the entire column. Since medical care is practically nonexistent, a foot wound may eventually lead to death. The Russians believe these mines are not just an effective tactical weapon for slowing down mujahadeen infiltration and supply, but they also terrorize the tribal peoples who support the insurgents.

Kandahar Province south of Kabul and Parvan Province to the north were the zones of Russia's 1982 "winter offensive." Russian tactics included the destruction of villages. Heavy casualties, according to Indian, Pakistani, and mujahadeen reports, were inflicted on the civilian population. Civilians near other strategic targets have also suffered. The Russian Air Force has repeatedly bombed towns in the Shomali area north of Kabul. These attacks have not just been alleged by the guerrillas (and the U.S. State Department); they have been covered by Western and Third World reporters in Kabul, and photographs of aircraft on sorties have even appeared in the Western press. The Russians are reported to be worried about guerrilla attacks from Shomali against their vital air base at Bagram and on the overland supply route from the Russian border to Kabul.

Because the rural population provides its own sustenance through farming and herding, Russian attacks have long-lasting effects. Destruction of crops, herds, and agricultural equipment make it less likely that people will survive, much less thrive and support partisans. Two million+ refugees attest to the effectiveness of the Russian terror-and-scorched-earth tactics.

The basic Russian infantry unit is the battalion, which has the following weapons for its 400 men:

Assault rifles—Nearly every Russian infantryman has an assault rifle. The most recently issued version is the AK-74, a 5.45-mm weapon similar to the United States M-16. It weighs as much as the old 7.62-mm AK-47 of Vietnam fame (8.8 pounds). The AK-74 has a slightly greater effective range than the AK-47 (500 meters versus 400) and a higher effective rate of fire (100 rounds per minute versus 90). Its chief advantage is the lighter weight of the ammunition (4.7 pounds per 100 rounds versus 6.2 pounds). Its drawback is the need to carry two calibers of ammunition, as the older machine guns use the old 7.62-mm rounds. The AK-74 has a severe disadvantage in that the Afghans prefer to snipe at targets farther than 500 meters, outside the effective range of the AK-74. The only way the Russian infantryman can respond is to fire off a lot more bullets, thus nullifying their ammunition-weight advantage. The AK-74 is, however, well suited for fighting in urban areas because of its high rate of firepower.

Machine guns—Each battalion has over 60. The type most used is the 5.45-mm RPK-74, which is a heavy-duty version of the AK-74. Its practical rate of fire is 120 rounds per minute. Each battalion also has perhaps a dozen "heavy" machine guns that use the same ammo as the older AK-47. Machine guns can be used effectively up to 1,000 meters.

Rocket launchers—Until recently, each squad had one RPG-7 rocket launcher (27 per battalion). These weapons fire an antitank rocket grenade. The Russians have introduced a new version similar to the United States's throwaway LAW (light antitank weapon) rocket launcher. These weapons have a disposable launching tube. Fire once and toss the container. This is unlike the earlier version for which the soldier kept the launch tube (like the old bazooka) and loaded new rockets. Their range is between 200 and 300 meters, and they are useful only in urban areas. These weapons are issued like hand grenades. The troops take as many as they can use in a particular situation.

Armored vehicles—The Russians are plentifully supplied with all kinds of AFVs (armored fighting vehicles). The infantrymen have their BMP personnel carrier (30 per battalion), which carries 11 men and a small cannon in the turret. The BMP is cramped and uncomfortable, making long-distance travel extremely difficult. Also, the Russians can't really fight Afghan tribesmen from inside the vehicle. If the idea is to deliver rested infantry in working condition, a truck serves the purpose far better than a "BUMP" (United States troop jargon for BMP). The Russians also have plenty of tanks. In addition to being as cramped and uncomfortable as the BMPs, the tanks are difficult to keep running in the rugged terrain and are exceptionally vulnerable to antitank rocket attacks from above. Worse yet, the tank cannon carries only 40 rounds and, because of Russian turret design, the barrel cannot be raised or depressed sufficiently to deal with combat in the hilly terrain. With their limited usefulness and high maintenance requirements, the plentiful Russian armored vehicles have proved a dubious asset.

Mortars—Each battalion has six 120-mm mortars, which are quite effective as artillery in mountainous terrain. Smoke and illumination shells can be fired quickly and accurately. The only limitation is ammunition supply, as each round weighs over 40 pounds.

Grenades—The various types of Russian hand grenades are not useful for much besides urban fighting. Afghan guerrillas don't build bunkers.

Mines—The Russians use several small, light (under a half kilogram) wooden or plastic antipersonnel mines. They have been spread around liberally, particularly by air over partisan travel routes. They are effective, although they cannot be used safely anywhere the Russians might go.

Special weapons—An automatic grenade cannon (the AGS-17) fires a 12-ounce 30-mm grenade up to 800 meters. Its effective rate of fire is about 100 rounds per minute. Each battalion has six cannons, which can be lugged by two men. Another effective antimujahadeen weapon is the antiaircraft artillery with which the infantry regiment is normally equipped: Four self-propelled, quad-barreled, 23-mm automatic cannons called ZSU-23-4s. This weapon gives a three-second burst that sends 40 seven-ounce, high-explosive shells 3,000 meters. Its only drawback is an overheating problem that limits the burst to three seconds.

Chemical weapons—The Russians consider that chemical weapons are normal, to be used "where applicable." They are regarded most suitable for use in the enemy's rear, away from friendly forces. Because of adverse world opinion, chemical weapons have not been used in Afghanistan as extensively as they would be in a major war. Usually delivered by artillery or aircraft, the effects of nonpersistent chemical agents do not last more than a few hours. Fatalities among unprotected personnel range to 30 percent, with nonfatal injuries (some permanent) rising to 90 percent. Chemicals are less effective in high winds, cold temperatures, and bright sunlight. Cold, windy, and brightly lit Afghanistan is not ideal chemical warfare country, but then these conditions make the use of a chemical weapon hard to verify, and the Afghans have no really effective protection against it.

Artillery—Each Russian division has over 100 artillery pieces. Their use is limited in mountainous terrain, and they require large quantities of ammunition. For example, to destroy an enemy position covering an area 1,000 meters square requires nearly 300 tons of ammunition (60 truckloads). For this reason the Russians rely on aircraft for fire support in areas that are difficult to reach. Also, stories abound of poorly directed Russian artillery. The Russians are excellent when they can use artillery en masse, but the kind of accurate fire control needed to battle guerrillas strains their capabilities. The Russians have killed a lot of their own infantry with massive and inaccurate artillery strikes. This doesn't improve the troops' morale.

Aircraft—The principal ground-attack aircraft are the MiG-27, the MiG-21, the SU-7, and the SU-25. Their normal combat radius (with maximum weapons load) is about 500 kilometers. A weapons load varies from about one ton for the SU-7, two tons for the MiG-21, and three tons for the MiG-27, to about five tons for the SU-25. The SU-25 (Frogfoot), a new aircraft designed for ground attack, has seen its first use in Afghanistan. Helicopters also are used, particularly the Hind Mi-24. At high altitudes the Hind's range is less than 100 kilometers, and its weapons load less than a ton.

MUJAHADEEN TACTICS: THE REALITIES OF TRIBAL WARFARE

Because of Afghanistan's geography and its historical-social situation, military cooperation beyond the tribal level rarely occurs. Operations are combined only for the immediate convenience of the groups involved. The degree of interinsurgent cooperation varies not from operation to operation but from hour to hour. Combat reports describe cooperative arrangements that have lasted for an afternoon, with one insurgent force withdrawing from engaged combat because the men had to return home by nightfall. This frustrates the grand strategists, but other rebel groups seem to understand the situation. Maybe next time *their* wives will want them home for supper. This is not combat in twentieth-century terms, but an Apache war party might have understood the concept, as well as an eighteenth-century Kentucky farmer with kids to feed. Call out the militia, but not for too long.

The largest effective insurgent operations group seems to be about twenty men, in other words, a tribal raiding party. Fire and maneuver are of the skulking variety. The raiding parties break contact quickly, but the survival rate is high for guerrilla light infantry facing the awesome firepower of Russian motorized rifle units. The guerrillas continually and successfully utilize the standard trick of simultaneously blowing a mine in front of the convoy and one at the rear. If the mines fail to take out a vehicle, then a brief spray of automatic fire just might. The Russians respond with ground fire and helicopters, and with artillery if a firebase is in the area. The guerrillas retire to the hills, harassed by helicopters.

The highland tribes are fiercely independent and adaptable. These traits, combined with the economic and social backgrounds of the tribesmen, produce effective and resilient insurgents. Economic activity in the hills consists of grazing flocks, some subsistence farming, and lots of smuggling. Flocks provide mobile, though very water-dependent, food sources. Smuggling sharpens the sneaking and peeping skills successful raiders use; so in this instance, normal living trains troops. In Afghanistan this isn't the only example of how day-to-day living hones combat skills.

The luxury industry, among the hill tribesmen, is the making and appreciation of fine guns. A son of the hills comes of age when he gets his gun. Visitors in the markets of highland Afghanistan and Pakistan often hear an eruption of semiautomatic and automatic gunfire, as the arms salesman displays his wares to an appreciative audience.

The life is harsh and tough. One former hill tribesman, now an officer in the Pakistani Army (he has relatives in both Iran and Afghanistan, the border being largely irrelevant), recalled a childhood game of standing on one ridge and trading shots with a cousin on the next ridge. The object of the sport was to "just miss the other's ear. Of course such a game is dangerously insane," the officer concluded, "but I want you to understand that's how we are raised." A major part of tribal socialization is to learn how to use a rifle, and use it accurately, from the age of five.

Another excellent contemporary "folktale" describes a goat-shooting contest. Now, no self-respecting hill tribesman would waste a precious .30-caliber round on a goat (that's knife work) unless prestige is at stake, like fame, honor, and a goat dinner for the winner. The goat is on a long rope tether so that it can't move far. But there is one catch: The goat is "maybe a thousand meters away." The competitors get one shot apiece. However, if you're in the goat shoot, you'd better not be third in line because the goat is usually dispatched by either the first or second marksman. If you can shoot a goat at 1,000 meters, you can shoot a Russian at 1,000 meters. Besides, the Russian offers a bigger target.

In many places Afghan bolt-action Enfields are superior to the Russian automatic rifles (AKMs and AK-74s), especially at great distances (like the goat shoot) when the Enfield's excellent long-range accuracy can be utilized. The guerrillas also have AKs, acquired on the black market from defecting Afghan Army troops and from dead Russians.

In the cities there have been minor shoot-outs in both Herat and Kabul, but they are rare. City dwellers tend to deal in terror actions against Russian troops and PDPA sympathizers. A bomb here, an assassination there, something to keep the occupiers occupied, for the Russians are going to hold the cities, at least by day.

THE REDEYE: MiG AND HIND HUNTING IN THE HINDU KUSH

The United States-made Redeye missile is one of several hand-held, man-portable, antiaircraft missiles available on the world arms market. The SA-7 Grail is the Redeye's Russian equivalent. Redeye missiles, fired from disposable launchers averaging four to five feet in length, utilize infrared trackers that locate and home in on aerial heat sources such as the hot exhaust of a passing jet aircraft. The missile chases the aircraft, flies up the jet engine, and explodes—at least, that's the idea. They are not very accurate, and their effective range is two to three kilometers. But if deployed in numbers or in ambush sites of known aircraft ingress and egress, they can provide ground forces with some protection against air attack. Since they are tail-chasers, Redeye teams have to be deployed in front of moving columns or outside defended areas if they are to take out the aircraft prior to attack; this exposes the teams to ambush or ground attack. (The new United States-made Stinger, a vastly improved Redeye, can lock on to the front of an aircraft, which reduces the need to deploy antiaircraft [AA] missile teams away from a unit.) There are several countermeasures aircraft can take, such as the Israeli tactic of dropping flares behind the planes. New United States and Russian aircraft, including helicopters, have flaps and devices (the American system is called "The Black Hole") that channel the exhaust up and away from the aircraft to some degree; this gives the missile a smaller heat source and may confuse its guidance system.

What does all this have to do with Afghanistan? Quite a bit, both politically and militarily. The Russians enjoy absolute air supremacy; MiGs strafe and rocket mujahadeen with near impunity (the occasional captured .51-caliber AA machine gun or 23-mm AA cannon provide some competition); Sukhois drop mines and Hinds chase guerrillas. Thus the Russians have a great deal of tactical flexibility. Missiles like the Redeye would restore some balance to the air war as well as give the mujahadeen a great way to publicize their situation: Blown-up pieces of aircraft make nice newspaper photographs.

The high valleys of the Hindu Kush would be ideal terrain for using these missiles. Aircraft can enter and exit the valleys lengthwise only; mujahadeen missile teams would simply deploy on the ridge near the valley mouths or in the passes, and wait for the MiGs to fly by. Even if they were to miss, the pilots would not take as much time to line up their targets, which would increase the likelihood of missing the mujahadeen.

At higher elevations, helicopters approach, and sometimes exceed, their operational altitude limits; this means they must stick to the valley floors and fly below the ridgelines. Hind helicopters shoot the exhaust skyward, an advantage if the opposing missile team is down below. In cases where the ground is in the sky, however—i.e., where the mujahadeen are higher than the helicopter and are firing down—directing the exhaust upward makes for a bigger target—and a bigger explosion.

MUJAHADEEN SOLDIERS

The hills are warrior country where military exploits and tales of heroic combat provide a daily source of pride and honor. But the orientation remains decidedly individual or, at the most, tribal. The Afghans regard the regular army as an instrument of the government, not the populace, so there is little sense of military tradition. The source of authority remains the head of the family or the tribal elder.

The mujahadeen fighter springs from this background. His age may range from twelve to the late fifties. He (the mujahadeen are predominantly male) is an excellent shot, by necessity and tradition, thoroughly acclimatized, and inimitably tough. He will fight on his own or in a small group, and has no fear of fighting to the last. He regards death in battle as an honor. This isn't romantic heroic stuff, it's a reality for a people whose way of life is so intensely difficult, dangerous, and threatening that combat against an immediate aggressor provides a break in the tedious struggle for existence. It's more pleasant to fight Russians and steal their food than it is to fight the weather and slowly starve.

RUSSIAN SOLDIERS

The average Russian soldier in Afghanistan is a Slav from either a Russian or Ukrainian SSR, or perhaps from the Baltic states. He is a young conscript, ranging in age from nineteen to twenty-three (generally age twenty), but reasonably well versed in the fundamentals of combat. He usually comes from a small town or a farming community, and while literate, has little more than a basic education. He received a smattering of military education in the Young Pioneers (a rough equivalent to the Boy Scouts) and is in excellent physical shape. He has little respect for sergeants, who are generally ineffectual. He is treated with contempt by his officers, and responds in kind. He has been trained from infancy either to quickly obey orders or find a way to avoid them. He's more inclined to believe rumor or gossip than official announcements of what is going on. Most of his training has been with his unit (infantry, artillery, or tank battalion). He is cynical about what the system is supposed to do contrasted with what is stated officially. Serving a two-year term of duty, of which usually one year will be in Afghanistan, he is capable of being an excellent soldier if given the proper leadership and combat experience. Neither of these is likely to be found in Afghanistan.

LEADERSHIP IN THE FOURTH AFGHAN WAR

On paper the Russians have a substantial military advantage over the Afghan partisans. But wars are not won on paper or with purely numerical and material advantages. The key element is the fighting ability of the soldiers. This fighting ability is directly related to the quality of the leadership. It is an ancient military truth that "there are no bad troops, only bad officers." In Afghanistan the effects of good, and bad, military leadership can be seen.

Russians

Senior Russian leaders are accustomed to the exact planning of operations and to precise adherence to those plans. Junior leaders are expected to exercise considerable "activity" (see definition below) in carrying out these orders.

The Russians place great faith in so-called scientific leadership. They believe in planning and are not keen on what we would call initiative. The word used to represent initiative can be translated literally as "activity." In other words, when in doubt do what you are already doing more energetically. Do not think for yourself.

A nation obsessed with control of all aspects of society naturally extends this policy to military affairs. The average Russian officer has learned very well by rote the drills and procedures. His theoretical education is often lacking. The officers and troops have no training for any nonplanned course of action.

This Russian orientation can be useful and even successful under some conditions. After all, the Russians defeated the Wehrmacht in World War II using the same principles they utilize today. There are, however, several significant differences between the war with the Germans and the present conflict with the Afghan partisans. The World War II battles were generally large, set-piece affairs. The Germans took their heaviest losses when they stayed in one place and allowed the Russians to bludgeon them to pieces. Also, it took the Russians nearly a year of combat, and thousands of disastrous losses, before they gained sufficient experience to fight the Germans effectively. Still, when the Russians mixed it up with the Germans in fluid battlefield situations, they invariably came out second best. The Germans practiced a high degree of individual initiative, probably more so than any other army in this century. The Afghan guerrillas are not an army, they are a collection of fighters, but fighters with a very high degree of individual initiative.

The thing a Russian leader fears most is encountering a situation not covered by orders. Battle plans are laid out meticulously; they try to cover every conceivable eventuality, but combat always produces the unexpected. Russian soldiers will fight heroically when cornered, but when they are on the move and faced with an unanticipated situation, they tend to freeze and their officers have no option but to order more "activity." This is the reason for the legendary Russian penchant for continuing to attack or defend even after all hope of success is lost. Such suicidal actions occur if the officers are performing as they are trained. Often even the officers become immobilized. This is particularly evident in the early stages of a war. Later the usual wartime punishment for unsuccessful officers (a firing squad) becomes recognized as the likely alternative to a lack of "activity."

When fighting partisans, it is not always possible to enforce such wartime discipline. The situation is far less clear than were the massive set-piece battles of World War II. It is difficult to maintain discipline among officers if one is not sure just when a failure occurred. The need to be flexible and exercise initiative in the face of resourceful partisans leaves the Russian leaders at a severe disadvantage. Thus, in Afghanistan most Russian operations are heavily planned sweeps of partisan-held areas. The guerrillas generally react by sniping at the Russians or detonating a few mines as they avoid becoming a fixed target.

Russian parachute units are allowed more flexibility and initiative. Given the nature of parachute operations (dropping into a murky situation), paratroopers must be trained to think for themselves. These troops are also selected more carefully and are trained to have a high opinion of their combat abilities. The parachute officers, however, are still cast from the same mold as are all other Russian officers, so the parachute units are only marginally more effective against the partisans.

Afghans

Afghan tribesmen exhibit a high degree of initiative in their daily lives. Eighty-five percent of the population is rural, and hunting, fighting family feuds, and enduring hard times are all considered normal activities. Banditry and smuggling further sharpen wits. The leader of all these activities is the most proficient warrior.

Such leaders are willing, and often eager, to expose themselves to danger. The tribal code of warrior honor practically demands it. But the Afghans are not eager to die. Once they realized how dangerous Russian military units could be, Afghan partisans became numerous bands of elusive warriors, always in the way but rarely remaining in the line of fire. This classic application of guerrilla-warfare techniques was possible only because the Afghans had thousands of resourceful and energetic leaders.

A major disadvantage of independent leadership is that it is not responsive to coordination and central direction. Fierce loyalty to family, clan, and tribe short-circuits any leadership beyond such restricted circles. A long-term concerted action would require an agreement that would circumvent generations of tribal and family feuds, not to mention plain old distrust and animosity. Unfortunately for the Russians, some of these agreements, although temporary, have been made and kept. Reported guerrilla attacks against the Afghan Army in Kunar Province were carried out by temporarily united mujahadeen groups. Their success sparked a Russian counteroffensive.

The texture of Afghan leadership creates an armed force similar to grains of sand. The Afghans are unlikely to form a force strong enough to hurt the Russian Army seriously. Yet the widely dispersed Afghan bands, rarely more than a few dozen men, are too tough individually and too numerous to be crushed by the usual Russian steamroller.

THE TIMETABLE FOR A RUSSIAN TAKEOVER (THAT HASN'T QUITE TAKEN)

Note: This timetable was compiled from reports by the Associated Press, *The New York Times*, Anthony Arnold's *Afghanistan: The Soviet Invasion in Perspective* (Hoover Institution Press), and notes provided by the Afghan Forum in New York.

(1) 1978—Taraki and Afghan Communist Party take power with Russian support; insurgency begins.

(2) February 15, 1979—United States Ambassador Adolph Dubs is abducted by antigovernment agents and killed during "rescue" when Afghan security forces storm the room in which he is being held. United States recommends negotiations with abductors. On February 16 the United States government accuses Moscow of playing the decisive role in the shoot-out that led to the slaying of Ambassador Dubs. Russia denies the charge, but admits its representatives were present. *The New York Times* reports, ". . . uncertainty exists over whether Dubs was shot by abductors or by government security aides." Russians are sus-

pected of wanting to embarrass antigovernment Afghans as well as remove the knowledgeable and well-connected Dubs.

(3) Spring 1973—Moscow starts discussions with Amin about removing the ineffectual Taraki; unbeknownst to Amin, the Russians begin to prepare for the political resurrection of the Parcham Faction of the Communist Party and Babrak Karmal.

(4) May 1979—Kremlin begins to refer to Afghanistan as a "member of the socialist community," code words for application of the Brezhnev Doctrine. Russian advisers begin taking over operations at Kabul's Bagram Air Base.

(5) Mid-August 1979—General Ivan G. Pavloskiy, commanding general of all Russian ground forces, arrives with an entourage of fifty officers. He will remain for almost two months.

(6) September 1, 1979—Taraki attends a nonaligned nations conference in Havana, Cuba.

(7) September 11, 1979—Taraki returns to Kabul.

(8) September 12, 1979—Taraki is forced to resign by Amin in a power move set in motion while Taraki was gone.

(9) September 14, 1979—Taraki allegedly attempts to assassinate Amin in the presidential palace; the plot fails.

(10) September 16, 1979—Amin assumes Taraki's office.

(11) September 18, 1979—About sixty are killed in a coup, which assures Amin of power; some speculate Taraki has been wounded or killed in the fighting.

(12) October 8, 1979—Other sources suggest that on this date the wounded Taraki was killed by strangulation.

(13) October 10, 1979—Kabul *Times* reports Taraki is dead of an illness.

(14) Early October 1979—General Pavloskiy's crew departs. Russian reservists in areas bordering Afghanistan are called to active duty.

(15) November 7, 1979—Soviet National Day. Kabul *Times* reports Afghanistan's role as a "continuation of the Great October Revolution." No eyebrows are raised.

(16) November 28, 1979—Lieutenant General Viktor Semenovich Paputin, a Kremlin deputy minister of interior, arrives for consultations on "mutual cooperation and other issues of interest." His high-level visit is not publicized until he has been in Kabul for three days. (One source for this timetable believes Paputin is really a top official in the KGB.)

(17) Mid-December, 1979—Russians airlift at least two battalions of infantry plus heavy weapons (light BMD personnel carriers and

some artillery) to Bagram Air Base. The battalions are probably drawn from an elite airborne division stationed in the Tashkent area.

(18) December 17, 1979—Amin's nephew, Assadullah Amin, chief of the Afghan intelligence service, is wounded by an assassin. He is taken to Tashkent for treatment. (Six months later he will return to Kabul to be executed by the Karmal regime.)

(19) December 18 and 19, 1979—The airlifted Russian battalions assume covering positions in the Salang Pass as the 357th Motorized Rifle Division, allegedly accompanied by KGB military units, begins to move south from the USSR.

(20) December 21–22, 1979—A reinforced Russian airborne regiment arrives at Bagram Air Base.

(21) December 22, 1979—Finally realizing his regime is under attack, Amin moves to the more-defensible Dar-ul-aman Palace. Unfortunately, the strategic and tactical momentum of the Russian invasion cannot be stopped. Russian advisers to Afghan tank detachments have made certain that the tank batteries have been removed for "maintenance purposes." Other Russian operatives have destroyed communication links outside Kabul, further isolating Afghan Army garrisons that might oppose the assault.

(22) December 23–24, 1979—Kabul's transportation and communications facilities are controlled by Russian troops. The infantry occupies the civilian airport and control tower. Commandos take over the government's central communications complex.

(23) December 25–26, 1979—The Russian buildup at Bagram Air Base continues. New motorized rifle units move to the Russian-Afghan border.

(24) December 27, 1979—Visiting Uzbek SSR minister of water resources hosts a reception for Afghan government officials at the Intercontinental Hotel. As the party concludes, the dignitaries are arrested. Meanwhile, Russian advisers to the Afghan Army host a cocktail party for their Afghan counterparts. The guests get drunk. Explosions go off outside, and the Afghans discover they're imprisoned in the building.

(25) December 27, 1979—H hour arrives at 19:15 (7:15 P.M.). Three Russian assault battalions hit the Dar-ul-Aman Palace, but run into stiff opposition, the first they've encountered in the capital. It won't be the last. Approximately 1,600 Russians attack President Amin and the palace guard (about 125 Afghans). Amin and his guards fight it out until midnight, indicating that even the "civilized" members of Afghan society know how to fight (in fact, Amin had the reputation of being

a good shot). The Russians' loss: 25 killed and 225 wounded. Resistance sources later report that no Afghans survived.

(26) December 28, 1979—Two more motorized rifle divisions cross the Afghan border. Another four move into reserve positions along the USSR-Afghan frontier. Fifty thousand Russian troops are in Afghanistan.

QUICK LOOK AT INDIA AND THE SIKHS: ETHNIC STRUGGLE ON THE SUBCONTINENT

Polyglot India has a long tradition of ethnic tolerance, at least as long as the ethnic groups know their places. The old caste system, now illegal, has been replaced by *jatis,* a more flexible caste-by-any-other-name system based on job status and religion. A number of India's provinces still have this social structure to a significant degree.

Many Indian provinces can communicate with other provinces only in the lingua franca of English.

India also has a tradition of rabid religious violence. Punjab Province is notorious for Hindu-Sikh conflicts. The Sikhs, an ascetic but militant ethnoreligious group, are demanding that the Punjab be an "autonomous Sikh state." New Delhi opposes the demand, envisioning the beginning of another division of the subcontinent, as happened with Pakistan. The Sikhs have a long, brilliant military tradition. The Akali Dal, the Sikh political party, is turning to armed street demonstrations and terror.

The Indian Army's June 1984 assault on the Sikhs' Golden Temple in Amritsar and associated violence may have killed as many as 2,000 people. The attack shocked Sikh sympathizers and radicalized many moderate Sikhs. This simmering Sikh rebellion could be far bloodier and much more sustained than the Assamese ethnic violence on the other side of India. Sporadic fighting occurred in 1982. In one 1983 outburst, according to some unverified reports, in less than two weeks as many as 4,000 Bengali immigrants were killed and another 10,000 to 20,000 were forced to flee.

PART 2

Africa

All Africa is divided into three parts. In the north lies the Saharan, Arab-dominated slice. In the south sits South Africa, the apartheid state of the white tribe. In between lie states in various stages of anarchy, chaos, starvation, and warfare—the results of powerful tribalism and colonialism. The few exceptions manage to maintain their sovereignty by difficult political and economic trade-offs. Some of the genuine middle African success stories, such as the Ivory Coast, still suffer from graft, a high debt load, and lack of transportation.

Africa's mix of colonialism, neocolonialism, potent tribalism, religious conflicts, foreign troops, modern weapons, economic decline, political aspirations, mounting international debts, racism, nationalism, and pan-nationalism creates extreme volatility. And Africa's human resources and relatively untapped natural resources make it an inevitable arena for geopolitical competition. This section will look at three African conflicts: Libya in Chad, Zaire and the battle against disintegration, and South Africa versus its neighbors and itself. These conflicts, while reflecting regional problems, also illustrate the larger troubles plaguing the African continent.

5. Libya and Chad: Qaddafi's Saharan Sandbox

INTRODUCTION

Colonel Muammar Qaddafi, the radical leader of Libya, seeks to build an empire at the expense of his neighbors. Chad, an impoverished African nation, is one of his recent attempts.

SOURCE OF CONFLICT

Colonel Qaddafi gets a lot of press coverage. There are a couple of reasons. Number one, because Qaddafi thinks he knows how to use the Western press to his advantage, he makes himself available to networks and newspapers. Through the media, the colonel thinks he can propagandize the Western masses with his titillating message of violence and arrogance. The second reason Colonel Qaddafi gets media attention is that he's a very convenient enemy—flamboyant, egotistical, arguably insane, fascistic, murderous, and, most important of all, demonstrably weak.

Colonel Qaddafi has bankrolled coups, assassinations, and revolts in at least nine countries. His one possible success was a coup engineered in starving, pitiful Upper Volta, but even that tragicomic affair has been a questionable victory. So much for covert, Qaddafi-led revolution.

Overtly, the colonel's forces have tended to do even worse. In 1978 the Egyptians beat the Libyans badly in their short border war. The Tanzanian Army routed the 2,000-man Libyan Legion in 1979 in Uganda. On at least two occasions weak Sudanese forces have flushed Libyan troops out of a disputed border region. Forced to withdraw from an initial fling in Chad, the colonel returned backing dissident forces in the name of (choose one or several possible reasons): socialist revolution, Islamic nationalism, anticolonialist solidarity.

WHO'S INVOLVED

Libya—Approximately 3,000 combat troops in Chad prior to the fall 1984 withdrawal agreement. Perhaps 10,000 auxiliaries, troops, and logistics personnel along Libya-Chad border.

Chad dissidents—French-educated elites who have been in power in N'Djamena. Nominal leader is Goukouni Oueddei. Three thousand to 4,000 soldiers.

Chad government—French-educated elites who constitute the sometime government of the Republic of Chad, based in N'Djamena. Nominal leader is Hissen Habré. Four thousand-plus soldiers.

France—Former colonial power in Chad. Approximately 3,000 military personnel in country, prior to the fall 1984 withdrawal agreement. Two thousand of the troops are ground combat forces.

Zaire—Approximately 2,000 Zairian soldiers are performing logistics and security missions for the N'Djamena government. Zaire's government is no friend of Qaddafi, and it owes France a favor (see Zaire chapter). Zaire also has aircraft (Mirage 5s) deployed in Chad.

Wild Cards

Russia—Russia needs Libya's arms market (hard currency) and can use Libya's influence among terrorists, but this is a marriage of convenience that Moscow could conclude has become permanently inconvenient.

Sudan and Egypt—Intervention by these other Libyan target states —for example, a direct attack across the Libyan frontier—could collapse the colonel's sand castle.

Nigeria—With 80 million people and an economy in shambles, Nigeria is a target for subversion and disruption, but the Nigerians have a history of not putting up with Qaddafi's interference. According to the Nigerian government, Qaddafi has tried to incite Moslem rebellion in Nigeria. Chadian rebels have fired on Nigerian patrol boats sailing on Lake Chad. This might backfire. Nigeria may be on the economic ropes, but it has a decent army and is a superpower by African standards.

GEOGRAPHY

Libya has a population of around 3.5 million and an area of 1,820,000 square kilometers. Tripoli has a population of approximately 850,000; Benghazi, 350,000. The country has significant oil deposits. One of Libya's most significant climatic features is the *ghibli,* a dry, hot, dusty southern desert wind occurring in spring and fall. The winds last one to four days; temperatures can rise as much as 20 degrees Celsius in a few hours. Almost all activity, including revolution, ceases.

Libya borders Egypt, the Sudan, Chad, Niger, Algeria, and Tunisia. Colonel Qaddafi has sponsored rebels and dissent in every one of his immediate neighbors.

Chad is the inland keystone to central Africa. It borders Libya to the north, Sudan to the east, the Central African Republic to the south, Niger to the west, and Cameroon and Nigeria to the southwest. Mountains cover the northwestern corner of the country and the area south of Abéché. Lake Chad, which divides Chad from Nigeria, is a vital water source, for most of the country is desert or arid pasture.

Chad has a population of 5 million and an area of 1,330,000 square kilometers. The population is fairly evenly divided between Moslems in the north and animists (followers of old tribal religions) in the south. Christians make up about 10 percent of the population, most of them living in the south. Nearly 340,000 people live in or near the capital, N'Djamena. French is the official language, though Arabic is spoken in the north. The animists speak several tribal dialects.

Less than 5.5 percent of the land is arable. Eighty-two percent of the population is classified as rural, but over 90 percent is engaged in subsistence agriculture. Even city life is a rural existence. Herding cattle is a major industry. The life expectancy in Chad is around forty-three years. Poverty and lack of facilities plague the country. Roads are a telling statistic—of Chad's approximately 28,000 kilometers of road, fewer than 300 kilometers are hard-surfaced.

HISTORY

Chad

From the ninth to the sixteenth centuries, the Sao tribes controlled most of Chad, Niger, and parts of the Sudan. Their black central African kingdom was under constant pressure from Arabs and black Islamic converts to the north. By the seventeenth century the Arabs were in nominal control of the country.

The French entered Chad in 1891 and attacked several of the southern Islamic fiefdoms. Chad became part of French Equatorial Africa until FEA was disbanded in 1959.

In 1975 a military coup toppled the fifteen-year-old regime of N'Garta Tombalbaye. Fighting broke out between the new junta and various rebel groups, the strongest led by Moslem rebel leader Hissen Habré. A coalition government in which former junta leader Félix Malloum and Habré shared power proved to be unstable. Nigeria mediated a truce in 1979, and Goukouni Oueddei was installed as a compromise leader. Religious rioting and the massacre of southern Moslems shook Goukouni's government. Nigeria once again tried to mediate, but in 1980 the cease-fire broke down. Habré, and a coalition of southern tribes, finally overthrew Goukouni in 1980. One of the major reasons for this overthrow was the Libyan report of January 6, 1981 (released after the Habré-led coup), that Goukouni and Qaddafi had decided to merge Libya and Chad. This, combined with Libya's interest in the potentially mineral-rich Anzou Strip, added to a series of internal disagreements that brought about the 1980 overthrow of Goukouni by Habré and a coalition of southern tribes. Sudan and Egypt supported Habré during the final stages of the civil war.

Libya

Arab armies overran Libya in the seventh century, driving the Berber tribes away from the coast and deeper into the desert. The Turks exercised nominal control over Libya from the sixteenth to the twentieth centuries. "Nominal" hardly describes the situation. Moslem pirates operated from the Libyan coast, and Sanussi tribes and religious sects controlled the oases in the interior.

In the early twentieth century, Italy wrested control of Libya from the Turks. The Italians had grand designs, which included settling huge numbers of Italian immigrants along the coast. Mussolini's visions of a new Roman Empire (similar to Qaddafi's visions of a new Arab empire) gave the Libyan project additional impetus, but then his failure in World War II lost Libya entirely.

Significant oil reserves were discovered in 1959. King Idris, leader of the Libyan resistance to Italian colonialism and head of a postwar constitutional monarchy, was deposed by a military coup in 1969. Colonel Qaddafi assumed power as "Leader of the Revolution." His adventures in Chad began with border incidents in the Anzou Strip. Several incidents occurred in the early 1970s. Libyan troops, according to several published European reports, were operating in Chad in 1977. Libya launched an "unofficial" invasion in 1981 and experienced two troop withdrawals, one in 1981 and one in 1982. Spring 1983 produced the next round of Libyan intervention. France responded by sending paratroops to support the republican government.

As of fall 1984, Chad is divided in half, roughly along the 16th parallel. But the parallel is an imaginary line in the sand. In the past there have been several "red lines" that were to separate the combatants. Sooner or later someone crossed the line. Water and oases are what count. The Libyans and the rebels use Faya (Largeau) as a base and staging area. The government and French forces are in the south, using N'Djamena as their prime staging area.

Colonel Qaddafi's fall 1984 deal with King Hassan of Morocco, the "unification" of their nations, is an act of desperation. As the petrodollars dry up and the anti-Qaddafi resistance increases in Libya, the colonel needs friends—as well as a cover for temporary withdrawal from Chad. King Hassan, who is well on his way to defeating the Polisario insurgency in former Spanish Morocco, also serves his own interest. Loss of Qaddafi's support knocks a major financial and propaganda prop from beneath the Polisario guerrillas. Looked at in a classic Machiavellian scenario, Libya and Morocco have turned on their neighbor Algeria, a nation that continues, as of fall 1984, to support the Polisario.

The Morocco-Libya agreement opened the door to a "mutual withdrawal" of French and Libyan forces from Chad. French mobile forces pulled back to outposts within 250 kilometers of N'Djamena. Chad's republican government claimed that Libya had made no withdrawals. France's code name for the withdrawal operation was that of a mud fish that burrows deep in the sand when the water disappears but returns to the surface when the floods come. This little fish tale informs West Africa that French troops can also reappear, especially if they have never left. The political situation in France, and the fragile situation in Chad, seem to favor continued French military involvement.

LOCAL POLITICS

Chad

Political parties are banned. As in many Third World states, the parties don't matter as much as the elites and the tribes.

Hissen Habré—President and leader of Republic of Chad; former rebel leader.

Goukouni Oueddei—Former president; current rebel leader.

GUNT—French acronym for Goukouni's forces.

Libya

Colonel Muammar Qaddafi has no official title; he's referred to as Leader of the Revolution.

Green Book—Qaddafi's revolutionary manifesto. Combines Islam, romance, Marxist jargon, and the colonel's insights into life. Required reading in Libya.

General People's Congress—Pseudolegislative forum run by executive General People's Committee and Colonel Qaddafi.

Jamahiriyya—"Republic of the Masses" in Arabic. Qaddafi's name for the Libyan government.

National Front for the Salvation of Libya—Anti-Qaddafi group formed in 1980 by former Libyan diplomat Mohammed Yosef al-Maghariaf. One of 11 Libyan opposition groups.

PARTICIPANT STRATEGIES AND GOALS

Libya—Qaddafi appears to be a man who relishes irony as long as it isn't visited upon him, which makes his anticolonial and anti-imperialist rhetoric so interesting. Imperialism isn't new and it isn't a European invention. Libya's annexation of northern Chad smacks of the kind of imperialism, of the Arab variety, that was anathema to black Africans long before the Portuguese planted flags along the West African coast.

As a youth, Qaddafi saw the results of Italian colonialism and knew the ugly history of the Ottoman occupation of Libya. No doubt this plays a large part in shaping his view of the world, along with doses of messianic Islam and a romantic quest for power. Qaddafi has stated repeatedly that he was called upon to be a great world leader. Unfortunately, from the colonel's perspective, he has few to lead.

Sure, Libya has oil, which pays for all the tanks and fighter-bombers as well as bankrolling terrorists. Libya also has a long Mediterranean coastline that outflanks NATO's Italian defense zone and bypasses Crete and the Turkish Straits. This interests Muscovites looking for air and naval bases, and frightens Romans, Londoners, and others. But with a population in the neighborhood of 3.5 million, in a country strung along the coast with the Sahara Desert to its back, and sharply divided between Arabs and desert tribesmen, the colonel doesn't have much to work with. Therefore, he tried an *anschluss* with Egypt and was refused. Now he looks to the Sudan, Tunisia, the Arab world in general, and gets swatted away.

However, Qaddafi is an armed gadfly. Neighboring Chad has had an unsettled Saharan border dispute with Libya that goes back to Ottoman days. (Before that no one cared about borders.)

Chad may have uranium deposits in its northern area. That sounds good to the colonel; the deposits might lead to A-bombs, and uranium is certainly worth some money. Chad might also be a nice place finally to show some Libyan armed muscle. Surely all these newfangled Russian weapons will defeat those backward southerners and show the rest of central Africa that Qaddafi is someone to be reckoned with. The Libyans would be beating the French in battle, a feather in the helmet even better than the 1984 embassy shoot-out in London. Libya stands up to those nasty former European big shots; that should be worth some votes at the next conference of nonaligned nations. Finally, Chad's worthless sand and poverty can be worth something, if you know how to look at maps. Chad sits like a big keystone, touching all the central African states. It also extends the Libyan border with vulnerable Sudan, and could place the Libyans in direct contact with Sudanese rebels in the south. And it puts Libya in contact with that big prize, Nigeria.

Once again there's a war in a nowheresville that is now a violent somewhere.

Since a war is going on among Chad's elites, Libya has only to choose the side that needs an ally.

Republican Government of Chad—Hang on with French and United States support, then make a deal with the rebels that excludes Qaddafi. The goal of both sides is to achieve governmental consensus and stop the fighting. But since Chad is so poor, the government and the elites would then face the impossible problems of its drought-stricken reality.

France—Contain Qaddafi with the smallest expenditure of men and matériel. The goals are to establish a consensus government in Chad and show other former French African colonies that France can be depended upon to be a reliable supporter when provocateurs like the colonel cross those tenuous African borders.

The former colonies demand economic, political, and military support in exchange for raw materials sold at favorable prices to France, and domestic markets with lower tariffs for the old colonizers manufactured goods. It looks like the old colonial situation, but with some very significant changes. The local elites are in charge of the local economic apparatus. If the old colonial power doesn't come through, they threaten to cancel the bilateral economic agreements and start dealing with the Reds, or the Japanese, or the Americans, or whichever country is anathema to the old colonialists. The former colonial power usually comes through with aid, and the situation trundles along until the next military or economic crisis. Chad is of little economic importance to France, but not so the Cameroons or several other African countries. Chad's elites understand the power game; as a result, the French poodle gets wagged by the Chadian tail.

SUPERPOWER INTEREST

	Political	Military	Historical	Economic
Russia	Medium to Low	Low	Very Low	Low
US	Medium	Low	Very Low	Low

Political—There is only one area of superpower interest and confrontation, the political. Russia has an arms investment in Qaddafi's sideshows as well as a lot of Third World political rhetoric. The United

States' interest is in keeping Egypt from being cut off from the rest of Africa by hostile states. This means supporting Upper Egypt, i.e., the Sudan. Hence, United States AWACS aircraft fly surveillance missions over the Sudan and relay intelligence to the French.

Note: The power that should be shown on the chart is France. The French are very involved in all of western Africa. Such a chart would read Political: High; Military: Medium; Historical: High; Economic: High. France perceives Chad as a test of French will in Africa. The former African colonies are watching to see if Paris will provide the support it has promised. If Paris reneges, France will lose a lot of political leverage. Hence French paras and fighter-bombers.

POTENTIAL OUTCOMES

1. 40 percent chance: French troops and political pressure stabilize the combat lines. A political deal, involving power-sharing (and francs in politicians' pockets), is cut between the dissidents, the republican government, and Paris. The colonel is excluded, but he calls it a victory anyway. Goes to 70 percent if French troops remain in Chad through 1985.

2. 30 percent chance: Rebels press for all-out victory by launching a new push to the south. If this occurs and the French still have troops in Chad, there's an 80 percent chance of a republican-French victory; a republican victory means the rebels are dispersed and the Libyans driven back into their country in shame; rebel victory means a new government in N'Djamena and a temporary success for Qaddafi, including recognition of the Libyan annexation of northern Chad. The new government would ultimately make a deal with the French.

3. 15 percent chance: Republican government launches an offensive to the north. If this occurs and the French still have troops in the field, there's a 95 percent chance of a republican-French victory.

4. 10 percent chance: French domestic politics force a withdrawal of French ground troops and air units. If this occurs, a rebel victory over the republicans is an 85 percent likelihood unless the Nigerians (see outcome 5) intervene.

5. 5 percent chance: The Nigerians intervene. Nigeria occupies southern Chad, backs a convenient government, and pushes Libya back into the north.

COST OF WAR

This has been an unremitting, low-budget bloodbath. Many of the most bloody actions were more massacre than warfare. This endemic disorder causes many more deaths by dislocation and privation. One could make a case that corruption is a bigger killer than military action, if only because there appears to be more local talent for corruption than for organized military action. We estimate that fewer than 2,000 people have been killed in action in Libya since 1975. This figure includes all combat deaths—Chadian, Libyan, French, and other participants. Another 2,000 civilians may have been killed in massacres, compared with the approximately 100,000 people who have starved to death in Chad during the same time period. Several Western press reports suggest the figure is much higher. Some of those starvation deaths may be directly attributable to the war; most of the starvation, however, is the result of poor agricultural techniques, corruption in the food distribution system, and the prolonged drought.

DESERT FEVER: ISLAM, DESERT CULTURE, AND REVOLUTION

The people of the desert have always been feared by neighboring city dwellers and farmers. The desert dwellers were free of overlords, and equally free of any steady, reliable source of sustenance. The desert people were admired for their ability to survive where others must surely perish. They reciprocated this respect with a proud disdain for those who did not live free. This attitude led to banditry and frequent revolution.

Nomads are best dealt with on their own terms. Throughout the Middle East (and the world), wise leaders learned to strike a deal with those whom they could not control. To remain in a constant state of conflict with the nomads merely provided a ready ally for any potential rebels among the settled population.

Nomads lead a leisurely, and somewhat desperate, life. They live simply because they must. Home is what you can carry. When times are bad, nomads hunker down and do what they do best, which is survive. When times are good, they indulge in their favorite sport, which is called war.

Throughout history, nomads have become a menace whenever changing climatic conditions either gave them enough surplus wealth to become full-time warriors, or caused privation that drove them in desperation into settled lands.

The nomads of the Arabian desert did not experience the changes in climate that pushed Asiatic nomads into China and Europe. In Arabia the catalyst was religion. Islam arose in the seventh century, and within 100 years the nomad-led armies of Islam had spread from the Atlantic in the west to the Pacific in the east. Arab-led armies reached down into the jungles of Africa and north into Russia.

While the Huns, Tatars, and other wandering warriors of Asia eventually were subdued, Islam sustained the Arab nomads. Islam continues to feed them spiritually and politically. The vigor of Islam rests partially in the independent spirit of its Arab nomad roots. While "civilization" and wealth from oil may weaken this physical independence, the psychological advantage remains.

The revolutionary spirit of the Islamic nomad resides in a religious and cultural conservatism that gives the movement stability over time. The spiritual conservatism provides a long historical identity and a sustaining religious relevancy; the cultural conservatism, however, can provide the framework for a violent reaction to material change brought about by contact and trade with other cultural groups. This reactionism, usually based on a "Golden Age" notion of simpler times and purer values, creates a very substantial danger to neighboring states. The religious rebellion in Iran brought the lesson home hard to the other gulf states. Russia, with its large Moslem population, also became nervous.

What the Arab nomad revolutionaries created in the seventh century has not fallen into history's dustbin. The Arabs believe that if they are threatened enough, they can rise again and mold the surrounding world in their own image. After the events in Iran, no one can totally discount such an event.

QUICK LOOK AT THE SUDAN: FURTHER LIBYAN ADVENTURES

The war in the Sudan varies in intensity from low simmer to sudden boil. There are several reasons. A quick look at the map shows that a pro-Russian takeover in the Sudan would cut off Egypt from the rest of Africa. The Sudan has a large population that Colonel Qaddafi of Libya would like to control. Libya's rich, but it has so few people. Taking the Sudan would give the colonel a nation to lead. The Sudan may have huge oil deposits; it is also a potential breadbasket.

A long civil war waged by dissident Christian and animist groups in the southern Sudan ended when General Gaafar Mohammed Numeiry, President of the Sudan, offered a compromise peace settlement that tacitly gave the dissidents the right to continue their religious practices. Colonel Qaddafi, however, in seeking to upset Numeiry's pro-Western government, began offering military and financial support to Sudanese Islamic religious zealots. To head off an Islamic revolution, Numeiry decided in 1983 to make Islamic religious law the civil law of the Sudan. This pleased the Islamic zealots, but angered the Christians and the animists. Qaddafi started shipping guns to the Christians and the animists. The civil war resumed.

Every once in a while, a Libyan Army unit will cross the Sudanese border. A couple of times the Sudanese have caught these units and defeated them. Now the colonel prefers surprise air raids and subversion. United States AWACS aircraft, vectoring Egyptian fighters, have put a dent in this tactic. The AWACS have the ability to detect the approaching Libyan bomber, pinpoint the originating air base, and, if Washington gives the command, order a retaliatory strike by United States carrier-based planes that will hit the Libyan base before the jet returns from its attack. This is called deterrence.

QUICK LOOK AT SOMALIA AND THE HORN: THE OGADEN WAR

Somalia juts out from Africa like a finger pointing toward the Arabian Sea. Oil tanker traffic to and from the Persian Gulf, as well as access to the Red Sea and the Suez Canal, give Somalia, the French protectorate of Djibouti, Ethiopia, and South Yemen a strategic position. Air and naval bases in the African Horn can be used to support forces in the Arabian Peninsula, or to close the entire region to merchant traffic.

The strategic Bab al-Mandeb Strait separates South Yemen and Djibouti. France keeps a Foreign Legion reaction force in Djibouti. It is supported by a squadron of fighter-bombers and a naval contingent. The Somali port of Berbera was once a major Russian port of call and naval supply center. The Russians now use South Yemen.

This area of East-West competition is wracked by the same internal squabbles afflicting the Arabian Peninsula as well as some of the post-colonial problems endemic to Africa.

The Somali-Ethiopian War, also called the Ogaden War, results from the late nineteenth-century colonial division of Somali tribes. Ethiopia is fighting another perennial war in the secessionist province of Eritrea. The Eritreans believe they were arbitrarily made part of Ethiopia. They have been fighting the central government in Addis Ababa for over twenty years. There are two major Eritrean resistance organizations: the Eritrean Popular Liberation Front (EPLF) and the Eritrean Liberation Front-People's Liberation Forces (ELF-PLF). The Russians supported the Eritrean rebels against the Ethiopian central government until a Marxist-oriented clique took power in Addis Ababa. Moscow dropped its support for the Eritreans posthaste. Since then, Cuban forces and Russian officers have been directly involved in Ethiopian offensives into the Ogaden Desert and into Eritrea.

Ethiopia and Somalia both have dormant claims to Djibouti. The French Foreign Legion unit in Djibouti keeps the claims dormant.

6. Zaire: And Quiet Flows the Congo

INTRODUCTION

Zaire fights several wars. First, there's an internal war, fought among the country's elites over who will control the government. Second, there are the tribal conflicts, often between Zairian provinces that but for colonialism would be different tribal nations. Then come the wars of outside interests, like the Angolans who sponsor to some degree the regular Katangan invasions, which become minor border wars. Sometimes this favor is reciprocated by Zaire, which from 1975 to 1982 sponsored a revolt in Angola's Cabinda Province. Finally, there's the war between Zaire and the International Monetary Fund (IMF), which tries to cycle cash from the relatively wealthy of the world to the definitely poor. Zaire is losing this economic war, in large part because of the endemic Zairian governmental corruption. Economic aid has a way of ending up in the Swiss bank accounts of the Zairian elites. Almost every nation in middle Africa suffers from similar problems, the only differences being in degree.

SOURCE OF CONFLICT

Zaire's problems are classic examples of the twentieth-century results of nineteenth-century colonialism. In European parlors borders were drawn on the basis of who had explorers and troops wherever and/or whoever was currently in political hock to whom. Tribal areas, cultural development, and language were given little consideration. The racist colonialists thought the natives were all "wogs," and that the empire's troops could bring order out of any chaos. But empires break up. The Belgians tried to keep the Congo and succeeded for fifteen or so post-World War II years. But it is a big task to control the tens of millions of people in central Africa. Central Africans have trouble doing it and they live there. Zaire has more than 200 different ethnic groups. The four major tribes constitute only 45 percent of the population. Zaire should have been several countries, but then history's filled with should-haves.

Here's the gist of the problem: When the colonial power leaves, there's inevitably a power vacuum, no matter how well prepared for independence the country seems to be. The colonial physicians, engineers, and other skilled personnel often leave with the colonial army. If no locals have been trained to take their places (for example, in 1960 Zaire, then called the Belgian Congo, had three native MDs), economic and political disruption follow. The colonial powers made either weak attempts (Britain in Nigeria) or none at all (France and Belgium) to give their former colonies a sense of national identity or the technical means to run a country and an economy. This neglect has been a cause of great suffering.

When there is no effort or desire on the part of a newly independent people to reorganize the country into nations along tribal lines, the real bickering starts. It is exacerbated if single tribes are divided by national boundaries—like the Somalis, many of whom are located in Ethiopia. Zaire, compared to other former middle African colonies, had a diversified economy when it achieved independence, but seven years of warfare from decolonialization in 1960 to 1967 stymied development. The invasion of Shaba in 1977 by the Angolan-backed Katangan gendarmes began another series of internal and external conflicts.

WHO'S INVOLVED

Zaire—Central government of President Mobutu; located in Kinshasa.

Zairian ethnic and religious groups, over 200—They aren't unified players in the political game, but separately they cause constant internal disputes. The government's game is to play the groups off one another; its policy of "national homogeneity" is a political masquerade.

Katangan rebels—Remnants of old Katangan gendarmerie, leftist elements from Angola. Still organized into a combat force and waiting in Angola. Originally participated in civil fighting in 1960 and 1961 and were defeated. Still a well-disciplined mercenary organization that could be a danger to Angola or anyone who harbors it.

Wild Cards

Angola—Outside sponsor of Katangans.

Cubans—Possible reinforcements to Katangans.

French Foreign Legion—The French say that when it comes to police work in Africa, one Foreign Legionnaire provides the same stabilizing influence as 100 Cubans. The Legion is a better mercenary outfit and doesn't carry the same heavy political baggage that comes with Cubans. Still, there is some merit to the Russian assertion that the French are the Cubans of the West.

GEOGRAPHY

The Belgian Congo has been renamed Zaire. The Congo River has been renamed the Zaire River. The local currency is now called the zaire. *Pays, fleuve, monnaie*—country, river, money—Zaire is referred to as the land of the three Zs. But in anybody's alphabet, Zaire remains the same equatorial land of 2.3 million square kilometers that it was when King Léopold II of Belgium was the sovereign.

Terrain varies from grasslands and savannas to mountains to tropical rain forests. The population is almost 32 million with 30 percent living in cities. Kinshasa has a population of more than three million. Over half the people are Christian, the remainder are members of tribal syncretic and animist sects.

Zaire borders Angola, Zambia, Tanzania, Burundi, Rwanda, Uganda, Sudan, the Central African Republic, and the Congo. It has large deposits of copper and cobalt as well as zinc, manganese, gold, and other minerals. The Shaba region, especially the mining area of Kolwezi, is particularly rich in mineral deposits. Shaba, formerly called Katanga, borders on Angola and Zambia.

Some statisticians estimate that Zaire has 13 percent of the world's potential hydroelectric power. Its land and climate make it a potential African breadbasket, but so far, agricultural development has not even kept pace with expanding domestic food needs.

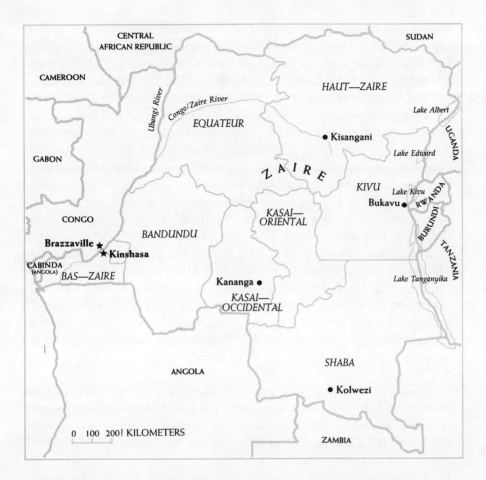

Zaire suffers from a "Balkanized" economy, an economy divided by mismanagement, separated by either poor or nonexistent transportation systems, language differences, and tribal mistrusts.

HISTORY

Migrating Bantu tribes from Nigeria entered the Congo Basin around 700 A.D., driving earlier inhabitants south and east. The Portuguese explorer Diogo Cão surveyed the Congo River's estuary in 1482. This was the heartland of the Bakongo Kingdom. Because of the thick jungle and native tales of wild interior tribes, few Europeans attempted to penetrate beyond the coast. Besides, the Bankongos supplied them with slaves and ivory. The hinterland remained relatively unexplored by Europeans until Henry Morton Stanley (of "Dr. Livingston, I presume" fame) passed through present-day Zaire in the 1870s. Belgium's King Léopold II, after hiring Stanley as an explorer and adviser, claimed the Congo area at the Berlin Conference of 1885.

The Congo was Belgium's most important colony, but the Belgians did little to improve native education or living standards. Their primary interest was in extracting Zaire's plentiful natural resources and shipping them to resource-poor Belgium. There were several native anticolonial movements, most of them religiously inspired, including Kimbanguism and the Kitawala sect.

French African decolonialization in the fifties made Belgium's already shaky hold on Zaire completely untenable. Zaire (then still called the Congo) became independent on June 30, 1960. Patrice Lumumba became prime minister and Joseph Kasavubu, president. Peace lasted less than a week. The army mutinied, Belgian troops acted to protect colonials living in Zaire, and Katanga Province (now Shaba), under the leadership of Moise Tshombe, seceded from the new republic. United Nations peacekeeping forces showed up, but Lumumba demanded they be placed under his direct control. The UN commander refused on the grounds that that was not part of his mandate. Lumumba then startled the world by requesting direct Russian aid.

This was too much. Exercising his powers as president, Kasavubu tried to fire Lumumba, but Lumumba refused to leave the government. He tried to remove Kasavubu. Colonel Joseph Mobutu (the current president) led a military coup that toppled the unmanageable government. Mobutu threw out all East Bloc diplomats and advisers, put Lumumba in prison, then returned Kasavubu to power. Meanwhile, Lumumba died from mysterious causes; he was probably assassinated by his rivals. But Lumumba has his memorial—the KGB-run Patrice Lumumba University in Moscow for "students from the developing world."

In 1961 Zaire was in shambles. The reborn Kasavubu government faced a half dozen dissident groups, chief among them being a "pro-Lumumba people's government" in Kisangani, run by the ex-vice-premier and Lumumba loyalist Antoine Gizenga; Maurice Tshombe down in Katanga, and a Baluba-tribe separatist rebellion in Kasai. Confusion, combat, negotiations, and UN troops brought on the Baluba rebellion. Gizenga and his followers returned to the government, but Katanga held out until 1963.

Katanga's reintegration and the UN withdrawal in 1964 didn't produce internal stability. A tribal rebellion erupted, directed by former Lumumba ally Pierre Mulele. Another revolt broke out in Kivu Province, led by another Lumumba faction. In July 1964 Tshombe was named head of the central government. He directed a counterattack on rebel strongholds and got strong support from Belgium.

In late 1965 political infighting resulted in the fall of the Tshombe regime. Mobutu, now a lieutenant general, led another military coup. He installed himself as president, a position he still holds as of summer 1984. In July 1966 white mercenaries and Katangan rebels, many of them former members of the national army and police forces, launched another drive on the central government. Combat ensued and was renewed a year later. By late 1967 the insurgency had been defeated and the Katangans withdrew into Angola.

They returned in 1977 with a fast-paced invasion that overran Shaba Province. Mobutu asked for French and Belgian assistance. He was provided with a regiment of the Moroccan Army, which pushed back the rebels into Angola. The rebels fought a series of holding actions, avoiding pitched battles with the Moroccan forces. In May 1978 the rebels launched another offensive, this time directed at the mining town of Kolwezi. This was a most calculated invasion, one designed to strike at Zaire's economy. When the rebels took Kolwezi, they machine-gunned Belgian and French technical advisers and mining personnel as well as Zairian civilians. As many as 200 foreigners and 5,000 Zairians may have been killed. France responded by sending the Foreign Legion. The Legionnaires and the Zairian Army routed the rebels and drove them from Shaba. Belgium provided a paratroop battalion.

Since 1978 the Zairian government has been plagued with economic difficulties that compound some of the internal tribal contentions.

As of summer 1984, the Katangan conflict is in a quiet phase. Katangan rebel groups remain in their Angolan havens. Some bandit activity around Lake Tanganyika may be caused by former rebels on the lam.

Accurate figures for Zaire's war with the IMF are hard to obtain, but sources cite inflation rates of 35 percent to 40 percent as low-ball estimates. International debt is around $2 billion. This figure compares with a 1980 GNP of slightly more than $6 billion. Internal development is at a standstill despite President Mobutu's policy of "national homogenization," an alleged attempt to forge a national identity for Zaire. The actual policy is to spread around as many economic goodies as possible among the tribes while keeping the elites in the federal district of Kinshasa supplied with new Mercedes. This works when copper prices are high. When they aren't, the country's consensus begins to break down.

Mobutu does feel confident enough about the internal and external situations that he has lent Chad and France 2,000 to 3,000 troops for duty in Chad. But then, he also owes France a thank-you for the Legion's assistance in 1978. In Chad his troops are given an opportunity to train and gain field experience. This could be very valuable should the Shaba invasion occur that we predict for 1986–1987.

LOCAL POLITICS

Zaire, nominally a federal republic, is a strongman dictatorship backed by the army and a consensus of tribal leaders.

Mobutu Sese Seko—The former Joseph Mobutu, now President of Zaire, referred to as "the Guide." He is a dictator backed by the army. Still appears to be the only consensus leader.

Popular Movement of the Revolution (MPR)—Only legal political party, a Mobutu front.

Katangan rebels—Remnants of old Katangan gendarmerie, some renegade Lumumba backers, leftist elements, now perhaps 2,000 strong. They are essentially an exile army in Angola. Evidence shows Cuban and East Bloc advisers have trained and rearmed the rebel units, but some of these guys were first-class French and British-trained mercs to begin with.

The Bakongo—Largest ethnic group with 2.5 to 3 million members. A Bantu tribe, they are only 10 percent of population, which illustrates the ethnic diversity of the country.

Baluba, Balunda, Mongos—Other major Zairian Bantu tribes.

Manbetu-Azande—Major Zairian Hamitic tribe.

Lingala—A Zairian patois, the language used by the Zairian Army and the closest thing to a national language. Government "nationalization policies" encourage its use. Zaire may have as many as 650 local languages and dialects.

Kimbanguism—Syncretic tribal religion, full name, "The Church of Christ on Earth by the Prophet Simon Kimbangu." Three to four million members.

In 1969 Kimbanguism was recognized by the World Council of

Churches. Current head of the government is Diangienda Kuntima, a son of founder Simon Kimbangu.

PARTICIPANT STRATEGIES AND GOALS

Zaire's central government—Continue to play the internal pay-off game and hope the IMF doesn't close the bank. The government must ensure that the Shaba region is adequately defended to forestall another invasion. Shaba is economically vital to Zaire's existence and everyone knows it. As for internal politics, the increasing use of the Lingala language and educational development are crucial to national survival, but these programs will take a long time and a lot of political stability to be successful.

Katangan rebels—Bide their time and wait for another opportunity to return to Shaba. Goal is to put their gang in power.

SUPERPOWER INTEREST

	Political	Military	Historical	Economic
Russia	Medium	Low	Very Low	Medium
US	Medium	Low	Low	Medium to High

Political—This isn't a big superpower arena. Political interest ranks as high as it does because of superpower relationships with other middle African black states—Russia with Angola and the United States with Nigeria—though United States-Zairian bilateral relations are strong. Zaire supports the Camp David accords and United States mediation efforts in southern Africa. (Worth noting is the United Nations' political investment in Zaire—UN action saved it as a national entity in 1960, but Zaire is no longer a major UN concern.)

Military—Zaire doesn't figure into East-West military power balances.

Historical—Very little historical interest from either Russia or the United States.

Economic—Economics is another ball game. Russia has significant cobalt supplies and allegedly went around buying up cobalt and copper prior to last Katangan invasion. The United States and the West (especially France and Belgium) rely on a steady supply of Zairian raw materials, especially cobalt.

POTENTIAL OUTCOMES

1. 60 percent chance: Same old suffering continues, with new Katangan invasion. Date for new invasion is sometime in 1986 or 1987.

2. 10 percent chance: Successful tribal federation system is established. Goes to 40 percent if Zaire avoids bankruptcy.

3. 30 percent chance: Area disintegrates into separate nations with Katanga a viable independent country. Goes to 40 percent after 1986 if Zaire goes into bankruptcy; to 60 percent if Mobutu dies before 1988.

COST OF WAR

In this part of the world, the depredations of war take a distinct second place to the ravages of daily life. Famine and disease are killing millions annually. Most of the forces are armed with light infantry weapons, many of them obsolete World War II surplus. Communications gear is practically nonexistent. Most troop losses come from disease and privation, not enemy action. The major result of all this armed posturing is to prevent the civilians from getting on with their lives. Oh yes, the soldiers often regress to common banditry. Welcome to the Dark Ages.

THE DOGS OF WAR—WHITE MERCS IN AFRICA

The image of the white mercenary relentlessly laying waste to black African soldiers is part myth and part fact. Mercenary soldiers are still used in many parts of the world. Indochina, the Persian Gulf, Latin America, and Britain are a few examples. But in Africa it's a little different. In Africa the white mercenary has the advantage of the *myth* of the white mercenary.

African soldiers, if properly trained and led (by whites or blacks), are as effective as any others. This has been demonstrated many times. Nigeria in particular has some outstanding light infantry units. South Africa has several elite black commando units. Bushmen from Namibia serve as trackers in South African forces. These sons of Kalahari hunter-gatherers are arguably the world's best light-infantry scouts. But most African nations usually provide neither proper training nor leadership. The typical white mercenary has served in a Western army and may even have combat experience. Then there is a psychological advantage: The white mercenary believes he is superior to the African soldier, and most African soldiers agree.

South Africa extends the myth to cover all white soldiers, particularly South Africans. The South African Army devotes considerable attention to training its troops and selecting the most effective military leaders. The South African troops are used in a very professional manner, no matter who the opposition is. But then, one mark of professionalism is not to underestimate the enemy. The net effect sustains the myth of the superior white soldiers and, in South African eyes, whites in general. As long as white soldiers have the edge in training and leadership, the myth will retain its basis in fact.

7. Boer Wars:
Africa's White Tribe

INTRODUCTION

This chapter will look at South Africa's internal apartheid war and one of the regional multistate guerrilla struggles in which it is involved, the Namibian War. These regional battles involve the nationalist ambitions of several tribal groups located in the Republic of South Africa (RSA), Angola, Namibia (South West Africa), Zimbabwe, and Mozambique. Neighboring Botswana and Swaziland are also indirectly involved.

The economic dominance of white South Africans and their state's noxious apartheid laws are under intense political and military fire from both inside and outside the RSA. Still, the ideological and racial issues all too often mask an underlying tribalism and sustained historical rivalries.

Both the internal and regional conflicts of South Africa are of special interest to the rest of the world because of geopolitical considerations. Southern Africa occupies a strategic position. Naval units based near the Cape of Good Hope can sweep into the South Atlantic or into the Indian Ocean. The VLCCs (very large crude carriers), which cannot squeeze through the Suez Canal, must circle the Cape on their way to European oil refineries. Southern Africa is rich in strategic mineral deposits. South Africa mines nearly 70 percent of the non-Communist world's gold. Neighboring Zimbabwe possesses some of the world's highest-grade chromium deposits.

SOURCE OF CONFLICT

Desperate problems beset southern Africa, problems that too often are perceived solely as a confrontation between white and black faces.

Nor should these conflicts be portrayed as a common East-West confrontation with "the forces of democracy opposing Soviet imperialism,"
or "noble Cuban soldiers defending the Angolan revolution against
Western puppet forces." In fact, racism and ideology are less important
causes of South Africa's conflicts than a troubled history of colonialism
and tribalism.

Brutal British colonial mismanagement, Zulu wars, and Boer resistance to both set the stage for a twentieth-century economic and political takeover that put the racist and patriarchal Afrikaner clans in
charge of the Republic of South Africa (RSA). In the seventeenth,
eighteenth, and nineteenth centuries, the Boers curled up inside their
circled-wagon *laagers* to fend off tribal attacks or British colonial intrusions. Now the Afrikaners use crude and cruel race laws to control their
opponents. As once the Boers were brutally uprooted from their farms
by British troops and placed into detention camps, so now they uproot
other tribes and transport them to poverty-pocket "homelands" that
are little more than large detention camps. The black tribes are kept out
of the political and economic structures. This political and economic
exclusion is called apartheid; it is, in reality, little more than a system
of state slavery. "Nonwhites," a category that includes blacks as well
as "coloreds and Asians," get few educational opportunities. Nonwhite illiteracy runs about 65 percent. White illiteracy is practically
nonexistent.

The Boer and white South African defenses are in place—military,
economic, and political. The social rings of apartheid are the Boers' new
wagons. The Afrikaners have made their nation into one big laager and
to them the laager means survival; it is the Boer tribal totem. And
besides, Boer reasoning goes, we're not doing anything different from
what goes on in other African countries. Look how the black tribes
mistreat one another. And where were the Western liberals when the
British were destroying us? (See History.) No one looks out for Boer
interests except us. We're criticized simply because we're white and
economically successful.

The Boers are right about one thing—black Africa is notoriously
undemocratic and its tribes are mutually exploitative. Black African
tribes murder one another with little remorse; the white African tribe
can't, or won't, change this.

The Boers, however, are caught in a bind. They want to be accepted
by the West as a Western nation, and they want economic integration
with the West. But they want to be "African" as well, which to them
means absolute tribal dominance over the local competition. The Boers'

version of tribal dominance is apartheid, state-sanctioned and supported slavery. South Africa's economic success is based on cheap black labor. The black laborers do the dirty work for their white employers, but have no voice in the nation's government and very little say about their wages. Supported by the peculiar theology of their Dutch Reformed Church, the Boers believe this is the way God planned it.

Other industrialized countries have learned that laborers' demands cannot be ignored forever. The nationalist aspirations, economic interests, and human rights demands of other South African tribes are intensifying. Black radicals can get weapons and international support. The physical isolation the Boers once had no longer exists in a world of instantaneous communication. South Africa is no longer a forgotten end of the earth. Apartheid can't be hidden, and the Western world doesn't approve of slavery.

Street demonstrations, guerrilla action, and Western repugnance for apartheid put added pressure on the laager. Yet it may well be too late for political compromise.

The regional wars in Mozambique, Zimbabwe, Namibia, and Angola are also driven by a nationalism that is strongly affected by the desire for tribal dominance.

WHO'S INVOLVED

Republic of South Africa (RSA)—Has three capitals, a legacy of the British incorporation of the Orange Free State, the Transvaal, and the Cape Province into South Africa. Pretoria is the administrative capital; Cape Town, the legislative; Bloemfontein, the judicial.

South African opposition groups—Major group is the African National Congress (see Local Politics).

Namibia—Former German colony of South-West Africa, given to South Africa after World War I as a League of Nations mandate. Marxist-oriented Namibian liberation front based in Angola is SWAPO (South West Africa People's Organization). SWAPO is recognized as legitimate representative of Namibia by the UN and the Organization for African Unity.

Angola—Former Portuguese colony, still fighting its own civil war with UNITA (see below) and some remaining dissidents in its oil-rich Cabinda Province. The MPLA (Movimento Popular de Libertação de Angola, Popular Movement for the Liberation of Angola), a Marxist faction, is in control in the capital, Luanda. The MPLA now is officially called the MPLA-PT (MPLA Labor Party). As of summer 1984, the leftist regime is backed by 25,000 Cuban troops.

"Front-line states"—Other neighbors of South Africa: Mozambique, Zimbabwe, Botswana. Mozambique is ruled by the Marxist-oriented revolutionary organization FRELIMO (Frente de Libertação de Moçambique, Front for the Liberation of Mozambique).

United States—supports a South African withdrawal from Namibia accompanied by a Cuban withdrawal from Angola. Several United States oil companies, notably Gulf Oil, are very active in Angola.

Great Britain—Former colonial power in South Africa. Used tactics of detention camps and starvation to defeat Boers in Boer War.

Cuba—Estimated 25,000 troops in Angola in 1984.

UNITA (National Union for the Total Independence of Angola)—Angolan rebel group, led by Jonas Savimbi, backed by South Africa. South African Army has provided direct logistics and combat support. Has claimed as many as 35,000 troops in the field.

FNLA (National Liberation Front of Angola)—Rebel group formerly active in Cabinda Province and northern Angola. FNLA was supported by Zaire.

Wild Cards

Russia—South African forces have captured a number of Russian military advisers in Angola.

East Germany—Has military advisers in several African countries, including Angola.

International church and human rights groups—Their antiapartheid policies have affected Western attitudes toward South Africa. These groups could cause increasing political and economic pressure on South Africa.

Wild wild card in Namibia

West Germany—West Germany could get involved due partly to German colonial ties to South West Africa, now Namibia, and the existence of 30,000 German Namibians. There is a precedent for limited West German involvement in the backwaters of the Kaiser's old empire. In the late 1950s and early 1960s, the Bonn government located the African survivors of imperial Germany's World War I East African

Army, and paid the kaiser's colonial troops an unexpected pension. The West Germans made a lot of friends.

GEOGRAPHY

The Republic of South Africa (RSA) encompasses over 1.2 million square kilometers. The country borders on Namibia, Botswana, Zimbabwe, Mozambique, and Swaziland. The RSA completely surrounds the independent Kingdom of Lesotho. The South African government, as part of its racist apartheid policies, has organized several "independent tribal homelands," including Transkei, Bophuthatswana, Venda, and Ciskei. These homelands are supposed to be totally separate political entities. They are, in fact, dumping grounds of black South Africans and vassal states of Pretoria. Few countries recognize the independence of these states.

The whole of southern Africa is a huge plateau dropping from eastern Angola and Zambia down through Zimbabwe and Botswana, and looping around Namibia and South Africa. The plateau parallels the coastline, with the distance to the sea ranging from 40 to 200 kilometers, and its edge is called the Great Escarpment. Elevation varies from just under 1,000 meters to about 2,000 meters. Rainfall varies widely. The Kalahari Desert in Botswana and Namibia receives very little precipitation. Parts of the eastern plateau receive a great deal of rain, from 75 centimeters to over 120 centimeters. The Natal coast is exceptionally fertile, but the topsoil of the plateau is thin and more suitable for cattle grazing and herding than agriculture.

Southern Africa holds vast mineral reserves. The world's largest gold-ore vein runs from the Orange Free State into the Transvaal. Zimbabwe has large deposits of chromium. South Africa and Namibia have huge deposits of diamonds. Other minerals found in abundance include copper, manganese, iron, platinum, silver, nickel, tungsten, and uranium. Coal reserves are in the range of 75 to 80 billion tons.

Major rivers in the southern African loop are the Orange River, running west through South Africa's Cape Province, then defining the RSA's southern border with Namibia; and the Limpopo River, which runs northeast and east, separating Transvaal Province from Botswana and Zimbabwe. The Limpopo cuts across southern Mozambique and empties into the Indian Ocean. Kruger National Park, a huge game preserve and conservation zone, separates the RSA and Mozambique along their border north of Swaziland. This park has been the scene of a number of guerrilla actions. Mozambique claimed South African-sponsored dissidents used base camps in the Kruger. South African security forces have fought African National Congress forces trying to infiltrate through the Kruger from Mozambique. Stopping such guerrilla infiltration through the Kruger was for both sides a major part of the 1984 RSA-Mozambique disengagement agreement.

The southern oil tanker routes from the Persian Gulf parallel the coastline of southern Africa. Naval units wishing to interdict this oil traffic could be based in Mozambique's port of Maputo or the South African ports of Durban, Port Elizabeth, and Cape Town. Walvis Bay, the Atlantic port claimed by South Africa but surrounded by Namibia, could also support naval units. Angolan ports have been regular anchorages for Russian blue-water naval forces.

See appendix, The Tribes of South Africa, for population figures and breakdown by tribes.

HISTORY

This section will outline briefly the history of the Republic of South Africa, then will discuss the Namibian War.

Click-language speakers are the earliest known inhabitants of southern Africa. The Bushmen and Hottentots were hunter-gatherers and primitive herders. Bantu speakers entered the Transvaal region sometime before 1000 A.D., pushing Bushmen and Hottentots south and west into the Cape and the Kalahari Desert. In the fifteenth and sixteenth centuries, Zulus and Xhosas settled the eastern portion of the RSA and Mozambique from the Limpopo River and Zimbabwe border to the coast. The Portuguese explorer Bartholomeu Díaz rounded the Cape of Good Hope in 1498. In 1652, under the sponsorship of the Dutch East India Company, the ancestors of the Afrikaners, or Boers, arrived from the Netherlands. The Boers and the Xhosas didn't clash until a hundred years later, when Boer farmers encountered Xhosa parties in the vicinity of the Great Fish River, between present-day Port Elizabeth and East London. This was a clash of migrations—the Boers were going north and east, and the Xhosas were heading south.

Neither side could get the best of the other. Both groups depended on herding and agriculture for existence, and both needed the land, but the Boer firearms and the Xhosas' numbers led to an uneasy stalemate.

The British destroyed the stalemate in 1795, when they grabbed the Dutch Cape Colony in the name of Holland's Prince of Orange, an exile in Britain hiding from the French Revolution. The Boers, many from families already 150 years out of Europe's mainstream, chafed under British rule. But it took the British twenty-five years to get down to the business of a policy called "anglicization." This meant elimination of the Afrikaans language and elimination of Afrikaner schools and churches.

The Boers began to leave. The largest migration took place in 1836, when 10,000 Boers left the Cape en masse. This was the Great Trek of the *Voortrekkers.* Moving farther north on the great plateau, they found an empty plain marked by piles of skulls and burned-out *kraals,* Bantu homes. The Zulus had been busy.

In the second and third decades of the nineteenth century, the Zulu Army was the Southern Hemisphere's most formidable war machine. Formed by the raw military genius of the Zulu chieftain Shaka (also spelled Chaka, 1787–1828), the Zulu *impis,* the rough equivalent of regiments, ran roughshod over the whole of southeastern Africa. Shaka was one of the world's most brilliant military leaders, ranking with Alexander, Hannibal, and Napoleon. He seems to have been that most unusual person, a "first-thinker," someone who actually creates a tradition rather than creating from a tradition. He invented Zulu tactics, developed a grand strategy of conquest, created the Zulu Army organization, and designed weaponry. He was also a megalomaniac. Human sacrifice was already a Zulu tradition, but Shaka is said to have set the record when one day he had 12,000 captives and slaves slaughtered at his whim.

The Voortrekkers and their slaves arrived during the aftermath of the Zulu offensives. At the Battle of Blood River in 1838, the Boers decisively repelled a Zulu attack. The Zulus withdrew to their northern tribal kingdom and left the plateau to the Boers. Each side respected the other's power; an uneasy peace ensued, bloodied by occasional raids.

The Boers formed two independent republics—the Transvaal (1852) and the Orange Free State (1854). But British demands, and the discovery of diamonds at Kimberley in 1870, once again put the Boers under the English thumb.

The Zulus didn't like the British intrusions either. The British decided to hit them first. In December 1878 they invaded KwaZulu, Zululand. On January 22, 1879, the impis dealt the British Empire its most severe defeat in a colonial battle. At the Battle of Isandhlwana, Zulu forces under Cetshwayo smashed the British imperial troops and opened a path for the invasion of Durban. Unfortunately, the Zulus proceeded to fritter away their opportunity by attacking the small British outpost at Rorke's Drift, the famous "Alamo with survivors." The British reorganized, stopped the assault, and by July 1879 had destroyed the Zulu Army in the Battle of Ulundi. This was the death knell of Zulu military power.

Now the British turned to the Boers. The first Anglo-Boer War (1880–1881) gained London economic rights in the Boer republics. The second conflict, the Boer War (1899–1902), gained Britain the entirety of South Africa—at an ugly cost. The Boer commandos, operating as horse-mounted guerrillas, fought a bitter partisan war. The British defeated the Boers by starving them. Unable to beat them on the battlefield, the English burned the Boers' farms and herded over 120,000 women and children into detention camps. The camp conditions were terrible. Over 26,000 Boer women and children died. Six thousand-plus Boer troops were killed, out of a guerrilla force of 35,000. The British lost 8,000 men out of an army of 290,000. The two Boer republics were incorporated into the British colonies of Cape and Natal, and the Union of South Africa was formed as a British dominion.

South African forces fought in World War I, and South African diplomats participated in the Treaty of Versailles peace conference. As part of the spoils of war, the League of Nations gave South Africa an administrative mandate over the former German colony of South-West Africa, known today as Namibia.

Afrikaner political strength began to grow in the late 1930s. They organized and took advantage of the colonial democratic political machinery. The RSA sent troops to help Britain during World War II; they served most notably in North Africa against Rommel. In 1948 the Afrikaner National Party took control of the dominion's parliament. The National Party's apartheid policies were developed to ensure that all political and economic power remained securely in white hands. The Afrikaners decided to dispense with dominion status, and the republic was officially born in 1961.

After World War II, the United Nations assumed responsibility for all former League of Nations mandates. The league's "mandate" system was essentially a way of dispensing with territory that the "First World" nations found troublesome. From the point of view of the mandated, it smacked of a new kind of colonialism.

Since World War II, UN policy has been to turn the mandates into self-governing countries. The UN officially terminated the RSA's mandate over Namibia in 1966. The RSA maintains it is preparing Namibia for independence (see Participant Strategies). In the 1960s Ovambo tribal dissidents decided the preparations had been taking too long. In 1966 SWAPO began guerrilla raids into Namibia. In 1973 the UN recognized SWAPO as the "authentic" representative of Namibia.

To the north of South Africa, Portugal controlled Angola and Mozambique until it abandoned its 300-year-old colonies in the mid-1970s. The new African governments in Angola and Mozambique proposed advancing the black revolution to their brothers in South Africa.

With the MPLA-Cuban victory in 1976, SWAPO moved its operations base from Zambia to Angola. After the Portuguese withdrew from Angola, the guerrilla war for control of the former colony at first favored the pro-Western UNITA forces. Part of UNITA's success was a result of South African logistics support. The South Africans wanted to ensure that a non-Communist regime came to power in Angola as well as one that would not give SWAPO a sanctuary. Until 1984 and the tentative South Africa-Angola disengagement agreement, South Africa continued to provide UNITA with arms and logistics support, and the South African Defense Force (SADF) launched occasional raids on SWAPO base camps. South Africa maintained a small number of troops on the Angolan side of the Angola-Namibia border.

As of summer 1984, South African support for insurgent groups in Angola and Mozambique has either ceased or been sharply curtailed since the cease-fire initiatives. A breakdown in the cease-fire, or the failure of the Cubans to withdraw from Angola, could renew Pretoria's support.

The political situation with Zimbabwe remains hostile, but pragmatic economics force the Zimbabwe government to deal with the RSA. Botswana remains economically dependent on Pretoria.

RSA forces have withdrawn from border posts in Angola and have returned to base areas in Namibia. SWAPO units, though badly beaten by the South Africans, still have the ability to strike into Namibia. Though some Cuban forces appear to have left Angola, down from a high of 25,000 troops, in 1975 it took a Cuban mercenary force only one third that size to reinforce successfully the Angolan Marxist units.

On the Mozambique border, as of summer 1984, the African National Congress (ANC) has claimed responsibility for several bombing attacks against transportation facilities, oil storage tanks, and police and government buildings. The South African government has in turn counterattacked ANC supporters in Lesotho and Mozambique.

The RSA continues its policy of establishing tribal homelands in the least productive areas of the country. South African police units have forcibly removed black villagers to these new areas. (The homelands have a Russian *gulag*-like reputation.) Black moderates as well as radicals refer to them as concentration camps.

Human rights and church efforts to persuade countries and companies to "disinvest" in RSA have produced minimal results.

LOCAL POLITICS

South Africa

Apartheid—Boer policy of enforced racial separation. Population is divided into whites, Coloreds (includes mixed black and white), Asians (Chinese and Indians, except for Hong Kong Chinese who have enough money to become "white"), and blacks. Whites get all the advantages, like wealth and democracy. Blacks get herded onto reservations. The South African parliament is all white. The judiciary has no power to review parliamentary acts. Various "councils" for Coloreds and blacks have been established to give the veneer of democracy to these groups. The councils have been abolished when they started demanding reforms.

National Party—Afrikaner party in power since World War II. Creators of apartheid system. Some moderates are calling for change in rigid apartheid system.

Herstigte Nasionale Party (Reconstituted National Party)—Far right-wing splinter of National Party. Religiously oriented, Calvinist, strong advocates of rigid apartheid.

Conservative Party of South Africa—Formed in 1982. Another National Party splinter group. Opposes all calls for power-sharing.

New Republic Party—Advocates a new federal republic with each racial group self-governing. Wants a multiracial central government with whites in control of principal positions.

Progressive Federal Party—Advocates a democratic federal system and elimination of apartheid. Many members are South African English.

African National Congress (ANC)—A banned party. Advocates "nonracial socialist system" and democracy. Has several wings. Principal sponsor of anti-South African government guerrilla activity. Originally nonviolent, after years of frustration now advocates violent overthrow of apartheid.

Pan-Africanist Congress (PAC, also called Pan-Africanist Congress of Azania)—Banned splinter faction of ANC. Advocates black-controlled government.

Indian National Conference of South Africa—Indian and Colored political party. Party itself banned, but some members participate in system through splinter groups.

Black People's Convention—Advocates black organization outside of "white racist political regime." Strong among urban blacks. Was part of the Black Consciousness Movement.

South African Black Alliance—Black and Colored coalition advocating nonviolent change in system.

Colored Labor Party—Asian and mixed-race party. Considered by the National Party to be an opposition group.

Colored Federal Party—Asian and mixed-race party that tends to be more progovernment.

Sullivan Principles—Code of conduct for United States companies doing business in South Africa. Formulated by Rev. Leon H. Sullivan, United States civil rights leader, Baptist minister, and a director of General Motors Corporation. The code dictates nonsegregation of work facilities, equal pay for equal work, and improved housing and schooling for all workers. As of summer 1984, of approximately 290 United States companies doing business in South Africa, 125 (representing over two thirds of the jobs) subscribed to the code.

National Union of Mineworkers—Increasingly powerful union composed predominantly of black gold miners. Led by Cyril Ramaphosa.

"Tribal homelands"—The concept behind these states is that if black tribes are recognized as being citizens of a nation other than South Africa, their disenfranchisement from South African politics is legitimized. (See Geography.)

Dutch Reformed Church—in South Africa the cultural as well as religious heart of the Boers. Extreme Calvinism (a very narrow interpretation unfair to John Calvin) concerning predestination of "God's Elect" is used to justify apartheid.

South African Defense Force (SADF)—The army, navy, and air force.

Broederbond—"Secret" Afrikaner society dedicated to Afrikaner cultural and political control.

De Beers—Giant South African mining consortium. Monopolizes, with Russia, the world's diamond business.

Rand Monetary Area-South African Customs Union—RSA-run economic group that includes Botswana, Swaziland, Lesotho, Namibia. The rand is the basic currency in the RSA.

SASOL—South African Coal, Oil, and Gas Corporation. Has been instrumental in developing coal gasification and liquefaction processes to produce oil from coal. The idea is to use the RSA's abundant coal reserves to overcome an international oil embargo instituted because of apartheid policies. SASOL plants have suffered several guerrilla attacks.

Steve Biko—Former head of Black People's Convention. Died from injuries received while being held by the South African police.

KwaZulu—Pretoria attempted to create a Zulu homeland, which the Zulus refused to accept.

Mogopa—Village west of Johannesburg from which black families were forcibly removed to new homelands in 1984. Mogopa has been used as an international symbol of the resettlement policy.

Soweto—Black African suburb of Johannesburg. Scene of several protests against apartheid and several brutal confrontations with RSA police.

Desmond Tutu—Anglican bishop and South African moderate. Major figure in national reconciliation effort between black tribes and Boers.

Namibia

Democratic Turnhalle Alliance (DTA)—South African-sponsored mixed-race party in Namibia. Includes part of white Republican Party. The RSA government sees the DTA as a moderate (and acceptable) alternative to the radical SWAPO.

Namibian National Front (NNF)—Multiethnic alliance. Boycotted last election along with SWAPO.

Ovambo tribe—Largest tribe in Namibia. Approximately 500,000 members (out of a population of 1.1 million). Christian Democratic Action Party is an Ovambo splinter group from DTA. SWAPO is predominantly Ovambo.

UN Resolution 435—1978 Security Council resolution calling for "early independence of Namibia through free elections under supervision and control of the UN."

PARTICIPANT STRATEGIES AND GOALS

Internal Situation

Boers—Radical Boer racists prefer to fight to the bitter end. South Africa, according to the radicals, is under a "total onslaught" (their words). To defend against this assault requires a "total strategy"— military might, psychological intimidation, and political apartheid. The trekkers in the Transvaal didn't bend—but back then the Zulus weren't armed with AK-47s. Boer moderates will accept change but want strong political guarantees of Boer existence and identity. Doubts that this moderation can be accomplished without their being "swamped in the black sea" allows Boer radicals to keep apartheid in place. The Boers also want to maintain their wealth; if apartheid ends, black labor won't be as cheap.

Since the Boers dominate South African politics, in the internal situation they are South Africa. As far as the radical Boers are concerned, the British imperialists can split for England and stay there— after they've served in the SADF. South Africa is short of white soldiers, and the RSA government can't keep reservists called up twelve months a year without paying an economic price. Black soldiers in the SADF have proved time and again to be superb soldiers, doing things like shooting Cubans in Angola. Many Boers, however, fear the demobilized black soldiers. Running a racist regime gets mighty tricky when the folks in charge discover how dependent they are on the oppressed. Still, the Boers will continue to practice apartheid until the race war starts or internal pressure from moderates and external pressure force it to end.

Black moderates—Several moderate groups look to the white English liberals, foreign governments, churches, and international human rights groups for support in forcing an end to apartheid. They demand democratic representation and an end to the homelands policies. They are willing to guarantee Boer rights. Once again, the sticky point is how this can be accomplished, given the violence Boer radicals and black radicals are capable of wreaking on one another and on well-intentioned moderates.

Black radicals—South African blacks, and a few whites, who think compromise with the Boers is impossible. Violence and war are the only solution, with the Boer regime being destroyed. After the leftist rhetoric is sifted out, this means killing the Boers.

United States and antiapartheid religious and human rights groups —Since 1981 Washington's policy has been "constructive engagement" —creating a dialogue with the Boers, urging them to deal with black African moderates, then opening the democratic process to all South Africans, black and white. This was to be a change from confrontational policies. Critics said past policies of open condemnation and threats of economic sanction only increased the Boers' paranoia and inflexibility. Many Americans oppose the new policy. Antiapartheid activists maintain the United States could drastically undermine South Africa's apartheid system by pressuring companies to disinvest and enforcing economic embargoes. Washington is firmly against apartheid, but the truth is that neither policy seems to have affected the Boers, who stubbornly show an ability to do without the West and ignore moral suasion. Some country (Israel, Taiwan) is willing to sell weapons to the South Africans. Some country (Saudi Arabia, Iraq?) is willing to sell them oil.

Namibian War

South Africa—Before the initial 1984 disengagement agreement between South Africa and Angola, Pretoria utilized military strikes into Angola, and sometimes based troops there, to keep SWAPO "off balance"; this meant denying SWAPO and its East Bloc advisers the time to build logistics and training bases in Angola. These attacks preempted SWAPO offensives into Namibia. With this strategy South Africa kept the initiative and maintained its troop units in concentrated strike forces, a tactical mode preferable to a thin defensive screen, which was the other option in Namibia. South Africa gave up this successful strategy in exchange for the Angolan disengagement agreement. South Africa wanted to disengage because:

(1) Angola, realizing it was slowly losing the war to South Africa and UNITA, agreed to the RSA demand that it deny SWAPO bases.

(2) The SADF was also beginning to feel the effects of extensive long-term combat (real physical and material fatigue).

(3) The South African economy was beginning to suffer the effects of its own costly war machine.

South Africa agreed to withdraw its troops and its support for UNITA. Many press reports indicate, however, that South Africa continues to provide UNITA guerrilla units with logistics support and advisers. This ongoing aid gives South Africa another trading card to exchange for Cuban withdrawal. All these military matters reduce to a political game: The RSA wants to ensure that Namibia's new government is reliable and pliant like Botswana's. This is the kind of independence Pretoria wants for Namibia. South Africa wants from Namibia what Russia wants from Poland. It doesn't want to run the post offices, but neither does it want dissent to spread. The RSA doesn't want the long Namibian border to become a sanctuary for guerrilla operations into South Africa. Finally, the Boers prefer to show once more that they can master black African military opposition as part of keeping the lid on at home.

UNITA—These Angolan guerrillas say they made "a pact with the devil"—the South Africans—because they had no choice. No one in the West supported them; Washington failed in 1975, though interestingly enough, many reports indicate that significant numbers of French-supplied arms showed up in UNITA's arsenals during 1976 and 1977.

The Marxist Angolan regime holding Luanda isn't the socialist democracy with which they wanted to replace the Portuguese colonialists. Instead of the Portuguese being in control, the Cubans, East Germans, and Russians are. UNITA's pro-Western guerrillas are socialist and anti-Communist, and very antiapartheid. South Africa is an ugly port in the storm, but it's still a port. UNITA claims it controls two thirds of the countryside and can keep its forces in the field with or without South African support. This is debatable. Realistically, the best UNITA can hope for is to maintain an active military presence in the countryside and wage an economic war against Luanda. By doing things like blowing up the Benguela railroad, which they claim to do regularly, they can force an "accommodation" upon the MPLA. The rebellion stops when the pro-Russian elements and Cubans go packing. Then some form of power-sharing begins.

As of summer 1984, pro-western FNLA guerrilla forces and former leader Holden Roberto seem to have reemerged in Northern Angola. The MPLA suspects that Zaire has had a hand in this resurgence. Former FNLA members opposed to Roberto have formed a splinter guerrilla group called Comira.

SWAPO—Tactically, these guerrillas want to do in Namibia what UNITA wants to do in Angola: stay in the field and wear down their opponents' political will. SWAPO says its goal is to establish a people's republic in Namibia, then move on to overthrow South Africa. This is good internationalist rhetoric, but it only stiffens Boer resistance to any kind of Namibian solution. SWAPO claims to be the sole legitimate representative of the people of South-West Africa. Any other political parties are referred to as puppets of the racist regime in Pretoria.

Angolan government (MPLA main faction)—The MPLA is getting tired of the war with UNITA, and getting tired of the Cubans. The initial South African disengagement, the withdrawal of South African forces operating in Angola, was met by implicit MPLA guarantees of Cuban disengagement. The MPLA have found themselves between a rock and a hard place: The Cubans limit their action, but if the Cubans go, then they lose their last bargaining chip. Angolan, South African, and United States representatives have met on several occasions to try to finalize, then implement, the cease-fire agreements.

United States—The United States is trying to act as a credible third party, but it is portrayed as the "protector of the South African racist regime." Maybe. But the United States has also been a reliable oil trading partner with the Angolans, and the Luanda regime is discovering that people don't live on ideology alone. The United States strategy is to move both sides from temporary disengagements to a permanent cease-fire. The United States wants the Cubans out. The United States also wants to see a free and open election in Namibia, which means a South African withdrawal. This tit-for-tat diplomacy is what the United States calls "linkage." All of this takes time, money, and a lot of luck. Once again, Washington may be dreaming.

Cuba—Angola has been one of the Cubans' steady-duty spots since 1975. Fidel pays his dues to Moscow by providing a mercenary army for service in the Third World. Put crudely, he exchanges human cannon fodder for cheap oil. This way Cuba gets directly involved in more armed conflicts than either superpower. It's a good game if you're El Jefe Máximo—the classic Latin tough guy, strutting his stuff on the world's stage. Shipping out the troops also helps Havana solve a chronic unemployment problem that can be hidden under the guise of "aiding worldwide socialist revolution." But Angola may be a free ride for the East Bloc. One source claims the Angolan MPLA government pays $100 a day for each Cuban mercenary. Most of Angola's hard currency comes from royalties on oil sold to the United States. Indirectly, American consumers may be paying for the Cubans. Fidel's pitching career may have been hampered by a lack of zip on his fastball, but when it comes to making Washington a city of fools, Señor Castro's a major-league ace.

SUPERPOWER INTEREST

	Political	Military	Historical	Economic
Russia	High	Medium	Very Low	Medium
US	High	Medium	Medium	High

Political—Russia, East Germany, and Cuba have played a high-profile, though not so high-stakes, political game in South Africa. The RSA is portrayed as the ultimate capitalist slave state. The communist bloc says the West's toleration and "encouragement" illustrates its true view of the Third World—it is a permanent slave colony and source of cheap raw materials. Russian shouting at South Africa also deflects criticism of its comparable human rights violations, such as Russian Slav racism toward Jews, Arabs, and Asians. The United States is very involved politically. United States domestic civil rights groups and United States human rights policies give RSA a high political profile. The United States's commitment to a Namibian cease-fire and its involvement with Zimbabwe are not solely motivated by East-West competition, but also by strong domestic considerations. The United States also wants to show the Third World that change can be effected by "constructive engagement" (peaceful coercion) and positive economic incentives.

Military—Surprisingly, both rate a Medium, despite RSA's protests to the contrary. Bases to intercept Cape traffic would be very useful to Russia during a war; but establishing them, even if the RSA collapsed, would be a long time coming. The United States is more concerned with the Persian Gulf and the Horn.

Historical—Contrary to its propaganda, Russia historically has had little interest in southern Africa, other than as a playground for arms sales and covert troublemaking. United States historical awareness is enhanced by the civil rights movement's interest in the RSA's long record of racial oppression.

Economic—Russia has gold and chromium mines in sufficient supply. If RSA production terminated (i.e., if the mines were blown up in terrorist raids), the Russians would almost have a corner on some strategic metals, which would be a shot in the arm for hard-currency sales. So Russia has a negative economic interest in South Africa. United States investment in the RSA and utilization of its natural resources are high, almost as high as those of Western allies.

POTENTIAL OUTCOMES

1. 40 percent chance: Race war arises in South Africa—organized rebellion against Boer state. Increases to 60 percent chance after 1987 if apartheid laws remain unchanged. If race war occurs, 60 percent chance of Boer pyrrhic victory—economy is destroyed, mines are closed, but a vestigial Boer state remains. Forty percent chance of Boer victory if Cubans or East Bloc forces intervene through front-line states or Namibia. If East Bloc forces participate, look for United States-British occupation of Cape Town and Durban.

2. 30 percent chance: No change from present internal-external situation, with possible exception of cease-fires in Namibia and Mozambique. The Mozambique-RSA cease-fire seems solid as long as the current Mozambican regime maintains power or as long as the drought, which began in 1981 and continues into summer 1984, grips southern Africa and continues to produce starvation and economic decline.

3. 30 percent chance: Mediation, led by the United States and Great Britain, moves Boers to change apartheid laws. Black moderates form coalition with political groups in homelands. Boers are guaranteed cultural and political survival in constitutional form. This chance decreases to 20 percent after 1987.

COST OF WAR

Based on GDP (gross domestic product) and a GDP–arms-expenditure analysis of a similar out-of-the-way nation (Australia), South Africa spends $1.4 billion a year above its "normal" defense requirements in order to wage war with its neighbors and its own black inhabitants. Though the RSA believed the Angolan and Mozambican disengagements would allow it to reduce defense expenditures, the proposed 1985 defense budget jumped 22 percent—to more than $3 billion. This is 15 percent of the RSA's total budget—a very high figure, especially since it doesn't include many police and internal-security items that are really paramilitary in nature. The economic cost to the entire South African economy is more difficult to measure, as the economy is based on cheap black labor.

The human cost is the loss of several thousand lives a year. A fair guess would be that 8,000 to 10,000 people a year are killed because of combat, apartheid violence, and the destruction of homes and food resources. This estimate also includes deaths in the tribal homelands administered by South Africa as well as the SADF, Angolan, Cuban, SWAPO, ANC, and Mozambican combat deaths. Civilian deaths in Angola and Mozambique are not included in the 8,000-to-10,000 estimate. How many people die as a result of UNITA-MPLA combat or of starvation brought on by economic dislocation and destruction, theft, economic mismanagement caused by ideological adherence to Marxist theory, or corruption, is at the present time anybody's guess. The figure of one million deaths caused by starvation and drought between 1981 and 1984 for the whole of southern Africa (including Zambia as well as the RSA and other states) gives some idea of the potential magnitude of the civilian casualties that could be attributed to the ongoing warfare and political instability.

THE TRIBES OF SOUTH AFRICA*

Click-language Speakers

Khoikhoi (also known as Hottentots)—About 200,000 lived in southern Africa as late as 1660. Tribe is now extinct, descendants have merged into the Colored South Africans.

San (also called Bushmen)—No longer found in South Africa. Forty thousand live in the Kalahari in Namibia and Botswana.

Bantu Speakers, Sotho Group

North Sotho (also called Pedi)—1.8 million in RSA. Live on reserves in eastern Transvaal.

South Sotho—1.6 million in RSA. Live near Lesotho (another one million live in Lesotho).

Tswana—1.9 million in RSA. Live in western Transvaal, eastern Cape Province, Botswana border.

*Population figures are approximate; tribal population figures vary widely according to source; Click-language speakers are included for historical purposes.

Bantu Speakers, Nguni Group

Xhosa—4.7 million+ in RSA. Live in Cape Province. Nominal residents of Transkei homeland.

Zulu—Five million+ in RSA. Live in Natal.

Swazi—500,000+ reside in RSA.

Ndebele—Several hundred thousand reside in the RSA, most near Zimbabwe border. Many have migrated to Zimbabwe.

Bantu Speakers, Tsonga Group

Tsonga—More than 800,000 reside in the RSA near border with Mozambique.

Afrikaans Speakers

Boers—Over three million. A white, rather heterogeneous tribe of Dutch, French Huguenot, German, and (apartheid to the contrary) black African ancestry adapted to the Dutch-Boer life-style.

English Speakers

Indians and Asians—Approximately 900,000.

Anglos—Approximately 2.4 million. Majority are South Africans of English descent, but there are also immigrants from several European countries.

PART 3

Asia

Most of Asia's wars are small and (uncompromisingly) brutal. Indonesia's imperial aspirations in the East Indies have produced several midget wars, including those in East Timor and the Moluccas, and Sukarno's failed war in Borneo. Drug profiteering motivates the perennial war in Burma, where nationalists and Communists have discovered that greed has an ideology all its own. The Laotian Communists, backed by Vietnam, wage a dirty little war with rural tribes. Chemical weapons have been used in this ugly conflict.

Some of the wars, ongoing and potential, are not so tiny. Vietnam has 200,000+ troops in Cambodia. The 1979 Chinese-Vietnamese border war may have cost China 40,000 casualties and Vietnam 8,000 to 10,000. India and Pakistan could fight again. China and India still have severe disputes over their Himalayan borders.

The Korean War was suspended in 1954. Across the DMZ, two of the world's most powerful ground armies face each other. Sometimes the war "un-suspends." In 1983 North Korean assassins killed several South Korean officials as they attended a meeting in Burma. While the Russians deploy SS-20 nuclear-armed missiles in Siberia, the Japanese grow increasingly nervous. The biggest potential Asian war pits Russia against China.

8. The Philippines: The Sick Man of ASEAN

INTRODUCTION

The Philippines was the first Asian nation to be deeply influenced by Western culture and economics. A Spanish colony taken by the United States in the Spanish-American War, the country was once one of Asia's most progressive and educated societies, possessing a strong foundation for the expansion of democratic institutions. While those democratic roots and aspirations still exist, since the coming to power of dictator Ferdinand Marcos, there has been no broad-based power-sharing among the Philippines' many ethnic and economic groups. A small number of wealthy families controls the destiny of the nation and is reluctant to share control. Several ethnic groups, most notably the Moslem Moros, fight a guerrilla war in the bush. The urban population agitates and demonstrates. There are terrorist incidents. The Marcos oligarchy, a broad-based anti-Marcos opposition, and the United States are the major players in this ongoing political drama. The United States has a vital interest in this area, and China and Russia show varying degrees of involvement. Pressure is building for a change of government. Several groups want absolute power (Marcos, the Communists); others want independent states; still others want democracy. The big question is who will replace the Marcos clique.

SOURCE OF CONFLICT

Nationalist ambitions, ethnic animosities, oligarchic oppression, and religious persecution influence the dozen or so continuing Asian wars. The Philippine conflict incorporates all those elements. There are two wars being waged: the jungle battles between Filipino Moslems, Communists, and the state; and the war of succession among the oligarchs.

A decaying oligarchic dictatorship has become the target of a cross-section of opposing forces that includes liberal democrats, business people, Communists (both pro-Moscow and independent), and the Moros, Moslem Malays of the southern Philippines.

The situation in the Philippines is quite different from that in Iran just prior to the collapse of the shah. The secessionist Moros can be likened to a Kurdish tribe (see Arabian Peninsula chapter for a description of the Kurds) that would use any ideology as a pretext for revolt. But the Marcos oligarchy, while it may not be able to control the country, does have a demonstrable base of popular support among conservative Catholic and Spanish-influenced Filipinos; the shah lacked significant popular support. Up to now, the Filipino resistance groups have no galvanizing leader, like Khomeini, who could unite different opposition elements. The man who might have filled the bill, Benigno Aquino, was assassinated. Aquino had a reputation as a tough politician, but favored a pluralist government and open elections. This is called moderation. Khomeini's revolutionary ideology might be called moderate only compared with, say, Attila's or Stalin's.

WHO'S INVOLVED

Marcos regime—Dictatorship centered around Ferdinand and Imelda Marcos. Strong military backing, supported by old-line hispanicized families and some industrialists. Ferdinand's health may be failing.

Pro-Western Marcos opponents—Many have close United States ties. A wide range of people in this group, including the church, the middle class, and wealthy politicians from pre-martial-law democratic period. Object to Marcos for a variety of reasons, such as his authoritarian policies, corruption, neglect of the poor and social issues.

Anti-United States Marcos opponents—Filipino Communist groups, generally Maoist. Original external support came from China, now speculation has it coming from Vietnam and Russia.

United States—Has close historical ties with the Philippines. Maintains major air and naval bases. Will pay $900 million for basing rights through the late 1980s.

Moros—Filipino Moslems. Comprise three linguistic groups: the

Tau Sug of the Zamboanga Peninsula, the Magindanao of the Cotabato area, and the Maranao around Lake Lanao—all on Mindanao.

Wild Cards

Association of South East Asian Nations (ASEAN)—Southeast Asian economic community. Also provides for limited sharing of regional security responsibilities. Members are the Philippines, Malaysia, Indonesia, Singapore, Thailand, Brunei.

Indonesia—Moslem Indonesia might be able to influence the Moros, either for or against the Filipino government. A radical Moslem government in Indonesia, a Malay version of Iran's Islamic republic, might foment a Moro rebellion and offer to incorporate Mindanao into Indonesia. All of the Southeast Asians are wary of Islamic radicals. Indonesia, a predominantly Moslem country with what is essentially a secular state, is vulnerable to "Islamic revival." Malaysia, and along with it rich little Singapore, could also be caught in a convulsion sparked by Islamic radicals.

GEOGRAPHY

The Philippine archipelago covers 300,000 square kilometers, all lying within the tropics. Forest covers over half of the land, much of it jungle; and 30 percent of the land is arable. Nearly 65 percent of the country is mountainous. Jungle and mountains make ideal guerrilla terrain. The archipelago is 1,800 kilometers long from north to south. There are over 7,100 islands, but 11 islands hold 95 percent of the land and people. Luzon is the largest island. Manila, the capital with a population of more than six million, is located on Luzon. Luzon's central plain is the country's most productive agricultural region. Mindanao is the second largest island. Other important islands are Samar, Mindoro, Panay, Negros, and Palawan.

Approximately 52 million people inhabit the islands, 91.5 percent of whom are Christian Malays. Eight out of nine Christians are Roman Catholics. Moslem Moros make up an unusually significant 4 percent. These Moslems, for a variety of geographical and ethnic reasons, have not been assimilated into the population, nor have they been accommodated politically. The Moros inhabit the southern Sulu Archipelago and western Mindanao. There are some Moslem groups in northern

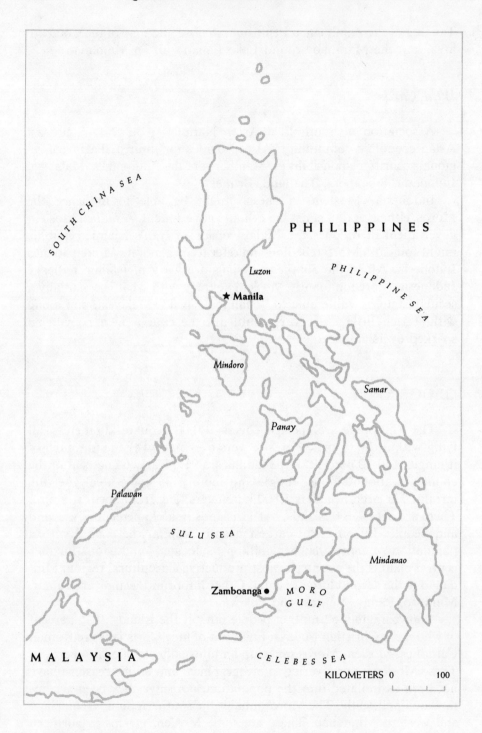

Luzon. Many Malay Filipinos also claim Chinese ancestry. The Chinese have been trading in the Philippines since the eighth or ninth century.

Nearly ninety different languages and dialects are spoken in the Philippines, a diversity not unusual in island nations. These languages include the designated national tongue, Pilipino, a Tagalog-derived language, Tagalog, Cebuano, and Ilocano. English is spoken widely. Less than 2 percent of the country speaks Spanish.

Literacy in the Philippines is a remarkably high 80 percent, but among Moros, the literacy rate drops dramatically, one Christian missionary group says to about 30 percent. Even if the literacy figure were higher, the disparity is indicative of the Moros' disadvantage compared with the rest of the population.

HISTORY

Negrito island peoples first settled the archipelago 25,000 years ago. Malays came to the Philippines in several waves from 100 B.C. to the eighth and ninth centuries. Then the Chinese began to arrive. Arab traders showed up in the thirteenth and fourteenth centuries, introducing Islam to the southern islands.

In 1521 the Spanish explorer Ferdinand Magellan claimed the islands for Spain. In that same year Spanish troops defeated Manila's Moslem ruler, Rajah Sulayman. A typical Spanish colonization ensued, with forced conversions to Catholicism and division of the land into large family holdings. The Spaniards fought several low-grade native insurgencies. Areas of Luzon became thoroughly hispanicized. The mountains and the south were largely ignored.

In 1898 the United States received the islands under terms of the treaty ending the Spanish-American War. In 1899 an insurgency led by Emilio Aguinaldo brought United States combat troops. Aguinaldo was captured in 1901, but the war sputtered on for another year. The war introduced American Marines to the machetes wielded by Moro and other insurgent forces. The United States-issue .38-caliber pistol wouldn't stop a charging Moro. The Moro might die from the gunshot but not before delivering a generally fatal blow. Because of this the United States started using the .45-caliber pistol.

The United States declared its control would be temporary, and from the beginning, its efforts were directed at preparing for Filipino self-rule. In 1935 the Philippines became a self-governing common-wealth.

World War II, the Japanese occupation, and the subsequent United States struggle to recover the Philippines devastated Manila and the countryside, but the country did become independent in 1946. Despite American aid, recovery was slow and hampered by the Huk rebellion, a Communist-influenced insurgency from 1945 to 1953.

The first Filipino administrations of Magsaysay, Garcia, and Macapagal were elected democratically. Marcos's first election in 1965 appears to have been legitimate. Since that time, the president's powers have become increasingly authoritarian. In 1972 Marcos declared martial law to oppose an alleged insurgency organized by the Communist New People's Party. Martial law was nominally lifted by a series of acts between 1980 and 1982, but elements of martial-law decree were still enforced in 1984. Combat incidents involving the New People's Party and the Moro National Liberation Front (MNLF) began to increase in 1979.

As of summer 1984, the Philippine government and ruling elite are facing a growing insurgency in the south. Government forces battle Moro rebels and Communist elements. Seventy percent of the country's armed forces are deployed in the south.

Elections held in May 1984 confirmed the power of the anti-Marcos opposition. Despite attempts by Marcos supporters to hamper (and, in some alleged cases, rig) elections, the opposition managed to gain over 40 percent of the vote. Democratic opposition forces have a strong base of support in the middle class and in the United States. Leftist elements call for armed revolt, but the Philippine Army has managed to keep a lid on significant terrorist activity. Government instability increases. Demonstrators are becoming familiar sights in the streets of Manila.

Economic decline exacerbates the situation. The GDP may decline by 2 percent in 1984 and 1985. The country faces a staggering debt load of over $20 billion. Debt and government corruption have forced significant devaluation (20 percent+) of the Philippine peso.

LOCAL POLITICS

Marcos oligarchy—Ruling elite centered around sickly Ferdinand Marcos and his wife, Imelda.

New Society Party (KPL)—Marcos's "popular front" formed after imposition of martial law.

Pilipino Democratic Party, Lakas ng Bayan (PDP-Laban)—Liberal coalition party, cofounded by Aquino.

United Nationalist Democratic Party—Coalition of moderate anti-Marcos forces.

MNLF—Moro National Liberation Front. Political and military arm of Moro militants.

New People's Army—Military arm of the outlawed Philippine Communist Party. Strength figures vary from 4,000 to 8,000 troops. Regional headquarters are located in northern Luzon, on Samar, and in Mindanao.

Filipino labor movements—Mainly dominated by anti-Marcos left-wing leaderships. Include May 1 Movement, National Federation of Labor, Philippine Alliance of National Labor Organizations, Association of Democratic Labor Organizations.

Benigno Aquino—former senator and opposition leader, assassinated August 21, 1983. Often referred to by his nickname, "Ninoy," he claimed in 1981 to have headed the Filipino "equivalent of the CIA." Wife is Corazón Aquino.

Datu system—The "headman" system of the Moros. Originally a flexible way of allowing a man with natural leadership abilities to become a tribal leader, over the years it became rigidly hereditary. New Moro activists in MNLF see the hereditary datu system as part of the cause of Moro political failure.

PARTICIPANT STRATEGIES AND GOALS

United States—The United States cannot risk an Iran-style debacle in the Philippines. Association with the Marcos regime is inevitable when the United States successfully negotiates for basing rights, but American support for the Marcos government isn't nearly as strong as that government portrays it to be. The United States wants a stable Philippine government and favors a return to democracy. Pressure on the Marcos regime can backfire if moderate forces are not strong enough to resist anti-United States radicals. One possible strategy would be to prepare to utilize other Asian bases in Guam, Tinian, or Japan, so that should an anti-United States government come into power, American defenses in the Pacific do not suffer. What the United States wants to avoid is Russian occupation of Subic Bay and Clark Field. The Russians are already using the old United States base at Camrahn Bay in Vietnam as a major Southeast Asian naval and air facility. The best United States tactic would be to support an immediate return to free, general elections while armed Communist resistance to the Marcos regime is still small.

Marcos regime—One theory making the rounds concerning the assassination of Aquino is that Marcos feared being "Diem-ed"—shot by the United States CIA (as was South Vietnamese Premier Diem in 1963 under orders from President Kennedy) and replaced by the moderate Aquino. So Marcos struck first. Whether or not Aquino was murdered on Marcos's direct order may never accurately be determined, but the ruling Marcos elite is struggling for self-preservation. The 1984 elections or those promised for 1987, with a return to a United States-style presidential election, could preserve it by appearing to give the people what they want, or by being rigged. And elections can be used like carrots in front of horses; they're always just ahead.

Business and labor unrest can usually be quieted with fat tax and wage payoffs, but the Philippines are already in debt. The Marcos regime used to make a policy of giving out fat contracts to friends to maintain support, but when there's no more easy money, the support can dry up. The Marcos government must play on Filipino Catholic and United States fears of a Communist takeover, and yet keep a rein on the countryside so that the insurgency doesn't get out of hand. The goal is to stay in power and keep the money flowing into the pockets of corrupt politicians.

Moros—The Moslem insurgency is mainly limited to western Mindanao. Mindanao and Sulu are essentially occupied by the Philippine Army, which gives the Moro militants lots of targets. It also makes their villages and *barrios* vulnerable to immediate reprisal. MNLF-Moros also fight the old, ingrown datu system (see Local Politics). Part of the struggle is an "Islamic revival." Currently 400+ Filipino Moslem students study in Egypt.

There are three competing Moro strategies. The MNLF seeks total independence; it wants to toss the Catholics off Mindanao, and says the time to strike is now, when Manila is in turmoil. An alliance with the Communists would be acceptable to some members of the MNLF. A third group wants a positive acculturation program in which Moros become more integrated into Filipino society but retain their religion and customs. They regard Marxist atheism as anathema to Moro life. The last group maintains that a revolt at this time would be doomed to failure. They favor independence, but suggest that rather than suffer defeat at the hands of a stronger-than-it-seems central government, it is better to wage a low-grade guerrilla war and wait for a better opportunity.

Pro-Western Marcos opponents—Many of the Marcos regime's liberal opponents believe time, Filipino public opinion, and United States public opinion are on their side. Citing the Philippines' history of democratic institutions, they believe they could win if a just and open election were held, and maintain their strong showing in the May 1984 election is proof.

The strategy of "it's either us or the Communists" might play well in Washington. The risk is that the United States may not have as much power as the liberal opposition believes.

Not all Marcos's opponents have given up reasoning with the regime. This group includes leaders in the Catholic Church. The pope's condemnation of poverty in the Philippines and his plea for democratic reforms have had an effect. The economic decline will force the Marcos regime to either accept reform or face armed chaos. Opponents taking this point of view don't believe the Marcos oligarchy is interested in committing political suicide.

Anti-United States Marcos opponents—The Communists' main theater of military operations is Mindanao. They would like nothing better than an open alliance with the MNLF; this would popularize the revolt. The Communists have also been associated with terrorist activity and street demonstrations in Luzon. Communist propaganda attacks the presence of large United States corporations in Mindanao, exploiting existing labor unrest. For the Communists, the Marcos regime is an ideal opponent. It serves as a lightning rod for mass public dissent; Marcos's destruction of the democratic processes in the Philippines has been an excellent issue. The Communist goals are to get rid of United States bases in the Philippines and take control of the government.

Indonesia—Indonesia has wars of its own, but a destabilized Philippines would be a huge threat to Jakarta. The instability could spread to easily agitated minorities in Indonesia. The South Moluccans and the Timorese are already looking for guns (see Quick Look at Indonesia). Should a Communist-MNLF front be publicly organized, look for Moslem Indonesia to try to mediate between Manila and the Moros.

SUPERPOWER INTEREST

	Political	Military	Historical	Economic
Russia	Medium	Medium	Low	Low
US	High	High	High	Medium to High
China	High	Medium	Medium	Medium

Political—Russia would love to see the Philippines under the control of an anti-United States regime, but there are other more pressing Muscovite Asian concerns. The United States has a high political investment in the Philippines, since the country was America's only true colony. Indochina and the Sino-Russian border are China's chief foreign policy concerns, but the Chinese regard events in Southeast Asia as being in their area of primary concern.

Military—Russia is currently settling into Camrahn Bay in Vietnam; Philippine bases would be nice but aren't a major Russian priority. Philippine bases at Subic Bay and Clark Field give the United States tremendous strategic flexibility. China is interested in Southeast Asian stability and does not want an expansion of Vietnamese or Russian influence.

Historical—Not a Russian stamping ground. The United States has a long and intimate interest. China is always interested in its "overseas Chinese" communities, especially those in Asia—the Philippines has an important Chinese community.

Economic—Not a primary Russian concern. The United States could live without the Philippines, but there is significant investment in its economy. China may become more involved should oil deposits in the South China Sea prove significant.

POTENTIAL OUTCOMES

Outcome note: Initial probability of a Moro-central government war is 40 percent if Marcos dictatorship stays in power. There's a 65 percent chance of government success in putting down the insurrection.

1. 35 percent chance before 1988: Marcos regime is removed, either by coup, United States pressure, or "controlled elections." Moderate, pro-United States government gains power. Moro conflict is contained by military pacification. Thirty percent chance of Moro autonomy in western Mindanao if moderates take over.

2. 25 percent chance before 1988: Radical leftists replace Marcos or short-term moderate regime; move to throw out United States bases. If this occurs, the probability of a Moro war drops to 10 percent for first year because of radicals' overtures to Moros. If autonomy for western Mindanao is part of Moro political package, war likelihood drops to a steady 2 percent. If this is not part of the deal, chance of a Moro war jumps to 50 percent one year after radicals gain power.

3. 20 percent chance: Marcos oligarchy maintains power through

1988 (with perhaps a new front man). Likelihood of a Moro war moves from 40 percent to 50 percent in 1988.

4. 15 percent chance: Military take-over.

5. 5 percent chance: Political chaos in Manila produces United States military intervention. Moderate regime is installed by United States. Likelihood of Moro War jumps to 80 percent as Moros take advantage of unsettled political situation; 25 percent chance of United States getting involved in a guerrilla war.

Wild Card Outcome

China, Taiwan, Vietnam, and the Philippines all lay claim to islands in the central South China Sea that may sit on huge oil fields; though unlikely, this could bring about a local naval war with concurrent "sponsored terrorism" in the opponent's country.

COST OF WAR

The active fighting against the Moros has not been expensive because of its low level. Direct military costs related to the insurgency run between $200 to $300 million a year; the cost of increased police forces would add to this figure. Since 1980 there have been fewer than a thousand casualties. The economic costs have been greater because of corruption and government inefficiency and are a major cause of economic stagnation and general poverty. The economic costs caused by the dictatorship in terms of corruption, mismanagement, and systemic inefficiencies can only be guessed.

QUICK LOOK AT INDONESIA: INDONESIA, EAST TIMOR, AND THE MOLUCCANS

The Indonesian central government in Jakarta has been waging a quiet but ugly war on the island of East Timor. After the former Portuguese colony went through several upheavals, including a short-lived leftist rebel front, the Indonesians invaded in 1975, claiming that (1) East Timor had been Indonesian all along (debatable, since Indonesia was created out of former Dutch colonies); and (2) a pro-Communist government in East Timor would not be tolerated. A new East Timorese liberation front, named Fretilin, has been created, but it has not had much success. The East Timorese have no allies, little opportunity to acquire weapons, and no public relations firm trying to interest the Western press.

The South Moluccans, at least those exiled in Holland, do understand the impact of media attention. Hijacking Dutch trains, blowing up Dutch school buildings, threatening the assassination of Indonesian ambassadors, the South Moluccans know how to grab headlines in the West. But they have not been successful at creating an active guerrilla movement in the islands to challenge the Indonesians. In 1984 United States press reports have indicated the radical Moluccans may look to the East Bloc for guns. Unfortunately for the Moluccans, the East Bloc is reluctant to give them guns because the Russians don't want to offend the Indonesians.

The Moluccans believe they were promised an independent state when the Netherlands turned loose the Dutch East Indies. Decolonization of the East Indies, however, was not a planned or calculated Dutch policy. It was brought about by a Japanese invasion; and post-World

War II Holland, with its home country shattered by the Germans, was in no mood properly to oversee the division of its old Far Eastern island empire. Javanese and Sumatran imperialists (the Moluccan names for the Indonesian government) took advantage of a power vacuum and assumed control. Forty years later the Moluccans remain angry.

9. Korea: The Strange Kingdom

INTRODUCTION

For centuries Korea was an isolated kingdom, walking a wary path between the local superpowers, China and Japan. Since World War II, Korea has been split in two: a xenophobic Communist dictatorship in the north and a pro-Western oligarchic dictatorship in the south. The two Koreas may want to reunite, but their political positions divide them and their political sponsors won't let them. The Russians see North Korea as a buffer state. United States interest is primarily economic and sentimental, but the United States is involved because the Korean Peninsula is Japan's front yard. The Chinese want to limit Russian influence; Peking would love a neutralized and unified Korea.

The disparate living standards between North Korea and South Korea increase the chance for instability in the north. South Korea has been an economic success story but has a dismal human rights record. The north's human rights record is worse. Slowly, North Korea's military dictatorship in Communist trappings is turning into a hereditary autocracy in Communist trappings. North Korea, lacking economic muscle or ideological appeal, resorts to terrorism and saber rattling against the south. Everyone wants reunification, but on his terms. Military standoff makes decisive action unlikely, but the potential for a very bloody war, a repeat of the last shoot-out in Korea, remains all too real.

SOURCE OF CONFLICT

Sixty million Koreans are separated by an armistice line and superpower interests. A post-World War II decision divided the country into

Communist and non-Communist halves. An unsuccessful Communist military invasion in 1950 produced the current stalemate. The 1950 war was never officially ended; only a cease-fire and an armistice were agreed to in 1953. The North Korean government is controlled by a military strongman, Kim Il Sung, who has dynastic ambitions. He plans to have his son, Kim Chong Il, succeed him as dictator.

Kim Il Sung is still obsessed with reunification on his terms, and he pursues it through military force and subversion. Economic prosperity in the more populous south makes subversion difficult and invasion unlikely to succeed.

Still, most people on both sides of the border desire reunification. To this end, there have been on-again-off-again talks between the two Koreas. Still North Korea wages a terrorist war against South Korea, including assassination of South Korean officials. The 1983 bombing assassination in Rangoon was just one of many such terrorist strikes.

American stands staunchly behind South Korea. Russia supports its neighbor, North Korea. China waits. Japan worries. It sees Korea as its front door.

A continued stalemate appears to be the most likely outcome of the current situation.

The Korean military situation is World War I again. Both sides still adhere to a doctrine of frontal assault until the objective is taken or the attacker is demolished. The front is 240 kilometers of mostly mountainous terrain. The largest open area is the 100-kilometer front only 24 kilometers north of the South Korean capital of Seoul. Both sides concentrate their best forces here.

Both sides realize that a battlefield decision would be difficult to achieve solely with conventional forces. The North Koreans have organized commando troops, numbering 100,000, trained to move by air and sea into South Korea's interior. Here the North Korean forces would attack logistical and other essential installations. South Korea has responded by organizing its own Special Forces, modeled after the United States Green Berets, who will return the favor. In addition, large militias are distributed throughout the territories on both sides. Over a million men are thus equipped in North Korea, and nearly five million in South Korea.

As long as there is an American presence in South Korea, there will also be substantial United States air power and nuclear weapons. If a war occurred, the North Koreans would most likely use chemical weapons. If so, no one should be surprised if South Korea, given its own sophisticated chemical industry, responds in kind.

The North Koreans realize that they would have to win fast. Thus any future Korean war will be massive and bloody, and probably short unless Russia or China intervenes. Should the North Korean Army take a severe beating, the only force holding the country together would be gone. Should the South Korean Army take a beating, look for intervention by the United States and, quite possibly, Japan.

WHO'S INVOLVED

North Korea—The same Communist government and leadership that fought and lost the 1950 war still hold power in the early 1980s.

South Korea—Many changes of government since 1950, with the potential for many more. Moving toward more military dictatorship in the 1980s.

United States—The guarantor of South Korean independence and its major trade partner.

Russia—Patron of North Korean Communist regime, partly because North Korea borders Russia and partly to deny the Chinese an ally.

United Nations—Because of resolutions in 1950, still a participant in defense of South Korea.

China—Provided manpower to produce stalemate during the war. Traditional patron state of Korea.

Japan—Although generally disliked by Koreans, a major trading partner and economic influence. Also shares many military problems, particularly Russian presence in the area. Also, Japan is allied with the United States.

GEOGRAPHY

The Korean Peninsula is 966 kilometers long and 217 kilometers wide. The eastern half is covered by a rugged, largely unpopulated mountain range. On the west coast lies a coastal plain containing most of the agriculture and population. The South Korean capital of Seoul, for example, contains 20 percent of the total population. The northern portion has more natural resources, and coal and ore mines have been developed during the past eighty years. The south was traditionally the breadbasket, with 22 percent of the land being arable and therefore farmed intensively.

Korea is infantry country—for infantry with very strong legs. Its dominant features are very steep hills forming one ridgeline after another. In the last thirty years the South Koreans have built up their road network. The North Koreans have not; there is a bare minimum of roads necessary to keep the agricultural and mining economy crawling along.

There are very few good ports on the east coast. The west and south coasts are much better off as they support a large fishing industry.

HISTORY

By the sixth century, Korea had left its feudal period and was a united kingdom. Being caught between China and Japan (and later Russia) developed Korean diplomatic skills and produced a strict isolationist policy (much like Japan's from the seventeenth to the nineteenth centuries).

Japan annexed Korea in 1910 as a result of Russia's being driven out of the Russo-Japanese war of 1904–1905. Japan tried to eradicate the Korean language and culture and turn the Koreans into second-class Japanese. They succeeded in the second endeavor. Their attempts to delete Korean culture merely created a vehement dislike of the Japanese by the Koreans that persists to this day.

World War II ended the Japanese occupation. Because Russia borders Korea, Russian troops replaced Japanese forces in the northern part of the country while American troops landed and took the southern half. A "temporary" administration was set up in the north. This administration was quickly turned over to a Russian-trained Communist named Kim Il Sung. The United States wanted to replace its occupation forces with a democratic Korean administration. Elections were held under UN auspices in 1948, but the Russians wouldn't let the UN election commission into the north. Syngman Rhee, a longtime champion of an independent Korea, was elected president in the south. The UN proclaimed Rhee to be the president of the provisional Republic of Korea. Kim Il Sung and the Russians denounced Rhee's election. In June 1949 the United States withdrew all but a small contingent of advisers.

Things were different in the north. China has always had a significant Korean population. Many Koreans joined forces with the Communists during the Chinese civil war. When this war ended in the late 1940s, quite a few of these soldiers returned to North Korea and joined the North Korean Army.

Communism appealed to many Koreans, as they had suffered severe economic deprivation under the Japanese occupation. Two generations had passed since Korea had governed itself, and much had changed in the world. The Communists had succeeded in Russia and China. For the young and the visionary, it seemed the way to go.

The major Western influence in Korea up to that time had been German missionaries, who were not expelled by the Japanese because of the alliance with Hitler. Impressed by the missionaries' good works, many Koreans developed an affection for things German, ranging from industrial efficiency to baked goods, beer, and Beethoven.

In 1950 the Communists in North Korea saw that the Americans had all but left. The United States also made a severe political blunder. In January 1950 the Senate Foreign Relations Committee "drew the line in the water" when it said that United States defense interests ran from the Sea of Japan and the Strait of Taiwan down through the China Sea to Malaya. Kim Il Sung felt that this implied the United States wasn't interested in a confrontation on the mainland; the American defense line didn't include Korea. A Communist-inspired insurgency in South Korea was going well but was taking too long. Thus, in June 1950 the North Korean Army crossed the border to hasten the revolutionary process. This was a grave misunderstanding of United States intentions, but it is one that is often made by dictators used to hearing nations speak with one voice. Hearing and interpreting the many voices of a democracy requires experience and subtlety.

America responded by driving the North Koreans back from Pusan and landing in their rear at Inchon. The Chinese Communists, seeing their ally's defeat and fearing a United States drive into Manchuria, attacked across the Yalu River, driving the United States forces back. The lines stabilized around the 38th parallel. Three years later the Chinese and the North Koreans agreed to an armistice. The Chinese Army was a wreck; the Americans were tired. The battle line remained.

In the north a Communist bureaucracy took over, eliminating absolute privation but spreading poverty to all except the senior bureaucrats and the members of the armed forces. A classic military dictatorship under Kim Il Sung took shape. Attempted coups by various factions were put down in the late 1950s and 1960s.

In the south eight years of generally corrupt and ineffective civilian government were followed by a military dictatorship. Unlike the North Koreans, the South Korean military did not try to take over everything. A general revulsion with the corruption of the civilian government led to the takeover. Thus the military enforced clean (by local standards) government.

Aided by an admirable Korean work ethic, a desire for education, American loans, and a proximity to the flourishing Japanese economy, the South Korean economy began to take off.

Consider the military and political effects of the differences in the Korean economies. North Korea occupies 55 percent of the peninsula, but has only one third of the population and one fifth of the GDP. South Korean military spending is more than twice North Korea's. North Korea keeps conscripts in uniform twice as long as does South Korea —five years. Total armed forces are about equal, with South Korea having superior weaponry.

Koreans are courageous and diligent fighters. The Korean people are very keen on hard work, physical fitness, careful planning, and unquestioning respect for authority. Koreans believe in a fighting code akin to Japanese Bushido. As demonstrated in the Korean and Vietnam wars, Korean soldiers make formidable adversaries. In a Korean-versus-Korean conflict, considerable bloodshed can be expected.

The Korean War has never officially ended. Since the armistice, in effect since 1953, North Korea has never renounced the use of force and in fact advocates a second invasion of the south. Large buildups in North Korean military forces in the past ten years indicate a willingness to try for another military solution to the stalemate.

However, North Korea has participated in reunification talks with South Korea. While the government of North Korea may not want such a reunification, the people on both sides of the border would welcome it.

The North Korean government has two important characteristics. First, it is the creature of one man, Kim Il Sung. He seems determined to pass power on to his son and thus establish a dynasty. Second, North Korea is very much a military dictatorship, with all power and privilege derived through participation and support of the armed forces. Military control is absolute and cannot be questioned.

South Korea also has a military dictatorship, but it must share considerable power with civilian leaders of industry and with the general population. Some analysts refer to this as "military authoritarianism," but that minces words. Call it a dictatorship that isn't absolute and doesn't try to be, but don't fail to call the present government a species of dictatorship.

LOCAL POLITICS

North Korea—The economy is controlled by the state and the state is controlled by Kim Il Sung. In typical police-state fashion, all benefits flow from enthusiastic participation in the running of the state. Because the government is the army, as long as Kim Il Sung controls the army, he (or his heir) controls North Korea. At any one time 12 percent of the working male population serves in the armed forces.

South Korean military—The army has a lot of power and control. It can always invoke the threat from the north in order to stay in command. Generals have a way of suddenly becoming president.

Industry—Call it Big Business, but it's really Corporate Korea. The Korean work ethic gives businesses a real tool and a lot of power.

KCIA—Korean Central Intelligence Agency, a power unto itself in South Korean affairs.

Various Christian churches and religious groups—Though small in number (perhaps 15 percent of the population), they are having a liberalizing effect on the political atmosphere.

Student activists and democratically minded opponents of the Seoul government—They make a lot of noise, but have little impact on the population as a whole. A basic conservatism, traditional subservience to authority, and economic prosperity make the people content with the current government. The only experience with democracy was not favorable (corruption and economic stagnation).

PARTICIPANT STRATEGIES AND GOALS

Common Strategies and Goals (North and South Korea)

For economic and nationalist reasons, both Koreas desire reunification, but on their own terms. So strong is this urge that both sides will put aside their animosities and actually discuss it. As a practical matter, it is unlikely that either the north or the south could be successful in a military attempt at reunification.

North Korea—Pyonyang, at least as long as Kim Il Sung calls the shots, will remain impoverished and militarized. The arms programs will come first and economic development will get the dregs. North Korea will continue to pursue a strategy of violence, including assassination, terror, and armed threats, to try to frighten the south into capitulation.

South Korea—The south pursues a dual strategy, maintaining a strong and reliable army while vigorously expanding the economy in heavy industry and consumer goods. The South Koreans figure that leading the good, or at least demonstrably better, life is the best revenge as well as the best propaganda. While both North and South Korea attempt to stir up revolution in the other side's population, it appears that the economic success of the south has the better chance of subverting the north.

United States—South Korea is a valuable base for United States electronic intelligence, but with the American-Chinese detente (and the subsequent sharing of intelligence information), China has proved to be a better spot for electronic eavesdropping on Russia. The United States wants to keep enough combat power in the region to ensure that North Korea doesn't attack the south and that some overly aggressive South Korean government doesn't decide to attack the north. United States strategy seems to be one of waiting: waiting for Kim Il Sung to die, waiting for the south to get so rich that angry northerners revolt and sue for reunification, waiting for the Japanese to start paying their share of the defense burden.

Russia—The Kremlin would not willingly give up a satellite. Russia would just as soon keep North Korea poor and militarized, so it would remain dependent on Russian arms and economic largesse. A militarized Russian ally is always useful to the Kremlin, like having a pit bull on a leash. North Korea gives Russia the ability to threaten Japan and China without directly involving Russian troops.

China—The Chinese would love to have a demilitarized Korean Peninsula and a united, neutral Korea. Getting Russia and the United States off the peninsula would create a pliant buffer state between China and Japan. Should a war break out, the odds are that Peking would remain neutral. This would mean that the next Korean War would involve the Russians and the Americans, which would be fine with China as long as the Russians didn't win.

SUPERPOWER INTEREST

	Political	Military	Historical	Economic
Russia	Very High	High	High	Low
US	High	High	Medium	Medium
China	High	High	High	Medium
Japan*	High	Very High	High	Medium

*Economic superpower; included because of proximity to conflict.

Political—This is Russia's backyard. Although Korea is an obscure corner, Russia always takes its borders seriously. The United States is committed to the defense of South Korea and keeps an infantry division and a corps headquarters there. South Korea is the edge of the United States-Asian defense perimeter. China has an interest in neutralizing a Russian ally and using Korea as a buffer state between it and Japan. Japan sees Korea as a political and military buffer state between it and China and Russia.

Military—Russia's major threat in Asia is China. North Korea gives Russia a military card to play against the Chinese. The United States is interested in maintaining its South Korean ally and protecting Japan. Compared with the fronts in Vietnam and Russia, the Korean Peninsula is viewed by the Chinese as a minor front, but they desperately want it to remain peaceful. The Japanese see the peninsula as the classic invasion route to Japan.

Historical—Russian involvement goes back several hundred years. The United States started taking an interest only because of its victory in World War II and later in the Korean War. China and Japan have a long and intimate historical involvement in Korea.

Economic—North Korea is an economic burden for Russia. For the United States, South Korea is a valuable trading partner, in both high- and low-tech goods. China appears to be interested in developing trade with economically progressive South Korea. South Korea and Japan are competitors, but bilateral economic involvement is growing.

POTENTIAL OUTCOMES

1. 68 percent chance through early 1990s: Continuation of the status quo.

2. 10 percent chance: Political breakdown in North Korea, civil war and reestablishment of a Communist government by the Russian Army.

3. 10 percent chance through early 1990s: Peaceful reunification of Korea—low chance, given the unlikely acquiescence of Russia and the differences in political systems.

4. 5 percent chance before early 1990s: Unsuccessful North Korean invasion and return to current status. As long as Kim Il Sung has the means, it's a possibility.

5. 5 percent chance before early 1990s: Political breakdown in North Korea, civil war, and reunification with wealthy South Korea.

6. 1 percent chance: Successful North Korean conquest of South Korea. Unless South Korea weakens considerably in military strength, it's very unlikely.

7. 1 percent chance: Unsuccessful North Korean invasion and subsequent reunification by South Korea. Not as long as the Russian army is on the North Korea border, but there is a chance . . .

COST OF WAR

The Korean War of 1950–1953 killed over two million people, military and civilian, and injured three million more. The cost of that war exceeded $20 billion. Another war would be at least as costly economically, although less deadly in human terms if the Chinese or Russians do not intervene. The prospect of such a war precipitating a larger one between the superpowers (the United States, Russia, China) increases the potential costs more than tenfold.

In East Asia, military operations have always involved enormous losses. The nineteenth-century Chinese Tai-Ping rebellion caused nearly as many deaths as World War II (more than 50 million). The Chinese civil war killed millions more. Even the relatively minor Korean War killed over a million (mostly Chinese) just in combat operations. The massacres in Cambodia during and after the Vietnam War amounted to several million deaths. In actuality, the Vietnam War has not yet ended, and the killing continues. The potential for large-scale slaughter between Russians and Chinese and Chinese and Vietnamese is high. The economic costs would be so high as to become meaningless. A second Korean War would be a $20 billion affair (based on United States, South Korean, and North Korean participation) if it stayed conventional and lasted only two weeks or so.

QUICK LOOK AT BURMA:
THE HIGH ROAD

Opium trading has been a way of life in Burma's Golden Triangle.

Growing poppies is easy, moving the narcotic is simple, and the payoff is huge. The Golden Triangle region is mountainous, jungle covered, and isolated. It is also the site of a continuous drug war with strong political overtones.

The war has been going on for about forty-five years. Forces involved include former Burmese Communist rebels who have turned to the drug business, Chinese Nationalist Kuomintang troops who were operating in China's Yunan Province and could not escape to Taiwan, Laotian royalists who fled the Communist Pathet Lao takeover in Vientiane, some Pathet Lao troops, and of course a sprinkling of just plain mountain bandits. The Burmese government looks the other way as long as the graft continues to flow, or until the various bandit groups come out of the hills and try to set up their own "Burmese governments."

The United States Drug Enforcement Administration (DEA) might also be considered a player. The DEA continually pesters the Burmese and Thai governments to go after the big drug smugglers. The drug smugglers fight it out, retreat, or call on their erstwhile political allies. It's just another sideshow of the great Indochina War.

Here's a quick list of the players in this game:

"Red Flag" Communists (Trotskyites)
"White Flag" Communists (Stalinists)
Karen National Unity Party
Karen National Defense Organization
New Mon State Party
Chin National Organization

Arakan Liberation Party
Kechin Independence Army
Shan State Army
Parliamentary Democratic Party
KMT Opium Armies
Lah Opium Tribes

Heroin sold in Europe and the United States subsidizes a number of
Asian warlords.

QUICK LOOK AT RUSSIA AND CHINA: THE BIGGEST BORDER WAR

There's certainly enough to argue about, for the Russian-Chinese border is the world's longest. And there are dozens of disputes over where the border should be, disputes over tiny parcels of land, like islands in the Amur River, and disputes over not-so-tiny pieces of real estate, like the whole of eastern Siberia. Most of the disagreements date back to nineteenth-century Russian land grabs.

Russia keeps over 400,000 troops, army, KGB, and MVD security troops along this extensive border. Modern tanks and equipment are backed by an array of tactical nuclear weapons. More than 1,000,000 Chinese army troops and militia face the Russian forces. China's units are for the most part foot soldiers or truck-borne light infantry.

Significant combat has erupted over a dozen times since 1966, the most grievous along the Amur River line. The recent deployments of SS-20 missiles, the same nuclear-armed missiles Moscow has deployed in Europe, threaten both China and Japan. The Chinese are starting to modernize their air and ground forces, but the process is slow and expensive. The Chinese have chosen to build massive civil defense projects. Their strategy remains one of simply surviving in such huge numbers that any invader will be absorbed. From the other side, the Russians feel that their long lines of communication to Vladivostok (in particular, the Trans-Siberian Railway) are highly vulnerable to sabotage or quick Chinese air strikes.

Neither side wants a war, but the historical and ethnic tensions for a major conflict are there and will continue to exist. The tensions between Peking and Moscow are exacerbated by the peoples in between.

Several central Asian tribal groups are trapped between the Russian Slavs and the Han Chinese. Moscow has been carefully wooing China's Kazakh and Tadzhik minorities. This is a dangerous game, for restive minorities can be exploited by either side. The example of other central Asian tribes that are successfully resisting superpower dominance (i.e., Afghanistan) could cause problems for the Russians. Chinese propaganda, directed at Russia's central Asian minorities, consistently underlines this.

QUICK LOOK AT HONG KONG, MACAO, AND TAIWAN: THE CHINA SYNDROME

In 1997 the British lease with China on 95 percent of the Hong Kong colony runs out. Only tiny Hong Kong Island and a thin slice of the peninsula are excluded. Britain has concluded that a remnant colony isn't worth the trouble. The 1984 treaty negotiated by Britain and China, which returns control of Hong Kong's "foreign policy" to Peking, seems to satisfy the negotiations. China covets Hong Kong for both historical (it removes a blot from the Opium War) and economic reasons. Hong Kong's rampant capitalism brings needed cash and credit to mainland China. The sticky point is the status of the Hong Kong Chinese. They may demand their own government. They could toss out the colonial administration prior to 1997, then try to renegotiate with Peking.

Portugal would love to have China take Macao, the Iberian enclave long noted for the manufacture of firecrackers; but Macao's open port serves mainland China's interests, and the Portuguese shoulder the burden of its operation. China will take Macao when the Chinese decide they want to pay for it.

Then there is the big island, Taiwan, the sometime Republic of China, enclave of the Kuomintang. Taiwan is the richest, most productive province in China. That's the way the mainland Chinese Communists see it. And the younger Taiwanese aren't so sure the mainlanders are wrong. Taiwan will not, however, sacrifice its success. From 1949 to 1960, the U.S. Seventh Fleet kept the "two Chinas" from attacking each other, and the likelihood of a return to open warfare is almost nil. Still, reunion will take some time. If the mainlanders show they can keep Hong Kong an open, relatively free, and going concern, then the Taiwanese may be ready to make a deal.

PART **4**

The Americas

Every continent has a certain style of warfare. In the Americas a remarkably constant cycle of suppression-revolution-suppression exists in nations where wealth and democracy are for the few, and poverty and disenfranchisement for the many. This pattern is most characteristic of the Latin American nations, although Canada follows it to a limited degree with its French minority. The United States is not perfect, but compared with most alternatives, it serves as a standard of comparison, or a final destination, for the ambitious poor throughout the world.

Seeking to maintain its enviable life-style, the United States gets nervous about all the revolution and, in recent years, the foreign intrigue lurking in its neighborhood. Suddenly, after years of neglecting regional social and economic problems, the United States finds it cannot safely ignore a string of brushfire conflicts near the strategic Panama Canal and south of vulnerable Mexico.

The wars in the Americas may seem puny compared with ongoing and potential conflagrations in other parts of the world. However, their geographical proximity to, and often involvement with, one (and sometimes more) of the world's superpowers make them of great concern.

10. El Salvador, Nicaragua, Honduras: Revolutionaries, Commandantes, and Pistoleros

INTRODUCTION

Revolutionaries battle other revolutionaries, and both fight the old *patrónes* in Latin American nations that never made democracy work for anyone but a small, wealthy minority; that isn't democracy, that's oligarchy. For a host of cultural, economic, ethnic, and geographical reasons, violent administration of and quick changes in local government have been the centuries-long norm in Latin America.

The United States Monroe Doctrine in the early 1800s put such mayhem off-limits to nations outside the Americas, but it didn't prohibit the United States from intervening economically and militarily. Many of the nations affected by this intervention saw little difference between American and European interference. Then the local tough guys might have needed to be kicked around by the U.S. Marines. Central America has long suffered from "the *Pistolero* Effect," in which oligarchs or bandits in the guise of revolutionaries (or *not* in the guise, as the case might be) toss out the reigning fascists and bring in their own clique. These revolutions bring about few changes.

Recently the Monroe Doctrine has been more difficult to enforce. Russian guns and Cuban advisers have started mixing with the locals. For this reason, political trouble and social problems once ignored have become international concerns.

SOURCE OF CONFLICT

Central America, Spain's colonial backwater, long avoided twentieth-century tides of social, economic, and political change. Dual mar-

ket and barter economies, the *patrón* (pronounced pah-trone) system
of land ownership (vesting all authority in the large-estate landowner),
submission to outside economic interests, and governmental failure to
integrate the hinterlands into the national economic and political fabric
produced countries needing not one but several revolutions. But revolutionary slogans and firepower cannot solve problems created by 450
years of neglect. Solutions require education, capital, and stability. All
of these take peace and time. In Central America peace and time are
in short supply.

Central America's basic political situation remains unchanged.
Genuine social revolutions are being co-opted by outside interests that
have little commitment to the betterment of the people. Inequitable
distribution of wealth, lack of social and economic opportunity for all
but the elite, and inhumane military regimes created a social and political climate in which rapid revolutionary change was inevitable. However, can the revolution make change stick? After the rebels toss out
the government, *they* are the government. Then their real problems
begin.

Old political debts are one of the new government's biggest headaches. Revolutionaries turn to outside sources for arms. Getting weapons from the outside is like getting a loan from the Mafia. When you
owe, you really owe. Though the revolution arises for indigenous reasons, the outside source exerts a strong influence upon the revolutionaries. The revolutionaries must then resist their own allies, the agents
of the outside supporter. The outside supporter demands its payoff. It's
an old tactic. For example, the United States organized and funded
Panamanian revolutionaries, then extracted the Canal Zone as pay-
ment. Seeing the same old imperialism in this ploy, supporters of the
revolution began to fall away, charging their former cohorts with "selling out the revolution." The remaining revolutionaries must face the
reality of running the country. They are forced to make unpopular
decisions, and they may decide to pay their political debts at the expense of a frustrated populace. These rebels, now called the government, become increasingly isolated. The old revolutionary vanguard
turns into the new elite. Commissars become patrónes.

The current Sandinista regime in Nicaragua is in hock to Havana
and Moscow. Though the last thing Nicaraguans need is more conflict,
Moscow is demanding anti-Americanism and military support for the
Marxist guerrillas next door in El Salvador. The United States perceives
this as a threat, especially as the fighting closes in on Mexico. Suddenly,

the populist anti-Somoza revolution, a revolt backed by the Carter administration, has become a superpower game.

The Russians aren't the only ones pulling guerrilla strings. When the Sandinistas talk about the CIA controlling the *contras* (the Sandinista name for the anti-Sandinista guerrilla fighters), they aren't far off the mark. But the revolutionary who refuses superpower beneficence has a tough time. Edén Pastora, the former Sandinista and five-star revolutionary hero, defected from the Sandinista junta because of the overwhelming East Bloc influence. He doesn't want to get into the same kind of debt relationship with Uncle Sam. Pastora refuses to deal with people he considers to be controlled by Washington. As a result, his organization, ARDE, frequently runs out of money. Some ARDE cadres, intrigued by CIA support, have run out on Pastora.

The conflicts in Central America won't start World War III, but they are important to the superpowers. The isthmus is the strategic neck of the Western Hemisphere.

So, where are those who want to deal with the fundamental human problems underlying these armed disputes? Moderates—and there are many who want change without bloodshed and fascism (of either the Red or patrón variety)—are shot by right-wing death squads or assassinated by left-wing terrorists. When the shooting starts, the old local elites run to Miami and live off the money they hid in the Grand Caymans. The revolution turns sour and the radicals, after killing or driving off the moderates, start tooling around Managua in Mercedes.

The peasant who spilled his blood for the revolution sees his new farm taken over by "the State," which looks to him like a new patrón. Back in the woods, the Indians continue to starve.

The revolutions will succeed only if there is peace. With Russian and American interests in the balance, peace in the Central American backwater is a very distant prospect.

WHO'S INVOLVED

United States—The Colossus of the North. Tends to support whoever claims to be anti-Communist and can provide local stability.

Cuba—Has trained revolutionary cadres throughout Latin America.

Russia—The United States is in Turkey; why can't Russia be in Mexico? Supports whichever group will use force to hamper or destroy

United States interests. If the group claims to be Communist, that's even better.

Nicaraguan Sandinista regime—The remaining "revolutionary vanguard" and political elites of the anti-Somoza revolution. Somoza was the former pro-American dictator in Nicaragua.

United States-backed anti-Sandinista groups—The overt "covert army" backed by the United States, trained, supplied, and sometimes led by the CIA, and based in Honduras.

Left-wing anti-Sandinista rebels—A collection of moderate democrats, socialists, and revolutionaries who have revolted against increasing Communist subversion and domination of the Nicaraguan revolution.

Honduras—In comparison with Nicaragua, a moderate democracy, but only in comparison.

The El Salvador government.

Left-wing Salvadoran guerrillas and terrorists.

Right-wing Salvadoran groups and death squads.

Wild Cards

Contadora group—Mexico, Venezuela, Colombia, and Panama. Nations seeking negotiated solutions to Central American conflicts.

American adventurers—Civilian Military Assistance group, et. al. (See Local Politics.)

GEOGRAPHY

Central America can be described as a mountain range dividing two coastal plains. Flat, swampy, and largely covered by tropical forest, the Caribbean coastal lowlands form the eastern margin. Hurricanes, poor soils, and insects discourage settlement. The region is populated only by Indians and the poor.

The Pacific coastal plain is narrower than its Caribbean counterpart. Weather patterns give it tropical wet and dry seasons. There are more deciduous forests and some open grasslands. The western plain is widest around the Gulf of Fonseca between El Salvador, Nicaragua, and Honduras.

The mountains sweep down the isthmus in a long arc of parallel ridges. The western range is volcanically active. The eastern range,

especially in Honduras and Guatemala, is rugged. The back-country is culturally and economically isolated. Mayan Indians in the Guatemalan highlands remained relatively untouched by the dominant Spanish society well into the twentieth century. The mountain regions and the relatively empty wetlands provide excellent rebel staging areas.

The people of El Salvador, Guatemala, Costa Rica, and Honduras cluster in the *tierra templada,* a temperate, less disease-ridden zone that runs roughly 800 to 1,800 meters above sea level.

The mountains break around Nicaragua's lake district. Nicaragua's largest population centers lie along the shores of Lake Managua and Lake Nicaragua.

Nicaragua is the largest Central American country, with 148,000 square kilometers. Honduras covers 112,000 square kilometers and tiny El Salvador, nearly 21,500 square kilometers.

Coffee is the region's primary export crop, followed by bananas and other agricultural products. Dependence on these crops makes national economies highly vulnerable to price fluctuations. A shift of 15 to 25 cents in export coffee prices can have a major effect on these countries.

About 24 million people live in Central America. Over 90 percent of Honduras's 3.8 million people are mestizo, of mixed Indian and European ancestry. El Salvador has 4.8 million inhabitants, of whom 89 percent are mestizos. Nicaragua has almost three million people. Mestizos make up 69 percent of its population; 17 percent are white European, 9 percent black, and 5 percent Indian.

In all these countries, even in revolutionary Nicaragua, the Europeans generally control the political processes and the economy.

Rapid population growth gives another dimension to the area's problems. The regional rate of increase is more than 3.2 percent per year. Honduras has a whopping 3.6 percent plus growth rate. Already struggling, Honduras has another 125,000 or so mouths to feed every twelve months. A decline in infant mortality rates, the result of improved nutrition and health for children, has helped produce these high growth rates. Also, the powerful Catholic Church opposes birth control programs.

Population growth also presents difficulties for land reformers. More and more peasants must be settled on smaller and smaller farms. This problem is already apparent in El Salvador, which has the highest population density in the Western Hemisphere, about 234 people per square kilometer. If the birthrate isn't controlled, revolutions of any kind simply won't be able to solve the problem of poverty. Another ten years at the present birthrate will make any productivity increases or revolutionary redistribution of wealth meaningless.

HISTORY

Regional

Spain conquered Central America between 1502 and 1540. The *conquistadores* didn't find much gold in Nicaragua, El Salvador, and Honduras, but they did take the best agricultural lands and established large private land holdings for the Spanish overseers. The Indians either retreated into the hills or became slaves.

Nicaragua, El Salvador, and Honduras were provinces under the captaincy general of Guatemala. In 1821 they broke with Spain during the Latin American revolt.

At first, Mexico tried to keep all the Central American provinces in one large union under its control, but El Salvador insisted on Central American autonomy. Mexican forces invaded El Salvador in 1823. El

Salvador, looking for an ally, asked the United States government to make it a state. The United States was cool to the idea, but a revolution in Mexico led to a Mexican withdrawal. Later that year the five Central American provinces of El Salvador, Nicaragua, Honduras, Costa Rica, and Guatemala formed the Federal Republic of Central America. The union dissolved in 1838, with much bickering and recrimination. Several union proposals have been made since the breakup, but they have failed to arouse much enthusiasm.

British and German investments in the 1850s, primarily in coffee plantations, returned some capital to the region, but they also tied the local economies to one or two crops. In the twentieth century, large United States firms began to acquire banana and coffee plantations. Native businessmen and politicians often became the local representatives of foreign investment interests.

As long as foreign powers stayed away, as long as United States citizens weren't threatened, as long as American business interests weren't complaining, and as long as national borders weren't violated, Washington could not have cared less about Central America.

El Salvador

El Salvador has a history of frequent revolutions. Since the 1930s, all but two governments have been led by the military. In 1979 a civilian-military group overthrew President Carlos Humberto Romero. Young officers and Christian Democrat allies formed a junta in early 1980. They began a series of economic reforms that included the expropriation of all estates larger than 1,250 acres, nationalization of export marketing, and nationalization of the banks. The right wing objected and many wealthy landowners left the country. The left-wing opposition, centered around the FDR (Democratic Revolutionary Front), refused to join the government. Members of the radical PLF (Popular Liberation Forces), who were already waging a low-level war in the countryside, saw their opportunity in the splintering of the center and right opposition. The civil war was on.

As of summer 1984, El Salvador continues to suffer the disruption and violence of two separate but related wars. The political right and political center fight an overt guerrilla war against the rebel left. This is a main-force guerrilla war. There is also a terror war. The far right wages a death-squad battle against the center and left-wing elements that have not gone underground. The far left murders its centrist and right-wing opponents. In between, the moderates die, along with peasants, students, American nuns, and journalists. The political compass points in several directions at once: army coup d'état, open elections, more civil war, internal collapse.

The presidential election of moderate Christian Democrat José Napoleón Duarte in May 1984 gave moderate groups some hope. Members of the leftist guerrilla groups even talked openly of possible negotiations with the new government. The question remained, however, Who negotiates with whom and about what?

Rightists and some moderates believe that since the left first boycotted, then tried to disrupt the elections by violence, the left should not be allowed to participate in the new government. Leftists maintain that the election was rigged and that their candidates would have been killed had they participated. Rightists counter that their candidates were shot at by the left. Duarte faces a huge task. His reform policies are vulnerable to disruption by the right and the left, his government is continually weakened by the threat of military takeover, and the entire economy of El Salvador is totally dependent on United States aid. Duarte, however, appears to be an adroit politician.

Nicaragua

In the seventeenth, eighteenth, and nineteenth centuries, Spaniards in Nicaragua fought a number of battles with the Miskito Indians of the Caribbean coast. Great Britain supported the Miskitos and even controlled a small strip of the eastern coast until the late 1800s.

After the breakup of the Central American federation, Nicaragua experienced nearly 100 years of instability. American adventurers, the notorious William Walker being the most prominent, fueled the ongoing disputes between polarized liberal democrats and supporters of the old patriarchal elite.

The United States intervened on occasion. United States Marines were in and out of Nicaragua between 1912 and 1933. The 1912 intervention was allegedly spurred by possible German imperial intrigue in Nicaragua. Britain and the United States feared the establishment of German naval bases in the Caribbean. Just how real this threat was remains debatable. Franklin D. Roosevelt finally withdrew the Marines as part of his Good Neighbor Policy (and because the United States was deep in the Great Depression).

Before the Marines left, they placed Anastasio Somoza García into power. The Somoza family became incredibly corrupt. By the mid-1970s the Somozas may either have owned or been directly involved in 50 percent of the businesses in the country. They controlled Nicaragua until 1979, when Anastasio Somoza Debayle was overthrown by the Sandinistas.

The 1979 revolution was a popular one. Businessmen, church groups, peasants, the middle class, and ideological opponents banded together to topple the Somoza regime.

Since that time, the Sandinista junta has become increasingly militant and anti-United States. East Bloc advisers have entered the country. Nicaragua doubled, then tripled the size of its armed forces. The reason given was to thwart a United States invasion. The Sandinistas frightened Honduras and shook Costa Rica's complacent world view. CIA-sponsored contras now operate from Honduras and from base camps inside Nicaragua. Former Sandinista revolutionaries have broken with the regime, and their own guerrilla groups operate from inside Nicaragua and from Costa Rica. Sandinista attempts to control the Miskito Indians of the Caribbean coast backfired and produced an Indian revolt. The Sandinista junta has imposed press censorship and shut down the offices of human rights groups that have objected to junta policies.

As of summer 1984, the regime grapples with growing economic failure while battling internal and external foes. Press censorship of even moderate opponents casts doubt on the credibility of Sandinista-run elections. The defections of Sandinista heroes like revolutionary socialist Edén Pastora begin to confirm suspected Russian-Cuban de facto control. The Russians donate guns, but they haven't come forth with the requisite economic aid. Yet the regime can and does call upon the country's still powerful antipathy to the old Somoza clique—and hostility to former Somoza supporters like the United States. The contras and their supporters in the United States are having trouble getting fiscal support from a suspicious Congress. The 1984 assassination attempt on Edén Pastora split ARDE into several factions.

Honduras

Honduras has been a comparative island of tranquillity. Maybe its tranquillity is a product of quiet despair at the endemic poverty.

Honduras did receive a visit from the U.S. Marines in 1912, and partisan left-right political clashes typical of the region do occur. In

Honduras, however, these clashes have never produced the polarization found in Guatemala, El Salvador, and Nicaragua. Though plagued by military coups, Honduras has enjoyed periods of stability. The Andino administration ruled from 1932 to 1948. Ever since their highly successful national strike in 1954, Honduran labor unions have held a great deal of political power.

Guerrilla activity in Honduras has been minimal, though spillover fighting along guerrilla infiltration routes around the Gulf of Fonseca (between El Salvador and Nicaragua) has been a source of concern.

As of summer 1984, Honduras has increased its regional role by providing sanctuary to anti-Sandinista Nicaraguans. Bilateral military and economic agreements with the United States create risks and opportunities. Dissidents point out that United States bases provoke Nicaragua and make Honduras a target. But the Honduran government seems to have concluded that some degree of armed conflict with Nicaragua is inevitable, so it's better to be armed and prepared. Along with military aid the Hondurans demand economic and developmental assistance. (Here's the argument: Either Honduras gets the entire package or it will become another El Salvador.)

The 1969 Soccer War between El Salvador and Honduras didn't end officially until 1980, when the two countries finally agreed to settle lingering border differences. Rivalry over a series of soccer matches sparked the five-day fight. The real issue was Honduran so-called mistreatment of Salvadoran migrants. Given the threat of internal disruption in both Nicaragua and El Salvador, a Soccer War rematch isn't likely. The war, however, indicated several things. In main-force, conventional combat, the Salvadoran Army can be an effective offensive force. The Honduran Air Force also performed well in the war. In 1984 the Honduran Air Force, though limited to a squadron of high-performance fighter-bombers and outnumbered by the rapidly growing Nicaraguan Air Force, has a corps of superb pilots. The Hondurans believe this compensates for their weak ground forces. The Honduran pilots believe they are more than a match for any potential opponents, whether they be Guatemalan, Salvadoran, Nicaraguan, or Cuban and other East Bloc mercenaries flying for Nicaragua.

Costa Rica and Nicaragua

In Costa Rica the democratic government has been shaken by economic setbacks and terror spilling over from Nicaragua. Guatemala continues to wage an ugly, brutal, but successful counterguerrilla war in its upland Indian country.

LOCAL POLITICS

Honduras

Army—Strongest power group in the country.

Liberal Party (PLH)—Three main factions are the Rodista, FUL, and ALIPO. Also the National Party (PNH), National Innovation and Unity Party (PINU), Honduran Christian Democratic Party (PDCH), Communist Party of Honduras (PCH), Socialist Party of Honduras (PASO).

Morazon Honduran Liberation Front—Communist guerrilla group, allegedly supported by Nicaragua, which as of summer 1984 was beginning to conduct small raids in Honduras. Have seized a radio station in Tegucigalpa and denounced the United States presence in Central America. Could well be Havana and Managua's card, possibly traded for an end to Honduran support for Nicaraguan "contra" freedom fighters.

Other political groups—Association of Honduran Campesinos (ANACH), Honduran Council of Private Enterprise (COHEP), Confederation of Honduran Workers (CTH), United Federation of Honduran Workers (FUTH).

El Salvador

FDR, Democratic Revolutionary Front—Salvadoran leftists. Guillermo Ungo heads small opposition socialist democratic party. Rubén Zamora is a former Christian Democrat. Aligned with the FMLN as FMLN-FDR, forming part of the DRU (Unified Revolutionary Directorate).

FMLN, Frente Farabundo Martí Revolutionary Front for National Liberation—Guerrilla group alliance; chief is Salvadoran Communist Party. Three other members—the Popular Liberation Forces (PLF, a group with a Maoist orientation), the People's Revolutionary Army, and the Armed Forces of National Resistance—are splinter groups of the Communist Party. Fifth guerrilla group is Central American Revolutionary Workers Party. In mid-1983 an even more radical group, the Clara Elizabeth Ramírez Front, split from the PLF.

Arena Party—Nationalist Republican Alliance. Right wing, headed by Roberto d'Aubuisson. Salvadoran Authentic Institutional Party is another right-wing group.

Christian Democratic Party—Nominal moderates, headed by José Napoleón Duarte.

Salvadoran Army (Fuerza Armada)—Main source of political power in the country.

"Death squads"—name usually applied to right-wing terror groups that seek to make examples of those who oppose them.

Roman Catholic Church—Could act as a mediator between government and left.

Nicaragua

Sandinista-junta directorate—Headed by Daniel Ortega Saavedra. In March 1981 junta shrank from five men to three.

FSLN, Sandinista Front for National Liberation—Original umbrella group for opposition to Somoza.

Turbas—Pro-Sandinista street mobs. Used to terrorize opponents of the junta.

Other Nicaraguan political parties (activities restricted)—Nicaraguan Democratic Movement (MDN, headed by Alfonso Robelo), Conservative Democratic Movement (PCD), Liberal Independent Party (MLC), Social Christian Party (PSC), Social Democratic Party (PSD), Pro-Sandinista Socialist Party (PSN).

Coordinadora—Umbrella political organization of moderates and conservatives led by former Sandinista government leader and Nicaraguan ambassador to the United States, Arturo Cruz. Coordinadora may or may not participate in Sandinista-sponsored elections. Free press, open campaigning, voter registration, and freedom from harassment and attack by Sandinista *turbas* (in other words, guarantees of a free and democratic election), have been the sticking points. Like Cruz, Adolfo Calero and Alfonso Robelo, other insurgent leaders, once supported the Sandinistas.

Contras—Anti-Sandinista guerrillas. Main group is Nicaraguan Democratic Force, which fields 8,000+ troops, has some former Somocista National Guardsmen. Leaders are Chamorro, Bermúdez, and Calero.

Democratic Revolutionary Alliance (ARDE)—Anti-Sandinista

guerrilla group led by revolutionary socialist Edén Pastora; based in Costa Rica.

Misurasata—Miskito, Sumo, and Rama Indian organization. Leader is Stedman Fagoth Muller, who is currently exiled in Honduras. Miskitos may field as many as 3,000 guerrillas.

La Prensa—Nicaraguan opposition newspaper. Frequently shut down by Somoza; frequently shut down by the Sandinista junta.

Edén Pastora—Also known as Commander Zero. The Che Guevara of the Nicaraguan revolution, now opposes the Sandinista regime. He survived a 1984 assassination attempt which occurred while he was conducting a news conference from a base camp in Costa Rica.

General Augusto César Sandino—Nicaraguan national hero; fought U.S. Marines to a stalemate in 1920s and 1930s. When Marines left in 1933, he left the backcountry and made peace with the new government. Was murdered during dinner with President Juan Bautista. National Guardsmen, under the command of Anastasio Somoza, were the killers. The Sandinistas take their name from Sandino.

United States Congress, United States public opinion, American newspapers and TV networks—Considered by many participants to be the most important political battleground in Central America.

Civilian Military Assistance group and other private "military aid" organizations—Private groups of U.S. citizens, many of them Vietnam vets and other former military, who go to Central America to fight. Many are far-right anti-communist ideologues, some are democratic idealists, some mercenaries, some just "gringo pistoleros." Not a new phenomenon by any means. U.S. citizens have a long tradition of conducting their own foreign policies. American volunteers have fought all over the world for all kinds of causes, including communist revolutions. These particular volunteers circumvent U.S. restrictions on military involvement and military aid in Central America. Some of them are ill-trained macho "cowboys" who'll just get themselves killed. Some of them are experts who can, and have, advised and trained the Salvadoran army, the Honduran army, and Nicaraguan rebel fighters. A few have openly fought in Nicaragua and have allegedly attacked Cuban-manned installations. Accurate numbers of potential recruits are not available, but 800 to 1,000 volunteer troops isn't beyond possibility. It is doubtful that they would ever be deployed in large units. Most of them are "vacation warriors" who fly down to Central America from Miami, Houston, or New Orleans, and then fight for a couple of months. They are a genuine wild card whose effect is difficult to estimate. They are generally well skilled in what are, for Central America, some of the more esoteric aspects of warfare, like demolition, maintenance, fortification, and flying. A Salvadoran officer interviewed by NBC News said that when U.S. volunteers show up, his light machine gun availability rate (i.e., what percent of the guns assigned to his unit are working) jumps from about 50 percent to 100 percent. The volunteers know how to fix and maintain weapons, skills in which the poorly trained Salvadorans are weak. Small things like these make the difference in tactical combat, and over a long period of time tend to win wars.

PARTICIPANT STRATEGIES AND GOALS

United States—Wants to (1) defend the Panama Canal, (2) defend Mexico and the southern United States border, and (3) bring moderate, popular, and pro-United States governments into being.

Washington is trying to use economic and military aid to bring about social and political reforms in El Salvador, Honduras, and Nicaragua. Negotiations by opposing factions, free elections, and land reallocation are part of the policy. Debate in the United States over the degree of Russian-Cuban influence in these countries affects the use of American combat forces as well as the aid packages. A militant pro-Moscow dictatorship, it is argued, represents a physical threat to the United States, and merely substitutes one ruling oligarchy for another. Another side counters with the argument that Central American revolutions are inevitable and that anger at United States support for the old oligarchies is understandable. Anger doesn't make a country a Russian puppet. If the United States would stop supplying arms to the regimes in power and opened negotiations with the rebels, they argue, its policy aims would be far better served. The other side then responds that "the Bolsheviks would subvert the Mensheviks"—i.e., moderate democratic rebels, who would opt for genuine coexistence and reform, would be toppled by pro-Moscow extremists. So the arguments go. Washington fiddles while Central America burns.

The 1983–1984 bipartisan Central American policy commission chaired by Henry Kissinger was an attempt to overcome this policy hiatus. The commission's report reveals an understanding of the economic and social origins of Central America's problems, which are often glossed over by those who see the world as a struggle between the superpowers. The committee's recommendations stressed educational reform and highlighted the need for extensive development of basic transportation services and agricultural revitalization. Translated, this means teaching kids, building roads, and growing plants. But war kills teachers and kids, destroys roads, and burns cornfields.

What do you do in the short run, while people wage war against each other? The basic United States policy dilemma remains. Peace is essential to solving these human problems, but can Washington risk the coming to power of genuinely hostile, Moscow-backed and armed regimes if American military aid to pro-United States factions is withdrawn? Or should the United States gear up, as it seems to be doing in Honduras, to defend the region with American troops, since pro-United States elements can at best produce military stalemates? The flip side is that the left-wing rebels are only able to produce military stalemates as long as the United States continues to back the current government.

Essentially, Nicaragua, El Salvador, and Honduras represent three different strategies. In Nicaragua the United States withdrew its support from Somoza and encouraged the Sandinista revolution. In El Salvador the United States has practiced a policy of providing "just enough" military and economic aid to sustain the government. In Honduras America has built military support and training facilities and established a bilateral defense policy that promises to use United States troops to defend Honduras. The last policy may work as long as Honduras maintains a liberal democratic government, but should a dictatorship return to power, the United States will be back in the policy bind of supporting what could become an unpopular and oppressive regime.

Nicaragua

Sandinista regime—Try to defeat rebels militarily within the country, and solidify the regime's political control. Propaganda offensives against United States supporters of the anti-Sandinista rebels and against Honduras may help blunt or stop military supplies to them. But the rebels are not created by Washington. There is simply too much dissatisfaction within Nicaragua over the Sandinista junta's failure to carry out the aims of the 1979 revolution. What are the regime's goals? If it opts for open, free elections and allows a free press, then its goals are those of democratic revolution. Other goals of the regime concern the presence of 5,000 to 10,000 (the numbers vary widely) Cuban so-called technicians and advisers inside the country. The Sandinista junta wants to avoid direct negotiations with its own dissidents and prefers to negotiate with Washington. Direct negotiations with dissident former Sandinistas means that free elections, a free press, and freedom of religion are the issues. Talking with Washington lets the Sandinistas make impending invasions or border problems the issues, not their internal problems with other Nicaraguans. Washington is portrayed as an aggressor.

Anti-Sandinista opposition—The liberal socialists want the Sandinistas to fulfill the democratic promises made in 1979. They claim the Sandinistas have undermined the revolution, and do not accept a totalitarian regime led by a Leninist "revolutionary vanguard." These former revolutionaries field guerrilla forces, but they do not solicit the blessings of Washington. That would be a sellout to Yankee imperialism. But moderates and some old Somoza National Guardsmen with guerrilla forces in Honduras willingly accept United States aid. Many critics of American policy claim these contra forces are the creation of the CIA. The opposition forces maintain that their aim is to carry out the revolution of 1979, but that the current Sandinista regime is too much in league with Moscow to do anything except produce another Cuba. Both opposition groups believe constant economic and military pressure on the regime will either (1) force less extreme Sandinistas to toss out the extremists, then move to negotiations, or (2) eventually topple the regime. If they succeed in tossing out the Sandinista junta, these two opposition factions would have to work out their differences, either politically or militarily.

El Salvador

Government—Is the government the army or a hazy coalition of moderates and conservatives that is caught in a cross-fire between the extreme right wing and the left-wing guerrillas? Land reform has been a central issue. The government developed a strong land-reform policy, but its implementation has been sporadic and right-wing critics have tried to stop the program. Moderates in El Salvador, those who have not fled or been slain, press for a centrist "government of national reconciliation" that would try to incorporate all but the most extreme political elements. This is almost as impossible as trying to stop the right-wing death squads and the left-wing guerrilla raids and terror bombings. The government is trying to convince the peasants that reform is progressing, to stop left- and right-wing violence, and to ensure continued United States support. The government also claims that putting an end to outside support for left- and right-wing violence is beyond its means. Right-wing death squads are financed by wealthy exiles living in Miami and elsewhere. The left is supplied by Nicaragua and Cuba.

Right wing—Want to roll back land reform. Assassination and terror are their tactical methods. They say labor organizers and clergy who talk about the health needs of peasants are just troublemakers. They argue that the old patriarchal system provided stability.

Left-wing rebels—The rebels aim to "stay in the field." They will continue hitting isolated army posts, seizing and holding villages until the army responds, then tackling government main-force units when such units are vulnerable. Urban hit-and-run raids and economic disruption also play a part in their strategy. The rebels dynamite electric generators, bridges, and railroads, damaging the economy. Shooting up buses and trucks further weakens the transportation-and-distribution networks. And the right-wing rebels have no monopoly on terror. Assassination of key opponents remains a classic revolutionary tool; the idea is to shift the blame to someone else. Analysts are split over the left-wing rebels' willingness to negotiate. The Maoist PLF is thought to regard any negotiations as unacceptable. Many of the best guerrilla forces are loyal to the PLF. If the radicals control the movement, then the goal is absolute military victory.

Honduras—Has decided that military cooperation with the United States is its best strategy. Some degree of armed conflict with Nicaragua, or with Nicaraguan-backed guerrillas in Honduras, is inevitable. The Honduran strategy includes maximum appeals for United States economic assistance. Honduran democrats have tried to make a deal with the military and with the right wing for the maintenance of free elections. They argue that it is easier to get military and economic support from Washington if Honduras remains a democracy. United States support includes new weapons and supplies for the army, funds for capital investment, and a significant kick to the weak Honduran economy.

SUPERPOWER INTEREST

	Political	Military	Historical	Economic
Russia	High	High	Low	Low
US	Very High	Very High	High	High

Political—Moscow's political involvement in America's backyard gives it superb political leverage. Support for revolutionary movements scores with the Third World; subversion of these movements gives Moscow direct strategic military advantage. A demonstration of support by the United States that moderate reform (even in the middle of open warfare) is possible is a high priority worldwide. Protection of United States investments in region is vital.

Military—Moscow has a strategic opportunity to split North and South America and move that much closer to the Panama Canal. If the Kremlin can't control the Canal, it would like to be able to interdict it with land forces. United States defense of the Canal is vital to the American economy. Washington wants to stop the spread of anti-United States warfare to potentially vulnerable Mexico.

Historical—Russian awareness of the area begins with the 1954 Arbenz regime in Guatemala, a Communist government, and Fidel Castro in Cuba, but this isn't Russia's traditional territory. United States neglect of the region has alternated dramatically with a sudden frenzied concern that ends when American isolationism reasserts itself, or when the region becomes "stabilized" either through democracy (Costa Rica) or a strongman government (everybody else).

Economic—Russian interest barely rates. They can't really afford to subsidize Central America as they do Cuba. United States economic interests are outclassed only by those it has in Western Europe, Canada, and Japan, and in Persian Gulf oil.

POTENTIAL OUTCOMES

Nicaragua

1. 35 percent chance before 1988: War between Nicaragua and Honduras. If this occurs, there's a 75 percent chance of United States intervention in Honduras; a 40 percent chance of El Salvador entering fray because of proximity of the conflict and the threat of a Nicaraguan victory; a 15 percent chance of Guatemalan intervention on the side of Honduras.

2. 30 percent chance: Sandinista regime defeats internal and external foes militarily and politically. Goes to 50 percent if Cuban main-force units are introduced. Nicaragua becomes a mainland Cuba.

3. 25 percent chance: Pro-Moscow elements of Sandinista regime are suppressed, and moderates and left-wing rebels return to government. Open elections are held and Nicaragua becomes a socialist neutral nation—in other words, the aims of the 1979 revolution are achieved.

4. 10 percent chance: United States invasion of Nicaragua. Goes to 60 percent if Cuban main-force units are brought into Nicaragua. Result is that present situation is reversed, with new pro-United States government fighting a guerrilla war with former Sandinista regime.

El Salvador

1. 35 percent chance: Same old story—bloodshed, poverty, guerrilla war, coup d'état. United States continues program of giving just enough military and economic aid to sustain pro-United States forces and enrich crooked right-wing generals. Rebel supply sources in Nicaragua remain functional.

2. 35 percent chance: Moderate liberal democrats succeed in controlling right-wing elements, non-Communist left enters political process, reconstruction begins. Goes to 50 percent in 1986 if predicted massive United States economic aid materializes and President Duarte remains in power. Duarte has the rare combination of leadership skills, background, and intellect that, given luck, could form a strong coalition government out of the extremist chaos.

3. 18 percent chance before 1986: Outright rebel military victory. Goes to 65 percent if Sandinista regime wins outright victory in Nicaragua.

4. 12 percent chance before 1986: Right-wing military victory. Goes to 20 percent if Nicaraguan-Honduran conflict erupts.

Honduras

1. 35 percent chance of army coup d'état by 1986; 65 percent chance of stability of present regime through 1986. An ironic note: If the Sandinista regime in Nicaragua *loses* power or moderates in its policies, look for Honduras to begin to distance itself militarily from Washington. Economic reliance on the United States, however, will grow. Honduras will demand that American funds earmarked for military airstrips be spent on farm roads and civilian transportation facilities.

COST OF WAR

Most of the warfare consists of the national armed forces waging low-level combat against their own citizens. Add to this the endemic banditry, civil disorder, and insurgency characteristic of so many areas. Then you have several thousand deaths and injuries a year throughout the entire region.

The economic costs are equally high, with bloated military budgets and substantial harm to national economies.

QUICK LOOK AT ECUADOR AND PERU: BORDER WAR, INDIAN WAR, AND THE SHINING PATH

Peru and Ecuador share a long, mountainous, and ill-defined border. The population of the region—where there is any—consists of Indians living in small, isolated villages.

The simmering border conflict between Ecuador and Peru, which so far has featured minor infantry skirmishes and strikes by armed helicopters, isn't driven by national pride: There are strong indications that the border area sits on a significant pool of oil. The new Inca gold is Texas Tea.

The Indians don't particularly care for the mestizo and white soldiers of either side. Ecuador and Peru have both followed a policy of neglect that cannot be characterized as benign. The Indians lack basic medical care; their agricultural methods remain primitive. But the Indian peasants also want to be left alone. They are classic mountaineers.

The Indians present Marxist ideologues with a quandary. According to Marxist-Leninist theory, the Indians should be rebelling. Enter Sendero Luminoso, "the Shining Path." Founded by extreme leftist intellectuals in Lima, and with a slight bow to Mao and Trotsky, in the early 1980s Sendero Luminoso began a brutal series of terror attacks against the Peruvian government. The intent was to foment an Indian revolt. The intellectuals even called on the power of old Inca legends that say "sleeping" Inca kings will rise out of the Andes to kill the Spanish invaders. Naturally, the Leninists want the Indians to conclude that the Shining Path is that Incan resurrection.

To the Indians, leftist intellectuals from Lima are just central-government Spaniards spouting a different verse of the old saw "you be like us, or else." Sendero Luminoso hasn't been very successful at organizing the Indians. The Indians have killed a number of the would-be guerrillas, and in one instance they massacred a group of journalists mistaken for the left-wing outsiders.

Shining Path's founder is Abimael Guzman. He calls himself the "Fourth Sword of Marxism," an apocalyptic complement to Marx, Lenin, and Mao. Unlike other South American guerrilla groups, however, Shining Path doesn't seem to rely on outside advisers or arms shipments. This is probably because its hatred for Moscow is as intense as its hatred for the United States.

Summer 1984 estimates on Shining Path's strength ran from 2,000 to 7,000 guerrillas.

The Shining Path has exhibited a genuine nihilistic taste for general terror, and while a murderous problem for the Indians, they are also a threat to Peru's central government. Recent reports also mention Shining Path activity in Colombia, but that's already the stamping ground of the guerrilla organization M-19, which started as an urban-proletariat-oriented revolutionary group. Now, allegedly, M-19 is in the cocaine business.

QUICK LOOK AT BOLIVIA, CHILE, AND PERU: THE LINGERING WAR OF THE PACIFIC

During the War of the Pacific (1879–1884) Bolivia lost the port of Arica, its outlet to the sea, to Chile. This remains an unsettled issue. Bolivian calls for negotiations have gone unanswered; Chile says there is nothing to negotiate. But the argument over access to the sea through a national port isn't simply an issue of hurt national pride, and it isn't about an insignificant area (like Chile and Argentina's old dispute over islands in the Beagle Channel). When it comes to trade and tariffs, Chile and neighboring Peru hold Bolivia by the throat. This is a recipe for renewed conflict.

QUICK LOOK AT THE UNITED STATES AND CANADA: CONTROLLED ANARCHY ON THE ISLAND OF STABILITY

In parts of southern Missouri, Jesse James is still regarded as a hero. The United States has always been an easy place to stage a riot or rob a stage. But the United States government is difficult to topple because democracy provides a way to give at least the appearance of overthrowing the ruling cliques every few years. Being rich also helps the United States and Canada remain stable. Quebec's separatist Parti Québécois began to falter as soon as the French Canadians realized that because all the English and American companies were leaving Montreal for Toronto and Burlington, Vermont, a "Free Quebec" could get a nasty case of Third World poverty.

The chief reason for the democratic success of the United States and Canada is that they sit on a big island. The Mexicans to the south aren't the Germans; there aren't any Hapsburgs raising armies next door, no Russians live across the marsh. All the local barbarians were destroyed by disease and ended up in large desert relocation camps called Indian reservations. Besides, the Comanches could never get a sustained war together as the Goths could.

The entire North American system is designed to let the steam out of polarized positions by allowing for loud political debate and occasional riots. This is followed by a period of muddling compromise. Historically, the United States and Canada have had time to muddle through because there isn't a Hun at the doorstep. No one has ever heard of Attila the Eskimo. Mexico offers no threat, though when it does, the United States reacts *muy pronto*. When Pancho Villa shot up a couple of border towns, the United States sent the troops to the border, and Villa disappeared. The Atlantic and Pacific oceans serve as rather large English Channels. Even the threat of nuclear ICBM bombardment hasn't *yet* affected this perception of isolation.

11. Suriname and the Caribbean: Blood and Bauxite in a Backwater

INTRODUCTION

Suriname presents a new variation on an old problem: How do you keep the troops in the barracks when they think they should be running the government?

In 1980 the Suriname military, headed by Dési Bouterse and supported by foreign military and political advisers, seized control of the tiny South American nation of Suriname. The junta has encountered much opposition: the bulk of the population, antidictatorship exiles, and the Netherlands, Suriname's former colonial occupier. The Bouterse regime may not last long, but if it falls, it will probably be replaced by a like-minded group of military thugs if there is no outside intervention.

The dictatorship, the Dutch, the Brazilians, the Cubans, and the exiles all have different aims. Superpower interest and involvement in these intrigues increases world tension and may yet precipitate a superpower confrontation.

SOURCE OF CONFLICT

In December 1982 revolutionary leader Dési Bouterse sent a message to the people of Suriname and the world when he arrested sixteen of the former Dutch colony's most prominent citizens. The next day all but one were dead.

This is a short story of collapse, the collapse of a tropical idyll. Suriname was a small country with Chinese, Javanese, Creole, and Indian inhabitants, blessed with mineral resources, and funded to the tune of $100 million a year by a generous Dutch government. It had one of the highest per-capita annual incomes ($2,360) in the Third World. Now the strings and hangman's nooses are pulled by an ill-educated former physical-education instructor with a Leninist mistress.

The new regime replaced political and religious tolerance with the power of the submachinegun and pseudo-Marxism. Most of the Cuban advisers left for Havana after junta strongman Bouterse saw the assassination and replacement of Grenada's Maurice Bishop in October 1983 as a possible Cuban script for his own removal. Indications are, however, that the Cubans have not left completely. Cuban secret policemen built Bouterse's secret police force, and their influence remains.

In Suriname this strongman government took power in a former colony, repeating a common postcolonial pattern: Three to five years after independence, whoever controls the armory suddenly controls the country. Bouterse led a military faction that demanded the right to form a soldiers' union. On February 25, 1980, he overthrew the democratically elected but fragile and divided government. No formal combat took place. The troops simply left their barracks, surrounded key government buildings, arrested key government officials, and replaced the officials with army sergeants.

Bouterse's takeover is something more than an unfortunate series of brutal murders for several reasons. Suriname was the world's leading producer of bauxite (aluminum ore) until 1964. It now ranks fifth, but still has one of the largest reserves of the strategic mineral. Suriname's location, on the South American mainland near powerful yet politically fragile Brazil, makes it attractive for Russian-Cuban penetration. Suriname could provide naval air stations for destroying the oil routes from Venezuela and the tanker routes coming from the South Atlantic.

Brazil and the United States fear that Russia could establish air and naval bases in Suriname. Building such bases could trigger an invasion. Given the popular dislike of the dictatorship, there is little likelihood of a subsequent guerrilla war. However, the diverse ethnic nature of the country could lead to civil disorder. It would resemble gang warfare.

WHO'S INVOLVED

Dési Bouterse—Former PE instructor and army sergeant major who became the commander-in-chief of the eight-man revolutionary council, which means he controlled the militia in Paramaribo, the capital. Bouterse has a fourth-grade education and a very large ego. He has promoted himself to lieutenant colonel. Bouterse understands the dictator's basic equation: Gunfire subtracts the intellectuals and divides the bureaucrats. Fear multiplies.

Henk Chin A Sen—Former prime minister of Suriname. After Bouterse overthrew the Henck Arron government in 1980, he put in Chin A Sen as caretaker, then toppled him in February 1982. Chin A Sen is a moderate and is recognized as the leader of Suriname's massive exile community, 185,000 of whom live in the Netherlands.

The Surinamese bureaucrats: Forty percent of Suriname's labor force is in government service—still another inheritance from the Dutch.

Cuba—Out but not down. Most of the Cubans were expelled in late 1983. However, some secret police and intelligence types remain.

The Netherlands—The old colonial power is still respected politically and economically.

The Surinamese exile community: Between 200,000 and 250,000 strong, a large number, especially since only 360,000 people now live in Suriname. A thousand of the exiles are military personnel.

GEOGRAPHY

Located on the Atlantic Ocean, just east of the South Atlantic approaches to the Caribbean Sea, with French Guiana to the immediate east, Brazil's poverty-stricken northern provinces to the immediate south, and Guyana (formerly British Guiana and former home to Jim Jones, Jonestown, and the People's Temple) to the west, Suriname is a tropical land, with rain-forested lowlands, rivers, a balmy coast, and forested mountain ranges in its southern section. The Brazilian border area is primarily savanna, which becomes tropical jungle as one moves north toward the coast. There are few roads in the backcountry.

Since independence, the population has been declining steadily, mostly because of liberal Dutch immigration policies. Population estimate in 1980 was 355,000, with more than 180,000 concentrated in Paramaribo. Another 40 percent of the people live in the coastal towns; only 10 percent live in the hinterland.

The population reflects the racial mixture of the old Dutch empire:

32%: Creoles (European-Africans)
35%: East Indians (called Hindustanis by the locals)
15%: Indonesians

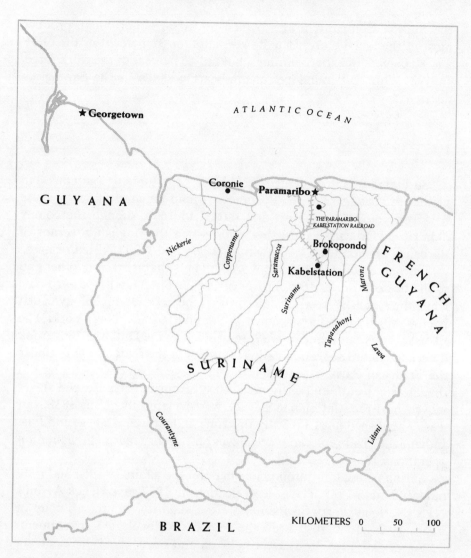

3%: Chinese
3%: Carib and Arawak Indians
2%: Europeans
10%: Bush Blacks (the offspring of escaped slaves)

Literacy is an unusually high 80 percent.

Moengo and Paranam are the two principal bauxite-producing areas. Both are near navigable rivers. The Suriname Aluminum Company (SURALCO), a subsidiary of United States-based ALCOA, and the Billiton Company, a firm owned by Royal Dutch Shell, produce most of the bauxite ore. Bauxite accounts for 31 percent of the GDP and 80 percent of export earnings, but only 6 percent of the work force. In 1981 Gulf Oil found petroleum-bearing sands in the Saramacca district.

HISTORY

Suriname was first sighted in 1498 by Christopher Columbus, but neither the Spanish nor the Portuguese found much use for it because it lacked gold. The English first settled in 1630, though the colony didn't begin to thrive until the 1650s, when the English governor of Barbados arrived with 1,000 white settlers and 2,000 African slaves.

Suriname's contribution to world trivia is that it was the other end of the tradeoff in the 1667 Treaty of Breda: The Dutch got Suriname while the English Crown acquired the rights to a Dutch colony called Nieuw Amsterdam, now known as Manhattan and New York. The British retook Suriname in 1799, returned it to the Dutch in 1802, took it back again in 1804, and finally restored it to the Dutch in 1814 under the Treaty of Paris. Several spectacular slave rebellions took place in the late eighteenth and early nineteenth centuries. The escaped slaves moved into the hinterland. Slavery was declared illegal in 1818, but wasn't abolished until 1863. By this time, indentured Chinese and East Indian labor had replaced black slaves on the very marginal plantation operations.

Suriname became autonomous in domestic affairs in 1954 and fully independent in 1975. The general elections in 1977 gave Henck Arron's NPS (National Party Suriname) a clear majority. Bouterse's coup of February 25, 1980, overthrew the democratically elected government.

As of fall 1984 Bouterse's hold on the reins of government are slipping, along with his confidence in Cuban support. Until October 1983 Bouterse was using his Cuban-trained and supported police force to weed out potential dissident intellectuals, and was closely scrutinizing relatives of exiled opponents who have not been able to get visas to leave Suriname.

Interestingly enough, because governmental corruption has increased dramatically, visas are for sale, but obtaining them entails risk and money. Fragmentary United States newspaper reports have indicated that in June or July 1983, Dutch intelligence agents working out of the Dutch West Indies informed Bouterse of a coup being plotted by exiled opponents. This may well have been a ruse to try to persuade Bouterse to trust the Dutch, but there is strong evidence that exiles in Holland and in the Caribbean have been acquiring Belgian-made weapons. Bouterse fended off a March 1982 coup led by Sergeant Major Wilfred Hawker. Bouterse had Hawker executed.

Bouterse felt very confident until the death of his friend Maurice Bishop of Grenada at the hands of Cuban-backed supporters. Bouterse had relied on Cuban assistance. He increased the Surinamese Army, which had declined in strength because of immigration, exile, and execution, to more than 2,000 men. Prior to Bishop's death, there had been reports of Cuban advisers in Suriname. Bouterse was convinced Castro would back him in both internal challenges as well as regional threats, such as an invasion by Brazil.

Bishop's assassination increased Bouterse's paranoia. Following some public advice Bishop had given him in October 1982 about his enemies ("You must eliminate them or they will eliminate you"), Bouterse concluded the Cubans were no longer his friends and he expelled them along with the local Russian consulate. However, not all the East Bloc personnel departed. Either Bouterse wanted to hedge his bet or internal Cuban police and intelligence contacts were too strong to be broken with one diplomatic stroke.

Exiles have told of random arrests by Bouterse's police, rising unemployment, and increasing public fear. Though one American estimate puts the number of political prisoners at a "mere" 150, exile leaders believe another brutal purge is in the works. Bouterse has killed his democratic political opponents, dispersed his army opposition, and now fears only reaction or retaliation from his former left-wing allies.

The economic situation continues to deteriorate. Bauxite production, already stagnating in 1980 and 1981, has slipped even more because of the loss of skilled personnel and the world recession. Suriname possesses large timber resources which the Japanese are reported to be interested in developing. The United States is Suriname's major trading partner, selling the country 32 percent of its imports and buying 41 percent of its exports.

LOCAL POLITICS

National Military Council—At the present time political parties are banned and all direction comes from the National Military Council

(NMR, Nationale Militaire Raad), which is directed by Dési Bouterse, Major Roy Horb, and Lieutenant Iwan Graanoogst.

Revolutionary People's Front—The NMR's offspring, which hopes ultimately to include all political factions.

Staten van Suriname—Prior to the February 1982 "final coup," this legislative council, had thirty-nine elected members, though the council had ceased to function effectively when the NMR overthrew Arron in 1980. The political parties that existed prior to 1982 reflected the country's ethnic hodgepodge. In fact, the parties represented separate ethnic groups, which was a major reason for the constant divisiveness. The Hindustanis have been a strong economic and political force, often angering the powerful Creole parties. Still, Suriname remained a surprisingly tolerant place, given the cultural and religious differences of its people.

The political parties are currently banned, but you will notice that each of them represents an ethnic group. Therefore, each party is a potential source of rebellion and a natural rallying point for ethnic aspirations. The following list shows each party and the ethnic group they represent.

Hernieuwde Progressive (HPP)—social democratic party, mainly composed of Hindustanis.

Kaum-Tani Persuatan Indonesia (KTPI)—Indonesian party.

National Party Surinam (NPS)—Creole party, was Henck Arron's power base.

Partij Nationalistische Republiek (NPR)—Creole party, split into two rival factions.

Vooruitstrevende Hervormings Partij (VHP)—Predominantly Indian party.

Pregressive Bosneger Partij—Bush Black party.

Progressive Surinamese Volkspartij (PSV)—Christian Democratic Party.

PARTICIPANT STRATEGIES AND GOALS

Bouterse—Stay in power. However, the sword of Damocles is held by a fraying string. The exile community is unforgiving. Castro waits as an only friend, unless the Brazilians want a deal. As for controlling the home front, Bouterse feels it is better to be feared than loved. The paranoid oppression increases.

The Netherlands—Return Suriname to a semblance of its former self without intervening directly and becoming labeled "imperialist." Internal Dutch politics won't allow for much use of the Dutch marines in the West Indies, though should Bouterse begin new round of killing, a quick visit to restore order might work. We estimate that the Dutch could bring over 1,500 marines into Suriname within a thirty-six-hour period, provided the United States or France supplied extra transport aircraft. The Netherlands Antilles provide a nearby base. (See Potential Outcomes.)

The Dutch are still popular with the Surinamese. The ideal outcome for The Hague would be if Bouterse requested more Dutch economic assistance, then agreed to disappear in wealthy exile. But this would require Bouterse's cooperation. Given the exile community's outrage at the December murders, Bouterse is likely to fear any deal that requires power-sharing. The Dutch government has no desire to hang Bouterse —that job is for the exiles. But a buy-off is unlikely.

Just waiting might be a good strategy, but this would mean more Surinamese would be killed or rot in prison. The Dutch government has a responsibility to its polyglot colonials in Suriname. Meeting this commitment may require covert cooperation with the exiles.

Brazil—Keep the Cubans and the Russians from gaining a toehold next to Brazil. Brazil may threaten to invade, actually do so, cut a deal with Bouterse against the Cubans, or cooperate in an exile-led guerrilla war across the border. Remember, Suriname is within MiG-23 range of the major Brazilian population centers.

Surinamese exiles—Return to power and punish Bouterse. Then rebuild Suriname's economy, once enviable by Third World standards. The least onerous method is to coax the Dutch government into supporting a covert move.

Cuba—Wait in the wings with weapons for anyone who is interested. Bouterse may still need Castro. Still, what once looked to the Cubans like an easy-to-influence regime is no longer so.

SUPERPOWER INTEREST

	Political	Military	Historical	Economic
Russia	Low	Medium to Low	Very Low	Very Low
US	Medium	High	Low	Medium to High

Political—The Russians have a flicker of an interest in a South American toehold, but Suriname's a terrible choice. Brazil and Venezuela are the prizes. Russian strategic penetration always arouses the United States.

Military—A potential Russian air or naval base near the South Atlantic sea-lanes can't be passed over lightly. The United States always has to consider threats to Venezuelan oil. Should there be a big conflict, Cuba is a big enough problem without having to divert air and naval forces to attack Suriname.

Historical—This isn't anywhere near the Russians' stamping ground. Historically, United States interests have fixed on the Caribbean and Central America.

Economic—The Russians aren't as threatened as the United States by a strategic mineral crunch. Their resource base is the Eurasian land mass and they don't have to protect vulnerable sea-lanes. As a sea power, the United States must consider mineral sources, to say nothing of such allies as Japan.

POTENTIAL OUTCOMES

1. 35 percent chance through 1986: Current dictator maintains control as the economic slide continues and the social oppression increases. Through 1987: 25 percent; past 1988; 15 percent.

2. 25 percent chance through 1986: Another strongman from the left or right replaces Bouterse either by assassination or forced exile, and nothing really changes except the personality responsible for the oppression. Becomes a 40 percent chance if covert Cuban activity is involved and a Grenada Exchange (the killing of one dictator and replacement of another more agreeable to Cuba) is made.

3. 18 percent chance through 1988: The Brazilians intervene to forestall a pro-Communist country on their borders, especially one near their volatile northern states. The boys from Brasilia restore opposition leaders who are favorable to the Brazilian regime, and Brazil becomes big brother. Price of Brazilian aluminum products becomes internationally competitive.

4. 15 percent chance through 1986: A coup is engineered by exiled army officers, possibly with covert Netherlands intelligence cooperation. Dutch involvement increases the chance for a return to democratic civilian leadership whose power base would be exile community. Goes to 40 percent if a conservative government is in power in Holland,

and overt Cuban support for the Surinamese dictatorship returns. If an exile coup is engineered, there is a consistent 80 percent probability that at some point Dutch forces will be involved as "reinforcements." Once the decision is made to support a coup, it won't matter if left- or right-wingers control The Hague—the marines will go. Doubters should take a look at Mitterand's France.

5. 7 percent chance: Castro "covertly" reenters the picture as disenchantment within Suriname grows and pressure from the exile community increases. The Cuban secret police back up Bouterse. Suriname becomes the long-sought South American mainland Cuban base.

COST OF WAR

The Dutch used to subsidize Suriname to the tune of over $100 million a year, 10 percent of Suriname's national income. The Dutch have cut back these subsidies drastically in response to the new government's violence against its citizens. Cuba and Russia can be expected to make up a small portion of these losses, although both countries are not noted for their generosity. Half the national income is derived from the export of raw materials, primarily bauxite. Talk of nationalizing the bauxite mines does not encourage additional foreign investment. The police state is expensive and the public employment sector of the economy is already huge. Over 40 percent of the work force is employed by the government. Half the national income goes into the government budget. Expect all this to result in a 20 percent decline in national income, or over $200 million a year.

Should there be a civil war or an invasion, the destruction of capital assets (housing, commercial establishments, government buildings, etc.) is possible. This could cause several hundred million dollars more in losses. Much of this money would be replaced by foreign aid.

Loss of life has not been exceptionally high, at least through fall 1984. Several dozen opponents of the government have been murdered and several hundred more are imprisoned. Invasion could push the death toll over 100; civil war could, because of the wide ethnic differences, cause thousands of deaths.

Prospects for a leftist guerrilla war are slight. The backcountry is lightly populated and neighboring nations are not friendly to the leftists.

The population does not have a history of violence, another vestige of the Dutch heritage.

MEANWHILE, ELSEWHERE IN THE CARIBBEAN

The countries of the eastern Caribbean have several common characteristics that make them prone to political instability, violence, and war.

Small Is Not Better: Many of these nations are small in size and population, as shown by the following table, which also shows the annual per-capita income. In comparison, the United States has a population of 65 per square kilometer, and a per-capita income of nearly $13,000 (Russia, $4,600; Japan, $9,600; Britain, $8,900; France, $10,600; Netherlands, $9,700).

Nation	Population	Per Square Kilometer	Per-Capita Income
Barbados (Br.)	250,000	582	$3,200
Dominica (Br.)	85,000	195	620
Grenada (Br.)	110,000	148	690
Guadeloupe (Fr.)	330,000	187	3,870
Martinique (Fr.)	325,000	296	4,640
St. Lucia (Br.)	130,000	208	850
St. Vincent (Br.)	110,000	325	520
Trinidad/Tobago (Br.)	1,200,000	235	4,370
Guyana (Br.)	820,000	4	688
French Guiana (Fr.)	63,000	0.7	2,880
Suriname (Dutch)	350,000	2.1	2,840
Bahamas (Br.)	250,000	18	3,300
Cuba	9,700,000	87	1,900
Dominican Republic	5,600,000	115	1,240
Haiti	5,100,000	202	294
Jamaica (Br.)	2,300,000	203	1,100
Puerto Rico (U.S.)	8,900,000	425	3,010

Shown in parentheses are the recent colonial associations (Br. = British; Fr. = French). Puerto Rico, given the large number of inhabitants who agitate to become the fifty-first state, really isn't a colony in the same sense as the Bahamas or Suriname. Just what Puerto Rico is remains a classic question—for the United States, the UN, and Puerto Ricans.

Size tends to create more stability than wealth does. It's a matter of arithmetic: It takes more troops to terrorize two million people than to terrorize two thousand. Thus the Caribbean's micronations are prone to the adventures of the powerful, the United States, Britain, and

France. The Cuban Communist regime is adventurous, but smart enough to avoid being foolhardy. When it has been foolhardy, its more powerful neighbor, the United States, has intervened.

Different Kinds of Independence: The independence of these nations varies. The British, Dutch and French controlled the area before the wave of decolonialization after World War II. The French states (Guadeloupe, Martinique, and French Guiana) are considered to be overseas departments of metropolitan (mainland) France. Like French citizens, the islanders may freely move to France and are eligible for relatively generous social welfare benefits. Anyone who gets out of line will either be arrested by the local gendarmes or face the tender mercies of the Foreign Legion. The Dutch treated Suriname in a like fashion as far as emigration and financial assistance were concerned. Suriname, however, is now an independent state, with the Dutch playing the role of a rich and, so far, indulgent uncle. The British were not as generous as the French and Dutch. Immigration was eventually restricted and generous social benefits were not forthcoming. It is the former British colonies that are most prone to disorder.

Our Gang: The small size of these islands enables small, organized groups, like the army or police, to take over easily. When there is no external authority to which the population can appeal, these takeovers can be long-lasting. Until the Russians became involved in Caribbean politics, the takeovers were generally right wing (conservative) or apolitical. The rulers operated on behalf of the wealthier families and generally avoided messy external political involvements.

Delicate Finances: The economies are very fragile, usually dependent on tourism, raw materials, and cash subsidies from foreign nations, often the former colonial power. The tourism income varies with the state of the North American economy and the perceived friendliness and safety of the tourist areas. Raw-materials income depends on the state of the world economy and competition from other producers. Cash subsidies vary with the providing nation's political and economic climates.

Revolution as a Career: High unemployment provides a pool of capable and willing followers for an armed leader who preaches change, especially in situations where only change will improve a stagnant economy and prospects for the young and ambitious.

Selling Friendship and Position: The Caribbean nations have little to offer their wealthier and more powerful neighbors other than friendship (respect foreign citizens' economic and social indiscretions) and position (cooperate militarily with your stronger neighbors). For many years Americans and Europeans had the islands to themselves as there was no competition for friendship and position. When Russia entered the act, there was a political war, and several shooting ones as well.

Scoundrels in Power: Small size, particularly when coupled with high unemployment, high education levels, national independence, and armed forces, produces a potential for tragicomic situations. The most apt comparison is to the frequent municipal political scandals in the United States in which a group of scoundrels gets elected by making the most outlandish promises, then does as it wishes with the municipal finances and civil rights. The day of reckoning on the undeliverable promises is delayed by paying off potential troublemakers. The worst abuses are often in the smaller cities. Without the restraint, and threat of intervention by state and federal governments, small municipalities can get out of hand. Haiti, a right-wing dictatorship, is a prime example of how bad things can get.

The Army to the Rescue: Think of what would happen if the corrupt city governments of the United States had ruled independent islands and kept small armies. In such isolation very little restrains local bully boys. The elected scoundrels cater to their favorite faction. Driven by jealousy or indignation, the army often deposes the civilian government in order to "straighten things out." The only solution is for the bully boys to control the armed forces closely. Such is the case in Haiti.

The Promise of Socialism: The socialist dictator (usually a Communist) has given socialism an undeserved bad name, for genuine socialism is fervently democratic. Socialist dictatorships have introduced two new versions of a couple of old ideas. First, there is to be no independent wealth. The state—that is, the leader and his gang—owns and controls everything. Second, this nifty new wrinkle is treated like a religion. Missionary activity is supported to convert the heathens (nonsocialist nations, especially those who economically oppress their citizens). Socialist dictatorships become fascist dictatorships with a propaganda shield, and the democratic socialist revolutionaries end up either dead or in exile.

The Perils of Diplomacy: Foreign affairs is a dangerous area for all nations, particularly small ones. The best approach appears to be "Keep your head down and your mouth shut." Haiti is a prime example of how a despicable dictatorship can stay in power by doing the "right thing" by its more powerful neighbors (in this case, the United States, Cuba, etc.), which means following the current party line of the more powerful.

12. The Falkland Islands: Cleaning up After Modern Colonialism

INTRODUCTION

The 1982 war between Argentina and Britain was another classic kind of dispute that could reoccur in many parts of the world. The immediate cause of the conflict was a dictatorship's need for an external event to distract the population; an old cause was the attractiveness of island bases for colonial powers. This gold-plated little war served primarily as a proving ground for the latest weapons and as a test of very different attitudes toward training and leadership. Third World military commanders had their inferiority complexes reinforced. Western powers renewed their confidence in their military prowess. In the wake of the Falklands/Malvinas War, Russia became less certain of its ability to blitz Western Europe with a conventional attack so awesome was the British demonstration of Western military flexibility.

In many ways the isolated corner of the earth occupied by the Falklands provided an ideal place to fight a war, if one can speak of an ideal place to kill. The battle was fought over a treeless, windswept, archipelago just north of the Antarctic Circle. With few civilians, no cathedrals, museums, or heavy industry, and no place to hide, the naval, air, and ground forces were limited only by their political objectives and their combat capabilities.

Argentine aspirations to be a significant power combined with their political instability to produce the war. It could happen again. Despite the anticipated costs, neither Britain nor Argentina seems willing to abandon its claim to the islands. Argentina wants to right a perceived, though ancient, injustice; Britain is willing to pay a high price to preserve the rights of British subjects.

SOURCE OF CONFLICT

The Falklands War is a classic case of a power being dragged into conflict as a result of past colonial activities. During the heyday of colonialism, Britain's possessions brought it great wealth and power; today the former colonies often create political headaches.

When constructing an empire, the British generally knew what they were doing, especially in terms of naval strategy. Islands like the Falklands play a significant role in maintaining fleets and merchant traffic. Naval powers have always found island bases to be an attractive alternative to messy continental involvement. Islands usually have a limited hinterland, thus limiting the need for large garrisons. Small island populations are easier to manipulate than large, dispersed continental populations. If there is a revolt, a naval blockade to cut off food and weapons followed by a swift marine assault usually put an end to the disturbance. In short, an island base tends to be less politically and militarily vulnerable than one on the mainland.

If the island is strategically located near a vital region, the power that controls the island can be commercially, politically, and militarily active without the greater costs and higher risks of continental involvement. Should the controlling power decide to move to the mainland, the island provides a natural logistics and command base. This principle governed Russian and Cuban interest in Grenada. (Grenada also offered the Cubans a classic staging area on their route to Angola.) Great Britain secured an empire using this geopolitical ruler. (South Africa, India, and the occasional deep penetration of the Sudan were large and expensive exceptions.) From island bases like Singapore, Hong Kong, and Malta, the Royal Navy could sail forth securely to protect commercial sea-lanes, project English power, and reinforce the inevitable disruptions in the continental possessions.

Even after massive decolonialization, a number of former island possessions still belong to the Crown. Some even are of extreme strategic importance, like Diego Garcia in the Indian Ocean. There are others of no significance other than beauty, for example, Anguilla. The damp and chilly Falklands, however, are a more dangerous anachronism. When the Argentine junta needed an outside conflict to maintain domestic control, the old Anglo-Spanish dispute over the Malvinas was renewed and marines replaced diplomatic negotiators.

There were actually two wars for the Falkland Islands. The war on the battlefield has been fought to a conclusion. It was primarily a naval conflict involving transport over long distances, high technology, gutsy Argentinian pilots, and well-trained and led British infantry. The second war, the political conflict, is back to a stalemate, that may be more difficult to resolve than the stalemate *before* the military conflict.

The Argentines had been planning an invasion for late 1984 or 1985. By then, Argentina's navy would have been reinforced by the acquisition of four more German submarines, and an entire squadron of French Super Étendards armed with antiship missiles would have been operational. And maybe, just maybe, there could have been a political breakthrough in England with the cost-conscious Thatcher government. The question then is, why did the junta attack in April 1982?

When diplomacy becomes deadlocked and a dictatorship's domestic support falters, a political analyst might expect the dictatorship to find a border dispute or some other conflagration that will mobilize the populace against an external enemy. I may be bad, says the dictator, but at least I'm one of you. A revival of old antagonisms keeps the gang in control. The Argentine junta also had in mind the Beagle Channel dispute with Chile. By hitting the Brits, the Argentine generals would show Santiago it ran the risk of war if it terminated discussions about the border problem in Tierra del Fuego. Finally, a successful war would cleanse the army in the people's eyes. After several years of the dirty internal war against leftist terrorists and political rivals, with political murders and army terrorism, the military knew its reputation was severely tarnished. Recovering the Malvinas would make it difficult for any subsequent Argentine government to prosecute the army for its crimes. The army would be too popular. The generals would be heroes, not criminals.

This analysis helps explain the Argentine junta's political situation in the spring of 1982. It does, however, finesse several powerful historical and ideological forces, such as an angry national desire to reclaim land allegedly taken by British "pirates," that also affected the Argentine decision. Still, a dictatorship beset with 120 percent annual inflation (one conservative estimate—the rate hit 434 percent in 1983), and international and domestic pressure to account for thousands of political murders, has immediate concerns about its own survival.

In light of these problems, the stalemated Falklands negotiations and the apparent British withdrawal of all but token defensive forces (interpreted as implicit recognition of Argentinian hegemony) created a situation in which invasion became a plausible political alternative for the dictatorship. That Britain's female leader consistently frustrated the junta's demands was an affront to Spanish *machismo,* adding fuel to the generals' smoldering plans.

The Argentine Navy believed that the invasion force would not be physically challenged by the British. The islands are too far from England, the war advocates argued. The British no longer have a big carrier, so they won't be able to provide enough air cover for their fleet. And besides, the war advocates maintained, the British have no taste for war. Thatcher's Labour party opponents won't let her send off a fleet to fight in the Third World.

The invasion and subsequent war resulted in a military disaster for the junta and paved the way for its political downfall. Ironically, Argentina's return to democracy was due in large part to the junta's military failure. This isn't surprising since the historical role and the general structure of Argentina's forces are those of a police army designed to occupy Argentina. The Argentine Army had no business masquerading as an expeditionary force to engage highly professional British ground troops.

Despite the conclusion of one round of hostilities, a permanent political resolution has not been reached. Negotiations to restore normal ties reduce the threat of armed conflict, but they do not guarantee peace. Unless there is a resolution of the sovereignty dispute, the possibility of renewed full-scale combat, air strikes, or terrorism remains. Even massive demographic change, brought on by, say, the influx of 100,000 new British settlers (highly unlikely), might render Argentine claims moot, but would not resolve the question of remnant colonialism.

WHO'S INVOLVED

Great Britain—With Margaret Thatcher's conduct of the war approved of by about 90 percent of the people, and with over 80 percent of the country in favor of maintaining a presence in the islands (according to English newspaper polls taken after the war), even a left-leaning Labour government would be hard-pressed to disengage immediately.

Argentina—The democratic government that replaced the junta continues to push for recovery of the Malvinas, albeit through peaceful means. But democracies use armies, too. Although the military junta has been discredited, weapons to replace those lost in the war are once again arriving from France, Israel, and second-hand sources (third parties suspected of fronting for Belgium, Holland, and perhaps Russian clients).

GEOGRAPHY

The Falkland Islands are typical of the remaining British colonial possessions. Isolated and sparsely populated, they hang on the edge of the South American continental shelf approximately 600 to 800 kilometers east of Patagonia and the town of Rio Gallegos in Argentina. The Falklands, with an area comparable to that of Connecticut and a population of less than 2,000 natives, are 600 kilometers from South America and 13,000 kilometers from England.

The island chain is about 225 kilometers from west to east, and 125 kilometers from north to south. There are several dozen islands in the archipelago, but only two are of consequence: West and East Falkland. The last is divided into two distinct regions—East Falkland to the north and Lafonia to the south. These regions are connected by a narrow isthmus running between the settlements of Darwin and Goose Green. Falkland Sound separates East and West Falkland. It varies in width from more than 50 kilometers in the south to less than 10 kilometers in its middle and northern reaches.

The weather is temperate in the summer, antarctic in the winter, with vicious southerly and southwesterly winds. The seas can be very heavy, but the Port Stanley anchorage and several anchorages in Falkland Sound can be used year-round.

Most of the islands are covered with rocky hills and large moorlike meadows of grass, ideal spots for raising sheep. There are few trees.

Fifteen hundred kilometers east and south of the Falklands lies the British possession of South Georgia Island. Britain's South Orkneys lie 850 kilometers south and west of South Georgia. The South Sandwich Islands, another British possession, are situated 600 kilometers east and south of South Georgia. These islands are uninhabited except for weather and research stations. South Georgia, the South Sandwiches, and the Falklands constitute Britain's Falkland Islands Dependencies.

Argentina claims South Georgia as well as the Falklands.

HISTORY

Under Juan Perón, dictator from 1943 to 1955, all Argentinian schools were required to teach that the "Malvinas are Argentine." Perón made sovereignty a point of national honor, maintaining that the Malvinas/Falklands were unfairly taken by Britain in 1833.

Discovery of the Falklands depends on whose history you read. Magellan, Vespucci, Hawkins, and others claimed the islands. The first European known to have put ashore was Captain John Strong in 1690. Strong was on his way to Chile. He named the islands for England's then First Lord of the Admiralty, Lord Falkland.

The Treaty of Utrecht in 1713 gave Spain a piece of paper that confirmed the control of its American territories, which included the Falklands, but the first settlement in the islands was directed by Antoine de Bougainville of France. In 1764 he claimed the islands for Louis XV, and established a colony north of what is today Port Stanley. Port Louis had over 200 colonists. The British, suspicious of the French, concocted their own expedition and established a small rival colony in the islands called Port Egmont. Under pressure, the French ceded all their rights to the Spanish, who promptly renamed the colony Puerto Soledad. In 1769, 1,400 Spaniards attacked the colony of Port Egmont and forced the British to leave under protest. The British returned, but in 1790 Spain and England signed the Nootka Sound Convention and Britain dropped its claims to disputed areas in South America and any adjacent islands.

Spain's collapse in the Americas and the loss of its colonies to New World revolutionaries (between 1810 and 1825) gave rise to a long period of anarchy and freebooting by pirates, traders, and whalers. The nascent state of Argentina, still using its revolutionary name, the United Provinces of Río de la Plata, tried to assert some authority, based on Spanish claims, and appointed a Malvinian governor who imposed economic restrictions on farming and trading interests in the islands. The British objected. The governor confiscated a large quantity of sealskins from the British.

The renegade action of an American naval captain turned the charged situation into a minor war. In 1832 a United States warship, the *Lexington,* arrived in the Falklands under the command of Captain Silas Duncan. Duncan recovered the sealskins, blew up the Spanish powder magazines, pillaged Puerto Soledad, and declared the islands to be "free of all government." The Silas Duncan Society (SDS) still honors the memory of this creative American anarchist.

On January 2, 1833, two British ships arrived in the middle of a fight between Falkland rebels, a group composed for the most part of freed convicts, and the crew of an Argentine frigate. The British kicked out the Argentines, ostensibly to establish order, then went about setting up a naval station. A group of gauchos, one of them a thief named Antonio Rivera, were later rounded up and shipped back to the mainland. The Argentines have described Rivera as a nineteenth-century guerrilla hero, and indeed he was a tough, unsophisticated thug.

With the advent of steam power, the Falklands took on some limited importance as a South Atlantic coaling station. The British cruiser squadron that in 1939 trapped the German pocket battleship *Graf Spee* in Montevideo sallied from the Falklands.

There's a rumor that Britain's postwar Labour government tried to sell the Falklands to Argentina in 1947, but at the time Perón wasn't interested in buying. In the fifties, when the Argentines did get around to making an offer, the Tories were in power and they declined.

In the 1960s Argentina, taking advantage of the rapid withdrawal of Britain from its colonies, renewed the on-again-off-again quest for the islands. In 1966 an armed Peronist gang attempted to circumvent the rather sleepy negotiations. They hijacked an airplane and flew to Port Stanley, where they were promptly arrested. In 1977 the British frustrated what may have been initial Argentine invasion moves by sending a nuclear sub and two frigates to the South Atlantic.

The constant sticking point in the negotiations was the will of the people; the Kelpers (British islanders) had no stomach for Argentine rule. Many of them could point to three or four generations of home-steading and farming. They argued that any claims Argentina might have had, based on Spanish claims or otherwise, had long since been rendered moot by human reproduction. The Falklands belonged to the Kelpers, and they wanted to remain with Britain.

Negotiations dragged on. The Argentines didn't believe the British were serious about the negotiations or about protecting the Falklands. Indeed, the British government was very ambivalent. As discussed under Source of Conflict, Argentina's internal politics set the stage for the Falklands War of 1982.

Briefly, the 1982 war pitted a poorly led and equipped South American police army against the best troops of a front-line European force. The British force, however, was not equipped for an expeditionary invasion outside of land-based air cover. NATO expects the United States's supercarrier task forces to carry the burden of non-European power projection. Britain's Harrier jump-jet carriers and agile antisubmarine frigates, while suited to rough North Atlantic and, thus, South Atlantic seas, were not the weapons a nation needs to launch an opposed invasion 13,000 kilometers from home. The long, slender, and fragile supply line from England could be cut or hindered by aggressive Argentine submarine action. The Argentine Navy and Air force had some outstanding pilots, and also some French Exocet antiship missiles. A few hot pilots could sink a lot of ships. Thus, despite the qualitative superiority of the British, the military outcome was still much in doubt, at least until strong marine and army infantry forces were ashore. Once ashore, the superbly trained British troops would have the advantage.

The Argentine invasion began on April 1 and 2, 1982, when marine and army detachments landed on South Georgia and East Falkland. Despite last-minute appeals from President Reagan, the junta rejected United States demands for a halt to the invasion. By April 5 a British carrier group was already sailing from Portsmouth. Shuttle diplomacy by United States Secretary of State Alexander Haig failed to achieve a solution. The British declared a maritime exclusion zone around the Falklands—in effect, a blockade—to be enforced by nuclear submarines.

By April 25 South Georgia Island had been retaken. Commandos landed in the Falklands on May 1 to begin gathering intelligence. May 1 also marked the beginning of aerial and naval bombardment against Argentine positions in the Falklands. On May 2, by order of the British War Cabinet, the Argentine cruiser *General Belgrano,* a former American warship, was sunk by a British submarine while outside the exclusion zone.

Argentina responded with vigorous air attacks and on May 4, sank the British destroyer *Sheffield* with an Exocet missile delivered by a Super Étendard. The game became a contest between Argentine jets operating at their maximum range, and British Harrier jump jets and frigates armed with surface-to-air missiles. Argentine air attacks subsequently sank five more British ships and damaged others.

On May 21 British forces began landing on East Falkland near Port San Carlos. On May 28, 400+ British paratroopers defeated over 1,200 Argentines in the Battle of Goose Green. On June 11 the battle for Port Stanley began. The Argentines surrendered on June 14.

As of summer 1984, the British goal of a Fortress Falklands is becoming a reality. A squadron of all-weather F-4s operates from the lengthened Port Stanley air base. The new airfield near Port Stanley will allow long-range transports to reach the Falklands from either Ascension Island or Africa, thus ending the awful logistics burden of in-air refueling. The British Vulcan long-range bomber strikes from the air base on Ascension Island had required as many as eighteen tanker sorties to complete, since tankers had to refuel tankers. The new airfield also serves a political function, since civilians will now be able to reach the Falklands without first flying to South America.

The brigade-strength garrison force has been whittled down, but the Kelpers are finding that peace has not brought back the old tranquillity. Troops need a place to carouse, and right now there are more troops than islanders. Most of the British soldiers live in large barrack barges, literally floating hotels complete with rooms, showers, gyms, kitchens, and recreation facilities. The soldiers have begun to refer to the Kelpers as "Bennies," a nickname based on their alleged similarity to a bumpkin comedy character on British TV. The Kelpers call the British troops "Whennies," mocking the soldiers' flair for beginning conversations with war-story-laden references to "when I was in Cyprus" or "when I was in Belize." So goes garrison duty among the friendlies.

After the war a new government took over in Argentina. Under the leadership of United States-leaning moderate democrats, the new government promised reform after the bitter experience of the terrorist war. The government purged the armed services by "decapitation," removing the admirals and the generals. If they had gone any lower in the ranks, they would have risked a counter coup led by the middle-class field and company-grade officers.

Tentative British-Argentine negotiations, conducted in July 1984, broke off because of British refusal to discuss sovereignty and Argentine insistence on raising the issue.

LOCAL POLITICS

Kelpers—Nickname for the very English natives of the Falkland Islands. They want to remain tied to Britain and not run the risk of being ruled by a Spanish government, much less one that is authoritarian. There are only 1,800 or so Kelpers, and their power to control their own destiny is limited.

Falkland Islands Company (FIC)—Development company with royal monopoly. Same idea as old Hudson Bay Company in North America. Owns two thirds of the farms in the Falklands. Controls the sheep economy.

The Radical Party—Raúl Alfonsín's moderate-democratic group that replaced the military junta in Argentina and defeated the Peronists.

Peronists—What is a Peronist? Is Peronism a fascist movement giving lip service to leftist ideas? A pro-union and populist movement with strong ties to the military? Or a convenient vehicle for a charismatic leader like Juan Perón? He was never required to define what he meant by "integral nationalism."

The Argentine military—Remains a potent political force even in a democratic Argentina.

Eva Perón—The real power behind Juan Perón. Her plasticized corpse has been returned to her homeland; don't cry for her, Argentina.

Isabel Perón—The second wife of Juan Perón. Returned from exile in Spain in 1984.

PARTICIPANT STRATEGIES AND GOALS

Argentina—Recovery of the Falklands isn't Argentina's biggest problem, but it is an issue all political parties can agree upon. The post-junta Argentine government maintains it is dedicated to cleaning up the aftermath of the terrorist war and the junta's murderous counterterrorist campaign, but the Falklands remain high on its agenda. Look for diplomatic pressure in the UN and renewed cozying up to Washington to try to bring United States pressure on Britain. The rearmament program continues unabated, not simply to show Britain that Argentina is capable of fighting over the Falklands, but also to make sure the military is prepared to face off with Chile over the Beagle Channel, or to show muscle to Brazil.

United Kingdom—Maintain a strong military presence in the Falklands while continually testing domestic support for that presence. The people of Britain enjoyed the Lion's Last Roar, but feel there must be some resolution, either permanent incorporation of the islands in the UK via resettlement, or some agreement with Argentina over mutual control. Resettlement isn't likely.

SUPERPOWER INTEREST

	Political	Military	Historical	Economic
Russia	Low	Low	Very Low	Very Low
US	Very High	Medium	Medium	Low

Political—Other than the possibility that the invasion would drive a wedge between the British and the United States, which it didn't, or that it would wreck the Reagan administration's currying favor with the Argentine government, which it did to a degree, this doesn't rank high on the Russian agenda. Still, the Russians missed an opportunity when they and their Cuban allies jumped on the bandwagon and supported the Argentine invasion. One can only imagine the political success they might have enjoyed with the European peace movement had they condemned the assault. United States interest hits a peak when the British are involved in a war, particularly when it pulls the Royal Navy out of its NATO role as subhunter and first line of defense in the BIG (Britain, Iceland, Greenland) Gap.

Military—Russia would have gloated if Britain had received a shellacking, but the prestigious Russian hardware wasn't on the line in the Falklands. (See Lebanon chapter for Russia's disaster.) For the United States the Falklands were of minor strategic interest. They rate higher because concepts for defense of the significant United States and NATO surface fleets were on the line.

Historical—This isn't an area of Russian interest, which is partly why Russia gave Chile's short-lived Marxist government little more than propaganda assistance and some security help. The Monroe Doctrine and the Rio treaty for hemispheric defense make this region somewhat significant for the United States, but Argentina isn't Central America.

Economic—Russia has no interest. It is of minor interest to the United States, since the United States is a sea power. Also, when the wheat deals come up, Argentina ignores American interests and makes its own deals.

POTENTIAL OUTCOMES

1. 78 percent chance: The situation remains deadlocked. The British complete Fortress Falklands preparations and assign a permanent two-battalion garrison force to the island. Major air base completed as well

as facilities for servicing submarines. The Kelpers (see Local Politics) chafe at the presence of British troops, who would vastly outnumber the locals. The Argentine government continues diplomatic efforts to recover the islands. Probability moves to 50 percent after 1990 if a democratic regime stays in power in Buenos Aires, because a stabilized Argentine democracy will make it easier for Britain to convince the Kelpers to accept Argentine sovereignty.

2. 11 percent chance: Britain makes immigration to Falkland Islands attractive by eliminating Falkland Islands Company. Argentina yells: Laborites scream at the cost to UK exchequer. Call this the demographic solution.

3. 5 percent chance: 1,800+ Kelpers are paid off by Britain and Argentina to resettle. Argentina gets control of the islands. This goes to 10 percent after 1988; drops to under 1 percent if oil is discovered in the Falklands.

4. 4 percent chance: Argentine government renews hostilities with occasional air raids and some special-forces activities on the island. Goes to 20 percent if military dictatorship topples the democratic regime. If this occurs, there's an 85 percent chance Britain will retaliate against the mainland; rises to 98 percent if Argentina develops a nuclear weapon and Britain locates its nuclear production-storage facilities (the destruction of Argentine weapons would justify the British hostilities in responding to the reaction of other South American nations).

5. 2 percent chance: Negotiations solve sovereignty issue, allowing a sort of dual monarchy in which islanders are given right of local government and Argentina, the control of "foreign affairs." Goes to 40 percent after 1990 if Argentina maintains a democratic government.

COST OF WAR

For the Brits the shooting part of the war cost a mere $665,000 per Kelper. Still, it was a small war. For both sides it cost a combined total of 1,100 dead and $4 billion. Britain could spend more over the long haul, but some of the expense can be written off as capital improvements. Port Stanley needed a new airport anyway.

POLICE ARMIES AT WAR

Armies generally are good at doing what they are trained and structured to do. There are many kinds of armies, and the type that a nation fields is dependent not simply on the population and wealth of the country, but on its perceived strategic needs. South American armies, like almost all Third World forces (the exceptions can be counted on one hand), are police armies designed to:

(1) Keep the population under control.

(2) Keep in power the government favored by the military.

(3) Put down any banditry in the hinterlands that may pass as a small-scale guerrilla war.

(4) Have enough defensive strength to deter the police army next door from trying anything more serious than a border incident.

For the most part, police armies are political animals ill-suited for fighting any kind of external war other than a border skirmish.

NEW TRUTHS, OLD LESSONS

Too often, the supposed new truths emerging from an event are either restatements of old, time-proven axioms or, much worse, terrible misconceptions drawn from an inaccurate understanding of the immediate events.

The Falklands War revalidated several strategic and tactical tenets and failed to establish anything dramatically new despite the use of up-to-date, sophisticated weapons systems.

Here are a dozen old lessons of warfare that the Falklands revalidated:

Old Lesson #1—Don't bring a fleet within range of an unsuppressed land-based air power. The British couldn't avoid doing so, and they lost ships.

Old Lesson #2—For every new offensive weapon there is a countermeasure. Exocet antiship missiles can be stopped by electronic or physical means. The British jury-rigged a helicopter to carry out electronic surveillance (the Searchwater system) when their picket destroyers began to get blasted.

Old Lesson #3—The most effective antiaircraft weapon is still another aircraft.

Old Lesson #4—You can never get enough information about your enemy.

Old Lesson #5—Most surface ships built since 1960 cannot take much physical punishment. They lack armor protection. This was one convincing argument for the resurrection of old United States battleships.

Old Lesson #6—Until new weapons systems perform under fire, no one believes they work. When the *Sheffield* sank, the Exocet missile's black-market price tripled. Qaddafi wanted to acquire some. This demonstrates that testing during peacetime is unconvincing.

Old Lesson #7—At this point VSTOL (vertical short takeoff and landing), aircraft like the Harrier are not in the same league as supersonic attack and fighter aircraft. The Harrier force did perform magnificently at what it was designed to do—support ground forces. The Harrier is of marginal value in defending a fleet because it lacks range and speed to close with attacking aircraft. The British pilots were superb, however, and "ground loitering," waiting on the ground near the expected place of attack, did decrease reaction time. Likewise, the Harrier technique of "viffing" (vectoring in forward flight), cutting on the vertical exhaust jets while flying forward, proved to be a valuable tactic. Any pursuing Argentine aircraft couldn't duplicate the Harrier's radical turn.

Old Lesson #8—Supersonic aircraft based on big carriers are still the best means of ensuring fleet security. If the British had had even one United States-style supercarrier armed with F-14s and E-2c early-warning aircraft, there would have been fewer ships lost, since the fleet's detection and defensive combat zone would have begun at the Argentine coast. But then had the Brits possessed such a carrier, the Argentines might have decided not to attack. Buying weapons that frighten aggressors is a way of saving money that would otherwise be spent on a war.

Old Lesson #9—Good infantry is worth three or four times as much as inferior infantry. Even attacking at odds of one to two or one to three, a veteran infantry force can defeat inferior infantry or militia troops. Caesar said that veterans are two to one against unblooded troops. The advent of accurate lightweight automatic weapons seems to have further improved the veterans' odds. Superior morale and training can be decisive weapons; fanaticism and courage don't make up for poor leadership.

Old Lesson #10—The press, including television, can be used effectively (though perhaps unwillingly or unwittingly) to confuse your enemy. Britain manipulated its own press with stories of the arrival of Royal Navy subs off the Falklands. The Argentine junta believed them, and this restricted reinforcement by sea. In reality, British subs took much longer to arrive.

Old Lesson #11—Once your organized resistance to an invasion ceases, it's good to have a plan for converting any remnant forces into guerrilla bands. The original Port Stanley British garrison (though only a Royal Marine platoon) didn't have to surrender. Members of the unit could have escaped and evaded the lackluster invasion by the Argentine marines and army. The British government would have had a valuable political tool (long-term resistance) around which to rally domestic support. The odds are good that the Argentines would have wasted a lot of effort in tracking down the marines hiding out in the countryside. But then, the Argentines didn't use the time they had to dig in and prepare defensive positions.

Old Lesson #12—If you're Great Britain, there's no ally like your long-lost colony, the United States. The British might well have lost the campaign without some very quick American aid. The United States supplied 12.5 million gallons of aviation fuel, state-of-the-art AIM-9L air-to-air missiles, Shrike radar-seeking missiles, Harpoon antiship missiles, and shoulder-fired Stinger antiaircraft missiles (one of which shot down an Argentine fighter-bomber; see chapter on Afghanistan for more on Stingers). The United States also provided Great Britain with 4,700 tons of airfield matting for reinforcing temporary landing strips. Britain received new submarine-detection devices, communications satellite aid, and possibly (though denied by the U.S. Department of Defense), intelligence from American spy satellites. All this cost the United States $60 million, a figure that excludes the cost of the aviation fuel and the Sidewinders. The question is, if the United States gets in a comparable crisis and experiences similar massive shortages, who will bail it out?

PART 5

Europe

We notice, study, deplore, and condemn wars in many parts of the world. The most dangerous battleground, however, is Europe itself, that source of the most destructive weapons, armies, and military thinking. Why are the Europeans so bloody-minded and catastrophic in their warfare? We do not know the answer, but we must accept the potential for a European-caused Armageddon. This section examines the most dangerous military and political situation our planet has ever faced, and what our chances are of surviving it.

13. Albania and Yugoslavia: Continuing the Balkan Tradition

INTRODUCTION

Currently, frictions between Albania, Yugoslavia, and various ethnic groups within Yugoslavia have the potential for turning into a world-class conflict. One more time. World War I began here, as well as many other major wars throughout history.

Over a dozen major ethnic groups live in the Balkans. Each has its internal divisions. These factions, large and small, are torn between the advantages of unity and the desire for ethnic independence. For example, the formation and continued existence of a united Yugoslavia is a historical oddity. Normally, Yugoslavia would be divided, like the rest of the Balkans, into many diverse and mutually antagonistic states. Some economists in Yugoslavia claim the standard of living has dropped nearly 40 percent since Tito's death. If this is the case, such poor economic performance does not bode well for internal political stability.

Russia considers the Balkans part of its "Slavic Protectorate."

As always, the Balkans are a major crisis waiting to happen.

SOURCE OF CONFLICT

Three significant geographic features characterize the Balkan Peninsula and have directly affected the region's political history:

(1) Most Balkan rivers follow erratic courses and are not navigable.

(2) Rugged mountains are the dominant terrain.

(3) There is a dramatic absence of geographical centers (one or two

central areas with good surface routes to the rest of the country) around which a national state can coalesce.

These three geographic ingredients are a recipe for strategic isolation. Even in the twentieth century the absence of a significant, navigable river system makes large-scale trade expensive; prior to railroads and highway systems, the lack of navigable streams cut off the more easily developed coastline from the backcountry. The presence of mountains exacerbates this difficult situation. Without one or two geographic centers, which even in mountain countries can exist in the form of fertile transverse valleys, every valley or hill becomes its own ethnic, cultural, and, usually, political center. The creation of Yugoslavia did not solve the Great Balkan Problem of who rules whom and what constitutes a Balkan nation state.

Grating against central Europe and the eastern Mediterranean, the Balkans occupy a strategic and sensitive position. Any potential conflict in the peninsula dramatically affects the European power balance. This has always been the case. Before the Warsaw Pact-NATO division, there existed Axis versus Allies, Grand Alliance versus Triple Entente, Ottoman Turkey versus everyone. Everyone worried about the Balkans.

Yet superpower geopolitics is only one cause of the difficulty. Local ethnic groups, some quite small, violently object to the cartographer's status quo. They see themselves as belonging to a nation state other than the one in which the last war left them. Agitation and instability begin at the local level.

The current problem of ethnic Albanians in Yugoslavia is but one example of several dozen similar conflicts that continue to simmer and occasionally erupt into combat in the Balkans. Such unrest cannot be taken lightly. A Serbian eruption during the Austro-Hungarian Empire led to World War I.

Yugoslavia and Albania are nominally Communist states. For socialist brothers, they have radically different genes. Yugoslavia is a fragile ethnic composite, while, with the exception of a significant Greek community in the south, Albania is largely Albanian. The Albanians maintain that Yugoslavia's Kosovo Province with its 1.2 million Albanians belongs to "Greater Albania"; they feel that the Serbo-Croatian variety of Slavic imperialism keeps Kosovo separated from its legitimate rulers in Tiranë (Tirana).

The Yugoslavians, however, seek to keep the delicate balance created by Tito. If one province slips from the fold, then what's to keep the entire flock from scattering? If Yugoslavia divides into several countries, they become a collection of weak petty republics. Then Big

Brother Slav (Russia) moves in. Who knows? The Italians might return from across the Adriatic.

If Albanians in Kosovo were the only issue, then the Balkan problem wouldn't be insurmountable. But Macedonians, Serbs, Croats, Montenegrins, Slovenes, Bosniaks, Greek minorities, Turkish minorities, Bulgars, Magyars, even a few displaced Austro-Germans, all with strong national and ethnic aspirations, are part of the Balkan powder keg.

WHO'S INVOLVED

Albania—The xenophobic regime of Enver Hoxha (pronounced Hod-yah) has kept a heavy lid on Albania. Of the 3.9 million Albanians in the world, 2.53 million live in Albania, 1.2 million in Yugoslavia's Kosovo Province.

Yugoslavian government—The federation's executive oligarchy made up of members from each ethnic state. The position of chief of state annually is rotated.

Albanian minority in Yugoslavia—Eight percent of the total Yugoslav population. Terrorists have caused a Serbian "flight" from Kosovo Province. Kosovo residents earn an average annual income of around $1,000—one third the Yugoslavian norm.

Other Yugoslavian ethnic groups—The federation experiment may not work now that Tito's gone, but the Serbs, Croats, Slovenes, Macedonians, Bosnian Moslems, and Montenegrin Slavs know that collective strength keeps out the Russians. The federation up until 1984 has allowed the groups who have their own republics a degree of ethnic independence.

Greece and Greek minorities—Greece's border claims against Albania remain unresolved. With 280,000 to 300,000 Greeks in Albania, an Albanian grab for Kosovo might shake the Greeks into reaching for "northern Epirus," which is what Athens calls southern Albania.

Wild Cards

Russia—Pan-Slavism was an old Russian ploy prior to the Comintern, and in some ways it's still a better mask than Communism. But the South (Yugo) Slavs will buy it only if sold at gunpoint.

Italy—Italy is increasingly willing to involve itself financially, politically, and militarily in foreign disputes. Control of the other side of the Adriatic becomes especially important if the Russians are involved.

Bulgaria—Stalinist Bulgaria covets Macedonia.

Hungary—There are lots of Magyars in Vojvodina Province.

Libya—Yes, indeed, Colonel Qaddafi has been taking young Moslems from Albania and Yugoslavia and bankrolling an "Islamic" education. Boom!

GEOGRAPHY

Yugoslavia occupies 256,410 square kilometers, an area about two thirds the size of California, and it has a population of 24 million. The Socialist Federal Republic of Yugoslavia consists of six republics: Croatia (capital in Zagreb), Slovenia (Ljubljana), Montenegro (Titograd), Bosnia and Herzegovina (Sarajevo), Macedonia (Skopje), and

Serbia (Belgrade). Serbia has two autonomous provinces, Vojvodina and fractious Kosovo. Belgrade serves as the federal capital.

The most important land routes between the Aegean Sea-Bosporus and central Europe run through Yugoslavian territory. The Adriatic coastline is rocky but has good harbors. The Donau (Danube) River, the most important waterway in central and southeastern Europe, flows through northeastern Yugoslavia and past Belgrade.

The populous and agriculturally developed lowlands, running north and northwest from Nis and Paraćin in the east to the Zagreb region in Croatia, contain river plains, some swamps, and a few minor mountain ranges. Tito and his partisans visited this area to either recruit or shoot Axis soldiers. For permanent guerrilla campsites, the partisans preferred the other two thirds of the country, the rough and rugged mountains, especially the Dinaric Alps, which parallel the Adriatic coastline. The Julian Alps cover the northwest corner. Kosovo Province also contains some of those rough and rugged mountains.

Albania is significantly smaller than Yugoslavia, approximately 28,500 square kilometers, or about the size of Maryland. Tiranë (Tirana), the capital, is the only city of any size. About 180,000 people live in Tiranë. Durrës (the ancient Illyrian city of Epidamnos and the Roman Dyrrachium) is the only significant port, though Vlorë can handle shipping. For the most part, Albania is rural and undeveloped, despite Hoxha's insistent propaganda to the contrary. The Gheg Albanians live to the north of the Shkumbi River; the Tosk variety live to the south.

Mountains, many with conifer forests, dominate Albania. The northern ranges are an extension of the Montenegrin Dinaric Alps. The 20 percent or so of the country that is coastal plain is infertile and often swampy; malaria once scourged visitors and, for all the World Health Organization knows, it may still.

Armies have always been able to move through Albania. The great Roman road that crossed ancient Illyria, the Via Egnatia, attests to that. The difficulty lies in controlling the mountainous backcountry and digging out the armed clans that inhabit it. Falling back into the mountains and cutting themselves off from invader or landlord is the classic Albanian tactic.

HISTORY

As a political entity, Yugoslavia is relatively new. It came into existence at the end of World War I with the defeat of the Austro-

Hungarian Empire. The Great Powers wanted to solve the perennial Balkan problem of what to do with the small, fragile, yet strategic southern Slavic states, so they established a kingdom of Serbs, Croats, and Slovenes with Serbian King Peter I as ruler. Yugoslavia combined the former Austro-Hungarian provinces of Croatia, Slovenia, Bosnia, and Herzegovina with the previously independent states of Montenegro and Serbia. Macedonia, the other present-day Yugoslav republic, was originally part of Serbia.

It is impossible to attempt to do justice to the rich, violent, and intriguing histories of Yugoslavia's republics prior to World War I within the constraints of this book. But let's be pithy—the history is one of short periods of stability punctuating long sentences of petty internecine conflict over land claims and ethnic rights, and paragraph-length episodes of outside imperial powers dividing the squabbling Balkan countries. In the main, Serbia got the best of the others, but the Croats, Slovenes, and Macedonians have all had their turns in the driver's seat. The Montenegrins for the most part have held out in their mountainous niche against the influx of Serbs, Turks, Germans, etc.

In April 1941 the Germans invaded Yugoslavia. The then ruler, Peter II, established a London-based government in exile. Within Yugoslavia two rival partisan armies emerged: the Communist National Liberation Army, a multiethnic group under Marshal Tito, and the Yugoslav Army of the Fatherland, or Chetniks, of Drazha Mikhailovich, also multiethnic but with strong Croatian support. The Chetniks fought the Germans and the Communists, and made the mistake of noticeably cutting deals with the Nazis. Tito waged a consistently anti-Nazi, nationalist campaign, no mean feat considering that there was no such thing as a Yugoslavian national. This is the key to Tito—his communism was very secondary to his nationalist mission. During World War II, over two million Yugoslavs lost their lives, more than half of them slain by fellow Yugoslavs. With the defeat of both the Germans and his Chetnik adversaries, Tito became premier in 1945. He severed his close relationship with Moscow in 1948 and closed the Macedonian border to Russian-backed Greek Communists who sought to topple the Athens government. As Tito saw it, the most imminent imperial threat came from the east. Western governments, the United States in particular, were slow to recognize the truly nationalist aims of Tito.

Albania is similar in many respects to the other petty Balkan states, Montenegro in particular, in that it has a long history of clans retreating into the wilderness and maintaining some self-determination and a definite identity. Albania claims to be the descendant of the ancient kingdom of Illyria, a contemporary of the early Greek city-states. It is a reasonably valid claim; certainly it is an important element of the Albanian national myth and Albanian pride.

Albania is one of history's greatest losers. With the brief exception of 1443 to 1478, when Albania's national hero, Skanderbeg, drove the superior Turkish forces from the country, from Roman times to 1912 Albania was occupied by some foreign power. An independent state of sorts did exist in the interior as Roman power waned, but the Byzantines soon appeared, then Venetians, Turks, and more Turks.

The Ottoman policy of passing out fiefs to soldiers and civil servants gave many countries under their reign a legacy of rapacious feudalism. There was little interest in long-term development of a country, since, in all but a few rare cases, the fief could not be passed on to an heir. Albania was no exception. Already poor and backward, Albania was further impoverished by Turkish rule.

During the Balkan Wars (1912–1913) and World War I, Albania was a battleground for Greek, Bulgarian, Serb, Austrian, Italian, and other forces. After World War I, a civil war among various mountain clans sputtered. When a battle stopped, the mountain clans' vendetta tradition kicked off a new round of fighting. In 1925 Ahmed Zogu declared Albania to be an independent republic. By 1928 Zogu had made himself king. Renewed Italian intrigue, sparked by Mussolini's quest for a New Rome as well as Albania's oil deposits, culminated in an invasion in 1939. Albania was the springboard for Italy's bungled attack on Greece. Germany's attack on Yugoslavia was precipitated by Italy's impending loss in the Balkans.

By 1944 Hoxha's Albanian resistance group had driven out the Axis armies. The Albanians won without the benefit of an invading Russian or Allied army. In 1946 Albania declared itself a Communist republic with Hoxha as premier. A strict Stalinist, Hoxha broke with Yugoslavia when Tito broke with Russia. When Stalin died, Hoxha became an even more virulent Stalinist. Khrushchev and his revisionist gang had destroyed the old wartime Communist camaraderie, or so it appeared to him. In 1961 Albania withdrew from the Warsaw Pact and became Communist China's European ally. Hoxha admired Mao's revolutionary fervor and extremism. Since Mao's death the Chinese relationship has gone sour.

Currently, Bulgaria claims parts of Grecian Thrace, Grecian Macedonia, and Yugoslavian Macedonia. Greece claims parts of southern Albania, not to mention its claim against Turkey and Bulgaria. Yugoslavia thinks all of Macedonia should be Yugoslavian. Many Macedonians on both sides of the border think Macedonia should exist as a separate state and maybe even be an empire like the one Alexander the Great, a Macedonian, had. Albania claims Yugoslavia's Kosovo Province. Yugoslavia believes Italy's control of Trieste is not quite proper. Landlocked Austria can still make a case for Ljubljana as being Laibach, Austria, not to mention the question of control of the southern Tirol. But that gets us out of the Balkans.

As for Kosovo Province, ethnic Albanians demand to be "liberated from the tutelage of Serbia" despite huge Yugoslavian investments in the province. The Kosovian Albanians are very wealthy when compared with native Albanians, but strong demands for ethnic identification don't seem to be satisfied by economic development. Belgrade thinks there must be outside agitation from Albania and Russia, with possible aid from Bulgaria. However, discontent has long been a phenomenon in Kosovo. There were student disturbances in 1968, demonstrations in the provincial capital of Pristina in 1976, and a number of riots, some of the worst occurring in 1981. In the last decade over 65,000 Serbians have left Kosovo because of "harassment by Albanians." The Albanians claim they cannot get jobs. The Albanikos, an ill-defined resistance group in Kosovo, have participated in several public demonstrations; Belgrade fears they are the vanguard of a revolution.

Finally, there is the Greek view. The Greeks refer to southern Albania as northern Epirus; in 1981 a number of Greek groups estimated that Hoxha held nearly 20,000 Greeks in Albanian jails or labor camps. Albania denied the accusation. Greece has never formally relinquished its claim to northern Epirus, though it seems to want to leave well enough alone. It is no secret that the Greeks fear trouble in Kosovo could turn the Balkans into a madhouse.

LOCAL POLITICS

Albanian Workers Party—Communist Party of Albania.

Ghega—Northern group of Albanians. Speak the Gheg dialect.

Tosks—Dominant southern group of Albanians. Speak the Tosk dialect.

Enver Hoxha—Albanian Communist leader. He survived all Khrushchev's and Tito's alleged attempts to remove him. Of Albanian Moslem background, violent anticlerical and opposed to all religions.

Alleged "founder of the world's first atheist state." Fancies himself a philosopher.

Ramiz Alia—Albanian political figure and potential national leader of Moslem background. Served with Yugoslavian partisans in World War II.

Mehmet Shehu—Was supposed to be Hoxha's replacement, but he died in 1981 from "mysterious causes," purportedly associated with a coup attempt.

Albanikos—Albanian ethnic "irredentists" (Yugoslavian political description meaning roughly, "people we don't like") living in Kosovo Province in Yugoslavia.

Decree number 4337 of the Presidium of the People's Assembly— Entitled "On the Abrogation of Certain Decrees," it was passed on November 22, 1967. This was Hoxha's deathknell for religion in Albania. It finalized the creation of "the first atheist state in the world." In 1967 the Albanian government closed nearly 2,200 churches, mosques, and shrines. Country was supposedly 70 percent Moslem, 20 percent Orthodox, 10 percent Catholic.

League of Communists of Yugoslavia—Yugoslavian Communist party. Voters elect delegates to bicameral assembly. Federal Executive Council is executive branch; position of premier is rotated. Essentially, it is a nine-member collective presidency.

1974 Yugoslavian constitution—Says that the federal state is composed of "voluntarily united nations" and implies that these nations have the right to pull out of the federation, but autonomous regions, such as Kosovo, do not have such a right. Here lies the rub.

Tito—Josip Broz (1892–1980), the godfather of all Yugoslavs, whose legacy even after his death still plays an enormous role in Yugoslavian politics. Anti-Nazi resistance hero who led the partisan movement from 1941–1945, a true Third World leader, a pain in the side of Russian imperialism. Stressed that the only Balkan Slav state that could survive was a federation. Believed infighting would bring in strong outsiders to divide and conquer the Balkan Peninsula.

PARTICIPANT STRATEGIES AND GOALS

Albanikos and other Albanian ethnics in Kosovo—Keep up the pressure on Belgrade to make Kosovo a republic—strikes, sabotage, threats to Serbs. Goal: a separate republic that would then unite with Albania.

Albania—Provide political, propaganda, monetary, and perhaps armed support to Albanikos.

Yugoslavia—Stop the development of Albanian ethnic terrorist cells while stressing the comparative wealth of Albanians in Kosovo vis-à-vis Albanians in Albania.

Bulgaria—Keep demanding that Macedonia be given to Bulgaria. Try to stir up ethnic disturbances.

Russia—Bide its time while supporting ethnic disaffection in Yugoslavia. Support the Albanikos and the creation of a Greater Albania. When Hoxha dies, destabilize subsequent leadership, then move in. Goal: ports on the Adriatic and a land route to the Adriatic through Bulgaria and Greater Albania.

Greece—Support Belgrade diplomatically to ensure Balkan stability. Failing that, prepare to recover northern Epirus and block a Bulgarian grab for Macedonia. Goals: Ensure that Greek minority in Albania is protected, stop Russian penetration of Balkans.

Italy—Support Yugoslavia diplomatically. Goal: Keep the Russians from acquiring a direct land route to the Adriatic.

SUPERPOWER INTEREST

	Political	Military	Historical	Economic
Russia	Very High	High	High	Medium
US	Medium	High	Low	Low

Political—This is one of the old and new czars' ulcers. Breakdown and disruption among ethnic groups may give ideas to other groups under Russian hegemony, as well as give the Russians the opportunity to intervene and establish "order." United States interest lies in maintaining the Yugoslavian buffer state and its helpful neutrality.

Military—The Russians covet air and naval bases on the Adriatic and closer to Italy. The United States wants to keep Russia from obtaining these bases and increasing the air and naval threat to NATO's Mediterranean shipping routes and supply lines.

Historical—The Balkans have been a graveyard for failed Russian foreign policies as well as Austrian, and there are a lot of bones to prove it. United States historical interest begins with OSS operations in World War II, and with Tito's closure of the border to Greek Communists in 1948.

Economic—Russian economic interest is rated somewhere between

Medium and High because the area is near COMECON countries. The United States has little economic interest in the area—there are no oil wells.

POTENTIAL OUTCOMES

1. 45 percent chance: Occasional riots and sporadic terrorism continue, with Albanian ethnic resentment exacerbated by the Hoxha government, the KGB, and perhaps Libya. Yugoslavia continues to deny the ethnic Albanian demand that Kosovo be an Albanian republic within Yugoslavia (see Local Politics, 1974 Yugoslavian constitution); Belgrade buys off resentment by increasing local autonomy and granting a larger Albanian voice in Belgrade, and the Albanian minority in Kosovo accepts the payoff. Increases to a 65 percent chance if Hoxha dies before 1985; grumbling by Macedonians also increases.

2. 35 percent chance: The same situation described in outcome 1 continues except that rioting leads to a military crackdown by Yugoslavia and the Albanian revolt is crushed. Should this happen, Yugoslavs have an 80 percent chance of victory with a 10 percent chance of stalemate and a 10 percent chance of Albanian rebel success. If Albanian rebels begin to win, look for intervention by the Albanian Army and a Yugoslav counterattack on Albania with a 60 percent chance of support from Greece. Call this the Third Balkan War of this century.

3. 10 percent chance: Yugoslavia capitulates to ethnic Albanian demand for a separate republic. Albanians in Montenegro and Macedonia request they be included in this new republic. If an Albanian republic is created, there's a 10 percent chance that it will remain part of Yugoslavia, a 90 percent chance that it will withdraw from the federation and precipitate that Third Balkan War mentioned in outcome 2. Obviously it isn't in Belgrade's interests to make Kosovo an Albanian republic.

4. 5 percent chance: Russia steps into Albanian revolt to support socialist brothers from attack by deviationist Yugoslavs. If Yugoslavia resists more than two weeks, a second Afghanistan begins for the Russian Army. No kidding. The mountain folk are armed, dangerous, and ready to resist. Greece offers Russian defectors a far more attractive sanctuary than does Pakistan or Iran.

5. 4 percent chance: Russia invades, and Italy, with United States support, crosses the Adriatic, Greece invades southern Albania, Yugoslavia resists Russian troops and Bulgarian lackeys. Myriad of nego-

tiated withdrawals begins. If this occurs, there's a 1 percent chance for World War III.

COST OF WAR

In the struggle between the Albanikos and Belgrade there have been several hundred dead and wounded, a few thousand imprisoned and fewer than $100 million of economic disruption. However, the potential for enormous loss exists should another Balkan War break out. The Balkan peoples have historically pursued their conflicts vigorously. Given the historical trends in Balkan warfare, the human cost would be several million dead, many more millions injured. Economic cost would be over $200 billion in property destruction and lost earnings.

14. Spain and Catalonia: European Tribes

INTRODUCTION

The friction between the inhabitants of Catalonia Province and the Spanish government is an example of unresolved ethnic and historical rivalries in many European states. Ethnic and historical realities create a war of words that frequently turns to bombs, bullets, and occasional civil war. The map of Europe shows central states, but certain populations beg—and sometimes shoot—to differ. This is a dispute that is over 2,000 years old with no end in sight.

SOURCE OF CONFLICT

Local issues can ignite large wars. World War I is an ideal example. Ethnic nationalism in the Balkans put the fuse to a Europe primed for armed conflict. Often the local issues that set fire to a region appear to be petty grievances, like demands for use of a language or local autonomy for an ethnic group no one has heard of since the Middle Ages. It leads one to conclude that the Middle Ages are still with us.

And they are. Europe, like the rest of the world, is inhabited by tribes, lots of them, some very large (perhaps 150 million Russian Slavs), some very small (25,000+ Slavic for example).

What is meant by a tribe? One definition is ethnic group. Who is a member of an ethnic group? Almost anybody who says he or she is. Ethnic groups identify themselves by:

(1) A relationship (usually involving oppression) with another ethnic group that says, "You are different from us."

(2) Shared religious beliefs.

(3) Shared linguistic heritages (sometimes the same language but different dialects).

(4) Historical identification, often involving a "golden age." Almost without exception, each of Europe's unassimilated groups can look back into history and find a gilded era when it was in control of the countryside. History somehow went wrong.

Today throughout the world, some tribes form "nation states" by reaching a consensus based on geographic, economic, historic, or ethnic considerations. Generally, these tribes finished fighting in so distant a past that everyone has forgotten who killed whose cousin. There is also a second group: those recently at war in which the bloodshed was so bitterly exhausting that the tribal councils are resigned to cooperation. Other tribes form their states—and keep them—with armed force (Russia and South Africa for example). This strategy works for a while, provided the dominant tribe continues to field large, militant occupation armies or is wealthy enough to buy stability by paying off those who threaten it (Saudi Arabia for example). If the dominant tribe slips up, rebellion results.

Europe's tribes are still trying to sort themselves into nations. This is a dangerous business, especially when Germans get involved. See Quick Look at Germany.

Western humanists would like to think that democracies are immune to the tribal disease. The idea is that democracies stage planned rebellions called elections that seek to reestablish the consensus. This works to some extent, but the demands of ethnic groups are sometimes very difficult to accommodate.

Sometimes accommodation is possible. Take the United Kingdom for example. The Celtic tribe of Wales has historic, linguistic, and religious roots that differ from those of the dominant Angles. Wales today is an occupied country with significant social and economic grievances, but it is pacified by parliamentary representation, not armies. England failed to use that form of pacification with a former colony now called the United States. Remember "taxation without representation"?

Not all European tribal demands are so well met. Northern Ireland is an ugly sore. Corsicans throw bombs; Basques assassinate all kinds of Spaniards; Flemings and Walloons square off in bitter brick-throwing street demonstrations. Then there are the problems waiting in the wings: Celtic Bretons angry with the central Frankish state in Paris; Tirolers who, never quite happy with Vienna, look at the Sud Tirol and wonder if Italy will turn their southern brethren into pasta lovers.

This doesn't begin to address the tribal problems of an Eastern Europe that "sits beneath the Russian Army." (See the chapter on the Balkans for a taste of real tribal trouble.) The Russian Slavic state was always an ethnic hodgepodge. Now that the Bolshevik Revolution is over and the Germans have been fended off for a while, the ethnic and nationalistic desires of the Ukrainians (who did have a little revolt going until 1954), Latvians, Lithuanians, et al., will have a chance to simmer. One shouldn't forget the already smoldering Poles. The Hungarians got parboiled in 1956, but they appear to have worked out an economic leave-us-alone deal with Moscow. The Russians are well aware of this tribal threat to their empire. They are also afraid of their central Asian tribes (see the chapter on Afghanistan).

Not only do European tribal conflicts debilitate their own provinces and destabilize the nation states the tribes currently inhabit, but in a nuclear-armed Europe, a local tribal demand can demolish everything. Gone are the days when a folk rebel simply burned the other guy's castle and salted the wheatfields.

The Catalans and their relationship with Madrid serve as a remarkable illustration of the dynamics of European tribal politics. Unlike the Basques, the Catalans have controlled their terrorists and struck a working economic and cultural bargain with Spain. But no astute Spanish politician should take their stability for granted. They do not have the size and power (yet) to create their own nation. However, forming 17 percent of Spain's population, and having 25 percent of the GNP, the Catalans possess the size and power to do a great deal of damage to someone, should they elect to do so.

As tribes go, the Catalans haven't been one of Europe's big winners, not at least for 400 years, but they certainly cannot be counted among tribal Europe's losers. Catalans have a large measure of wealth and power to complement their sense of ethnic identity.

The Catalans' twentieth-century intrastate quarrel with Madrid doesn't have the same geopolitical implications for Europe that it did 500 years ago. Geographically Catalonia isn't situated so that a disturbance in Barcelona could become the Sarajevo of World War III, although the Spanish Civil War (1936–1939) did serve as a diplomatic and military test bed for World War II.

Catalonia versus Madrid, when compared with other ongoing European intrastate conflicts, is remarkably restrained. As we've said, unlike the Basques, the Corsicans, or the IRA in Ulster, the Catalans have their terrorists under control. While anarchist members of the now fractious NCL (see Local Politics) as well as other radical separatists do occasionally extort "revolutionary taxes" from businesses afraid of being bombed, in Catalonia they get sent to prison by the Catalans.

The Catalans, unlike the Tirolese or Albanians, do not spill across existing national borders. The Catalan population lives in one political region, with the Balearics as an island offshoot. Such cohesiveness reduces the degree of nationalistic grief and raises the group's power vis-à-vis the central state government.

Economically the Catalans seem to have struck a reasonable bargain with Madrid. Politically they have a great deal of autonomy. So, what is the problem? Don't you know that Catalonia was never meant to be part of Spain?

Stated simply, the problem is unresolved nationalism.

WHO'S INVOLVED

Madrid (Spanish central government)—The heir to the power structure imposed on the Iberian Peninsula by the Castilians. Whether run by Franco and his Falange, by the socialists, or by a Bourbon king, Madrid is still the central government.

Catalonia—An autonomous region of Spain. Once a separate kingdom that maintained its own empire.

Wild Cards

The Valencians—The tribe south of Catalonia. Catalans say the Valencians are Catalans, because of language similarities; Valencians disagree (but despite what the Valencians say, their language *is* very similar to Catalan).

The Basques—Northwestern Iberian tribe that speaks a non-Indo-European language. Many Basques demand their own country. There are also Basques on the French side of the border. Currently they are the most violence-prone tribe on the peninsula. If terrorists succeed in tearing the Basque country away from Madrid (unlikely), then the Spanish pastiche might come apart. Unlike Catalonia, the Basque region could not stand alone economically because it is saddled with economically weak heavy-manufacturing industries.

France—The French have tried to placate the Basques by allowing them to use southern France as a sanctuary, but as of summer 1984, the door seems to be closing. The French, confronted with separatist violence in Corsica, may act in conjunction with Madrid to squelch the Basques, or the Catalans if they become restive. The French have another reason for changing their policy of tacit support for the Basques. Closing the border to Basque radicals accommodates Spain, which will soon be a member of the EEC. Going along with Madrid on the terrorist issue gives France a negotiating card when the time comes to discuss Spanish demands for entry, especially in the volatile areas of agricultural products and fishing.

GEOGRAPHY

Catalonia, with a population of six million and an area of 31,930 square kilometers, occupies the northeastern corner of the Iberian Peninsula. Catalonia is divided into four provinces: Lérida to the northwest, Tarragona to the south, Barcelona in the center, and Gerona in the northeast. Heavily industrialized metropolitan Barcelona is the cultural center and regional capital. Nearly three million people live in Barcelona. Rural Catalonia farms and grows grapes. Nearly one third of Spain's wines are produced in the region.

Catalonia's Pyrenees Mountains are very rugged, with some peaks approaching 3,000 meters. The Mediterranean coast has a number of excellent harbors and superb beaches.

Over half the population of Catalonia speaks Catalan, a Romance language similar to Provençal. Catalan is also spoken in the Balearic Islands. A dialect of Catalan, Valencian, is spoken in Valencia to the south. The Valencians, however, consider their language to be separate and not a dialect. They refuse to submit to Catalan linguistic imperialism.

HISTORY

Until the late fifteenth century, history was kind to Catalonia. Catalonia ruled an empire. Then the whip changed hands. Alas, a proud tribe never forgets.

Greece, Carthage, and Rome placed trading colonies along the Catalan coast. The Greek colony of Emporion (the Spanish Ampurias) was a major center of Mediterranean trade. The Carthagians in the third century B.C. founded Barcelona, named after the general Hamilcar Barca. The Romans eventually conquered Catalonia and made Tarraco, present-day Tarragona, the regional capital.

Arabs invaded the Iberian Peninsula in 711 and by 715 had conquered the area, including Catalonia. Toward the end of the eighth
century, Frankish counterattacks against the Arabs began in earnest.
Charlemagne created the Spanish March, ruled over by the Counts of
Barcelona. Tied to Charlemagne's empire but separated by the Pyrenees,
the Catalans waged war against the Moors; the Counts of Barcelona
were in reality their own bosses. Unlike in other feudal regions, there
were numerous rich peasants who owned their own land, further establishing a tradition of independence. Many of these burghers entered the
already extensive foreign-trade business. By the twelfth and thirteenth
centuries, Catalan merchants rivaled those of Venice and Genoa.

In 1060 the Catalans drew up in one document, The Book of Us-
ages, a civil code which recognized the equality before the law of the
nobility and bourgeoisie. The Catalans claim it is a democratic charter
that precedes England's Magna Carta. The Cortes Catalanes emerged,
a guild-oriented parliament with three branches: bourgeoisie, nobility,
and Catholic Church. This evolved into the Generalitat. By the end of
the fourteenth century, Catalonia had something approaching parlia-
mentary-style self-government.

The politics of the eleventh through fifteenth centuries were marked by political marriages that formed links to Aragon and Castile. There were also occasional border skirmishes. From 1230 to the mid-fifteenth century, the Catalans succeeded in building a trade-based empire that included Aragon, Valencia, the Balearica, Corsica, Sardinia, Sicily, the boot of Italy, and parts of the Balkan Peninsula. This was a golden age. Then marriage put John II of Aragon on the throne. The Catalan rebellion (1461–1472) against Aragon failed. When Aragon and Castile were united in 1479, Catalonia waned. The province rebelled against central Madrid's authority during the Thirty Years' War (1618–1648) and during the War of the Spanish Succession (1701–1714). Backing Archduke Charles of Austria against Philip V in the latter conflict— and losing—drew a stiff penalty. In 1716 Catalan laws and documents were forbidden and Catalonia was placed under the law of Castile.

Napoleon's invasion of Iberia gave the Catalans the opportunity to request "provincial individuality," but the new Spanish liberals of the Cortes were strong centralists. During the second half of the nineteenth century, Barcelona became industrialized and developed into a center of socialist and anarchist activity.

The early twentieth century saw a rebirth of Catalan nationalism, often under the guise of socialist unity. In 1932 Catalonia succeeded in establishing a separate regional government, which won limited autonomy from Madrid's Cortes. During the civil war, the Catalans backed the Republicans against Franco and lost, though there was a lot of hidden support for the Fascists. Franco, definitely a Spanish centralist, punished Catalonia by forbidding it to use the Catalan language, though practically the ban proved unenforceable. Catalan nationalist opposition groups, based in southern France and Paris, received international support from many anti-Fascist groups. With the death of Franco and the establishment of a constitutional monarchy, this support started to decline. In 1976 and 1977, Madrid began to return a degree of regional autonomy to Catalonia and the rest of Spain.

In Madrid Franco may be gone, but he casts a long shadow. The present Spanish government is a liberal parliamentary democracy under a constitutional monarch. The leading political parties are typical of Western Europe: the center-right Christian Democrats and liberal-democratic socialists. The mainstream parties are strong centralists but support regional autonomy, up to a point.

Catalonia today is an autonomous part of Spain. When Franco ruled Spain, the Catalans weren't allowed to fly the Catalan flag. This has changed, and so has the official language. Catalan is now used officially by the government and businesses of the region. The Catalans fought a long time for this linguistic autonomy; now they are living with its economic costs. Forty percent of the population has immigrated to Catalonia within the last three decades; new immigrants do not speak Catalan, and under the new laws they fear becoming second-class citizens.

In 1984 the nationalist Catalan party, Convergencia i Unio, won a decisive victory in regional Catalan elections. The party won 72 of the 135 seats in the regional parliament. The Catalans are demanding more direct control over their region than Madrid (which, as of summer 1984, is controlled by the Socialist Workers Party and Prime Minister Felipe González) is willing to dispense. But ethnic and nationalistic frictions still remain, as far as the Catalans are concerned, at the level of nonviolent politics.

LOCAL POLITICS

Juan Carlos I—King of Spain, a Bourbon, ruler of Spain's constitutional monarchy.

Spanish Socialist Workers Party (PSOE)—The ruling group in Spain. A typical European moderate socialist-democratic party, led by Prime Minister Felipe González.

Convergence and Unity Party (CiU)—Convergencia i Unio, the regional Catalan party, led by Jordi Pujol.

Reformist Party—Formed in 1983 as an alternative to the Popular Alliance Coalition and the socialists. A national party that strongly favors increased regional autonomy. The party's leader is Miguel Roca, who is also second-in-command of the Convergence and Unity Party.

Other Spanish political parties—Popular Democratic Party; Popular Alliance Coalition (AP); Communist Party (split into two factions, one Euro-Communist, one pro-Moscow); the Union of Democratic Center Party, a former center-right coalition, no longer exists.

The Cortes—Spanish parliament.

Guardia Civil—Spanish paramilitary police. Acts as counterterrorist force. Was regarded as tool of Francoist oppression. Basques, and some Catalans, call it an occupation army.

ETA—Euzkadi Ta Azkatazuna, meaning Basque Homeland and Liberty in the Basque language, Euskera. ETA is the radical Basque separatist-terrorist group. Two main factions: ETA Politico-Militar is less militant, ETA-Militar more murderous. Euskadiko Eskerra is a political party affiliated with ETA-PM.

Basque National Party (PNV)—Moderate Basque group.

Andalusian Socialist Party—Regional Andalusian party.

The Generalitat—Catalonia's autonomous regional government.

Republican Left of Catalonia (CRC)—Regional Catalan party.

National Confederation of Labor—Remnants of the once two-million-strong Spanish army of anarcho-syndicalists (disciples of the anarchist Bakunin) still alive in Catalonia.

Montserrat—Monastery in mountains northwest of Barcelona. Long a center of Catalan intellectual and linguistic resistance, it maintains a thousand-year tradition of intellectual guerrilla warfare.

PARTICIPANT STRATEGIES AND GOALS

Madrid—Preserve Spanish central authority by meeting the "soft" Catalan demands for economic aid and developmental subsidies. The current central government in Madrid is trying to live with autonomy, but it is against it for two reasons. Autonomy can be very expensive because government structures and services are duplicated. These duplicate governments also provide additional power bases for any kind of opposition, national or regional.

Catalonia—With 17 percent of the population of Spain (versus 2 percent for the Basques), continues to show that economic subsidies from Madrid and recognition of Catalan linguistic and historical uniqueness are a cheap price for quiescence. Union with Spain is better than a civil war, but wouldn't a Catalan UN seat be nice, even one like the Ukraine has?

Basque terrorists—Disrupt the Madrid central government by terrorism, causing reactionary oppression that will draw other groups (like Catalans) into a civil war.

SUPERPOWER INTEREST—SPAIN VS. CATALONIA

	Political	Military	Historical	Economic
Russia	Low	Very Low	Very Low	Very Low
US	Medium	Low	Very Low	Low

Political—Rates a nudge because the Russians are always interested in stirring up someone else's troubles as long as the stirring won't spill over into Russia. Moscow has supported the Basques, though very quietly. The United States is interested in keeping Spain as a stable trading partner and as a location for B-52 bases. Internal disruption in Spain is a nuisance to American policy. United States interest would rise if Spain were to increase its participation in NATO.

Military—Area doesn't really rate interest.

Historical—The United States has had a long relationship with Spain, but when Washington looks at the Iberian Peninsula, it sees only Spain and Portugal. Figuratively, Catalonia isn't on the map.

Economic—A blip for the United States since Spain, and Catalonia, occupy strategic positions for United States trade.

POTENTIAL OUTCOMES

Boredom for voyeurs of violence, fodder for the forces of utilitarian understanding.

1. 96.5 percent chance: A big vote for the status quo.

2. 3 percent chance: Catalans press for full "secession within union" —a Catalan state tethered militarily and economically to Spain. Catalonia gets a UN seat.

3. Less than .5 percent chance (but still a possibility): Basque terrorists succeed in starting a civil war; Catalan extremists pitch in to help.

COST OF WAR

The Spanish civil war devastated Spain and Catalonia. Since that conflagration, the Catalan-Spanish confrontation has cost fewer than 100 lives. Everyone is tired of fighting.

In all of Europe's separatist violence (including that in Northern Ireland, Corsica, Kosovo, the Tirol, the Basque region, etc.), the cost in lives has been relatively small, fewer than 10,000 since World War II. The economic cost has been much higher. The economy of Northern Ireland has essentially been stalemated because of violence. Other parts of Europe given to sustained ethnic violence have suffered similar economic losses.

EUROPEAN ETHNIC BREAKDOWN

The values in the first column represent the millions of people in that ethnic group in the world. The second column shows the percentage of the nation's population (Britain, France, etc.) that the ethnic group comprises.

Britain
(Population 55.9 million)

Group	Worldwide (millions)	% of country
English	46.4	83
Scots	5.1	9.1
Welsh	2.5	4.5
Irish	4.4	1.8

France
(Population 53.5 million)

Group		
French	46.1	73.8
Occitans	9.5	17.7
Bretons	1.1	2.1
Germans	94.9	1.9
Catalans	6.5	0.9
Corsicans	0.4	0.7
Basques	0.85	0.15
Flemings	5.5	<.01
Italians	55.9	<.01

Greece
(Population 9.4 million)

Group		
Greeks	10.2	96.4
Turks	41.3	1.8
Macedonians	1.5	1.1
Rumanians	20.1	0.5
Albanians	3.9	0.2
Bulgarians	8.3	0.2

Italy
(Population 56.9 million)

Group	Worldwide (millions)	% of country
Italians	55.9	96.5
Sardinians	1	1.8
Friulians	0.4	0.7
Germans	94.9	0.5
French	46.1	0.4
Rumanians	20.1	<.01
Albanians	3.9	<.01
Rhaetians	0.07	<.01
Catalans	6.5	<.01
Croats	5.4	<.01
Greeks	10.2	<.01
Slovenians	1.85	<.01

Netherlands
(Population 14.2 million)

Group		
Dutch	13.9	97.9
Surinamese	0.18	1.3
Frisians	0.3	0.7
Indonesians	0.1	0.7

Rumania
(Population 22.06 million)

Group		
Rumanians	20.1	83.9
Hungarians	12.7	7.7
Germans	94.9	2.7
Bulgarians	8.3	<.01

Spain
(Population 37.1 million)

Group		
Spanish	26.5	71.4
Catalans	6.5	16.2
Galicians	2.6	7
Valencians	1.5	4
Basques	0.85*	1.9

*This is based on Spanish Government figures. Some Basques claim the figure is 2 million

Switzerland
(Population 6.34 million)

Group	Worldwide (millions)	% of country
Germans	94.9	68.8
French	46.1	22.1
Italians	55.9	10.3
Rhaetians	0.07	0.8

Turkey
(Population 44.6 million)

Group		
Turks	41.3	90.9
Kurds	7.2	3.4
Arabs	128	0.7
Circassians	0.4	0.2
Armenians	4.5	0.1
Greeks	10.2	0.1
Georgians	4	0.1
Bulgarians	8.3	<.01

Yugoslavia
(Population 22.2 million)

Group		
Serbians	8.9	40.1
Croats	5.4	22.1
Bosniak Moslems	1.8	8.1
Slovenians	1.85	8.1
Albanians	3.9	6.1
Macedonians	1.5	5.9
Montenegrins	0.5	2.3
Hungarians	12.7	2.2
Italians	55.9	1.1
Rumanians	20.1	0.5
Bulgarians	8.3	0.4

QUICK LOOK AT GERMANY:
THE GERMAN PROBLEM

The German Problem has been with us for many centuries. German politics has directly or indirectly been the cause of most European wars since the first century. Currently Germans are divided among more than six nations: East and West Germany, Switzerland, Italy, Austria, and Russia. There are also large numbers in Luxembourg, Hungary, Czechoslovakia, Rumania, France, Yugoslavia, Belgium, and the United States—where there are more people of German extraction than any other ethnic group.

This lack of a unified German state has been the norm for the last 2,000 years. But, like most other tribes, the Germans have long sought, often through violence, to become united. The current division is most obvious in East and West Germany, divided largely to appease the Russians, who have been pummeled by Germans ever since the first Goths wandered south from Denmark looking for greener pastures. This third-century migration, the "Wandering of the Nations," plays an important part in German folklore and national aspirations. Many cultural myths affecting contemporary Germany derive from romanticized visions of tribal warriors and their disdain for non-German peoples. The Roman Empire fell in large part because of the years of conflict with the Germanic Teutons, Franks, and Goths. Throughout this period, when the Romans proved too tough, the Germans would head east and lay into the Slavs.

The *Furor Teutonicus* (German Fury) was its own undoing, for the Germans proved unable to get along with each other. While Britain and France (each containing a large German element), Turkey, and Russia became organized into nations, Germany degenerated into a very loose organization of petty states called The Holy Roman Empire. The First Reich united most of Europe under the leadership of the German emperor Charlemagne. The empire lasted less than half a century, and by 900 A.D. Greater Germany was on its way to being the political joke of Europe. This condition lasted more or less until 1871 when the Second Reich was formed by the humorless and efficient Kingdom of Prussia. The Holy Roman Empire was reincarnated as the Austro-Hungarian Empire. Maintaining this facade brought on World War I in 1914, the conflict that begat the Third Reich of the Nazis.

The Slavs, principally the Russians, have lost over 50 million lives to the various Reichs and seem determined to avoid a Fourth Reich. The Russian antipathy toward Germany has nothing to do with Communist ideology and everything to do with a long-standing fear of another German *Drang nach Osten,* movement to the east.

It is difficult for most Americans to appreciate the depth of these feelings in Germany's neighbors. Cultures that are themselves partially German (Britain, France, Italy, Scandinavia, Holland, Belgium, and the United States) are more at ease with Germany than are Slavic countries like Poland and Russia. The Slavs, considered culturally inferior by the Germans, never integrated with them as much as did the inhabitants of these other countries. To the Slavs the *nemetski* (figuratively, "speakers of gibberish," literally, "mute" or "tongue-tied") are an alien, hostile, and destructive force. The defeat of various German invaders, such as the Teutonic Knights in the thirteenth century, the "Franks" under Napoleon in the early nineteenth century, and the Nazis in the twentieth are high points in Russian history. Russian losses were enormous, and the Germans were not so much defeated as repelled. However, the German hordes still exist on the Slavs' western frontier. The Slavic nations' fear of Germany is not irrational, at least not to those Slavs whose kinfolk have fallen to German depredations over many generations.

Couple these feelings with the persistent Slavic inferiority complex toward the "efficient and cultured" Germans. The national aspirations of the Germans and the fears of their Slavic neighbors may produce yet another chapter in the tragic history of the German Question.

15. The Central Front: World War III

INTRODUCTION

In a very real sense, World War I isn't over. In 300 years, the flare-up called World War II will be seen as phase two of the Great Twentieth-Century War. That battle has been suspended since 1945. Everyone hopes that it won't begin again, for this time the consequences for humanity, in Tierra del Fuego as well as Berlin, could be devastating.

Today Russia, leading the Warsaw Pact Organization, and the United States, leading NATO (the North Atlantic Treaty Organization), confront each other most directly and precariously in central Europe across a line not too different from the one where Russian and United States tanks met in 1945.

From the Baltic to the Alps, the West German border has the heaviest concentration of troops and combat power in the world. This area is the Central Front. Although NATO defends a region that extends as far north as Norway and as far east as Turkey, the Central Front is aptly named. It is along this line that Russian and American troops may fight on German soil to stop, for example, a rebellion in Hungary. Absurd, but in European terms it has been a very common pattern for over 1,000 years.

What kind of war would it be? World War III would be without winners. Massive human and material destruction would occur even if nuclear weapons were—somehow—not utilized.

SOURCE OF CONFLICT

Two mighty self-defense organizations, NATO and the Warsaw Pact, watch Europe and each other. There are lots of reasons for this confrontation. The East German border is Russia's vital frontier against military and ideological threats. In Western Europe resides the largest concentration of population and economic power.

Most of the nations in Western Europe, as well as Greece, Turkey, Canada, and the United States, belong to the Atlantic alliance. NATO's European members provide most of the conventional combat strength.

Warsaw Pact power is Russian power. The pact's East European forces are numerically and militarily insignificant compared with Russia's. Hungarian and Polish units are of dubious political reliability.

It is the Russian empire in Eastern Europe, where non-Communist and anti-Kremlin politics are proscribed, that provides the greatest potential flashpoint for a military crisis. The Hungarians revolted once and the Russians quashed them. The Czechs got restive and the Russian tanks rolled. Now the Poles, a constant source of Russian paranoia, are simmering. The East Germans, Prussians by another name, have the highest standard of living in the East Bloc. Over 20 Russian divisions occupy East Germany. East Germany is Russia's strongest ally. The high standard of living and the army divisions, at least from the Russian perspective, are what ensure East Germany's compliance.

The Russians don't trust the Germans and the last thing they want is a reunified Germany, neutral or otherwise. They think a reunified, Communist Germany would still have to be occupied by Russian troops; otherwise within twenty years the Germans would end up just like the Chinese, armed and ready to fight Russians.

Strategies driven by other fears and historical concerns are part and parcel of the conflict on the Central Front. Russia's inferiority complex throughout history, respect for French culture, and fear of German technical achievement compounding a sense of peasant backwardness, increases the Kremlin's stubbornness. Russia has finally become a world-class success at military power. Fear of invasion by the capitalists (the West) and fear of the East (Moslems under Russian hegemony in the southern Soviet Socialist Republics as well as the Chinese) fueled the arms buildup; now the arms and military machine have become a source of Russian pride. So Russia seeks an iron-clad security Westerners find hard to comprehend, as well as recognition of Russian power.

As part of the strategy, the Kremlin tries to keep all potential enemies, including Eastern European allies, off-balance and incapable of decisive action. Espionage and propaganda are the tools of this strategy. Believing history has taught them that the best defense is a good offense, the Russians plan to defend themselves by preparing to invade Western Europe. The Russian Army, centered on the Group of

Soviet Forces Germany (GSFG), gives the Kremlin the means to make such a strategy more than plausible.

Western Europe and the United States follow slightly different strategies. The Western nations seek to achieve security through paradox: arming to the teeth while negotiating with Russia for disarmament. The West has tried to learn something from its experience with Hitler. Negotiations with heavily armed dictatorships about peace don't bear fruit unless both parties have the ability to hurt each other. Yet not so curiously, given the level of destruction an actual war would bring, Western Europe arms more heavily while becoming more pacifistic.

There are other divisions. The West seeks trade and open borders; both frighten the Russian government. The Russians perceive open borders as a form of subversion that will increase the level of agitation in their country and their satellites, and from an imperialist point of view, they are correct.

The increasing pacifism in the West is a result of living with the paradox of nuclear arms: The largest and most lethal mass of armaments ever assembled exists in the hope that it will never be put to use. If war came, it would be The Big One, a conventional war of awesome proportions that could go nuclear.

There are two schools of thought as to how this potential war could be fought. School one, the more common view, holds that World War III will be a free-wheeling mobile battle in which units of both sides will intermingle and slug it out in potentially uncoordinated combat.

School two foresees another World War I. So many troops deployed in so small an area could result in a loss of mobility. World War III becomes World War I with men in tanks instead of trenches.

During World War I, the fronts in Europe and Russia averaged 1,500 to 4,800 combat troops per kilometer. This produced a stalemate. One hundred men with machine guns and some artillery support could effectively defend one kilometer of front. An attack by a force six to ten times as large would eventually prevail, but not before the defender could bring up his numerous reinforcements. During World War II, troop densities declined to a maximum of 2,000. Today, most armies plan to have a maximum of 1,600 troops per kilometer of front.

The use of mechanized assault units during World War II enabled the attackers to breach the defenses before reinforcements could be brought to bear. The mobile defense was developed to meet the mechanized attack. Here the defender sent his own mobile units after the attackers. The decisive defensive battle then took place behind the front. A successful counterattack by the mobile defender would stall the attacker and perhaps restore the old front line. An unsuccessful mobile defense would leave the defender's forward forces trapped. Generally, the short leash imposed by supply considerations prevented even the successful attacker from going too far. However, a series of such attacks against an opponent with few mobile forces would eventually crush the defender. This is precisely what the Allies, particularly the Russians, did to the Germans.

On the Central Front each side is likely to mobilize over a million troops to cover a 1,000-kilometer front. Given the increased firepower of defensive weapons, the prospects do not look good for the attacker. Stalemate becomes increasingly possible.

All this is complicated by geographical and political factors which for the most part were not present during World War II. Mobile combat requires a lot of space for the defender to move around in. During World War I the defender's forces would be set up in a combat area 12 kilometers deep. Often less than half of the available defensive troops would be on the line opposite the enemy. Even during World War I it was recognized that "defense in depth" was the way to go. During World War II the mobile battle required a depth of about 60 kilometers.

Today, armies think they need about 70 kilometers of depth. The complication is that there is not that much depth available on the Central Front. The shortest distance between the East German border and the Rhine River is less than 150 kilometers. Furthermore, political demands force NATO commanders to plan and pledge to fight the Russians right at the border (Forward Defense), sacrificing the advantages of mobile defense. In practical terms, NATO commanders are able and willing to fight a mobile battle if war breaks out. Meanwhile, they have to be careful about what they say and do regarding mobile defense in depth.

The Russian response to this potential stalemate is to attempt to disrupt NATO's ability to deploy and control its forces by conducting surprise attacks and by rapidly moving assault troops. The idea is that if the defender does not have an opportunity to form a fighting line, the attacker will be all over West Germany before a defense is formed. This implies both sides will mingle, thus demoralizing the half-prepared defender.

This scenario, which NATO accepts as highly possible, assumes that both sides will generally be cut off from sources of supply and support. The Russians hope to solve the problem by loading the assault forces with three to five days' worth of fuel and ammunition and hoping for a short war. NATO's solution is to avoid surprise. As insurance, NATO units train to fight in isolation, but not for as long a time as the Russians train theirs to fight.

In general, neither side has visualized the Russian assault forces ever becoming lost, disorganized, and demoralized. Yet this happened to several Russian units during their unopposed invasion of Czechoslovakia in 1968. Getting lost and demoralized is a long military tradition (particularly for the Russians).

An additional contribution to the potential great armored stalemate is the likely Russian use of chemical weapons. Historically, chemical weapons have slowed up operations and inflicted significant casualties on the attacker using them. It would take a drastic change in human nature to speed up operations in a chemical war. No matter how hard you train, the primordial fear of "invisible" chemicals in the area induces a caution that is difficult to overcome.

WHO'S INVOLVED

Russia—Four separate armies defend the vast area of Russia. The Central Front is covered by over two million Russian troops organized into about 100 divisions. This leaves almost half of Russia's armed forces (the Balkan, Asian, and Far East armies) on the other borders. Only about half of these divisions, one quarter of the total force, are available on short notice. The 100 Russian divisions on the Central Front must also keep an eye on their East European allies.

The Warsaw Pact Organization—One step short of being fictitious. The Russians control and command the East European armies who have about a million men organized in 40 divisions. The Russians do not trust these forces. They devote considerable effort to keeping current their plans to disarm and neutralize their "allied armies" if the need should arise. When it comes to invading Western Europe, East European combat value is questionable, especially from the Russian point of view. The Russians have considerable historical experience with reluctant allies and they tend not to trust them. Allied forces, like the Cubans, are great to have in Africa; they might not be as dependable if the objective were to be France. Currently the East Germans are considered the most reliable pact member, although the Russians allow them to form only six divisions. Poland was once the leading pact force, but no more. Czechs and Hungarians are also considered suspect and are watched over by Russian forces in their respective homelands. In wartime Russian officers and political agents would accompany, and often command, Warsaw Pact divisions.

NATO—The European nations belonging to NATO form a stronger alliance than the Warsaw Pact members. Over a million and a half troops are available immediately. West Germany contributes about one third of the combat power, followed by the United States with 25 percent, France and Britain with 18 percent each. The remainder come from Canada, Belgium, Denmark, and Holland. Although there are serious questions about the effectiveness of the Belgian, Dutch, and Danish contingents, the other alliance forces are quite reliable. Reinforcements from Spain, Portugal, the United States, and Canada would create an even more impressive and powerful army.

GEOGRAPHY

The battlefield is mainly defined by the 1,000-kilometer West German border with East Germany and Czechoslovakia. About one quarter of this border consists of the flat North German plain. To the south the terrain becomes more mountainous as one nears the Alps.

The natural geography hasn't changed much over the past 1,000 years. The human geography has. While East Germany has shown incremental change, since World War II West Germany has experienced a spectacular building boom. The number of roads has increased, as has the number of towns bordering these roads. Germans favor sturdy building materials, providing instant fortifications and cover for defending troops. Thus the natural geography becomes less important than the works of man.

The ground forces on the Central Front are mechanized. Open plains are fine to fight on but are less efficient for moving troops than roads or autobahns. The thousands of tracked vehicles marching across a stretch of open plain would quickly turn bare ground into an impassable quagmire. Roads are needed for rapid movement.

The Russians are preparing for a war of rapid movement. They plan to travel an average of 300 kilometers from the East German border to the Rhine. Without opposition, a mechanized division can travel 200 kilometers per day in friendly territory. Moving over unfamiliar and unscouted roads, with opposition of any degree, slows up the process considerably. Going through towns and cities brings the mechanized attack to a crawl.

Still, there is something to be said for rugged natural terrain. Mountain roads in the forest are easier to defend than highways out on the open plain. The defender has more places to hide and set up ambushes in the forested hills that cover most of Germany. The Russians, as many old World War II German generals are fond of pointing out, are "plains people." The Germans are more adept at trudging up and down their forested mountains. Indeed, this activity is a popular recreation with much of the population. The Russians know all this. Plans to exploit the most easily traveled "corridors" to the Rhine have been developed. The three major routes are the North German plain (actually two or three adjacent corridors), the Fulda gap (where the distance between the East German border and the Rhine is the shortest), and the Hof gap on the Czechoslovakian border. Lesser invasion avenues include the Meiningen gap and the Cheb approach. An aggressive Russian attack through Austria and up the Danube River valley is also possible.

Russian commanders expect to overcome geographical obstacles with a combination of mass and what they term "cleverness." By saturating portions of the roadnet with small units of armored vehicles, they expect to paralyze the defenders' ability to halt the larger Russian formations. Air-landed commandos would carry the shock deeper into NATO's rear. Such tactics require a great deal of finesse and good luck. That's why the Russians aren't so sure they can pull them off.

HISTORY

As the European tribes sorted themselves into nations (see chapter on Spain and Catalonia; European Tribes and its appendix The German Problem), one area, Germany, proved particularly difficult to organize. Three of the most destructive wars in human history have been fought over the political makeup of the German-speaking peoples. During the 1600s there was the Thirty Years' War, a conflict of such destructive magnitude that it was not matched until World War II. Both World War I and World War II were essentially caused by disputes over German borders. Today the German-speaking peoples are still divided. Most Europeans have a sense of history, and know what fury will be released if the Germans march again.

Until the late 1700s, the prospect of marching Germans was not a particularly fearsome prospect. For hundreds of years the then major powers of Europe, France and Spain, settled their differences through wars fought in Germany. Germans provided most of the victims and many of the soldiers. The idea of a unified German nation was not taken seriously. Their territory divided in petty kingdoms, like Bavaria, Hesse, and Prussia, the Germans were diligent but fractious. They would turn on a fellow German while giving slavish obedience to a foreign lord. If the German states appeared to be getting chummy, one could count on a short little Austro-Prussian armed dispute to disrupt them.

In the early 1800s, Napoleon brought the ideals of the French (and the American) Revolution to Germany. Germans rallied around the highly disciplined and successful Kingdom of Prussia and defeated the French. This was a major military, and minor political, victory. In 1871 the united German states defeated France. A new military reality was created.

Meanwhile, in Eastern Europe another political problem was festering. Ever since the third century, Germans had been pushing Slavs around. In the 1200s the pope officially sanctioned a crusade by German warriors against the heathen Slav. The Germans needed little encouragement. But the Russian Slavs organized into nations before the Germans did, and by the 1600s it was no longer easy for Germans to campaign in the East.

What was possible was the partitioning of the Slavic areas between German and Russian spheres of interest. Most of what is now considered Eastern Europe fell under the control of German or Turkish overlords. The Slavic peoples in those areas struggled for independence. Russia set itself up as the Big Brother of its little brother Slavs suffering under the alien German and Turkish rule.

Wars came and conquerors went, and the Slavic little brothers traded German and Turkish occupiers for Russian ones. In areas occupied by the more alien Turks, particularly in Bulgaria, there was and is genuine gratitude for Russian liberation. The other Slavic nations had identified more with the West, if not with the Germans in particular. This cultural empathy outweighed ethnic ties to their fellow Slavs in Russia. The Russians are aware of this and look upon these nations with a mixture of contempt and admiration. Contempt for their ingratitude for the Russian sacrifices to liberate them from German influence. Admiration because the Russians admire the cultural and technical accomplishments of the West.

Ironically, while the Russians have won most of their wars in the past 100 years and the Germans have lost most of theirs, the Germans have wrought more destruction on the Russians. Man for man, the German soldiers have been more skillful and deadly.

The Russians take great pride in their hard-fought victories, but they are not unmindful of the Germans' skill. They are aware of their weaknesses and strive to compensate for them. Thus the Russian cult of cleverness has arisen, which consists of the following:

(1) Deception—Make the enemy think you are stronger, or weaker in some cases, than you really are.

(2) Secrecy—What the enemy doesn't know about your forces he cannot use against you.

(3) Mass—If you cannot muster quality, then come up with quantity.

(4) Confusion—Attack the enemy decision makers and means of communication. Cut off the head and the body will fall. This policy is pursued in peace, through fostering revolution and dissent, and in war.

What does this imply about the current situation along the Central Front? There are two ways to view it. If you are a NATO pessimist, you focus on the 19 to 20 Russian divisions in East Germany that are ready to march west at a few hours' notice. An additional 11 divisions are stationed in Poland, Hungary, and Czechoslovakia. They will be delayed only by the time it takes them to move to the West German border. The East European armies have 17 divisions ready to march immediately. Thus NATO is faced with the prospect of 47 divisions storming across its borders in less than 24 hours.

Against this attack NATO deploys the equivalent of 26 divisions in West Germany with an additional 12 division equivalents in the West German territorial army, the reserve forces that remain under Bonn's direct control.

This is worrisome enough. It is the second act of this battle scenario that is truly frightening. In the days and weeks following the initial invasion, NATO can muster a further three dozen divisions. The Warsaw Pact can bring up 90 divisions, 60 of which are Russian. Added to this overwhelming force are:

(1) The expected Russian use of chemical warfare.

(2) The insertion of commando forces deep inside West Germany.

(3) Surprise air attacks on NATO bases.

How can NATO survive?

NATO's chance of survival can best be judged by considering how a Russian pessimist would view the situation. First, the East European forces are unreliable. Russian units may even have to be diverted to disarm some of these potentially mutinous units. The nine-division Warsaw Pact advantage becomes a disadvantage.

It gets worse. The Russian battle plan is highly dependent on surprise. The official Russian justification for their constant training to invade Western Europe is that their superior intelligence capabilities will enable them to detect NATO's invasion plans and thus make possible a Warsaw Pact preemptive strike. It is for this reason that so many Russian divisions are stationed in East Germany. Several thousand commando troops are also available for raids on key military NATO installations. Chemical weapons are most effective when used unexpectedly. In the Russian view, an attack without surprise is almost certainly doomed. Russia is, somewhat justifiably, in awe of the West's technical reconnaissance resources, satellites, and electronics. The battle they feel least confident about is the technological one, and this is the battle they must win before the war begins.

Failure to prevent NATO forces from mobilizing would put the carefully prepared Russian war plans at grave risk. The Russian style of warfare rests heavily on minutely prepared plans and strict adherence to timetables. Only combat experience gives troops a significant capability to overcome unexpected delays and obstacles. Lacking any substantial combat experience, Russian troops must have the initiative in the opening battle of a war. This initiative can be obtained through overwhelming superiority of force. The Russians lack any massive superiority of numbers in Europe. The only other source of superiority is surprise.

To gain this surprise the Russians rigorously follow their long tradition of following the rules. Their obsession with secrecy is well known. They also invest heavily in deception. Hundreds of thousands of troops and billions of dollars from the defense budget go toward concealing their true resources and intentions. The Russians purposely export weapons that appear identical to the ones used by their forces. Yet these weapons are of special manufacture and have significantly different characteristics than those their own troops use. This is why it may be a big mistake for the United States to rely on Russian weapons data based on equipment captured from the Arabs. Incorrect maps are issued within Russia, accurate ones are considered state secrets. Even the troops don't get real maps except for when on special training exercises or in actual combat.

Finally, how does troop quality compare? World War II demonstrated that, soldier for soldier, there was a substantial difference in combat capability between the Russians and the Germans. Historical analyses by Trevor Dupuy have shown that at the start of World War II the average German soldier was equal in destructive capability to nearly four Russian soldiers. Four years later the Germans still had a nearly two-to-one edge despite a steady erosion of German troop quality.

This observation, however, is not some kind of cultural constant. The German Army in 1941 already had nearly two years of campaigning behind it. One can make a case for the Russians having closed the gap, but it is highly unlikely that they have matched German (or Western) troop quality. This being the case, their inability to muster even a two-to-one troop advantage on the Central Front indicates they have little chance of achieving an offensive victory.

LOCAL POLITICS

NATO—The confrontation on the Central Front has been going on for over thirty years. Due to periodic Russian invasions of neighboring countries, and the long European memory of wars in general, there is acceptance among the NATO countries for the arms buildup. What is more frequently questioned is the degree and nature of the buildup. In most NATO countries, the major issues are:

(1) Cost—Defense is one thing, but so is a healthy economy and adequate funding for social programs. Increased military spending is difficult to achieve. The escalating expense of new weapons is exceeding defense expenditures.

Because Europeans want to produce more of their own weapons rather than buy them from the United States, there is a greater proliferation of weapon types, which makes cooperation on the battlefield that much more difficult.

(2) Manpower—Conscription is still the norm in most nations. Due to public pressure, the term of service has been reduced steadily until now it is little more than a year for most nations. Add to this the coming reduction of eligible manpower in the 1990s and there will be a concomitant reduction in the number of troops available.

(3) Nuclear Weapons—Most are controlled by the United States, although the French and the British have significant arsenals. With the United States homeland 5,000 miles to the west of the European battlefield, there is a great fear that United States commanders will be too hasty to "go nuclear." Even a so-called tactical nuclear war would be a holocaust for Europe. Little can be done about Russian nuclear weapons; American ones can be demonstrated against with some chance of success. At best, this causes strains in the alliance; at worst, it disarms the democratic West.

(4) Forward Defense—Memories of being "liberated" by the Russians (or Germans, for that matter) remain fresh in many European minds. Should Russian armies move west, the public desire is that they be stopped at the border. In theory, this is possible. In practice, it is not the most efficient way to defeat Russian ground forces. In light of this, NATO forces are moving to a more mobile defense that includes counterattacks deep into Warsaw Pact territory.

(5) Command Responsibility—Although the West German Army comprises about one third of the Central Front's combat power (compared with 25 percent for the United States), the commander of the Central Front forces has traditionally been an American. The United States continues to spend billions each year on defending Western Europe, and urges that Europeans take on more of this burden themselves. The Europeans suggest that the command structure of the Central Front forces become more overwhelmingly European. Such a move could encourage the United States to play a lesser role in the defense of Western Europe. Isolationism still runs deep in the American soul.

NATO's biggest enemy is fading memories. The generation that remembers the wars of the first half of this century is slowly passing from power. A new generation will take charge over the next thirty years. Whoever experiences war is more compelled to avoid it. Europe entered World War II very reluctantly. Hitler erred in how far he tried to exploit that reluctance. The potential causes of war described elsewhere in this chapter are more likely to occur if the leadership lacks a practical experience with war.

Yet outright fear of war doesn't work either. When it comes to maintaining the peace, pacifists and "peace governments" have dismal records. Chamberlain's Britain and America's Neutrality Acts didn't discourage Hitler or Japan. Peace demonstrators and antinuclear activists in New York or Bonn don't reduce the possibility of war in Europe. NATO must deal continually with local political conditions that relate to defense policies. NATO's military strategy has been and will continue to be affected by local shifts in political opinion, like those that follow elections.

Wars generally begin when one or both sides has become convinced that victory is possible. It never is. Violence begets violence in an endless spiral that becomes the historical reality we bend to fit our current desires. This transformation is less likely if the leaders have seen the reality of war.

Because West Germany is NATO's front line—a fact the Germans never forget—Bonn's political infighting has a big effect on the alliance. Therefore, we include a special list of these West German parties.

West German Political Parties

Christian Democratic Party (CDU)—Conservative party.
Christian Socialist Union (CSU)—Basically the Bavarian wing of the Christian Democrats.

Free Democratic Party (FDP)—The liberal-moderate group that has been the swing party in West Germany.

Socialist Party (SPD)—The liberal party in West Germany, it is still struggling with a century-old identity crisis. The SPD has two natures: a genuine old-line European socialist-progressive element of the parliamentary-democratic kind, and a radical left wing committed to more drastic economic and social change and experimentation. Today the left-wingers seem to be more "German Nationalist" than the moderates. The socialist-progressive wing remains internationalist and pro-NATO (though less publicly, of late).

The Greens—Coalition of environmentalists, leftists, anarchists, German romantics, dreamers, anti-NATO activists, antinuclear-power activists, and left-wing German nationalists. Originally a non-party party in the old German antiestablishment *ohne mich* ("without me") mold. Committed to "postmaterialist values." In 1983 gained enough votes to get into the Bundestag.

German Communist Party (KPD)—Pro-Moscow Communist Party. Spends its time on anti-American activities. Currently trying to form alliances with the Greens. The Greens are wary of the Communists.

Warsaw Pact

Russia's borders, and those of her "allies," are tightly sealed and all within are politically and socially repressed.

Russia is a country within an armed empire. One hundred million ethnic Russians hold sway over an involuntary conglomerate that includes another 300 million non-Russians. For 500 years of its independent existence, Russia has survived as an armed state. Even more so than the Kingdom of Prussia, Russia has survived, and at times thrived, through the use of force and threats of force. This force has been applied more diligently within Russia than without. Moscow reminds one of a military base. Uniforms are everywhere.

For more than just nostalgic reasons, many Russians mourn the loss of Stalin. For all his faults, including spilling the blood of millions of innocents, Stalin was seen as tough enough to maintain order. The Russian fear of anarchy and disorder is difficult for people in the West to understand. It is equally difficult for most Russians to accept fully the Western concepts of personal freedom and responsibility.

Russia is a very conservative nation. Cleverness is admired more than ingenuity. Most of Russia's military technology and doctrine have come from the West, often via invading armies. The doctrine of defending itself by attacking first was learned at great expense from the Germans and Japanese during the last eighty years.

Russia's (largely justified) feeling of technical inferiority and its geographical position make it fearful of surprise attack by one or more of its surrounding hostile states. Historically Russia has striven to extend its control over adjoining non-Russian states. Better that the enemy should march through non-Russian parts of the country before it gets to the heartland, the area centered on Moscow and points east. The Ukraine, the Caucasus, the Baltic States, parts of Finland, Eastern Europe, and most of Asiatic Russia are all protection for the true Russian state.

There is a Catch-22 to this "defense through conquest" strategy. The conquered states exact a price in the political, military and economic resources required to keep them compliant. This has been a drain on empires for as long as empires have existed. Russian armed forces are stretched ever more thinly as their empire grows. The cumulative resentment of the conquered also grows. Because of their experience of this century's wars, the Russian leadership thus far has been restrained, by their standards, in the use of military force. As their sense of reality regarding Russian military competence dwindles, Russian leaders will be more tempted to overextend themselves. Thus, miscalculation in the face of crises, the classic cause of conflict, will likely precipitate the next war.

PARTICIPANT STRATEGIES AND GOALS

In a sense this chapter has been a discussion of strategies and goals that compete yet often intertwine. We will break from the usual participant-by-participant analysis and refine some previous insights.

The proclaimed Russian doctrine for responding to a threat is to launch a massive high-speed attack on NATO forces. This is supposed to produce a Russian victory within a week. This approach was taught them by the Germans during World War II. However, the Russians are not Germans. To paraphrase several successful German World War II generals, "To beat the Russians you let them run by you and then kick them in the behind." Currently, the NATO doctrine of Forward Defense is to send all the troops to the border posthaste. The Russians really fear NATO will send its troops beyond the border. The debate swings now between driving into the Russian rear (that is, East Germany, Czechoslovakia, or other states) or fortifying the border.

Another lesson the Russians have learned from their run-ins with the Germans is to surprise and inflict paralysis on the defender by destroying his ability to communicate with and control his forces. The disruption would involve everything from electronic warfare to commandos landing in the enemy's rear. NATO intends to return the favor. It's a question of who will foul up the other's operations most effectively. Taking no chances, the Russians have trained their troops simply to plunge forward until they reach the Rhine (or other major objective), are dead, or receive new instructions.

Then there are the secret agents—assassins and saboteurs. This favorite Russian technique might prove to be very useful. Again, NATO hopes to do a little of this itself. United States Green Berets would drop into Hungary, Poland, Rumania, Czechoslovakia, and even Bulgaria. They would conduct sabotage operations, strike rail and roadnets, attack nuclear and chemical weapons dumps, and, perhaps most important of all, contact and supply East European partisan forces. Many of America's European-based Green Berets are second- or third-generation United States citizens whose parents or grandparents emigrated from the countries where these soldiers would fight should a war begin. They not only speak the local languages, but they may have relatives in their operational zones. The Green Berets cannot foment a rebellion, but they can increase the effectiveness of a rebellion and the subsequent anti-Russian guerrilla activity. Even if the conventional war ground to a halt and ended in a negotiated settlement or withdrawal, the guerrilla wars spawned by the conventional war could bother the Kremlin for years. Both Moscow and Washington are aware of this.

SUPERPOWER INTEREST

	Political	Military	Historical	Economic
Russia	Very High	Very High	Very High	High
US	Very High	Very High	High	High

Political—This is Russia's front yard. One of the issues Russia would go to war for (and has in the past) is political control of neighboring states. The United States has long-term allies in Europe, and most American voters are of European ancestry.

Military—Russians can become irrational in their pursuit of security, which is reflected by their massive military investment in this area. The Western European nations are America's primary military allies. The loss of Western Europe would leave the United States to face Russia and its allies on its own.

Historical—Russian involvement in Europe goes back several hundred years. The United States took a keen interest only in this century.

Economic—Russia is less economically dependent on its Eastern and Western European neighbors than the United States, though both rate a High.

POTENTIAL OUTCOMES

The Europeans have many reasons to avoid another major war. In the 1600s the Thirty Years' War caused such widespread death and destruction that a conflict of equal magnitude did not occur for over 200 years. Perhaps this will serve as a historical precedent, given the appalling destruction wrought by World War I and World War II. The Napoleonic Wars of the early 1800s featured many spectacular battles, but for the most part caused limited civilian and economic losses. World War I and its sequel gave Europeans a taste of what their ancestors had suffered from 1618 to 1648. Still, the Europeans face several situations that could lead to a large-scale bloodbath. The situations addressed in this section could be settled peacefully, or with considerably less violence than produced by a major war.

1. 65 percent chance: The continuation of the current situation. The human and economic stakes are too high, the risks of war too great. Europe has rarely gone so long without a war of some significance. Perhaps nuclear weapons do have a peacekeeping effect.

2. 15 percent chance before 1999: The war for German reunification. This is the most likely cause of a major conflict, as it involves patriotic fervor, militant Germans, and fearful Russians, always a volatile combination in Europe. Whether it would be started by East or West Germany is an open question. An East German revolt is one scenario. German "self-neutralization" (refusal to participate in either the Warsaw Pact or NATO) and an East German revolt tied to a West German attack is another. Russia is unlikely to allow any reunification, no matter the result of the war, unless the new Germany is unarmed, socialist, and nonaligned. Even this might not be enough for the Rus-

sians, though there is a certain precedent in the arrangement they made when they withdrew their occupying forces from Austria. The current occupants of West Germany are unlikely to agree.

3. 15 percent chance before 1992: The Great Uprising. Local rebellions in Russia's East European "ally" nations spread into a general uprising, and the fighting in Hungary, Czechoslovakia, and East Germany spills across the border. These allies have rebelled or been restive ever since they were liberated in 1945. In 1945 Yugoslavia successfully moved the Russian Army out of the country at gunpoint. In the 1950s East Germany and Hungary fought Russian tanks in the streets. In the 1960s Czechoslovakia was reoccupied, and the 1970s saw Poland get uppity. Rumania has been constantly uncooperative. Only little Bulgaria remains faithful. Russia has made concessions, but a permanent fix appears impossible. The East European allies are too corrupted by Western thought to have anything but contempt for their Russian overlords. Through the centuries, such testy allies eventually came to blows. If the Russians become too heavy-handed and the situation gets out of control, several allied states could rebel at once. The Hungarian Army resisted in 1956. The Russians feared the Czech Army would resist. The Russians hesitated to invade Poland in 1980 because of the volatile reputation of the Polish armed forces.

4. 5 percent chance: The Empire Crumbles. There are plenty of internal and external threats to the empire that is Russia. Should an explosive combination of these problems occur, the resulting civil and/ or imperial conflict could spill over into Europe. This would not be a Russian invasion of Europe, but a European invasion of (or "intervention in") Russia. This is the Russians' greatest fear and it lies behind their desire for security through strength. This is why many Russians, while chafing under the yoke of repression and economic deprivation, will ultimately tolerate a strong leader like Stalin. Before the revolution, Czar Ivan the Terrible (Stalin's role model) was often held up as an example of a leader who would prevent such an invasion.

5. 5 percent chance: Watch on the Rhine. The least likely event, an all-out Russian attack, is the one to which NATO devotes most attention because it is the biggest danger. Russian generals, however, tend to be very mindful of military history. No one who has done his homework has any great desire to go chasing after a German army inside Germany. Russian generals are also mindful of the Russian Army's dismal record of offensive operations in the early stages of a war.

COST OF WAR

This would be a multitrillion-dollar war with over 100 million casualties if the fighting went nuclear. Even if there were a comparatively restrained conventional conflict lasting a month or so, the total cost, including economic damage, could still be in the one- to two-trillion-dollar range. Because much of the undeveloped world depends on Europe for manufactured goods, there would be collateral losses in many other parts of the globe.

There has never been a time when Europeans were not heavily armed in defense of their territory. Thus it is difficult to say that the peacetime military budgets are excessive. Still, several hundred billion dollars a year are spent on military matters. Peace is very expensive.

A QUICK LOOK AT NUKES

The threat of nuclear war between the superpowers makes the Central Front the most dangerous area for potential conflict. Small nuclear weapons, called tactical nukes, are designed for use against enemy troops, roadnets, and supply centers. Large ones, called strategic nukes, are either "counterforce" weapons to knock out enemy strategic nuclear weapons systems, or "city-busters" for direct attack on enemy civilian and industrial zones. There are between 8,000 and 10,000 nuclear warheads in Europe.

Tactical nukes are nuclear weapons with relatively small yields, from less than one tenth of a kiloton up to about 50 kilotons. Some nuclear warheads of greater yield, even to 500 kilotons, are sometimes referred to as tactical nukes, but this is a terrible misnomer. The Hiroshima bomb was in the neighborhood of 20 kilotons. The explosion of a half dozen 10-kiloton weapons in Europe would produce a disaster.

If these weapons are so destructive, and expensive, why then, given the already huge stockpiles, do both sides continue to build and deploy them? There are several reasons. First, no one knows how many of the nukes would work if somebody decided to use them. The United States originally planned to transport its Pershing I nuclear missile on a large, tracked vehicle. Tracks give vehicles like tanks better off-road mobility, and would have allowed the United States missile units to deploy more easily through woods or on rough terrain. The Americans discovered, however, that the rough ride produced by the tracks shook the Pershing I's delicate components. Missile electronics would break down and the weapon wouldn't work. The United States now moves its Pershings around on huge trucks with oversized tires and superheavy-duty shock absorbers. The trucks in the 56th Field Artillery Brigade, the United States Pershing missile unit in West Germany, look like moon vehicles. They are large and cumbersome, but the missiles ride smoothly. Odds are that the United States missiles would work . . . maybe.

The Russians, however, still deploy a large number of their theater nuclear missiles on tracked vehicles. Russian missile technology is still inferior to that of the West. Allegedly the Russian missiles suffer from an already high breakdown rate. The tracked vehicles lugging SCUD nuclear missiles through Red Square may look impressive on TV, but they are a very bad way to carry a missile around if you intend to shoot it.

There is a second reason for continuing to build nukes. The Russians know that their tank forces, when concentrated for a break-through attack in a conventional war, make easy targets for NATO's tiny artillery-delivered nukes. A NATO "tactical nuclear pulse," a volley of interlocking 155-mm and 8-inch nuclear artillery shells (in the $\frac{1}{10}$-to-1-kiloton range), could stop a Russian tank-army attack with comparatively little damage and the radiation limited to the immediate area of the attack. The Russians want to make a NATO nuclear counterattack as unlikely as possible. They believe that if they deploy about 400 SS-20 intermediate-range nuclear missiles, whose only real function is to destroy command sites, airfields, and large transportation nets, NATO could never risk using tactical mini-nukes. The fact that command sites, airfields, and large transportation nets in Western Europe are located in or within blast range of heavily populated areas only increases the effectiveness of the Russian threat. NATO, in turn, responds that if there were no Russian tank armies threatening Western Europe with conventional attack, then there would be no mini-nukes. NATO responds further by building and deploying newer intermediate-range nuclear systems like GLCM (ground-launched cruise missiles) and Pershing IIs, which are improved Pershing Is with much greater accuracy and range. These new NATO missiles have guidance systems which, provided that they work as advertised, can deliver nuclear war-heads 800 to 1,500 kilometers and place them within 50 meters of the target. Now the Russians are no longer sure that enough of their 400-odd SS-20s, and SS-21s, and SCUD As, and SCUD Bs, and so forth, will work or survive a NATO GLCM attack.

The result is that a lot of money is spent on weapons and there are more nuclear systems in an already nuke-filled Europe. However, there is also no appreciable change in the tactical situation. A new balance has been reached. Fortunately, neither side has an advantage that increases its chance of victory. Gaining such an advantage could produce high political and military instability. Instability leads to disastrous wars. In such a twisted, paradoxical manner, a balanced arms race can actually be a stabilizing influence.

The new balance of power, however, is still precarious. The new weapons increase the amount of destruction that could result if war broke out. They also signal another round of weapons development and rearming. More money is spent on these terrible armaments. One begins to think that only economic and fiscal fatigue will produce real arms-control negotiations.

There is also a third reason for building nuclear arsenals, an abstract, yet most compelling reason politically. Nuclear weapons have become an international symbol of power and military prestige, what dreadnought battleships were before 1914. The only weapons system that competes with nukes is the big aircraft carrier (currently the United States is the only country that has such carriers, but the Russians are rapidly constructing two large nuclear carriers for fixed-wing aircraft). Building nuclear weapons becomes a demonstration of political commitment and determination. Russia deploys nukes to show off its military might, which it wants the world to recognize and respect. Russia deploys nukes to coerce psychologically the populations of countries it fears are out to destroy it. NATO continues to deploy nukes for purposes of bargaining in arms-limitation or reduction talks and to illustrate the alliance's political cohesiveness. If the United States, Great Britain, Italy, and West Germany can agree in peacetime to cooperate on ridiculously expensive weapons programs, then an opponent can be (dead) certain that they will cooperate in wartime. And if the act of buying the ridiculously expensive weapons produces peace, at an infinitesimal cost of a war, perhaps the cost wasn't so absurd.

Fearful poetic images of destruction, analyses based on psychobabble, adolescent romanticism, and historical ignorance won't rid the world of nuclear weapons. The atomic Pandora's box has been opened, and unless UFOs arrive and the alien visitors remove the nuclear weapons from the planet, they are here to stay. Only a politics based on equal power and a respect for both sides' fundamental needs and fears (based on an appreciation of two centuries of history) will forestall and prevent the battle on the Central Front. Russian fears and an aggressive response to those fears lie at the core of the conflict. Only time—a time of extended peace—can and will assuage both Russian anxiety and Western apprehension. The irony is that the existence of hyper-destructive nuclear weapons has bought Europe forty years of peace. Human social systems change slowly, but there is hope, through time, for evolutionary change in Russia's perception of Western Europe.

CURRENTLY DEPLOYED IN EUROPE

Country	Wpn Name	Type	Yield	Other Information
US				
	Pershing IA	SRBM	400 kt	Dual Capable
	Pershing II	MRBM	250 kt	2 Types of Warhead
	BGM-109A	GLCM	200 kt	Dual Capable
	Lance	SRBM	50 kt	Dual Capable
	M-110 203mm	Artillery	1–2 kt	
	M-109 155mm	Artillery	0.1–2 kt	
	Aircraft	Bombs	5–200 kt	
	Trident	SLBM	100 kt	MIRV (8)
Britain				
	Aircraft	Bombs	5–200 kt	
	Trident	SLBM	100 kt	MIRV (8)
France				
	MSBS M-20	SLBM	1,000 kt	
	Aircraft	Bombs	5–200 kt	
	Pluton	SRBM	10 kt	
	HADES	SRBM	10 kt	Replace Pluton
	SSBS S-3	IRBM	1,000 kt	
	ASMP	ASM	100 kt	
Russia				
	Various	SLBM	100+ kt	
	Aircraft	Bombs	10–2000 kt	
	SS-4	MRBM	1,000 kt	
	SS-5	MRBM	1,000 kt	
	SS-20 Mod 1	MRBM	1,500 kt	
	SS-20 Mod 2	MRBM	150 kt	MIRV (3)
	SS-20 Mod 3	MRBM	150 kt	
	SCUD A	SRBM	1 kt	Dual Capable
	SCUD B	SRBM	1 kt	Dual Capable
	FROG 7	SRBM	200 kt	Dual Capable
	SS-12	SRBM	200 kt	Dual Capable
	SS-21	SRBM	200 kt	Dual Capable
	SS-22	SRBM	500 kt	
	SS-23	SRBM	200 kt	Dual Capable
	SS-C-1B	GLCM	1,000 kt	Dual Capable
	S-23 180mm	Artillery	1 kt	

Notes: GLCM = ground-launched cruise missile; SRBM = short-range ballistic missile; MRBM = medium-range ballistic missile; ASM = air-to-surface missile; SLBM = sea launched ballistic missile. MIRV = multiple warheads (number per missile in parenthesis). Dual Capable = can be used with nonnuclear warheads.

CONVENTIONAL FORCES

The following chart compares conventional weapons systems and divisions in place in Europe as of December 1983. The division totals include all divisions—Categories I–III for Warsaw Pact, active and reserve for NATO.

CONVENTIONAL FORCES CURRENTLY IN EUROPE

	NATO	Warsaw Pact
Main Battle Tanks	13,500	42,600
Atck Helicopters	560	960
Antitank Guided Wpns Launchers	12,300	32,200
Armored Personnel Carriers	33,000	75,000
Artillery Pieces/Heavy Mortars	11,000	35,000
Ground Divisions	86	176
High Perf. Jets Fighter/Ftrbmbrs	3,100	6,550

PART 6

A Databank on Wars Present and Potential

This section presents a statistical survey of current active and potential wars. There are two charts. One shows the conflicts themselves (The World in Conflict) and another, the basic economic and military information for all countries (The Nations of the World).

African Nations
1 Liberia
2 South Africa
3 Gabon
4 Guinea-Bisseau
5 Madagascar
6 Ivory Coast
7 Central Afr. Rep.
8 Mauretania
9 Botswana
10 Cameroon
11 Djibouti
12 Congo
13 Rwanda
14 Niger
15 Senegambia
16 Upper Volta
17 Ghana
18 Somalia
19 Mali
20 Benin
21 Sierra Leone
22 Tanzania
23 Comoro Is.
24 Zambia
25 Sao Tome & Princ.
26 Chad
27 Swaziland
28 Nigeria
29 Lesotho
30 Cape Verde Is.
31 Malawi
32 Seychelles Is.
33 Togo
34 Burundi
35 Zaire
36 Kenya
37 Uganda
38 Zimbabwe
39 Angola
40 Equatorial Guinea
41 Guinea
42 Ethiopia
43 Mozambique

American Nations
44 United States
45 Canada
46 Panama
47 El Salvador
48 Jamaica
49 Colombia
50 Brazil
51 Bolivia
52 Uruguay
53 Guyana
54 Paraguay
55 Peru
56 Mexico

57 Venezuela
58 Argentina
59 Chile
60 Ecuador
61 Trinidad
62 Guatemala
63 Haiti
64 Costa Rica
65 Honduras
66 Dominican Rep.
67 Belize
68 Suriname
69 Nicaragua
70 Cuba

European Nations
71 Italy
72 Belgium
73 Norway
74 Germany, West

75 Britain
76 Luxembourg
77 Spain
78 France
79 Iceland
80 Denmark
81 Netherlands
82 Portugal
83 Greece
84 Turkey
85 Malta
86 Cyprus (Greek)
87 Switzerland
88 Sweden
89 Ireland
90 Finland
91 Austria
92 Yugoslavia
93 Cyprus (Turk.)
94 Albania

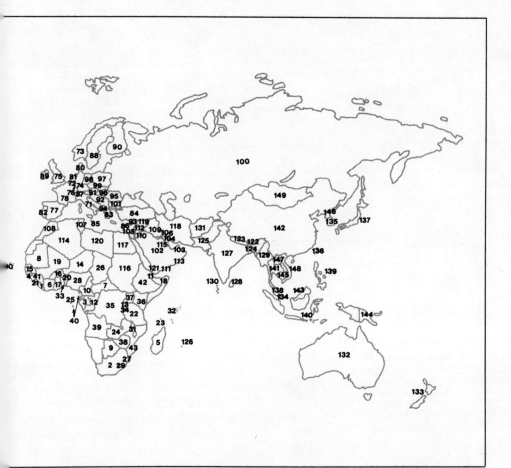

16. The World in Conflict

The World in Conflict chart is arranged according to the participants in the conflicts. Most wars have two participants; many have three or more. Each is a separate entity with its own combat forces, goals, and ability to escalate or stop the war.

The key element in the chart is the **Danger Level.** This is our estimate of the overall danger of this conflict to world peace. Each conflict is a serious matter for the participants, but each has a varying degree of potential for escalation to a wider, even worldwide conflict. The **Danger Level** measures this potential.

The other data summarize political and military aspects of the conflict and the human costs in casualties and refugees.

Special lists follow to sort out the most striking estimates.

Wars in general are not noted for meticulous record keeping. We have collected the data from a wide variety of sources and can make no claim to the reliability of many. But this information gives you a good picture of the state of the current wars. Keep in mind that many of the numbers are subject to frequent revision as new information appears.

Preceding the chart are notes on the abbreviation and methodology, and following it are notes on the conflicts.

TERMS AND ABBREVIATIONS

Averages & Totals—Averages and totals for each column as appropriate, gives you a sense of proportion for each value for each nation.

Conflict—For an active war the common name has been used.

Rank—Numerical ranking of the danger level of each conflict, from 1 on up.

Side—The identity of the combatants, with the country name and Insurgents used for most internal revolutions. Note that wherever two or more groups are allied in a conflict, they are grouped together by a letter: A, B, C, with the government-allied participants coming first. Each major participant has been listed. The degree of participation often becomes murky as military advisers and technicians are often indistinguishable from combat forces. Russia is prone to sending personnel from its satellite nations. Currently there are twice as many Eastern European military technicians overseas than Russians. East Germany and Bulgaria are current favorites, the Germans no doubt for their efficiency and the Bulgarians for their strong loyalty to Russian aims.

Began—We cover operations since 1945, so the earliest start date is 1945. Many of these conflicts have been going on for hundreds of years, but we felt the numbers would be more reliable if we began counting no earlier than 1945.

Type—Gives an indication of the nature of the conflict, using letter codes that are presented in order of increasing importance. The abbreviations, in no particular order, are:

I: Ideological, including religious
R: Political-social revolution
S: Separatist movement
T: Territorial dispute
H: Historical antagonisms

Dngr Lvl—Danger Level, the relative danger to world peace represented by a participant in a conflict. The higher this value, the more likely the participant's warlike activities could trigger more widespread death and destruction. The key components of the formula used are the next three indices.

Int—Intensity Index, measures the level of severity of the conflict:

0: Very-low-intensity terrorist activity
1: Serious predisposition to armed conflict
2: Sustained terrorist activity
3: Guerrilla activity
4: Sustained guerrilla activity
5: State of war, continuous operations

6: Lower-scale conventional operations such as in the Falklands or Lebanese wars

7: Medium-scale conventional war, like the Iran-Iraq conflict

8: Full-scale conventional warfare, such as a nonnuclear superpower clash

9: Nuclear exchange

Each side in a conflict will often have a different intensity level. This reflects different goals and means. A strong government, when faced with opposition, will bear down on it more severely than an emerging opposition group.

Prob—Probability index, expressed as a percentage chance that the side will be engaged in active combat in the conflict at any given time in the next few years. Each side will often have a different probability index, reflecting differing predispositions to settling conflicts with violence.

Esc—Escalation Index, the possibility of the conflict spreading either vertically (intensifying) or horizontally (involving more areas or countries):

1: No international impact beyond the nation(s) involved

2: Potential threat to neighboring states

3: Significant threat to neighboring states

4: No international impact beyond the nation(s) involved, with some chance of superpower involvement

5: Potential threat to neighboring states, with more superpower involvement

6: Significant threat to neighboring states, with significant superpower threat

7: Multiregional threat with superpower interest

8: As number 8 above but more so

9: Overwhelming international importance

Gov Form—Government Form, an indication of the type of government of the side:

Mon: Functioning monarchy
Dem: Functioning democracy
Dic: Dictatorship
M: Military government
OP: One-party rule

Soc: Soviet-style socialist regime

Jun: Junta (military leadership, applied to insurgent groups when no better information is available on the most likely type of leadership contained

Combinations of these forms of government are shown as such.

Gov Sta—Government Stability, rates the government on a scale of 1, highly unstable, to 5, highly stable. It reflects the quality of the national leadership and whatever national governing organizations exist. A more stable national leadership usually means more predictable performance by that nation in pursuing or stopping its conflicts.

Combata—Combatants, the approximate number in thousands of troops directly committed to the conflict. This number is often debatable, as the deployment of forces is usually flexible in "peacetime" wars. Other priorities like keeping your civilians in line and facing down other aggressors keep the order of battle (mix of units) in the immediate combat area quite flexible. The total forces involved in all conflicts can often exceed the number of troops available for each nation because a nation can have more potential conflicts on its hands than its available forces can handle. This is a particular fear of the Russians, surrounded as they are by numerous hostile nations.

Qual—Quality of the forces involved in the conflict. A nation often has available troops of vastly differing quality. The best troops are usually sent against the most dangerous enemy. Less qualified (but often more loyal) troops are used against restive civilians. Rated on a scale of 1, extremely poor, to 5, excellent.

Endur—Endurance, the ability of each side to sustain the conflict at the current level of intensity, assuming current political conditions continue. A single nation involved in multiple conflicts usually shows different endurance levels for each conflict. Rated on a scale of 1, poor, to 5, excellent.

Losses—The number of casualties incurred in thousands. This number includes killed, wounded, and missing, but not prisoners (assuming they survive). Covers the period from the beginning of the conflict (1945 for those wars that predate that year). Conflicts with fewer than 1,000 casualties are assigned the number 1,000 (shown as 1 on the chart). This is based on the reasonable assumption that it won't be long before this nominal number of casualties will be exceeded.

Refugees—Number of persons displaced by the conflict, internally and internationally, in thousands. These are people who were forced out of their homes either by the fighting or the threat of it. It does not include the much larger number of people who remained in their home areas as the fighting overcame them.

Super—Superpower alignment, the primary source of diplomatic and more tangible support, Russia or the West (the Western nations led by the United States). These allies represent the most substantial assistance a nation can have. The degree of assistance varies from situation to situation.

Supt—Support, the degree of support that nation is receiving from Russia or the West. A 1 represents little more than moral support. A 9 indicates substantial military and economic aid. Many conflict participants have other allies in the region, but nearly all take their lead, or are heavily influenced by, the positions of the superpowers.

NOTES ON THE CONFLICTS

Aegean Shelf—Dispute over potential offshore-oil deposits is exacerbated by long historic antagonisms and the recent declaration of independence by the Turkish Cypriot community.

Afghanistan—See chapter on Afghanistan.

Angola—Negotiations now in progress between South Africa and Angola could settle matters in Namibia and possibly Cabinda but probably not in Angola itself, for the antigovernment UNITA movement appears well entrenched in a classic Maoist "liberated zone," with the country virtually partitioned. It is possible that only the presence of Cuban troops, plus some 1,000 to 2,000 Soviet and East German advisers, maintains the allegedly Marxist regime in power.

Beagle Channel—A democratic regime in Argentina, Chilean willingness to resolve the issue, and deft papal mediation appear to have ended the danger of Argentine adventurism over these insignificant islands with possible offshore-oil deposits. This is a significant step from the situation that saw war virtually imminent in the late seventies.

Belize—Argentina's defeat in the Falklands in 1982 appears to have cooled Guatemalan irredentist ardor, but the matter is of long standing. Britain made emergency reinforcements to its 1,500-man garrison in 1972, 1975, and 1977, in the face of saber rattling from Guatemala. Nevertheless, recent developments in negotiations may lead to a peaceful resolution. Meanwhile, Britain is building up the new Belize armed forces and the country has received promises of aid in the event of invasion from either the United States *or* Cuba!

THE WORLD IN CONFLICT

Conflict	Rank	Side		Began	Type	Dngr Lvl	Int	Prob	Esc	Gov Form	Gov Sta	Combata	Qual	Endur	Losses	Refugees	Super	Supt
Averages & Totals....						16	5	62%	5		4	26,964	3	4	50,812	48,929		
Aegean	138	Greece	A	1945	TH	6	1	50%	5	Dem	3	250	4	3	0	0	West	1
Aegean	137	Turkey	B	1945	TH	6	1	40%	5	MJun	4	500	4	3	0	0	West	1
Afghanistan	69	Afghanistan	A	1978	IH	20	5	80%	4	MDic	2	48	1	5	50	4,000	Russia	9
Afghanistan	6	Russia	A	1978	IH	47	7	90%	6	Soc	5	152	4	5	30		Russia	9
Afghanistan	29	Insurgents	B	1978	IH	28	6	90%	5	Jun	5	200	4	5	1,000		West	6
Angola	54	Cuba	A	1975	I	22	6	60%	5	Dic	3	25	3	5	1		Russia	9
Angola	59	Angola	A	1975	I	22	5	70%	5	OP	2	80	2	5	12	1,200	Russia	9
Angola	73	S. Africa	B	1975	I	19	6	50%	5	Dem/Dic	4	2	5	4	0		West	2
Angola	125	Insurgents	B	1975	I	9	3	60%	1	Jun	4	40	2	3	3		West	2
Beagle Chan	159	Argentina	A	1945	T	4	6	50%	1	Dem	3	225	5	3	0		West	1
Beagle Chan	150	Chile	B	1945	T	4	6	60%	1	MJun	4	140	5	3	0		West	1
Belize	160	Britain	A	1945	T	4	6	50%	1	Dem	5	20	5	3	0		West	9
Belize	171	Guatemala	B	1945	T	3	5	50%	1	MJun	3	25	3	3	0	250	West	1
Burma	165	Burma	A	1948	SIH	8	3	70%	1	OP	4	160	3	5	3		West	5
Burma	128	Insurgents	B	1948	SIH	15	4	57%	4	OP	4	20	2	5	5		Russia	2
Cabinda	94	Angola	A	1975	SI	15	5	60%	4	OP	3	8	3	5	1	50	Russia	9
Cabinda	55	Cuba	A	1975	SI	22	6	60%	5	Dic	5	2	2	5	2		Russia	9
Cabinda	131	Insurgents	B	1975	SI	8	3	55%	4	Jun	4	4	2	5	1		West	2
Cambodia	12	Vietnam	A	1978	HI	35	7	80%	5	Soc	4	160	4	3	125		Russia	6
Cambodia	95	Cambodia	A	1978	HI	15	5	60%	4	Dic	2	20	2	3	150		Russia	7
Cambodia	108	Insurgents	B	1978	HI	12	4	60%	4	Jun	3	40	3	5	2,000		West	4
Central Ame	30	Honduras	A	1945	TI	28	5	90%	5	Dem	3	15	3	2	0		West	8
Central Ame	70	Nicaragua	B	1945	TI	20	4	80%	5	OPJun	3	50	3	3	0	2,000	Russia	8
Chad	21	France	A	1965	ITH	31	6	85%	5	Dem	5	3	5	3	1		West	8
Chad	60	Zaire	A	1965	ITH	22	5	70%	5	Dic	4	3	5	3	0		West	5
Chad	74	Nigeria	A	1965	TSI	19	6	50%	5	Jun	3	150	2	3	0		West	3
Chad	53	Chad	A	1965	ITH	23	5	75%	5	OP	2	6	2	5	40	100	West	7
Chad	25	Libya	B	1965	TSI	30	6	80%	5	MDic	4	60	2	5	4		Russia	6
Chad	42	Insurgents	B	1965	ITH	26	6	70%	5	Dic	3	5	2	5	12		Russia	5
China	174	Taiwan	A	1945	I	3	8	5%	6	OP	3	500	4	3	10,000	0	West	2
China	173	Mainland	B	1945	I	3	8	5%	6	OP	5	1,500	4	5	20,000	5,000	West	2
Colombia	62	Colombia	A	1948	RSI	21	5	85%	4	Dem	4	60	3	5	250	500	West	6
Colombia	133	Insurgents	B	1948	RSI	6	2	65%	1	Jun	3	4	4	5	25	45	Russia	4
Cyprus	190	Turks	A	1945	THS	2	1	40%	1	MJun	4	20	4	4	2		West	1
Cyprus	96	Turkey	A	1945	THS	15	6	50%	4	MJun	4	25	4	4	0	30	West	1
Cyprus	188	Greeks	B	1945	THS	1	2	60%	1	Jun	3	40	3	3	1		Russia	2

Conflict	No.	Party	S	Year	Code			%		Gov						Aid	Bloc	
Dhofar	48	Oman	A	1963	TSI	25	5	80%	5	Mon	4	20	3	5	2		West	7
Dhofar	71	S. Yemen	A	1963	TSI	20	4	76%	5	OPJun	4	25	4	5	4		Russia	4
Dhofar	98	Insurgents	B	1963	TSI	14	3	10%	9	Jun	2	1	5	5	3		Russia	4
El Salvador	118	U.S.	A	1979	ITH	10	9	80%	5	Dem	2	5	5	5	0	200	West	9
El Salvador	26	El Salvador	B	1979	IR	30	6	90%	5	Jun	4	22	3	5	30		West	8
El Salvador	14	Insurgents	A	1979	IR	33	6	70%	5	Dic	5	7	3	5	30		Russia	6
Eritrea	43	Cuba	A	1961	SHI	26	6	90%	5	MDic	3	10	2	5	2		Russia	9
Eritrea	15	Ethiopia	A	1961	SHI	33	4	70%	5	Jun	5	100	4	5	50		Russia	9
Eritrea	56	Insurgents	B	1961	SHI	22	6	90%	5	Dic	4	25	3	5	100	1,000	West	2
Ethiopia	44	Cuba	A	1974	ISH	26	6	70%	5	MDic	3	9	2	5	5		Russia	9
Ethiopia	16	Ethiopia	B	1974	ISH	33	4	90%	5	Jun	5	100	2	5	20	1,000	Russia	9
Ethiopia	85	Insurgents	B	1974	ISH	17	6	67%	4	Dem	3	60	3	5	1		West	4
Falklands	110	Britain	A	1982	T	12	5	40%	4	MJun	3	1	2	3	2		West	9
Falklands	109	Argentina	B	1982	T	12	5	40%	4	MJun	3	17	3	3	5		West	4
Guatemala	61	Guatemala	A	1960	R	21	2	86%	1	Dem	3	3	3	3	0	50	West	6
Guatemala	139	Insurgents	B	1960	R	6	6	60%	4	Dem	3	60	2	5	1		Russia	4
Guyana	175	Venezuela	A	1945	T	3	2	40%	1	Dem	4		1	3	20		Russia	1
Guyana	97	Guyana	B	1945	T	15	6	50%	4	Dic	3	3	2	5	1		West	6
Haiti	86	Haiti	A	1945	R	16	1	80%	4	Dic	3	20	1	3			West	2
Haiti	153	Insurgents	B	1945	R	4	4	80%	5	Dem	2	1	1	2	20		Russia	2
Honduras	77	Honduras	B	1980	R	17	1	70%	5	Dem	2	15	2	5	1		West	8
Honduras	161	Insurgents	B	1980	R	4	7	60%	3	Jun	3	3	2	2			Russia	5
Indo-Pak.	155	India	A	1947	HTI	4	7	15%	3	Dem	5	1,000	4	5	2,500	12,000	Russia	7
Indo-Pak.	154	Pakistan	B	1947	HTI	22	5	15%	3	Dem	3	900	4	4	2,000	3,000	West	6
Iran	57	Iran	A	1979	ISH	6	7	90%	4	OPDic	4	80	3	5	5		Russia	3
Iran	134	Insurgents	B	1979	ISH	54	8	65%	4	Jun	5	20	3	5	25		West	4
Iran-Iraq	2	Iraq	A	1980	ISH	71	2	90%	4	OPDic	4	700	3	5	500	100	West	7
Iran-Iraq	1	Iran	B	1980	THI	12	5	90%	8	OPDic	4	900	3	5	700	500	Russia	4
Israel-PLO	111	PLO	A	1948	T	33	9	80%	2	Jun	3	16	5	5	12	1,000	West	5
Israel-PLO	17	Israel	B	1948	T	27	7	30%	5	Dem	5	300	5	4	2		West	8
Korea	64	U.S.	B	1950	I	21	3	40%	6	Dem	3	50	4	5	100	5,000	West	9
Korea	39	S. Korea	A	1950	I	31	1	60%	6	MDic	4	1,100	4	5	1,000	3,000	West	9
Korea	22	N. Korea	B	1950	I	10	2	55%	6	Dic	2	900	2	2	2,000		Russia	8
Kosovo	117	Albania	A	1945	THI	5	3	80%	5	OPJun	4	150	4	4			Russia	1
Kosovo	147	Yugoslavia	B	1945	THI	6	1	65%	4	Jun	4	300	3	4	20		West	4
Kurdistan	135	Kurds	B	1979	SH	17	2	70%	4	OPDic	4	5	4	5	15		West	2
Kurdistan	78	Iraq	B	1979	SH	12	3	80%	4	Dem	3	12	3	5	3		Russia	5
Kurdistan	112	Turkey	B	1979	SH	35	5	80%	7	OPDic	3	2	3	5	2		West	3
Kurdistan	13	Iran	B	1979	SH	17	4	85%	4	Dic	1	50	3	3	50		Russia	3
Laos	83	Laos	A	1975	IS	17	4	85%	4	Dic	2	46	1	3	24	500	Russia	6

THE WORLD IN CONFLICT

Averages & Totals.....

Conflict	Rank	Side	Began	Type		Dngr Lvl	Int	Prob	Esc	Gov Form	Gov Sta	Combata	Qual	Endur	Losses	Refugees	Super	Supt
Averages/Totals						16	5	62%	5		4	26,964	3	4	50,812	48,929		
Laos	31	Vietnam	1975	IS	A	28	5	90%	5	Soc	4	60	4	4	12		Russia	7
Laos	136	Insurgents	1975	IS	B	6	2	65%	5	Jun	4	20	3	5	50		West	2
Lebanon	7	Syria	1975	HIS	A	41	7	80%	6	OPDic	3	40	3	3	20		Russia	8
Lebanon	145	UN	1975	HIS	A	5	1	85%	5	UN	3	6	4	3	1		West	6
Lebanon	49	U.S.	1975	HIS	A	24	7	40%	7	Dem	5	35	5	3	1		West	9
Lebanon	40	NATO	1975	HIS	A	27	6	60%	6	Dem	3	2	5	5			West	7
Lebanon	33	Lebanon	1975	HIS	A	28	6	90%	5	Dem	2	15	2	5	12	250	West	5
Lebanon	8	Israel	1975	HIS	A	41	7	80%	6	Dem	5	30	5	5	4		West	8
Lebanon	27	Armenians	1975	HIS	B	30	6	80%	5	Jun	3	25	4	3	1		West	2
Lebanon	65	Iran	1975	HIS	B	21	6	40%	7	OPDic	4	1	2	5			Russia	5
Lebanon	28	Phalange	1975	HIS	B	30	6	80%	5	Jun	5	15	2	5	40		West	4
Lebanon	76	PLO	1975	HIS	B	19	5	60%	5	Jun	3	15	5	4	15		Russia	3
Lebanon	32	Shiites	1975	HIS	B	28	5	90%	5	Jun	4	18	2	5	5		Russia	1
Lebanon	18	Druse	1975	HIS	B	33	6	90%	5	Jun	5	18	4	3	60		West	9
Lebanon	89	Russia	1975	HIS	B	16	6	30%	7	Soc	4	2	4	3			Russia	3
Lebanon	19	Sunnites	1975	HIS	B	33	6	90%	5	Jun	4	5	4	5	50		Russia	3
Libya	79	Egypt	1945	TIH	A	17	5	40%	5	OP	4	300	2	3	1		West	8
Libya	45	Libya	1945	TIH	A	26	7	60%	7	MDic	3	60	2	2	2		Russia	8
Libya	101	Sudan	1945	TIH	B	12	5	50%	4	OP	3	58	3	2	5		West	7
Malaysia	113	Malaysia	1968	I	A	11	3	75%	4	Dem	4	80	3	5	3		West	6
Malaysia	169	Insurgents	1968	I	B	3	1	55%	5	Dic	5	5	3	5	8		Russia	3
Malta	172	Malta	1980	TH	A	3	5	10%	5	Dem	4	3	3	5	0		West	6
Malta	90	Libya	1980	TH	B	16	7	30%	6	Dic	5	60	3	5	0		Russia	5
Maranon	162	Ecuador	1945	TH	A	4	6	50%	1	Dem	3	45	2	3	0		West	1
Maranon	176	Peru	1945	TH	B	3	4	40%	1	Dem	3	100	3	3			West	1
Middle East	4	Israel	1948	TIH	A	48	8	70%	8	Dem	4	400	5	3	1		West	8
Middle East	87	U.S.	1948	TIH	A	16	8	20%	8	Dem	5	110	4	4	1		West	9
Middle East	122	Lebanon	1948	TIH	B	9	5	30%	5	Dem	1	35	2	1	1		West	6
Middle East	50	Jordan	1948	TIH	B	24	7	40%	7	Mon	4	80	4	1	1		West	6
Middle East	11	Iraq	1948	TIH	A	36	8	60%	7	OPDic	4	25	3	3	1		Russia	7
Middle East	3	Syria	1948	TIH	B	48	8	70%	8	OPDic	3	200	2	2	4		Russia	8
Middle East	66	Egypt	1948	TIH	B	21	8	30%	7	OP	3	400	3	5	1		West	8
Mozambique	46	Cuba	1975	SI	A	26	6	70%	5	Dic	5	1	3	5	1		Russia	9
Mozambique	80	Mozambique	1975	SI	A	17	5	70%	4	OP	3	28	2	3	5		Russia	6
Mozambique	140	Insurgents	1975	SI	A	6	4	60%	4	Jun	3	10	2	5	12		West	2
Nagaland	170	India	1956	SI	A	3	3	85%	3	Dem	3	30	5	4	4		West	4
Nagaland	156	Insurgents	1956	SI	B	4	1	77%	4	Jun	5	8	5	5	12	100	West	2

Country	No.	Party	A/B	Year	Type			%		Gov					Aid	Bloc	
Namibia	47	S. Africa	A	1966	SI	26	6	87%	4	Dem/Dic	4	40	5	5	8	250	West	2
Namibia	88	Insurgents	B	1966	SI	16	3	85%	5	Jun	5	10	3	5	2	150	Russia	4
Nicaragua	20	Nicaragua	A	1981	I	33	5	90%	6	OPJun	3	50	2	5	5		Russia	9
Nicaragua	93	Cuba	B	1981	I	15	6	40%	5	Dic	5	4	3	5	1		West	8
Nicaragua	67	Insurgents	B	1981	I	21	4	70%	6	Jun	2	10	5	5	5		Russia	9
Ogaden	23	Cuba	A	1964	THS	31	6	70%	6	Dic	3	2	3	5	3		Russia	9
Ogaden	10	Ethiopia	A	1964	THS	39	6	87%	6	MDic	3	80	2	5	15		Russia	9
Ogaden	81	Insurgents	B	1964	THS	17	4	70%	5	Jun	4	10	3	5	16		West	4
Somalia	41	Somalia	B	1964	THS	27	4	90%	6	OPDic	3	100	3	2	25	2,000	West	3
Oman-U.A.E.	102	U.A.E.	A	1945	T	12	5	40%	5	Mon	3	25	2	4	1		West	3
Oman-U.A.E.	123	Oman	B	1945	T	9	5	30%	5	Mon	3	20	3	3	6		West	2
Pakistan	141	Pakistan	A	1972	SI	6	5	90%	1	Jun	4	500	4	5	3		West	8
Pakistan	100	Insurgents	B	1972	SI	13	3	70%	5	Jun	4	12	2	5	3		Russia	3
Pal Lib Org	107	Arafat	A	1983	I	12	2	70%	7	Jun	3	8	2	3	3	4	Russia	3
Pal Lib Org	116	Insurgents	B	1983	I	10	2	60%	7	Jun	2	10	2	5	1		Russia	6
Persian Gulf	104	Qatar	A	1945	TIH	12	5	50%	4	Mon	3	20	3	5	1		West	7
Persian Gulf	103	U.A.E.	A	1945	TIH	12	5	50%	4	Mon	3	25	3	4	1		West	7
Persian Gulf	9	Saudi	A	1945	TIH	41	5	60%	8	Mon	3	50	3	3	1		West	9
Persian Gulf	105	Bahrain	A	1945	TIH	12	5	50%	5	Mon	2	3	5	2	1		West	8
Persian Gulf	52	U.S.	A	1945	TIH	24	8	30%	8	Dem	5	45	4	4	1		West	9
Persian Gulf	5	Iran	B	1945	TIH	47	8	60%	8	OPDic	4	200	3	1	2		Russia	3
Peru	148	Peru	A	1980	R	4	4	90%	1	Dem	3	40	3	5	1		West	5
Peru	114	Insurgents	B	1980	R	11	3	75%	4	Dic	5	3	3	5			Russia	5
Philippines	142	Philippines	A	1972	SIR	6	5	90%	1	OPDic	3	60	3	4	50		West	4
Philippines	166	Marxists	B	1972	SIR	3	1	70%	4	Jun	5	5	5	5	5		Russia	5
Philippines	177	Moros	B	1972	SIR	3	3	80%	1	Jun	5	12	5	5	150		Russia	2
Poland	38	Russia	A	1980	IH	28	8	40%	8	Soc	4	800	4	5	0		Russia	9
Poland	82	Poland	A	1980	IH	17	5	40%	7	Soc	3	300	3	5	1		Russia	9
Poland	185	Workers	B	1980	IH	2	1	20%	7	Soc	3	1	4	1	1		West	4
Saudi Arabia	63	Saudi	A	1945	IS	21	4	85%	5	Mon	4	50	3	2	2		West	9
Saudi Arabia	152	Insurgents	B	1945	IS	4	1	65%	5	Jun	4	1	2	5	1		Russia	1
Sino-India	186	China	A	1962	T	2	7	20%	7	Dem	4	250	4	4	2	0	West	2
Sino-India	187	China	B	1962	T	2	7	20%	7	Dem	4	250	4	4	2	0	West	2
Sino-Soviet	151	China	A	1945	ITH	4	9	15%	8	OP	4	3,000	3	4	2		West	6
Sino-Soviet	24	Russia	A	1945	ITH	30	9	30%	9	Soc	4	500	5	5	2		Russia	9
Sino-Vietn	51	China	A	1979	TIH	24	7	40%	7	OP	4	700	3	4	60		Russia	3
Sino-Vietn	163	Vietnam	B	1979	TIH	4	2	30%	5	Soc	4	400	4	4	40		Russia	8
So Africa	34	S. Africa	A	1975	R	28	5	90%	5	Dem/Dic	5	66	5	5	1		West	4
So Africa	167	Insurgents	B	1975	R	3	1	70%	4	Jun	4	5	3	3	3	50	Russia	4
So China Sea	124	Vietnam	A	1945	TH	9	5	30%	5	Soc	4	10	4	2	1		Russia	6

THE WORLD IN CONFLICT

Conflict	Rank	Side		Began	Type	Dngr Lvl	Int	Prob	Esc	Gov Form	Gov Sta	Combata	Qual	Endur	Losses	Refugees	Super	Supt
Averages & Totals....						16	5	62%	5		4	26,964		4	50,812	48,929		
So China Sea	75	China	B	1945	TH	19	6	50%	5	OP	4	20	3	4	1		West	2
Sudan	91	Sudan	A	1983	ISH	16	3	70%	6	OP	3	58	2	5	50	0	West	7
Sudan	126	Insurgents	B	1983	ISH	9	2	60%	6	Jun	3	3	3	5	250	100	Russia	2
Suriname	129	Suriname	A	1980	R	8	2	85%	4	Dic	3	8	2	3	0		Russia	5
Suriname	168	Insurgents	B	1980	R	3	1	70%	4	Jun	3	1	4	3	1		West	3
Syria	35	Syria	A	1975	SI	28	5	90%	5	Soc	4	235	3	4	5		Russia	9
Syria	115	Russia	A	1975	SI	11	6	30%	5	Dic	4	6	5	4	5		Russia	9
Syria	132	Insurgents	B	1975	SI	7	2	60%	5	Jun	5	5	4	5	20		West	2
Tacna-Arica	182	Chile	A	1945	TH	2	6	30%	1	MJun	4	3	3	3	0		West	1
Tacna-Arica	181	Peru	A	1945	TH	2	6	30%	1	Dem	3	3	2	3	0		West	1
Tacna-Arica	178	Bolivia	C	1945	TH	3	6	40%	1	Dem	1	2	4	5	2		West	1
Thailand	84	Thailand	A	1965	RSH	17	4	85%	4	MJun	4	200	2	5	2		West	7
Thailand	120	Insurgents	B	1965	RSH	10	2	80%	5	Jun	4	9	4	3	5		Russia	4
Timor	143	Indonesia	A	1975	SI	6	5	90%	1	Dic	4	250	2	5	400	200	West	2
Timor	184	Insurgents	B	1975	SI	2	5	75%	1	Jun	3	50	3	3	50		Russia	3
U.S.-Soviet	68	Russia	A	1945	ITH	20	9	20%	9	Soc	4	2,000	4	4	1		Russia	9
U.S.-Soviet	119	U.S.	B	1945	ITH	10	9	10%	9	Dem	5	1,500	5	4	1		West	9
Uganda	149	Uganda	A	1979	SHIR	4	1	90%	1	Jun	2	10	1	3	12	200	West	4
Uganda	191	Insurgents	B	1979	SHIR	1	1	80%	1	Jun	1	6	1	3	60		Russia	2
Ulster	144	Britain	A	1969	HSR	6	5	90%	5	Dem	5	14	5	5	2		West	6
Ulster	130	Insurgents	B	1969	HSR	8	2	85%	4	Jun	3	1	4	5	2		Russia	2
Vietnam	36	Vietnam	A	1945	I	28	5	90%	5	Soc	3	400	4	5	4,000	5,000	Russia	8
Vietnam	183	Insurgents	B	1945	I	2	1	85%	1	Jun	3	12	4	5	2,000		West	3
We. Sahara	72	Morocco	A	1975	SI	20	5	80%	4	Mon	4	75	4	5	100		West	8
We. Sahara	99	Insurgents	B	1975	SI	13	3	90%	4	Jun	4	10	4	5	150	80	Russia	5
West Irian	146	Indonesia	A	1969	S	5	3	85%	1	Dic	4	200	5	5	1		Russia	2
West Irian	180	Insurgents	B	1969	S	2	2	90%	1	Jun	2	50	3	5	12		Russia	1
Yemen	157	N. Yemen	A	1972	TI	4	5	10%	6	OP	3	50	3	4	3		West	2
Yemen	158	S. Yemen	B	1972	TI	4	5	10%	6	OPDic	4	75	3	4	3		Russia	2
Yugoslavia	92	Yugoslavia	A	1945	SHT	15	1	50%	5	OPJun	3	4	5	5	1		West	6
Yugoslavia	164	Moslems	B	1945	SHT	4	1	60%	5	Jun	5	2	2	2	1		Russia	1
Yugoslavia	189	Croats	B	1945	SHT	1	1	30%	4	Jun	3	2	2	2	1		Russia	3
Yugoslavia	121	Albanians	A	1945	SHT	10	2	80%	5	Jun	4	2	2	2	1		Russia	1
Yugoslavia	179	Macedonians	B	1945	SHT	2	1	40%	5	Jun	3	2	2	2	1		Russia	2
Yugoslavia	192	Serbs	B	1945	SHT	1	1	20%	4	Dic	3	2	2	5	1		Russia	2
Zaire	58	Zaire	A	1978	RSI	22	4	90%	5	Dic	3	3	3	3	8		West	7
Zaire	106	Insurgents	B	1978	RSI	12	5	40%	5	Jun	3	3	3	3	8		Russia	4
Zimbabwe	37	Zimbabwe	A	1981	I	28	5	90%	5	OP	3	60	4	4	2		West	3
Zimbabwe	127	Insurgents	B	1981	I	9	2	70%	5	Jun	5	1	3	5	3		West	1

Burma—Although there is no unity among the dozen diverse ethnic and political groups in rebellion against Burma, their persistence has foiled all government efforts at putting an end to the long struggle.

Cabinda—The externally supported insurrection against the Angolan regime appears to be quite durable, if low level, and seems likely to continue for some time. Oddly, this struggle finds United States economic interests (oil fields in the Cabinda district) being protected by Cuban troops from a threat posed by an American friend, Zaire.

Cambodia—Vietnam has been unable to stamp out Cambodian resistance despite overwhelming military superiority. The recent formation of a shaky national front among the royalist, rightist, and Khmer Rouge movements may lead to an escalation in a war that Vietnam is not economically capable of supporting. This one is likely to drag on for some time and will probably intensify.

Central America—See chapter.

Chad—The seesaw conflict in Chad will probably continue unabated, with the government holding its own in the southern reaches only through considerable French and Zairian aid, while Libya maintains over 10,000 men in the northern areas it claims as a result of a treaty between Fascist Italy and Vichy France and uses this force to support 3,000 combat troops actively in the field with the Libyan-backed Chad rebels. No solution appears in sight and escalation is probable. Meanwhile, the virtual partitioning of the country, coupled with Qaddafi's Pan-Islamic and revolutionary aspirations, poses a potential threat for Nigeria with its populous, ethnically diverse, and Moslem north. In 1983 Nigerian patrol boats on Lake Chad were attacked by Libyan-backed Chadian rebels.

China—The fifty-year-old Chinese civil war is not yet over, and both sides maintain significant armed forces. The Communists occupy mainland China, while the Nationalists hold the island of Taiwan. Neither side is strong enough to invade the other. Major disorder in China could bring the Nationalists back. Stranger things have happened in China, and the Communists are now preaching the Nationalists' capitalist doctrines. Stay tuned.

Colombia—While the Colombian government has drastically reduced the death rate and the scale of a persistent insurrection by a broad spectrum of loosely affiliated groups, the long war has shown little evidence of ending, but not much of growing. However, recent contacts between the government and rebels suggest that a peaceful solution may be in the offing. Meanwhile, there is evidence that some of the rebels have been trading in their principles for a share of the lucrative United States cocaine market.

Cyprus—Historic ethnic antagonisms on Cyprus have recently been exacerbated by the unilateral Turkish-Cypriot declaration of a federal state. Renewed armed conflict is barely restrained by the presence of about 24,000 Turkish, 4,000 British, and 3,000 UN troops.

Dhofar—Though the Dhofari insurgents suffered a severe defeat in 1975 by Omani, British, and Iranian forces while South Yemeni attentions were focused on Ethiopia, they remain in the field, albeit in greatly reduced numbers, and there is a serious possibility of a revival of the once broadly based insurrection.

El Salvador—See chapter.

Eritrea—The presence of thousands of Cuban troops, plus hundreds of Soviet, East German, and South Yemeni military advisers in the late 1970s, turned what appeared to have been an imminent Eritrean victory into defeat, but various insurgent groups have persisted and remain strong and popular. The recent formation of a national front is likely to intensify the war at a time when Ethiopia is not only hard pressed internally (see Ethiopia and Ogaden), but nearly bankrupt and with little likelihood of securing further lavish Russian infusions of equipment and manpower.

Ethiopia—Approximately ten insurgent movements exist within Ethiopia, ranging from separatists in Tigre and Gojjam, to royalists, to separatists in Eritrea and Ogaden. All of them have been held in check largely by a strong stiffening of Ethiopian forces by Cuban, Soviet, and East German personnel, though none has shown a willingness to quit the field. The chaotic internal situation can continue for some time. Meanwhile, the government appears to be attempting to improve its relations with the West, if evidence of the departure of some Cuban forces is reliable.

Falklands—See chapter.

Guatemala—The insurgency lost considerable ground in the late seventies, but has begun to revive, due partially to a rising level of unrest in Central America as a whole, but primarily to unresolved domestic economic and social problems.

Guyana—Venezuela's claim to about 65 percent of Guyana surfaced in the early stages of the Falklands War. Although little has been heard of this claim since Argentina's humiliating defeat, Venezuela could revive it at any time for domestic political reasons. Should Venezuela choose to press its demands, Suriname, which has a similar claim on portions of eastern Guyana, would most likely be heard from as well.

Haiti—The success of the Duvalier regime in suppressing dissent obscures the enormous problems that plague this most poverty-stricken and repressed state in the Americas. The recent "succession" debate in the country suggests increasing tension, as does the recent need of the Dominican Republic to improve the security of its borders to prevent anti-Duvalier raids being conducted from its territory.

Honduras—This low-level insurgency has enormous potential for growth in a country with a new, shaky democratic government, great economic and social problems, and a serious lack of will or means to interfere with the anti-Sandinista Nicaraguan exile groups on its soil.

India-Pakistan—The Kashmiri question remains unresolved nearly forty years after independence, and there is little love lost between the two nations, which have fought three wars in the same period. Tensions are presently intensified by Indian silence about the Soviet adventure in Afghanistan. Rising Indian concerns about Afghanistan may, however, ultimately reduce tensions between the two countries.

Iran—The fundamentalist Moslem government of Iran is confronted by resistance from a broad range of groups, including Kurds (see below), rightists, monarchists, and leftists, some of whom are receiving aid from Iran's external enemy, Iraq. However, without unity among the insurgents it is doubtful that they can seriously threaten the regime.

Iran-Iraq—See chapter.

Israel-PLO—Israel's massive defeat of the PLO's forces in Lebanon in 1982 dealt that organization a serious military blow. The downfall of Arafat was the most obvious political result. Nevertheless, terrorist and guerrilla activity continues, though at a reduced rate. Internal strains within the PLO may prove more beneficial to Israel in the long run than the invasion of Lebanon. Note: PLO strength figures include about 6,000 to 8,000 in Lebanon; a roughly equal number scattered among other Arab states, most notably Tunisia and North Yemen; and small numbers in Israel itself.

Korea—See chapter.

Kosovo—See Yugoslavia-Albania chapter.

Kurdistan—Long-standing Kurdish grievances sparked a renewal of armed insurgency in Iraq, Iran, and Turkey. The unexpected result was a unique arrangement under which Turkish troops could operate in northern Iraq. Recently, however, contacts between Iraqi and Kurdish leaders appear to have resulted in a truce, so that both sides can better concentrate on coping with Iran.

Laos—Limited royalist and tribal resistance to a Vietnamese-imposed Communist regime appears to continue, with neither side likely to secure victory in the near future. Vietnam's situation is complicated by a major guerrilla war in Cambodia, a small one back home in Vietnam, the necessity of retaining 300,000 men on alert on the Chinese frontier, and internal economic chaos.

Lebanon—See chapter.

Libya—See chapter.

Malaysia—Although no longer representing the major threat to Malaysian stability that it did from 1948 to 1960, the revived Communist insurgency is being viewed with great seriousness by the Federation of Malaysia, which has cooperated with Thailand to coordinate operations against the rebels across their mutual frontier.

Malta—Libyan pipe dreams could cause Qaddafi to make a try for Malta, which would cause Italy, and probably Algeria and Egypt, to intervene. Many thought Libya would not go into Chad. Anything is possible, even likely, while Qaddafi is in power.

Maranon—A historic territorial dispute is kept alive in Ecuador for domestic political consumption and reasons of national pride. It is further complicated by occasional border clashes, with dangerous potential for adventurism.

Middle East—See chapter on Israel and the Middle East.

Mozambique—South African support for antigovernment forces is probably the principal reason they remain in the field, but the mutual economic benefits of "peace" seem to have resulted in the two countries settling their differences. This will probably lead to a collapse of the insurgency in the near future.

Nagaland—India continues to be unable to stamp out a tribal separatist movement that has peculiar links to the Western world through various evangelical Christian groups, and that also occasionally finds support among other minority groups in northeastern India.

Namibia—Negotiations sponsored by interested Western powers to secure Namibian independence from South Africa appear finally to have gone somewhere. An unusual series of recent contacts between South Africa and Angola, the real principals in the struggle, may represent a significant breakthrough in the search for peace. Note: About 50 percent of the South African personnel in Namibia are locally recruited blacks and whites.

Nicaragua—The insurgents are a hodgepodge of former Somozan

troops and disillusioned Sandinista rebels who run the gamut from ultra-rightists to ultra-leftists, plus a sizable dissatisfied Indian population which would probably be in arms against whoever was in power. These groups have not coalesced into a unified front. But they have had a serious effect on the stability of Nicaragua and have been operating both internally and from secure bases in Honduras and Costa Rica, with American blessings even though Congress has become increasingly reluctant to continue funding covert activities there. The insurgency is regarded with great concern by the Nicaraguan revolutionary government, which has made apparently conciliatory gestures toward the rebels and, more particularly, United States opinion. The situation remains, however, potentially one of the most explosive current conflicts.

Ogaden—Despite defeat in open war in 1977–1978, the Somali insurgency in the Ogaden persists. This has created an enormous refugee problem for neighboring Somalia, which may be at the root of recent Somali efforts to seek a negotiated settlement with Ethiopia, itself experiencing pressing problems internally and in Eritrea. Nevertheless, tensions remain high and could spark a renewal of open warfare between the two states to reaffirm or reverse Somalia's defeat in the field in 1979.

Oman-UAE—An old territorial dispute exacerbated by the efforts of the Sheik of Ras al-Khaimah, one of the emirs of the United Arab Emirates, to expand his territorial base, complicated by Iranian interests in Oman and the Persian Gulf.

Pakistan—The Pakistani government has been increasingly troubled by various tribal and political insurgencies. Baluchistan is a particular focus of unrest. Although at present the government seems capable of coping with the situation, the potential for a more serious problem remains high.

PLO-PLO—The internal split in the PLO has resulted in open warfare between pro- and anti-Arafat supporters. Having been forced to abandon his base in Lebanon for the safer atmosphere of Tunisia, Arafat appears in a precarious situation. Since Syria threw its weight behind the insurgent PLO elements, it is likely that this branch will end up as an instrument of Syrian ambitions.

Persian Gulf—See chapter.

Peru—This small-scale insurgency has been receiving increasing attention and the government has begun to take it very seriously. Although the rebels, mostly middle- and upper-class Maoist romantics, appear to have made little headway among the rural Indians, the latter are fertile ground on which to base a major insurgency. Note: There is evidence that the rebels are attempting to establish themselves in Colombia.

Philippines—See chapter.

Poland—The Polish government's success at suppressing dissent has lessened the possibility of Soviet action, but renewed calls for reform or a weakening of the military regime could touch off an invasion, particularly if Soviet domestic political problems become enmeshed with the Polish question.

Saudi Arabia—Strong religious and ethnic tensions mar the facade of stability and unity maintained by the Saudi regime, as revealed most recently by the 1979 assault on Mecca.

Sino-Indian—Although the frontier between the two Asian giants has been quiet for over twenty years, tensions still run high and each has informally associated itself with one of the superpowers in virtually all significant international issues. While a revival of open warfare is unlikely, it is not impossible, given the widely different political and diplomatic aims of both powers.

Sino-Soviet—Longstanding territorial and ideological disputes have been cooling recently, but a serious potential for war exists, particularly in the event of a Vietnamese disaster in a Sino-Vietnamese confrontation.

Sino-Vietnamese—Repetitions of the brief week's fighting in the spring of 1983 are likely, though a full-scale war is improbable but not impossible.

South Africa—See chapter, Boer Wars.

South China Sea—The scent of oil in the Paracels and other islands has China, Vietnam, and maybe the Philippines squaring off for a possible violent resolution of their differences.

Sudan—After nearly a dozen years of relative peace, a series of ill-advised decisions by the Nimeiry government (imposition of Islamic law and reorganization of provincial boundaries in violation of a 1972 "peace" agreement) has brought the southern Christian and animist separatists into open conflict again. The Anyanya II Movement has scored some recent successes in the field, and apparently is receiving material support from Libya and Ethiopia, while the government leans heavily on Egypt and the United States.

Suriname—See chapter.

Syria—Internal resistance to the Assad Alawite regime has been relatively low since 10,000 actual and suspected rebels were killed in Hama in 1982, but the revival of more serious resistance is highly possible in a country ruled by a minority comprising 15 percent of the population.

Tacna-Arica—A territorial dispute dating to Chile's victory in 1879–1884 is dusted off regularly for domestic political consumption and occasionally aired internationally by Peru and Bolivia.

Thailand—The government appears to have turned the corner in its efforts to suppress a persistent Communist insurgency. This is because of success in the field and in meeting the social and political needs of its people, friendlier links with China, and, paradoxically, the Communist take-over of Cambodia, which presented a particularly unpleasant example of a "worker's paradise" in action. Cooperation with Malaysia in conducting antiguerrilla operations along their mutual frontier has been of critical importance as well. Efforts against the private armies of various drug lords remain frustratingly inconclusive, however, and there also appears to be Libyan-sponsored unrest among the country's tiny Moslem minority.

Timor—Although perhaps the most poorly reported insurgency in the world, the anti-Indonesian movement on Timor seems to be surviving despite genocidal countermeasures, though it is not likely to achieve significant success either militarily or politically.

US-Soviet—While the danger of war between the superpowers is hardly as imminent as is generally believed, a very real possibility of war exists.

Uganda—The government has had some success in resolving the anarchy existing since the overthrow of Idi Amin, but many revolutionary, local, and tribal armies control important areas, and, like the regular army itself, they are virtually indistinguishable from the numerous bandit gangs that also infest the bush.

Ulster—There does not appear to be any solution in sight, since neither side is willing to undertake serious negotiations and neither is capable of securing victory.

Vietnam—A small-scale but persistent insurgency by remnants of the ARVN complicates Vietnam's internal situation, already suffering from economic disaster, the necessity of maintaining armies in Cambodia and Laos, and the threat of renewed war with China, thereby contributing to the overall difficulty of solving any one of the problems.

Western Sahara—Moroccan resources have been strained in the war with the Polisario insurgents, but they maintain control over the most valuable portions of the largely desert region, leaving the bulk of the territory, but little wealth and few people, to the rebels. The only significant threat to Moroccan control is the unlikelihood of the rebels securing open assistance from regular forces of their Algerian sponsors. Meanwhile, the possibility of a peaceful settlement has been improving.

West Irian—The persistent tribal resistance to Indonesian control is likely to go on for some time with neither side gaining any significant advantage. Although the war complicates Indonesian relations with Papua-New Guinea, there is little possibility of conflict between the two despite occasional border violations.

Yemen—Skirmishing on the long frontier between the ideologically hostile regimes of North Yemen and South Yemen is frequent, with a more serious conflict only a slight possibility.

Yugoslavia—See Yugoslavia-Kosovo chapter.

Zaire—See chapter.

Zimbabwe—Dissatisfied with postindependence political developments, a portion of the former anti-Rhodesian forces have taken to the field once more in opposition to the existing government. Although confined to terrorist actions at present, the insurgents may expand their activities, capitalizing on tribal differences, particularly if the regulars of the Zimbabwean Army operate with little discrimination against suspects. All of the foregoing may work in South Africa's favor.

LOW-LEVEL WARS

Here is a list of low-level wars that at the moment are being dealt with by domestic police forces. In the chart the "target" country is used as the name of the conflict. Some of the groups are not active in the target country, but operate against its officials and diplomats and even against third parties in other countries. Some of these movements are fronts for groups wishing to embarrass particular nations, rather than genuinely indigenous movements. At least one is based on a nonexistent ethnic minority.

Argentina: Leftist insurgents
Chile: Leftists
China: Tibetan separatists
Costa Rica: Leftist insurgents
France: Basque separatists, Bretons, Corsicans, Spanish anti-Basque activists, West Indian separatists
India: Mezo, Sikhs
Indonesia: Holy War commandos, South Moluccans
Italy: Red Brigades

Lesotho: Lesotho Liberation Army
Netherlands: South Moluccans
Portugal: Ultra-leftist insurgents
Soviet Union: Armenians, others?
Spain: Basques, Catalans, "Canary Islands Liberation Front,"
    Maoists
Turkey: Armenians, rightists, leftists
United States: Puerto Rican nationalists, rightists, leftists
Yugoslavia: Albanians, Croatians, Macedonians, and other nation-
    alists
Venezuela: Leftists

We can add countries that are involved in assassination-level wars.

Bulgaria: Assassination against exiled dissidents
Libya: Against exiled dissidents
Iran: Against exiled dissidents
North Korea: Against South Korean governmental officials and
    businessmen
South Africa: Against exiled dissidents
Russia: Against the Polish pope

SOME OBSERVATIONS ON THE POTENTIAL FOR VIOLENT POLITICAL ACTION: THE UNITED STATES AS A CASE IN POINT

In the chart we have attempted to indicate the places where war is likely to occur. But predicting wars is not an exact science. The potential for the large-scale, politically motivated violence called war exists in every society. A good example is the United States of America. Below is a list of *possible* foci for war or warlike action involving the United States. We are not suggesting that there is a high probability of any of the situations leading to war, but rather that a possibility does exist, however small, of an armed clash over the matters. Indeed, such clashes have occurred already on a small scale in the disputes marked with an asterisk.

Alaskan Secessionist Movement
American Indians*
The American Nazi Party*

Anarcho-Libertarian Political Movements*
Animal Rights Movement*
Antiabortion Movement*
Antinuclear-Power Movement*
Black American Revolutionary-Separatist Movements*
California-Arizona Water Rights Dispute
California-Nevada Boundary Dispute
California "Water Wars"*
Drug Lords*
Ethnic and Racial Minority Group Internal Disputes*
Hawaiian Nativist Movement
The KKK and Other Nativist Movements*
Mexican-American Secessionist-Irredentist Movements*
Pro- and Anti-Gay Rights Movements*
Puerto Rican Independence Movement*
Religious Cults*
Texas Secessionist Movement
Ultra-leftist Political Groups*
United States-Canadian Fisheries Disputes
United States-Ecuadorian Fisheries Disputes
United States-Secessionist Movement
Ultra-leftist Political Groups*
United States-Colombian Claims to Caribbean Islets
Virgin Islands Separatist Movement*

Neither should it be forgotten that the annual number of murders in the United States, currently more than 20,000, exceeds the combined annual death toll of most of the wars in the world, and that motor-vehicle-related deaths run about 50,000.

REGIONAL SUMMARY

A summary by region of The World in Conflict chart is shown below. It is readily apparent that Asia is the bloodiest region and the Middle East the most volatile. Africa is also dangerous, but most wars there are not likely to escalate to major significance. Europe, on which most of the world's military budget and attention are focused, is the most peaceful of the regions.

One conclusion that we can reach by looking at this chart is that World War III has been going on for some time now. The casualties

REGIONAL SUMMARY

	#	Dngr Indices Lvl	Int	Prob	Esc	Sta	Combatants	Qual	Endur	Losses	Refugees
Asia	38	11	4.7	57%	3.9	3.9	12,977	3.7	4.4	46,781	36,050
Middle East	56	23	5.2	65%	5.6	3.7	5,336	3.4	4.1	2,632	5,874
Africa	45	19	4.7	69%	4.7	3.6	1,753	2.7	4.3	993	6,030
Americas	33	12	4.7	61%	3.5	3.2	984	2.6	3.9	387	900
Europe	20	8	3.3	48%	4.9	3.6	5,915	4.2	3.2	20	75
	192						26,964			50,812	48,929

MOST DANGEROUS WARS

Rank	Conflict	Side	Began	Type	Dngr Indices Lvl	Int	Prob	Esc
Averages & Totals....					16	5	62%	5
1	Iran-Iraq	Iran	1980	THI	B 71	8	90%	8
2	Iran-Iraq	Iraq	1980	THI	A 54	7	90%	7
3	Middle East	Israel	1948	TIH	A 48	8	70%	7
4	Middle East	Syria	1948	TIH	B 48	8	70%	7
5	Persian Gulf	Iran	1945	TIH	B 47	8	60%	8
6	Afghanistan	Russia	1978	IH	A 47	7	90%	6
7	Lebanon	Israel	1975	HIS	A 41	7	80%	6
8	Lebanon	Syria	1975	HIS	A 41	7	80%	6
9	Persian Gulf	Saudi	1945	TIH	A 41	7	60%	8
10	Ogaden	Ethiopia	1964	THS	B 39	6	87%	6
11	Middle East	Iraq	1948	TIH	B 36	7	80%	5
12	Cambodia	Vietnam	1978	HI	A 35	7	80%	5
13	Kurdistan	Iran	1979	SH	B 35	5	80%	7
14	El Salvador	Insurgents	1979	IR	B 33	6	90%	5
15	Eritrea	Ethiopia	1961	SHI	A 33	6	90%	5

from all wars (including the few that have actually ended) exceed 50 million dead, wounded, and missing. The number of refugees exceeds that created during World War II, and the cost of the wars of the last forty years has more than matched the horrendous expense of World Wars I and II combined.

BAITING THE BEAR

Usually the Western press gives short shrift to the guerrilla wars that plague Moscow. Here's a list of the major insurgencies and, in some cases, outright wars that bother the Russians.

BAITING THE BEAR

Conflict	Rank	Side		Began	Type	Dngr Lvl	Indices Int	Prob	Esc
Averages & Totals....						16	5	62%	5
Afghanistan	1	Russia	A	1978	IH	47	7	90%	6
Ogaden	2	Ethiopia	A	1964	THS	39	6	87%	6
Eritrea	3	Ethiopia	A	1961	SHI	33	6	90%	5
Ethiopia	4	Ethiopia	A	1974	ISH	33	6	90%	5
Nicaragua	5	Nicaragua	A	1981	I	33	5	90%	6
Ogaden	6	Cuba	A	1964	THS	31	6	70%	6
Sino-Soviet	7	Russia	B	1945	ITH	30	9	30%	9
Syria	8	Syria	A	1975	SI	28	5	90%	5
Poland	9	Russia	A	1980	IH	28	8	40%	7
Mozambique	10	Cuba	A	1975	SI	26	6	70%	5
Ethiopia	11	Cuba	A	1974	ISH	26	6	70%	5
Eritrea	12	Cuba	A	1961	SHI	26	6	70%	5
Cabinda	13	Cuba	A	1975	SI	22	6	60%	5
Angola	14	Cuba	A	1975	I	22	6	60%	5
Angola	15	Angola	A	1975	I	22	5	70%	5
U.S.-Soviet	16	Russia	A	1945	ITH	20	9	20%	9

17. The Ability of the World's Nations to Wage War

Nations go to war for a variety of reasons. One of the more mundane, and critical, is a country's physical ability to wage war. Lacking the physical means, all the rhetoric and spleen of an enraged populace will not get an effective war going. To make this factor more obvious, and to illuminate current war-making capabilities, we have prepared a Nations of the World chart showing geographic, economic, population, and military statistics for all those countries capable in theory of military action. It will demonstrate rather starkly who can, and to what extent, wage war.

Information has been culled from many sources and is as accurate as possible. Many nations were either not forthcoming about the data or were simply ignorant concerning many of the numbers we collected for these charts. To avoid problems with corrupted data, we placed all of them in a computer model (utilizing the 123 spreadsheet program). By using formulas to generate additional data and sorting information to line up various categories by nation, we were able to smoke out many of the inconsistencies.

TERMS AND ABBREVIATIONS

The strength values shown demonstrate the relative combat power of nations. In a war these strengths can be modified greatly by surprise and superior strategy. Generally, the more powerful armed forces will prevail. This is particularly true if a relatively weaker power attacks a stronger neighbor. Examples of this are Germany in both world wars, Japan in 1941–1945 and Iraq in 1980.

NATIONS OF THE WORLD: REGIONAL AND BLOC SUMMARY

Averages & Totals	War State	Allies	Gov Stab	War Pwr	Atck Pwr	Long War Pwr	Tot Qual	Nukes	% Off	Area 1000 KmSq	Agr	Grz	For	Othr
	1.7	5.9	5.8	6,083	3,255	7,337	6.8	2.4	23%	132,278	21	16	27	33
National Summary										**Geographic Profile**				
Western Bloc	1.8	8.1	7.4	2,539	1,623	3,683	15	4	39%	47,609	21	16	27	34
Eastern Bloc	2.7	2.5	5.8	1,551	1,032	1,500	12	3	32%	28,742	27	14	30	26
Neutrals	1.7	5.8	5.8	1,993	600	2,154	5	2	18%	55,927	19	12	29	34
NATO	1.4	8.3	8.1	1,170	736	1,819	21	5	47%	3,396	31	20	23	25
NATO (w/o US)	1.3	8.0	7.9	898	472	1,432	17	4	41%	2,804	32	23	20	24
Warsaw Pact	1.7	2.3	6.8	679	472	683	18	5	44%	12,080	44	13	27	16
Russia	4.0	1.0	7.0	1,000	800	699	26	9	80%	22,401	10	17	35	38
On Russian Border	3.0	6.0	7.1	1,041	349	851	20	5	33%	13,704	18	5	28	49
Russian Enemies	2.4	6.2	7.5	1,570	598	1,601	22	4	33%	14,742	20	10	32	38
United States	2.0	9.0	9.0	820	656	724	38	9	80%	9,363	20	26	32	22
Pacific Allies	1.4	8.7	7.9	601	361	1,018	25	5	52%	16,449	17	23	33	23
Percentage Analysis														
Western Bloc	1%	37%	28%	42%	50%	50%	127%	58%	67%	36%	1%	0%	0%	4%
Eastern Bloc	55%	-58%	1%	26%	32%	20%	72%	16%	39%	22%	30%	-13%	11%	-21%
Neutrals	0%	42%	40%	33%	18%	29%	-21%	-9%	-22%	42%	-9%	-24%	7%	4%
NATO	-18%	42%	36%	19%	23%	25%	209%	94%	104%	3%	46%	30%	-14%	-26%
NATO (w/o US)	-26%	36%	36%	15%	15%	20%	152%	61%	74%	2%	50%	45%	-26%	-27%
Warsaw Pact	-4%	-60%	18%	11%	14%	9%	168%	95%	90%	9%	106%	-16%	-1%	-51%
Russia	129%	-83%	21%	16%	25%	10%	286%	277%	244%	17%	-53%	8%	29%	15%
On Russian Border	72%	2%	23%	17%	11%	12%	194%	91%	41%	10%	-16%	-65%	17%	48%
Russian Enemies	35%	5%	29%	26%	18%	22%	218%	86%	42%	11%	-7%	-34%	17%	15%
United States	15%	54%	55%	13%	20%	10%	463%	277%	244%	7%	-6%	66%	18%	-34%
Pacific Allies	-17%	48%	36%	10%	11%	14%	267%	95%	125%	12%	-21%	46%	21%	-31%
Africa	1.6	5.9	4.5	89	32	325	3	1	8%	20,959	21	20	25	30
Americas	1.9	6.3	6.3	949	694	1,162	6	4	24%	39,757	15	20	37	28
Europe	1.4	6.1	7.5	2,565	1,527	3,178	18	4	36%	28,064	32	19	27	22
Middle East	2.5	6.1	5.7	708	350	803	11	2	29%	13,653	15	7	4	75
South Asia	2.0	5.3	5.6	403	119	393	8	2	15%	5,821	32	4	29	31
Southeast Asia	2.0	6.2	6.7	1,369	533	1,477	15	3	35%	24,024	14	10	44	22
Percentage Analysis														
Africa	-8.0%	.0%	-22.5%	1.5%	1.0%	4.4%	-57%	-48%	-67%	15.8%	-2%	28%	-8%	-10%
Americas	8.2%	7.4%	8.7%	15.6%	21.3%	15.8%	-7%	-7%	3%	30.1%	-28%	26%	37%	-16%
Europe	-22.4%	3.4%	29.2%	42.2%	46.9%	43.3%	159%	58%	56%	21.2%	49%	19%	-2%	-32%
Middle East	40.4%	4.0%	-1.6%	11.6%	10.7%	10.9%	57%	-2%	23%	10.3%	-31%	-54%	-86%	125%
South Asia	14.6%	-9.6%	-3.3%	6.6%	3.7%	5.4%	19%	-8%	-35%	4.4%	52%	-74%	7%	-6%
Southeast Asia	14.6%	6.1%	16.1%	22.5%	16.4%	20.1%	115%	33%	52%	18.2%	-34%	-39%	63%	-34%

NATIONS OF THE WORLD: REGIONAL AND BLOC SUMMARY

Averages & Totals	3.8	5.4	35	4,674	54	42	3.3	12,375	26	4.9	2.6	3.6
			Population Profile				Economic Profile					
	Trans Net	MEI	Pop SqKm	Pop Tot	% Lit	% Urban	% Ind	GDP	% Frgn Trade	% Soc Exp	Per Cap	Qual Life
Western Bloc	6	6	28	1,322	77	64	6	$8,477	39	5	$6.4	6
Eastern Bloc	4	5	19	545	69	41	4	$1,989	14	3	$3.6	3
Neutrals	3	5	50	2,807	47	35	3	$1,910	22	3	$0.7	3
NATO	7	6	109	369	93	70	7	$3,596	23	6	$9.8	8
NATO (w/o US)	7	6	111	312	94	69	7	$2,210	24	5	$7.1	8
Warsaw Pact	6	4	20	240	98	60	7	$1,171	13	7	$4.9	8
Russia	4	7	12	272	98	62	7	$1,450	5	7	$5.3	4
On Russian Border	5	4	94	1,294	62	46	5	$1,641	18	5	$1.3	5
Russian Enemies	5	5	95	1,395	73	53	6	$2,528	20	6	$1.8	6
United States	9	3	25	234	99	74	9	$3,400	12	15	$14.5	9
Pacific Allies	7	5	15	254	92	74	7	$2,389	34	5	$9.4	7
Percentage Analysis												
Western Bloc	51%	5%	-21%	28%	44%	52%	69%	68%	46%	8%	142%	74%
Eastern Bloc	9%	0%	-46%	12%	28%	-1%	28%	16%	-47%	-29%	38%	-6%
Neutrals	-15%	-5%	42%	60%	-13%	-17%	-21%	15%	-17%	-4%	-74%	-14%
NATO	86%	4%	207%	8%	74%	66%	117%	18%	-13%	29%	268%	120%
NATO (w/o US)	85%	5%	215%	7%	75%	64%	107%	9%	-7%	5%	168%	114%
Warsaw Pact	66%	20%	-44%	5%	83%	44%	114%	12%	-49%	40%	84%	57%
Russia	5%	-26%	-66%	6%	83%	48%	109%	13%	-83%	40%	101%	11%
On Russian Border	19%	-18%	167%	28%	15%	9%	54%	20%	-31%	6%	-52%	42%
Russian Enemies	40%	-11%	168%	30%	37%	26%	77%	27%	-24%	18%	-32%	71%
United States	135%	-45%	-29%	5%	85%	77%	169%	19%	-53%	194%	449%	149%
Pacific Allies	74%	-16%	-56%	5%	71%	77%	123%	19%	28%	9%	255%	100%
Africa	2	5	18	380	23	19	1	$204	23	5	$0.5	1
Americas	4	5	16	641	69	54	4	$4,530	24	6	$7.1	4
Europe	6	6	29	811	93	63	6	$4,993	24	6	$6.2	7
Middle East	4	7	15	206	37	51	2	$507	48	7	$2.5	4
South Asia	3	4	173	1,007	30	26	2	$218	15	3	$0.2	1
Southeast Asia	4	5	68	1,629	67	41	4	$1,923	25	3	$1.2	4
Percentage Analysis												
Africa	-43%	-7%	-49%	8.1%	-57%	-55%	-65%	1.7%	-13%	-4%	-80%	-63%
Americas	-4%	-5%	-54%	13.7%	28%	30%	19%	36.6%	-9%	13%	167%	2%
Europe	69%	7%	-18%	17.4%	74%	50%	91%	40.3%	-10%	15%	132%	89%
Middle East	-6%	32%	-57%	4.4%	-30%	22%	-28%	4.1%	83%	35%	-7%	8%
South Asia	-35%	-13%	390%	21.6%	-44%	-37%	-40%	1.8%	-44%	-48%	-92%	-61%
Southeast Asia	16%	-17%	92%	34.8%	25%	-2%	25%	15.5%	-7%	-46%	-55%	20%

NATIONS OF THE WORLD: REGIONAL AND BLOC SUMMARY

Averages & Totals	Act Men	% Cadre	Mil Bud	% GDP	Bud Man	Bang per $	Bang M/Pop.	Bang T$/GDP	Reserves Men	p/mil	Act %
	28,636	68	757,734	6.1%	26	8.0	1.3	492	28,687	6.1	22
Military Capability											
Western Bloc	8,626	67	$426,373	5.0%	$49	6.0	1.9	299	9,919	7.5	37
Eastern Bloc	7,280	29	$242,782	12.2%	$33	6.4	2.8	780	7,830	14.4	26
Neutrals	12,730	70	$88,579	4.6%	$7	22.5	0.7	1,044	10,938	3.9	29
NATO	3,679	59	$159,706	4.4%	$43	7.3	3.2	325	3,803	10.3	44
NATO (w/o US)	3,702	53	$74,441	3.4%	$20	12.1	2.9	406	3,208	10.3	32
Warsaw Pact	2,906	40	$127,361	10.9%	$44	5.3	2.8	580	3,571	14.9	21
Russia	3,800	22	$214,000	14.8%	$56	4.7	3.7	690	3,800	14.0	5
On Russian Border	5,779	33	$53,173	3.2%	$9	19.6	0.8	634	5,915	4.6	35
Russian Enemies	7,827	35	$77,412	3.1%	$10	20.3	1.1	621	8,900	6.4	42
United States	2,136	100	$255,000	7.5%	$119	3.2	3.5	241	1,074	4.6	73
Pacific Allies	2,179	82	$93,824	3.9%	$43	6.4	2.4	252	3,917	15.4	61
Percentage Analysis											
Western Bloc	30%	-1%	56%	-18%	87%	-26%	48%	-39%	35%	22%	63%
Eastern Bloc	25%	-56%	32%	99%	26%	-20%	119%	59%	27%	134%	18%
Neutrals	44%	4%	12%	-24%	-74%	180%	-45%	112%	38%	-37%	31%
NATO	13%	-13%	21%	-27%	64%	-9%	144%	-34%	13%	68%	95%
NATO (w/o US)	13%	-21%	10%	-45%	-24%	50%	121%	-17%	11%	68%	45%
Warsaw Pact	10%	-40%	17%	78%	66%	-34%	117%	18%	12%	142%	-7%
Russia	13%	-67%	28%	141%	113%	-42%	183%	40%	13%	128%	-78%
On Russian Border	20%	-51%	7%	-47%	-65%	144%	-38%	29%	21%	-26%	56%
Russian Enemies	27%	-49%	10%	-50%	-63%	153%	-14%	26%	31%	4%	89%
United States	7%	48%	34%	-22%	351%	-60%	169%	-51%	4%	-25%	225%
Pacific Allies	8%	21%	12%	-36%	63%	-20%	82%	-49%	14%	151%	173%
Africa	951	80	$8,701	4.3%	$9	10.2	0.2	435	615	1.6	1
Americas	3,538	72	$274,413	6.1%	$78	3.5	1.5	209	3,398	5.3	31
Europe	10,883	51	$338,711	6.8%	$31	7.6	3.2	514	12,064	14.9	34
Middle East	3,327	58	$68,358	13.5%	$21	10.4	3.4	1,397	918	4.5	14
South Asia	1,963	91	$7,975	3.7%	$4	50.5	0.4	1,845	1,179	1.2	40
Southeast Asia	7,975	57	$59,576	3.1%	$7	23.0	0.8	712	10,513	6.5	40
Percentage Analysis											
Africa	3.3%	19%	1.1%	-30%	-65%	27%	-82%	-12%	2.1%	-74%	-95%
Americas	12.4%	6%	36.2%	-1%	193%	-57%	14%	-57%	11.8%	-14%	39%
Europe	38.0%	-24%	44.7%	11%	18%	-6%	143%	5%	42.1%	142%	54%
Middle East	11.6%	-13%	9.0%	120%	-22%	29%	164%	184%	3.2%	-27%	-38%
South Asia	6.9%	35%	1.1%	-40%	-85%	529%	-69%	275%	4.1%	-81%	79%
Southeast Asia	27.8%	-16%	7.9%	-49%	-72%	186%	-35%	45%	36.6%	5%	78%

NATIONS OF THE WORLD: REGIONAL AND BLOC SUMMARY

	Paramilitary Profile		%Pop	Army Profile						Air Force Profile				
	Tot	p/mil	Srv	Ult Men	Men Men	Mbl Divs	Men Div	AFV	Men/ AFV	Mbl Men	Cmbt A/C	Other A/C	Men/ A/C
Averages & Totals	43,502	9.3	2.2%	779,530	47,146	1,681	28.0	360,972	131	5,782	46,848	39,835	67
Western Bloc	12,013	9.1	2.3%	252,070	14,238	403	35	120,695	118	2,720	18,788	23,017	65
Eastern Bloc	12,828	23.5	5.1%	99,030	12,333	521	24	163,370	75	1,760	15,736	7,264	77
Neutrals	18,662	6.6	1.5%	428,430	20,575	757	27	76,907	268	1,302	12,324	9,554	59
NATO	816	2.2	2.2%	74,930	5,582	167	34	63,597	88	1,164	8,023	8,130	72
NATO (w/o US)	1,205	3.9	2.6%	62,810	5,095	141	36	45,320	112	782	4,644	4,153	89
Warsaw Pact	5,265	21.9	4.9%	47,900	5,054	168	30	87,065	58	933	7,904	3,780	80
Russia	5,600	20.6	4.9%	54,800	5,700	220	26	115,000	50	1,100	11,500	3,500	73
On Russian Border	10,887	8.4	1.7%	199,400	10,366	415	25	29,230	355	783	6,642	2,742	83
Russian Enemies	15,418	11.1	2.3%	221,350	14,478	505	29	47,757	303	1,083	8,711	3,957	85
United States	237	1.0	1.5%	50,000	1,600	44	36	31,000	52	1,000	8,700	12,400	52
Pacific Allies	1,411	5.6	3.0%	67,480	5,001	133	38	18,233	274	706	4,465	5,182	73
Percentage Analysis													
Western Bloc	28%	-2%	7%	32%	30%	24%	26%	33%	-10%	47%	40%	58%	-2%
Eastern Bloc	29%	153%	138%	13%	26%	31%	-16%	45%	-42%	30%	34%	18%	15%
Neutrals	43%	-29%	-30%	55%	44%	45%	-3%	21%	105%	23%	26%	24%	-11%
NATO	2%	-76%	4%	10%	12%	8%	20%	18%	-33%	20%	17%	20%	8%
NATO (w/o US)	3%	-58%	21%	8%	11%	8%	29%	13%	-14%	14%	10%	10%	33%
Warsaw Pact	12%	136%	127%	6%	11%	10%	8%	24%	-56%	16%	17%	9%	20%
Russia	13%	121%	125%	7%	12%	13%	-8%	32%	-62%	19%	25%	9%	10%
On Russian Border	25%	-10%	-19%	26%	22%	25%	-11%	8%	172%	14%	14%	7%	25%
Russian Enemies	35%	19%	7%	28%	31%	30%	2%	13%	132%	19%	19%	10%	28%
United States	1%	-89%	-32%	6%	3%	3%	30%	9%	-60%	19%	19%	31%	-22%
Pacific Allies	3%	-40%	37%	9%	11%	8%	34%	5%	110%	12%	10%	13%	10%
Africa	1,331	3.5	0.8%	47,400	1,470	78	19	10,211	144	70	941	1,766	26
Americas	1,971	3.1	1.4%	123,110	4,716	184	26	40,672	116	1,399	10,437	15,634	54
Europe	14,098	17.4	4.6%	164,430	17,764	549	27	213,106	83	2,604	21,146	11,953	79
Middle East	3,656	17.8	3.8%	31,510	3,785	138	32	51,217	74	352	4,199	3,664	45
South Asia	627	0.6	0.4%	157,845	2,896	97	30	6,859	422	165	1,293	1,528	59
Southeast Asia	21,820	13.4	2.5%	255,235	16,516	636	26	38,907	424	1,192	8,832	5,290	84
Percentage Analysis													
Africa	3.1%	-62%	-65%	6.1%	3.1%	4.6%	-32%	2.8%	10%	1.2%	2.0%	4.4%	-61%
Americas	4.5%	-67%	-36%	15.8%	10.0%	10.9%	-8%	11.3%	-11%	24.2%	22.3%	39.2%	-20%
Europe	32.4%	87%	112%	21.1%	37.7%	32.6%	15%	59.0%	-36%	45.0%	45.1%	30.0%	18%
Middle East	8.4%	91%	78%	4.0%	8.0%	8.2%	-2%	14.2%	-43%	6.1%	9.0%	9.2%	-33%
South Asia	1.4%	-93%	-83%	20.2%	6.1%	5.8%	6%	1.9%	223%	2.9%	2.8%	3.8%	-12%
Southeast Asia	50.2%	44%	15%	32.7%	35.0%	37.8%	-7%	10.8%	225%	20.6%	18.9%	13.3%	27%

NATIONS OF THE WORLD: REGIONAL AND BLOC SUMMARY

Type	Navy Profile							Manpower Distribution				
	Mbl Men	Cmbt Ships	Other Ships	Men/Ship	Tons	Tons/Ship	Men/Shp/T	Mbl Men	Incr %	Army %	AF %	Navy %
Averages & Totals	3,387	3,256	6,493	347	18,125	1,859	5.35	57,323	200%	82%	10%	6%
Western Bloc	1,587	1,382	2,692	389	14,556	3,573	9.2	18,545	115%	77%	15%	9%
Eastern Bloc	1,018	1,004	1,575	395	1,205	467	1.2	15,110	108%	82%	12%	7%
Neutrals	782	870	2,226	253	2,365	764	3.0	23,668	86%	87%	5%	3%
NATO	736	701	1,188	390	5,482	2,903	7.4	7,482	103%	75%	16%	10%
NATO (w/o US)	533	484	1,013	356	2,416	1,614	4.5	6,910	87%	74%	11%	8%
Warsaw Pact	490	479	809	380	620	482	1.3	6,477	123%	78%	14%	8%
Russia	800	845	940	448	845	474	1.1	7,600	100%	75%	14%	11%
On Russian Border	544	559	998	349	1,542	990	2.8	11,693	114%	89%	7%	5%
Russian Enemies	668	717	1,283	334	1,939	969	2.9	16,728	112%	87%	6%	4%
United States	510	429	412	606	9,496	11,292	18.6	3,210	50%	50%	34%	16%
Pacific Allies	390	320	607	420	3,745	4,039	9.6	6,096	180%	82%	12%	6%
Percentage Analysis												
Western Bloc	47%	42%	41%	12%	80%	92%	71%	32%		-7%	45%	45%
Eastern Bloc	30%	31%	24%	14%	7%	-75%	-78%	26%		-1%	15%	14%
Neutrals	23%	27%	34%	-27%	13%	-59%	-43%	41%		6%	-45%	-44%
NATO	22%	22%	18%	12%	30%	56%	-39%	13%		-9%	54%	66%
NATO (w/o US)	16%	15%	16%	3%	13%	-13%	-15%	12%		-10%	12%	31%
Warsaw Pact	14%	15%	12%	9%	3%	-74%	-76%	11%		-5%	43%	28%
Russia	24%	26%	14%	29%	5%	-75%	-80%	13%		-9%	44%	78%
On Russian Border	16%	17%	15%	1%	9%	-47%	-47%	20%		8%	-34%	-21%
Russian Enemies	20%	22%	20%	-4%	11%	-48%	-46%	29%		5%	-36%	-32%
United States	15%	13%	6%	75%	52%	507%	248%	6%		-39%	240%	169%
Pacific Allies	12%	10%	9%	21%	21%	117%	80%	11%		0%	15%	8%
Africa	27	50	444	54	124	252	4.6	1,566	-18%	94%	4%	2%
Americas	818	667	1,130	455	10,741	5,977	13.1	6,936	-2%	68%	20%	12%
Europe	1,581	1,597	2,692	369	4,318	1,007	2.7	22,947	5%	77%	11%	7%
Middle East	102	223	629	120	321	377	3.1	4,244	-36%	89%	8%	2%
South Asia	81	92	182	296	313	1,143	3.9	3,143	-20%	92%	5%	3%
Southeast Asia	778	627	1,416	381	2,308	1,130	3.0	18,487	16%	89%	6%	4%
Percentage Analysis												
Africa	0.8%	1.5%	6.8%	-84%	0.7%	-86%	-14%	2.7%		14%	-56%	-71%
Americas	24.2%	20.5%	17.4%	31%	59.3%	221%	145%	12.1%		-17%	100%	100%
Europe	46.7%	49.0%	41.5%	6%	23.8%	-46%	-49%	40.0%		-6%	13%	17%
Middle East	3.0%	6.8%	9.7%	-66%	1.8%	-80%	-41%	7.4%		8%	-18%	-59%
South Asia	2.4%	2.8%	2.8%	-15%	1.7%	-39%	-28%	5.5%		12%	-48%	-56%
Southeast Asia	23.0%	19.3%	21.8%	10%	12.7%	-39%	-45%	32.3%		9%	-36%	-29%

NATIONS OF THE WORLD: REGIONAL AND BLOC SUMMARY

Averages & Totals	2.9	2.8	2.3	1.7	1.8	3.1

Force Multipliers

	Ldrs	Eqp	Exp	Spt	Mob	Trad
Western Bloc	4.0	4.8	2.7	3.4	3.7	4.4
Eastern Bloc	3.6	3.1	3.6	2.1	3.0	4.4
Neutrals	2.7	2.3	2.3	1.4	1.1	3.0
NATO	4.5	5.4	2.5	4.6	5.1	5.6
NATO (w/o US)	4.1	5.0	2.2	3.9	4.4	5.3
Warsaw Pact	4.4	4.3	2.2	3.3	5.7	5.5
Russia	4.1	6.0	4.0	6.0	9.0	7.0
On Russian Border	4.6	4.3	3.7	3.6	3.6	6.9
Russian Enemies	4.8	4.6	3.4	4.1	3.7	6.7
United States	6.0	6.0	5.0	8.0	7.0	6.0
Pacific Allies	5.1	5.3	3.6	5.2	4.8	5.6
Percentage Analysis						
Western Bloc	40%	70%	20%	98%	104%	41%
Eastern Bloc	26%	10%	57%	18%	65%	39%
Neutrals	-7%	-20%	1%	-20%	-38%	-3%
NATO	57%	89%	10%	162%	182%	79%
NATO (w/o US)	43%	76%	-3%	126%	143%	69%
Warsaw Pact	51%	53%	-5%	92%	212%	75%
Russia	43%	111%	75%	245%	395%	123%
On Russian Border	58%	51%	63%	105%	96%	119%
Russian Enemies	67%	63%	47%	135%	105%	115%
United States	108%	111%	119%	360%	285%	91%
Pacific Allies	77%	88%	56%	200%	163%	77%
Africa	1.7	1.5	1.4	0.4	0.3	1.5
Americas	2.5	2.3	1.7	1.6	1.9	1.6
Europe	4.1	4.4	2.3	3.4	4.0	5.5
Middle East	3.2	4.0	3.7	1.4	1.1	3.9
South Asia	2.9	1.8	2.5	1.2	1.0	3.8
Southeast Asia	3.8	3.5	3.6	3.0	2.8	4.2
Percentage Analysis						
Africa	-40%	-48%	-40%	-77%	-82%	-53%
Americas	-14%	-18%	-24%	-6%	2%	-49%
Europe	41%	55%	2%	93%	120%	75%
Middle East	12%	39%	60%	-19%	-40%	23%
South Asia	2%	-37%	10%	-31%	-45%	21%
Southeast Asia	32%	23%	56%	73%	56%	33%

NATIONS OF THE WORLD: EAST ASIAN NATIONS

Country	Rnk	National Summary			War Pwr	Atck Pwr	Long War	Tot Qual	Nukes	% Off	Geographic Profile				
		War State	Allies	Gov Stab							Area 1000 KmSq	Agr	Grz	For	Othr
Averages & Totals		1.7	5.9	5.8	6,083	3,255	7,337	6.8	2.4	23%	132,278	21	16	27	33
China	3	3	6	8	638	191	300	16	9	30%	9,597	11	0	8	81
Vietnam	9	4	2	6	186	93	139	21	3	50%	333	14	?	50	36
Korea, South	13	2	9	7	137	82	194	22	5	60%	99	23	?	67	10
Korea, North	15	2	2	5	115	52	111	15	3	45%	121	17	?	74	9
Taiwan	17	1	8	8	102	41	199	22	6	40%	36	24	6	55	15
Japan	18	1	8	9	90	36	186	37	6	40%	372	16	3	69	12
Indonesia	28	3	7	7	29	5	54	10	3	16%	1,904	12	?	64	24
Australia	33	1	9	9	23	16	81	31	4	70%	7,687	6	58	2	34
Malaysia	46	2	8	7	11	4	35	11	3	40%	330	20	?	70	10
Singapore	48	1	9	7	11	3	44	19	2	30%	1	22	?	?	47
Thailand	49	2	7	8	10	5	32	4	2	50%	514	24	?	56	20
Philippines	52	3	8	4	8	1	29	8	3	12%	300	30	5	53	12
New Zealand	65	1	9	9	3	2	23	24	3	70%	269	4	50	15	20
Cambodia	69	4	4	2	3	1	16	10	1	20%	181	16	0	74	10
Laos	73	3	2	4	2	0	15	4	1	20%	237	8	?	60	32
Mongolia	76	1	2	7	2	0	13	7	1	23%	1,565	1	50	?	?
Brunei	107	1	6	7	0	0	3	2	1	10%	6	3	?	75	?
Papua-New Guinea	112	1	6	7	0	0	2	2	1	10%	475	2	?	?	22

NATIONS OF THE WORLD: EAST ASIAN NATIONS

| Country | Rnk | Trans Net | MEI | Population Profile | | | | Economic Profile | | | | | |
				Pop SqKm	Pop Tot	% Lit	% Urban	Ind	GDP	% Frgn Trade	% Soc Exp	Per Cap	Qual Life
Averages & Totals		3.8	5.4	35	4,674	54	42	3.3	12,375	26	4.9	2.6	3.6
China	3	5	5	110	1,059	25	20	4	$360.0	3.6	5.0	$0.3	3
Vietnam	9	5	4	171	57	75	19	3	$11.0	3.9	?	$0.2	2
Korea, South	13	6	3	415	41	90	60	7	$68.4	31.7	4.3	$1.7	5
Korea, North	15	5	3	158	19	90	38	6	$18.8	10.1	?	$1.0	3
Taiwan	17	5	6	497	18	90	77	7	$46.0	42.8	?	$2.6	6
Japan	18	9	5	320	119	99	76	9	$1,020.0	13.6	4.0	$8.6	8
Indonesia	28	3	4	85	161	60	19	2	$84.3	26.3	2.3	$0.5	2
Australia	33	5	4	2	16	99	86	9	$163.1	13.1	6.0	$10.2	9
Malaysia	46	4	4	45	15	45	29	2	$25.9	49.9	?	$1.7	4
Singapore	48	9	8	4,167	3	70	100	8	$15.1	137.1	?	$6.0	7
Thailand	49	4	5	99	51	70	25	2	$37.3	18.8	4.5	$0.7	3
Philippines	52	3	3	177	53	83	32	2	$39.6	14.1	2.4	$0.7	3
New Zealand	65	8	5	12	3	98	77	7	$24.0	24.6	11.2	$7.4	9
Cambodia	69	2	4	30	6	48	?	0	$0.7	0.3	?	$0.1	1
Laos	73	2	5	14	3	12	15	0	$0.3	10.2	?	$0.1	1
Mongolia	76	2	7	1	2	95	50	3	$1.2	?	?	$0.7	3
Brunei	107	2	4	40	0.23	45	?	2	$4.3	?	?	$18.5	6
Papua-New Guinea	112	1	2	7	3	15	13	0	$2.5	42.8	8.2	$0.8	3

NATIONS OF THE WORLD: EAST ASIAN NATIONS

Country	Rnk	Military Capability		Mil Bud	% GDP	Bud Man	Bang per $	Bang M/Pop.	Bang T$/GDP	Reserves		% Act
		Act Men	% Cadre							Men	p/mil	
Averages & Totals		28,636	68	757,734	6.1%	26	8.0	1.3	492	28,687	6.1	22
China	3	3,988	32	$22,800	6.3%	$6	28.0	0.60	1,772	4,490	4.2	100
Vietnam	9	900	10	$2,200	20.0%	$2	84.7	3.27	16,945	1,158	20.3	0
Korea, South	13	622	20	$5,173	7.6%	$8	26.5	3.35	2,008	1,558	38.0	10
Korea, North	15	785	10	$1,916	10.2%	$2	59.9	6.04	6,101	369	19.4	0
Taiwan	17	464	80	$3,323	7.2%	$7	30.7	5.67	2,219	1,668	92.7	50
Japan	18	241	100	$10,360	1.0%	$43	8.7	0.75	88	48	0.4	0
Indonesia	28	281	100	$2,926	3.5%	$10	9.8	0.18	340	35	0.2	0
Australia	33	73	100	$4,497	2.8%	$62	5.0	1.42	139	33	2.1	100
Malaysia	46	100	100	$2,077	8.0%	$21	5.2	0.72	416	81	5.4	100
Singapore	48	56	37	$852	5.6%	$15	12.4	4.22	698	181	72.2	100
Thailand	49	235	13	$1,562	4.2%	$7	6.6	0.20	278	560	11.0	17
Philippines	52	105	100	$878	2.2%	$8	9.3	0.15	206	118	2.2	100
New Zealand	65	13	100	$494	2.1%	$38	6.2	0.95	128	10	3.2	100
Cambodia	69	25	?	$60	8.6%	$2	43.3	0.47	3,714	65	11.8	0
Laos	73	53	?	$40	13.3%	$1	53.0	0.62	7,067	99	29.1	0
Mongolia	76	25	20	$244	20.3%	$10	6.8	0.97	1,381	40	23.5	0
Brunei	107	7	100	$125	2.9%	$18	0.9	0.47	25	0	0.0	100
Papua-New Guinea	112	4	100	$50	2.0%	$13	1.2	0.02	24	0	0.0	0

NATIONS OF THE WORLD: EAST ASIAN NATIONS

Country	Rnk	Paramilitary Profile Tot	p/mil	%Pop Srv	Army Profile Ult Men	Mbl Men	Eqtd Divs	Men Div	AFV	Men/ AFV	Air Force Profile Mbl Men	Cmbt A/C	Other A/C	Men/ A/C
Averages & Totals		43,502	9.3	2.2%	779,530	47,146	1,681	28.0	360,972	131	5,782	46,848	39,835	67
China	3	8,000	7.6	1.6%	156,400	7,600	335	22.7	16,850	451	528	5,300	1,500	78
Vietnam	9	1,550	27.2	6.3%	8,400	2,000	65	30.8	5,000	400	50	325	300	80
Korea, South	13	9,520	232.2	28.5%	7,700	2,020	51	39.6	2,250	898	100	650	360	99
Korea, North	15	1,800	94.7	15.5%	2,700	1,000	75	13.3	4,500	222	80	740	550	62
Taiwan	17	25	1.4	12.0%	3,900	1,884	38	49.6	3,000	628	165	510	400	181
Japan	18	5	.0	0.2%	26,000	197	14	14.1	1,580	125	55	530	430	57
Indonesia	28	112	0.7	0.3%	23,800	234	6	37.1	665	352	32	70	365	74
Australia	33	5	0.3	0.7%	3,400	63	3	21.1	900	70	26	175	245	61
Malaysia	46	455	30.3	4.2%	2,400	159	7	23.7	650	245	12	50	110	75
Singapore	48	40	16.0	11.0%	580	200	3	60.6	1,243	161	21	125	110	89
Thailand	49	72	1.4	1.7%	7,900	675	12	56.3	1,300	519	80	200	500	114
Philippines	52	109	2.0	0.6%	9,400	160	9	17.8	1,300	533	33	92	230	102
New Zealand	65	0	0.0	0.7%	600	13	1	13.4	310	43	6	33	62	61
Cambodia	69	?	0.0	1.6%	875	90	5	18.0	?	?	?	?	?	0
Laos	73	100	29.4	7.4%	500	150	8	18.8	75	2,000	2	20	32	38
Mongolia	76	25	14.7	5.3%	250	63	3	21.0	250	252	2	12	65	27
Brunei	107	3	10.7	4.0%	30	4	0	9.0	34	106	0	0	24	13
Papua–New Guinea	112	0	0.1	0.1%	400	3	0	17.0	0	0	0	0	7	14

NATIONS OF THE WORLD: EAST ASIAN NATIONS

Country	Rnk	Navy Profile Type	Navy Profile Mbl Men	Cmbt Ships	Other Ships	Men/ Ship	Tons	Tons/ Ship	Men/ Shp/T	Manpower Mbl Men	Distribution Incr	% Army	% AF	% Navy
Averages & Totals			3,387	3,256	6,493	347	18,125	1,859	5.35	57,323	200%	82%	10%	6%
China	3	R	350.0	335	560	391	725	810	2.07	8,478	113%	90%	6%	4%
Vietnam	9	C	8.0	14	64	103	46	592	5.78	2,058	129%	97%	2%	0%
Korea, South	13	R	60.0	31	68	606	147	1,481	2.44	2,180	250%	93%	5%	3%
Korea, North	15	L	73.5	37	51	835	45	507	0.61	1,154	47%	87%	7%	6%
Taiwan	17	R	83.0	43	69	741	297	2,653	3.58	2,132	359%	88%	8%	4%
Japan	18	R	36.6	82	186	137	422	1,575	11.53	289	20%	68%	19%	13%
Indonesia	28	R	50.0	21	120	355	168	1,189	3.35	316	12%	74%	10%	16%
Australia	33	R	16.7	18	35	315	148	2,792	8.86	106	46%	60%	24%	16%
Malaysia	46	C	10.0	10	80	111	45	498	4.48	181	82%	88%	7%	6%
Singapore	48	C	15.0	6	41	319	31	651	2.04	236	325%	85%	9%	6%
Thailand	49	L	40.0	12	51	635	55	867	1.37	795	238%	85%	10%	5%
Philippines	52	R	30.0	10	64	405	162	2,189	5.40	223	113%	72%	15%	13%
New Zealand	65	R	4.1	5	6	373	17	1,527	4.10	23	81%	58%	25%	18%
Cambodia	69	C	?	?	?	0	?	0	0.00	90	260%	100%	0%	0%
Laos	73	-	?	?	?	0	?	0	0.00	152	187%	99%	1%	0%
Mongolia	76	P	0.0	0	0	0	0	0	0.00	65	159%	97%	3%	0%
Brunei	107	P	0.5	3	15	28	1	50	1.80	7	0%	82%	7%	11%
Papua-New Guinea	112	P	0.3	0	6	50	2	267	5.33	4	0%	89%	3%	8%

NATIONS OF THE WORLD: EAST ASIAN NATIONS

Averages & Totals		2.9	2.8	2.3	1.7	1.8	3.1
Country	Rnk	Force Multipliers					
		Ldrs	Eqp	Exp	Spt	Mob	Trad
China	3	4	3	4	4	3	6
Vietnam	9	5	3	6	2	2	6
Korea, South	13	5	4	5	5	4	5
Korea, North	15	4	3	5	3	2	4
Taiwan	17	5	4	3	5	5	5
Japan	18	6	7	3	7	7	7
Indonesia	28	3	2	5	2	3	5
Australia	33	5	7	3	6	6	7
Malaysia	46	3	3	5	3	3	4
Singapore	48	5	5	4	4	3	3
Thailand	49	2	3	1	1	3	3
Philippines	52	3	3	3	1	2	4
New Zealand	65	5	5	3	5	3	6
Cambodia	69	4	1	6	1	1	4
Laos	73	2	2	4	1	1	2
Mongolia	76	3	3	2	1	2	3
Brunei	107	2	3	0	1	0	0
Papua-New Guinea	112	1	2	2	2	1	1

NATIONS OF THE WORLD: SOUTH ASIAN NATIONS

Country	Rnk	War State	National Summary Allies	Gov Stab	War Pwr	Atck Pwr	Long War	Tot Qual	Nukes	% Off	Geographic Profile Area 1000 KmSq	Agr	Grz	For	Othr
Averages & Totals		1.7	5.9	5.8	6,083	3,255	7,337	6.8	2.4	23%	132,278	21	16	27	33
India	4	2	5	6	301	90	200	27	8	30%	3,288	50	5	20	25
Pakistan	21	2	6	5	77	25	88	16	6	32%	808	40	22	3	35
Burma	47	3	6	6	11	2	33	8	1	20%	678	28	?	62	10
Bangladesh	54	1	5	4	3	1	28	8	1	10%	144	66	?	16	18
Nepal	63	1	6	9	8	1	18	14	1	25%	142	16	14	32	38
Afghanistan	66	6	1	2	3	0	17	6	1	15%	648	22	3	3	75
Sri Lanka	90	2	5	6	0	0	7	3	1	10%	66	25	?	44	?
Bhutan	136	1	7	6	0	0	1	1	1	0%	47	15	?	70	15
Maldives	142	1	6	6	0	0	1	0	1	10%	0	10	0	?	90
Mauritius	148	1	6	6	0	0	0	0	1	0%	2	50	?	40	7

Country	Rnk	Trans Net	MEI	Population Profile Pop SqKm	Pop Tot	% Lit	% Urban	Economic Profile Ind	GDP	% Frgn Trade	% Soc Exp	Per Cap	Qual Life
Averages & Totals		3.8	5.4	35	4,674	54	42	3.3	12,375	26	4.9	2.6	3.6
India	4	4	3	222	730	29	21	5	$160.6	4.5	1.8	$0.2	2
Pakistan	21	3	5	118	95	20	25	4	$31.0	7.4	2.1	$0.3	1
Burma	47	2	3	55	37	50	19	2	$5.6	8.4	2.7	$0.2	2
Bangladesh	54	5	7	667	96	25	9	3	$10.7	2.6	2.4	$0.1	1
Nepal	63	1	2	106	15	12	5	0	$2.5	3.2	2.0	$0.2	2
Afghanistan	66	1	4	25	16	10	15	0	$2.4	28.9	6.2	$0.2	1
Sri Lanka	90	4	4	244	16	82	22	2	$4.8	22.1	6.2	$0.3	1
Bhutan	136	1	1	28	1.3	5	3	2	$0.1	1.7	?	$0.1	1
Maldives	142	2	8	500	0.15	5	100	0	$.0	19.3	1.0	$0.2	1
Mauritius	148	2	7	450	0.9	60	44	2	$0.7	48.6	7.5	$0.8	2

NATIONS OF THE WORLD: SOUTH ASIAN NATIONS

Country	Rnk	Military Capability Act Men	% Cadre	Mil Bud	% GDP	Bud Man	Bang per $	Bang M/Pop.	Bang T$/GDP	Reserves Men	p/mil	% Act
Averages & Totals		28,636	68	757,734	6.1%	26	8.0	1.3	492	28,687	6.1	22
India	4	1,120	100	$5,556	3.5%	$5	54.2	0.41	1,875	337	0.5	100
Pakistan	21	479	100	$1,801	5.8%	$4	42.5	0.81	2,470	614	6.5	0
Burma	47	179	100	$176	3.1%	$1	61.2	0.29	1,918	30	0.8	0
Bangladesh	54	91	100	$161	1.5%	$2	47.7	0.08	717	20	0.2	0
Nepal	63	25	100	$31	1.2%	$1	111.5	0.23	1,360	115	7.7	100
Afghanistan	66	47	100	$208	8.7%	$4	14.5	0.19	1,253	28	1.8	100
Sri Lanka	90	17	100	$41	0.8%	$2	12.2	0.03	104	20	1.2	100
Bhutan	136	4	100	$1	1.0%	$0.3	8.0	0.01	80	15	11.5	0
Maldives	142	1	100	$1	3.3%	$1	3.9	0.03	131	0.02	0.1	0
Mauritius	148	1	100	$1	0.1%	$1	2.0	.00	3	0	.0	0

Country	Rnk	Paramilitary Profile Tot	p/mil	%Pop Srv	Army Profile Ult Men	Mbl Men	Eqtd Divs	Men Div	AFV	Men/ AFV	Air Force Profile Mbl Men	Cmbt A/C	Other A/C	Men/ A/C
Averages & Totals		43,502	9.3	2.2%	779,530	47,146	1,681	28.0	360,972	131	5,782	46,848	39,835	67
India	4	262	0.4	0.2%	116,100	1,295	34	37.8	2,600	498	115	795	800	72
Pakistan	21	110	1.2	1.3%	15,700	1,050	21	50.0	2,500	420	25	275	415	36
Burma	47	75	2.0	0.8%	4,700	193	15	12.9	110	1,755	9	16	95	81
Bangladesh	54	80	0.8	0.2%	13,900	103	5	20.6	56	1,839	3	21	22	70
Nepal	63	15	1.0	1.0%	2,000	140	4	39.9	50	2,794	3	0	9	33
Afghanistan	66	50	3.1	0.8%	1,900	65	15	4.3	1,500	43	10	180	150	30
Sri Lanka	90	20	1.2	0.4%	3,200	30	2	15.0	43	698	3	6	37	70
Bhutan	136	15	11.5	2.6%	180	19	1	19.0	0	0	0	0	0	0
Maldives	142	?	0.0	0.7%	25	1	1	8.0	0	0	0	0	?	0
Mauritius	148	0	0.0	0.1%	140	1	0	9.0	0	0	0	0	?	0

NATIONS OF THE WORLD: SOUTH ASIAN NATIONS

Averages & Totals			3,387	3,256	6,493	347	18,125	1,859	5.35	57,323	200%	82%	10%	6%
		Navy Profile									Manpower Distribution			
Country	Rnk	Type	Mbl Men	Cmbt Ships	Other Ships	Men/Ship	Tons	Tons/Ship	Men/Shp/T	Mbl Men	Incr	% Army	% AF	% Navy
India	4	R	47.0	67	37	452	200	1,923	4.26	1,457	30%	89%	8%	3%
Pakistan	21	R	18.0	22	45	269	93	1,381	5.14	1,093	128%	96%	2%	2%
Burma	47	C	7.0	1	33	206	8	232	1.13	209	17%	92%	4%	3%
Bangladesh	54	C	5.3	2	18	265	9	425	1.60	111	22%	93%	3%	5%
Nepal	63	-	0.0	0	0	0	0	0	0.00	140	460%	100%	0%	0%
Afghanistan	66	-	0.0	0	0	0	0	0	0.00	75	60%	87%	13%	0%
Sri Lanka	90	P	3.5	0	38	92	2	53	0.57	37	120%	82%	8%	10%
Bhutan	136	-	0.0	0	0	0	0	0	0.00	19	375%	100%	0%	0%
Maldives	142	P	0.2	0	10	15	2	200	13.33	1	2%	80%	5%	15%
Mauritius	148	P	0.1	0	1	50	0	160	3.20	1	2%	90%	5%	5%

Averages & Totals		2.9	2.8	2.3	1.7	1.8	3.1
Country	Rnk	Ldrs	Eqp	Exp	Spt	Mob	Trad
		Force Multipliers					
India	4	6	3	4	5	2	7
Pakistan	21	5	3	3	1	2	7
Burma	47	3	2	2	1	1	4
Bangladesh	54	3	3	4	1	2	4
Nepal	63	4	1	5	1	1	9
Afghanistan	66	2	2	5	1	1	7
Sri Lanka	90	3	1	2	1	1	0
Bhutan	136	1	1	1	0	0	0
Maldives	142	1	1	1	0	0	0
Mauritius	148	1	1	0	0	0	0

NATIONS OF THE WORLD: MIDDLE EAST NATIONS

Country	Rnk	National War State	National Allies	Summary Gov Stab	War Pwr	Atck Pwr	Long War	Tot Qual	Nukes	% Off	Geographic Profile Area 1000 KmSq	Agr	Grz	For	Othr
Averages & Totals		1.7	5.9	5.8	6,083	3,255	7,337	6.8	2.4	23%	132,278	21	16	27	33
Israel	6	4	8	9	235	165	154	48	7	70%	20	20	40	4	36
Iran	10	7	5	6	183	73	137	22	4	40%	1,647	30	8	11	51
Iraq	14	7	6	5	117	59	119	24	4	50%	432	18	10	4	68
Egypt	19	1	7	6	89	27	98	22	4	31%	1,002	3	?	?	97
Syria	27	2	4	6	32	10	56	10	3	30%	186	48	29	2	21
Algeria	44	1	5	7	12	4	34	8	3	30%	2,382	3	16	1	80
Jordan	45	1	6	8	12	5	34	16	3	40%	98	11	3	15	88
Saudi Arabia	51	1	8	6	8	3	29	11	4	40%	2,150	1	?	1	98
Morocco	58	3	7	6	6	2	24	4	2	10%	446	32	?	17	51
Lebanon	67	4	6	1	3	0	17	8	1	40%	10	27	?	?	64
Libya	68	4	4	5	3	1	17	4	3	20%	1,760	6	0	1	93
Sudan	70	3	3	4	3	0	16	4	1	17%	2,506	37	15	15	33
Yemen, South	72	2	3	5	2	0	15	8	1	20%	333	1	?	1	99
Yemen, North	78	2	7	6	1	0	11	6	1	24%	195	20	?	1	79
Tunisia	82	1	6	6	1	0	10	4	1	30%	163	28	23	6	43
Kuwait	85	1	8	6	1	0	8	5	3	20%	18	1	1	?	99
Oman	86	2	6	5	1	0	8	3	1	20%	211	1	1	?	99
United Arab Emir.	88	1	7	5	0	0	3	4	1	20%	84	1	1	?	99
Bahrain	106	1	5	5	0	0	3	4	1	10%	1	5	?	?	95
Qatar	108	1	6	6	0	0	3	2	1	10%	11	1	1	?	99

NATIONS OF THE WORLD: MIDDLE EAST NATIONS

Country	Rnk	Trans Net	MEI	Population Profile				Economic Profile					
				Pop SqKm	Pop Tot	% Lit	% Urban	Ind	GDP	% Frgn Trade	% Soc Exp	Per Cap	Qual Life
Averages & Totals		3.8	5.4	35	4,674	54	42	3.3	12,375	26	4.9	2.6	3.6
Israel	6	7	9	188	4	72	86	7	$20.6	27.2	8.1	$5.4	7
Iran	10	3	4	26	42	37	47	3	$102.0	14.6	12.7	$2.4	3
Iraq	14	3	7	30	13	30	66	2	$35.6	29.7	7.6	$2.7	3
Egypt	19	3	7	46	46	44	44	2	$29.5	10.8	6.5	$0.6	2
Syria	27	4	6	46	8.5	40	48	3	$8.9	23.6	7.5	$1.0	2
Algeria	44	4	6	8	18	58	52	3	$41.7	21.8	8.6	$2.3	3
Jordan	45	4	8	33	3.2	53	44	5	$2.6	22.0	7.4	$0.8	3
Saudi Arabia	51	2	6	4	9	15	28	2	$152.2	49.8	8.5	$16.9	6
Morocco	58	3	6	47	21	20	38	2	$14.9	17.0	7.1	$0.7	2
Lebanon	67	5	7	308	3.2	86	60	3	$3.5	25.3	9.1	$1.1	3
Libya	68	3	7	2	3.2	50	52	2	$33.0	47.4	7.0	$10.3	6
Sudan	70	1	7	7	18	8	20	1	$9.2	7.1	6.9	$0.5	1
Yemen, South	72	2	7	6	1.9	10	33	0	$1.0	25.0	?	$0.5	1
Yemen, North	78	1	5	26	5.1	15	11	3	$2.8	0.8	2.0	$0.5	1
Tunisia	82	5	7	39	6.3	50	49	3	$7.8	28.2	8.1	$1.2	4
Kuwait	85	5	9	72	1.3	60	99	3	$18.0	73.3	5.5	$13.8	8
Oman	86	5	8	5	0.97	10	10	1	$6.2	53.1	6.4	$6.4	4
United Arab Emir.	88	1	9	11	0.9	25	90	1	$9.6	176.0	3.0	$10.7	7
Bahrain	106	9	9	607	0.37	40	78	2	$2.0	211.0	5.0	$5.4	6
Qatar	108	6	9	18	0.2	25	71	3	$5.5	102.7	5.5	$27.5	6

NATIONS OF THE WORLD: MIDDLE EAST NATIONS

| Country | Rnk | Military Capability | | Mil Bud | % GDP | Bud Man | Bang per $ | Bang M/Pop. | Bang T$/GDP | Reserves | | % Act |
		Act Men	% Cadre							Men	p/mil	
Averages & Totals		28,636	68	757,734	6.1%	26	8.0	1.3	492	28,687	6.1	22
Israel	6	488	30	$6,461	31.4%	$13	36.4	61.85	11,409	9	2.4	29
Iran	10	850	7	$15,000	14.7%	$18	12.2	4.36	1,797	200	4.8	0
Iraq	14	480	15	$7,722	21.7%	$16	15.2	9.00	3,287	275	21.2	100
Egypt	19	410	43	$3,043	10.3%	$7	29.1	1.93	3,002	42	0.9	50
Syria	27	330	37	$2,548	28.6%	$8	12.4	3.73	3,560		0.0	0
Algeria	44	140	35	$848	2.0%	$6	13.9	0.65	282	101	5.6	?
Jordan	45	73	90	$465	17.9%		24.9	3.62	4,452	15	4.7	100
Saudi Arabia	51	77	100	$21,952	14.4%	$287	0.4	0.92	54	26	2.8	0
Morocco	58	144	60	$1,328	8.9%	$9	4.3	0.27	387	50	2.4	0
Lebanon	67	35	20	$576	16.5%	$16	5.1	0.92	840		0.0	0
Libya	68	73	25	$709	2.1%	$10	4.1	0.91	88		0.0	0
Sudan	70	58	100	$235	2.6%	$4	10.9	0.14	277	46	14.2	0
Yemen, South	72	26	30	$159	15.9%	$6	13.5	1.13	2,142	2	0.1	0
Yemen, North	78	22	60	$527	18.8%	$24	2.5	0.25	463	37	19.2	0
Tunisia	82	29	37	$119	1.5%	$4	8.7	0.16	132	25	4.9	0
Kuwait	85	12	81	$1,561	8.7%	$126	0.4	0.52	37	55	8.7	0
Oman	86	24	100	$1,772	28.6%	$75	0.4	0.68	107	12	9.2	0
United Arab Emir.	88	49	100	$2,915	30.4%	$59	0.2	0.65	61	5	4.6	0
Bahrain	106	3	100	$253	12.7%	$94	0.4	0.31	57	0.4	0.0	0
Qatar	108	6	100	$166	3.0%	$28	0.6	0.48	17	20	1.1	0

NATIONS OF THE WORLD: MIDDLE EAST NATIONS

Country	Rnk	Paramilitary Profile			Army Profile					Men/AFV	Air Force Profile			
		Tot	p/mil	%Pop Srv	Ult Men	Mbl Men	Eqtd Divs	Men Div	AFV		Mbl Men	Cmbt A/C	Other A/C	Men/A/C
Averages & Totals		43,502	9.3	2.2%	779,530	47,146	1,681	28.0	360,972	131	5,782	46,848	39,835	67
Israel	6	100	26.3	15.7%	670	450	18	24.6	11,600	39	37	675	365	36
Iran	10	2,550	60.7	8.6%	6,000	1,000	18	55.6	1,900	526	35	90	200	121
Iraq	14	450	34.6	9.3%	1,900	700	28	25.4	6,500	108	50	350	350	71
Egypt	19	278	6.0	1.6%	7,400	320	16	19.6	6,700	48	112	650	240	126
Syria	27	10	1.2	4.0%	1,200	280	9	32.2	6,300	44	40	600	360	42
Algeria	44	25	1.4	1.5%	2,700	220	8	28.6	2,150	102	12	340	145	25
Jordan	45	10	3.1	3.1%	550	80	5	17.4	1,900	42	8	120	75	38
Saudi Arabia	51	24	2.6	1.4%	1,600	77	5	14.5	1,700	45	14	206	796	14
Morocco	58	30	1.4	1.1%	3,000	175	5	37.2	2,400	73	13	100	225	40
Lebanon	67	60	18.8	3.0%	370	33	1	8.8	550	59	2	21	48	29
Libya	68	25	7.8	4.5%	500	100	7	14.9	4,500	22	12	565	403	12
Sudan	70	4	0.2	0.4%	2,900	55	3	17.7	805	68	3	36	70	28
Yemen, South	72	30	15.8	4.8%	250	58	4	14.5	770	75	3	128	36	18
Yemen, North	78	25	4.9	1.4%	600	45	4	11.3	1,150	39	1	75	19	11
Tunisia	82	9	1.3	1.5%	900	73	2	42.9	400	183	5	20	80	45
Kuwait	85	0	0.0	1.9%	400	22	1	21.9	825	27	2	60	55	17
Oman	86	5	4.6	3.4%	130	24	1	24.1	54	446	2	49	63	18
United Arab Emir.	88	1	0.6	5.5%	300	46	1	35.4	642	72	2	89	96	8
Bahrain	106	3	7.3	1.6%	80	2	0	23.0	146	16	0	0	9	33
Qatar	108	20	100.0	23.0%	60	25	1	41.7	225	111	0	25	29	6

NATIONS OF THE WORLD: MIDDLE EAST NATIONS

Country	Rnk	Navy Profile Type	Mbl Men	Cmbt Ships	Other Ships	Men/ Ship	Tons	Tons/ Ship	Men/ Shp/T	Mbl Men	Manpower Distribution % Incr	% Army	% AF	% Navy
Averages & Totals			3,387	3,256	6,493	347	18,125	1,859	5.35	57,323	200%	82%	10%	6%
Israel	6	L	10.0	28	75	97	21	203	2.09	497	2%	91%	7%	2%
Iran	10	L	15.0	16	19	429	90	2,583	6.03	1,050	24%	95%	3%	1%
Iraq	14	C	5.0	8	24	156	12	375	2.40	755	57%	93%	7%	1%
Egypt	19	L	20.0	42	62	192	63	604	3.14	452	10%	71%	25%	4%
Syria	27	C	5.0	20	12	156	7	209	1.34	330	0%	86%	12%	2%
Algeria	44	L	8.6	24	30	159	13	235	1.48	241	72%	91%	5%	4%
Jordan	45	P	0.3	0	6	50	0	8	0.17	88	21%	91%	9%	0%
Saudi Arabia	51	C	11.0	14	56	157	14	199	1.26	102	33%	75%	14%	11%
Morocco	58	C	5.5	5	19	229	12	492	2.15	194	34%	90%	7%	3%
Lebanon	67	P	0.3	0	15	20	1	60	3.00	35	0%	93%	6%	1%
Libya	68	C	6.5	32	53	76	50	593	7.75	119	62%	84%	10%	5%
Sudan	70	P	2.0	0	16	125	2	144	1.15	60	3%	92%	5%	3%
Yemen, South	72	C	1.0	7	25	31	11	341	10.90	62	143%	94%	5%	2%
Yemen, North	78	P	0.6	2	7	67	1	56	0.83	47	116%	97%	2%	1%
Tunisia	82	C	6.0	4	19	261	7	313	1.20	84	193%	87%	5%	7%
Kuwait	85	C	0.5	10	51	8	5	80	9.80	24	97%	90%	8%	2%
Oman	86	C	2.0	5	21	77	7	265	3.45	28	19%	86%	7%	7%
United Arab Emir.	88	P	1.5	3	48	29	2	47	1.60	49	0%	94%	3%	3%
Bahrain	106	P	0.5	0	29	17	1	41	2.40	3	15%	74%	10%	16%
Qatar	108	P	0.7	3	42	16	2	51	3.29	26	333%	96%	1%	3%

NATIONS OF THE WORLD: MIDDLE EAST NATIONS

Averages & Totals		2.9	2.8	2.3	1.7	1.8	3.1
Country	Rnk	Force Multipliers					
		Ldrs	Eqp	Exp	Spt	Mob	Trad
Israel	6	9	8	9	2	1	8
Iran	10	5	4	7	2	3	6
Iraq	14	5	6	7	4	2	4
Egypt	19	5	3	6	3	3	5
Syria	27	3	4	6	1	1	4
Algeria	44	3	2	5	1	1	5
Jordan	45	5	4	3	1	1	6
Saudi Arabia	51	3	8	1	2	2	5
Morocco	58	2	2	1	1	1	5
Lebanon	67	3	3	7	1	0	3
Libya	68	2	3	4	1	1	1
Sudan	70	2	1	4	1	0	5
Yemen, South	72	3	1	6	1	1	5
Yemen, North	78	2	3	5	1	1	5
Tunisia	82	2	1	1	1	1	5
Kuwait	85	3	7	0	1	1	0
Oman	86	1	6	1	1	1	5
United Arab Emir.	88	1	4	0	1	1	0
Bahrain	106	3	6	0	1	0	0
Qatar	108	2	3	0	1	0	0

NATIONS OF THE WORLD: EUROPEAN NATIONS

Country	Rnk	National War State	Allies	Summary Gov Stab	War Pwr	Atck Pwr	Long War	Tot Qual	Nukes	% Off	Geographic Profile Area 1000 KmSq	Agr	Grz	For	Othr
Averages & Totals		1.7	5.9	5.8	6,083	3,255	7,337	6.8	2.4	23%	132,278	21	16	27	33
Russia	1	4	1	7	1000	800	699	26	9	80%	22,401	10	17	35	38
Germany, West	5	1	9	9	285	200	466	58	6	70%	249	33	23	29	15
France	7	2	8	9	207	124	294	42	9	60%	547	35	26	25	14
Sweden	8	1	6	9	192	38	155	15	5	20%	450	7	2	55	36
Britain	11	2	9	9	164	131	220	51	9	80%	244	30	50	7	13
Switzerland	12	1	6	9	153	31	125	14	5	20%	41	10	43	24	23
Turkey	16	2	7	7	108	43	111	19	5	40%	779	35	25	23	17
Italy	20	1	9	7	79	26	139	21	5	33%	301	53	17	21	9
Poland	22	2	3	5	68	27	98	20	4	40%	313	49	14	27	10
Germany, East	23	2	2	8	54	24	94	32	4	45%	108	43	15	27	15
Yugoslavia	24	2	5	6	43	9	92	18	3	20%	256	32	25	34	9
Spain	25	2	8	7	42	10	78	12	4	25%	508	41	27	22	10
Czechoslovakia	30	2	2	7	26	12	58	13	4	46%	128	42	14	35	9
Netherlands	37	2	8	8	19	12	64	18	4	65%	41	70	9	8	13
Greece	38	1	7	7	19	8	50	10	3	40%	132	29	40	20	11
Romania	39	1	3	6	17	3	43	9	4	20%	238	44	19	27	10
Belgium	40	1	9	7	16	5	55	17	4	35%	31	28	24	20	28
Bulgaria	41	1	1	7	15	4	39	9	3	26%	111	41	11	33	15
Hungary	42	1	3	8	13	5	40	13	3	35%	93	74	?	10	16
Finland	43	1	6	9	13	2	40	32	4	15%	337	8	?	58	34
Austria	50	1	6	8	8	2	38	17	3	24%	84	20	26	36	15
Portugal	55	2	7	8	7	3	27	11	3	40%	92	48	6	31	15
Denmark	56	1	8	8	7	3	53	18	3	40%	43	42	7	35	9
Norway	57	1	9	9	6	3	60	14	3	50%	324	3	2	21	74
Albania	79	1	5	5	1	0	11	3	1	23%	29	19	24	43	14
Ireland	81	1	6	8	1	0	10	7	2	45%	70	17	51	3	30
Cyprus (Greek)	84	1	6	5	1	0	9	7	2	20%	6	47	10	18	25
Cyprus (Turkish)	93	1	6	6	0	0	6	9	1	10%	4	1	11	66	22
Luxembourg	115	1	9	9	0	0	2	7	1	40%	3	25	27	33	15
Malta	128	1	6	7	0	0	2	2	1	10%	0	45	0	?	55
Iceland	143	1	8	9	0	0	1	4	1	10%	103	0	22	0	78

NATIONS OF THE WORLD: EUROPEAN NATIONS

Country	Rnk	Trans Net	MEI	Population Profile		% Lit	% Urban	Economic Profile		% Frgn Trade	% Soc Exp	Per Cap	Qual Life
				Pop SqKm	Pop Tot			Ind	GDP				
Averages & Totals		3.8	5.4	35	4,674	54	42	3.3	12,375	26	4.9	2.6	3.6
Russia	1	4	4	12	272	98	62	7	$1,450.0	4.6	6.9	$5.3	4
Germany, West	5	9	6	249	62	99	86	9	$659.2	26.8	7.0	$10.6	9
France	7	9	5	99	54	97	71	9	$537.4	18.3	5.1	$10.0	9
Sweden	8	6	5	18	8.3	99	83	9	$98.8	27.1	10.5	$11.9	9
Britain	11	8	6	229	56	99	78	9	$473.4	20.5	9.9	$8.5	8
Switzerland	12	8	4	157	6.5	98	58	9	$96.6	26.9	6.0	$14.9	9
Turkey	16	4	5	63	49	62	45	4	$52.8	8.9	2.7	$1.1	4
Italy	20	6	5	186	56	95	70	9	$347.4	21.3	4.5	$6.2	8
Poland	22	8	8	118	37	98	58	7	$120.5	13.5	8.9	$3.3	5
Germany, East	23	8	7	157	17	99	76	8	$100.0	15.1	7.5	$5.9	7
Yugoslavia	24	5	5	90	23	80	39	5	$61.8	16.5	6.0	$2.7	6
Spain	25	5	5	75	38	97	49	7	$177.5	11.5	3.8	$4.7	6
Czechoslovakia	30	8	6	125	16	99	67	9	$85.0	15.5	8.0	$5.3	7
Netherlands	37	9	7	340	14	98	77	9	$137.0	48.4	8.1	$9.8	9
Greece	38	5	5	76	10	86	65	5	$38.4	10.9	2.8	$3.8	6
Romania	39	9	6	97	23	99	49	5	$90.0	14.0	5.0	$3.9	5
Belgium	40	9	9	328	10	97	95	8	$107.3	48.7	4.6	$10.7	9
Bulgaria	41	7	7	81	9	95	59	5	$30.5	27.7		$3.4	5
Hungary	42	7	8	118	11	97	51	7	$50.0	17.4	5.0	$4.5	6
Finland	43	6	4	14	4.8	99	59	6	$47.6	27.3	8.8	$9.9	8
Austria	50	7	6	91	7.6	98	52	4	$67.0	23.3	3.9	$8.8	8
Portugal	55	6	7	109	10	70	37	4	$23.6	17.4	3.0	$2.4	6
Denmark	56	9	8	119	5.1	99	80	6	$56.4	27.1	10.0	$11.1	9
Norway	57	9	8	13	4.1	99	57	8	$56.4	31.0	3.4	$13.8	9
Albania	79	4	5	98	2.8	75	34	3	$2.4	8.3	?	$0.9	1
Ireland	81	3	5	48	3.4	99	52	4	$17.1	46.7	7.4	$5.0	7
Cyprus (Greek)	84	4	6	89	0.5	90	45	3	$1.7	21.0	?	$3.4	5
Cyprus (Turkish)	93	4	6	54	0.2	85	40	3	$0.4	44.7		$2.0	4
Luxembourg	115	9	8	138	0.36	98	68	8	$3.4		5.0	$9.4	9
Malta	128	6	6	1,200	0.36	83	94	5	$1.2	35.4	6.6	$3.3	6
Iceland	143	5	2	2	0.23	100	87	3	$2.4	38.7	4.5	$10.4	8

NATIONS OF THE WORLD: EUROPEAN NATIONS

Country	Rnk	Military Capability Act Men	% Cadre	Mil Bud	% GDP	Bud Man	Bang per $	Bang M/Pop.	Bang T$/GL?	Reserves Men	p/mil	% Act
Averages & Totals		28,636	68	757,734	6.1%	26	8.0	1.3	492	28,687	6.1	22
Russia	1	3,800	22	$214,000	14.8%	$56	4.7	3.68	690	3,800	14.0	5
Germany, West	5	495	52	$18,934	2.9%	$38	15.1	4.60	433	303	4.9	100
France	7	493	51	$21,381	4.0%	$43	9.7	3.83	385	269	5.0	100
Sweden	8	1,264	26	$2,734	2.8%	$2	70.3	23.15	1,945	0	0.0	0
Britain	11	321	100	$25,168	5.3%	$79	6.5	2.93	347	91	1.6	48
Switzerland	12	1,124	13	$2,036	2.1%	$2	75.1	23.52	1,582	0	0.0	0
Turkey	16	569	14	$2,300	4.4%	$4	47.0	2.21	2,048	841	17.2	0
Italy	20	373	36	$9,788	2.8%	$26	8.1	1.41	227	237	4.2	?
Poland	22	340	44	$6,254	5.2%	$18	10.9	1.84	564	556	15.0	5
Germany, East	23	167	45	$7,700	7.7%	$46	7.0	3.18	541	385	22.6	5
Yugoslavia	24	240	36	$1,774	2.9%	$7	24.3	1.88	698	2,555	111.1	100
Spain	25	347	33	$4,929	2.8%	$14	8.4	1.10	235	653	17.2	0
Czechoslovakia	30	205	43	$3,774	4.4%	$18	6.9	1.64	308	200	12.5	5
Netherlands	37	103	53	$4,556	3.3%	$44	4.2	1.35	138	214	15.3	37
Greece	38	185	26	$1,805	4.7%	$10	10.5	1.89	491	403	40.3	25
Romania	39	190	43	$1,413	1.6%	$7	12.1	0.74	190	389	16.9	5
Belgium	40	95	66	$1,901	1.8%	$20	8.4	1.59	148	41	4.1	28
Bulgaria	41	163	42	$1,313	4.3%	$8	11.2	1.63	481	210	23.4	24
Hungary	42	105	45	$1,220	2.4%	$12	11.0	1.22	269	141	12.8	24
Finland	43	40	37	$809	1.7%	$20	16.1	2.71	273	66	13.8	100
Austria	50	50	36	$797	1.2%	$16	10.5	1.11	125	127	16.7	4
Portugal	55	64	39	$622	2.6%	$10	11.0	0.69	291	80	8.0	22
Denmark	56	37	42	$1,221	2.2%	$33	5.5	1.32	120	150	29.5	0
Norway	57	43	30	$1,696	3.0%	$39	3.5	1.45	106	242	59.0	48
Albania	79	40	45	$194	8.1%	$5	6.7	0.46	539	23	8.3	40
Ireland	81	15	100	$265	1.6%	$17	4.1	0.32	64	38	11.1	5
Cyprus (Greek)	84	10	80	$59	3.5%	$6	12.1	1.44	424	30	60.2	100
Cyprus (Turkish)	93	5	90	$5	1.3%	$1	81.0	2.03	1,013	16	77.5	28
Luxembourg	115	1	100	$43	1.3%	$61	1.1	0.13	14	14	3.3	36
Malta	128	1	100	$15	1.3%	$15	1.2	0.05	15	2	5.3	100
Iceland	143	0.10	100	$5	0.2%	$50	0.7	0.02	2	1	4.8	?

NATIONS OF THE WORLD: EUROPEAN NATIONS

Country	Rnk	Paramilitary Profile		Army Profile						Air Force Profile			
		Tot p/mil	%Pop Srv	Ult Men	Mbl Men	Eqtd Divs	Men Div	AFV	Men/ AFV	Mbl Men	Cmbt A/C	Other A/C	Men/ A/C
Averages & Totals		43,502	9.3 2.2%	779,530	47,146	1,681	28.0	360,972	131	5,782	46,848	39,835	67
Russia	1	5,600 20.6	4.9%	54,800	5,700	220	25.9	115,000	50	1,100	11,500	3,500	73
Germany, West	5	20 0.3	1.3%	13,750	540	18	30.0	11,890	45	200	1,127	441	128
France	7	92 1.7	1.6%	11,700	586	29	20.5	12,000	49	121	1,399	929	52
Sweden	8	500 60.2	21.3%	1,800	700	10	70.0	1,000	700	30	460	325	38
Britain	11	8 0.1	0.7%	11,800	238	16	15.2	7,250	33	97	882	1,088	49
Switzerland	12	500 76.9	25.0%	1,450	585	18	32.5	2,100	279	40	330	260	68
Turkey	16	125 2.6	3.1%	7,200	1,175	24	49.0	5,600	210	120	370	250	194
Italy	20	211 3.8	1.5%	11,700	445	10	44.5	6,000	74	110	705	823	72
Poland	22	635 17.2	4.1%	7,400	710	19	37.4	8,000	89	156	765	675	108
Germany, East	23	37 2.2	3.5%	3,500	446	6	74.3	6,600	68	67	394	700	61
Yugoslavia	24	4,000 173.9	29.5%	4,800	2,700	50	54.0	5,000	540	65	450	300	87
Spain	25	110 2.9	2.9%	7,500	850	13	65.4	2,000	425	50	300	600	56
Czechoslovakia	30	131 8.2	3.3%	2,900	348	12	29.0	7,550	46	57	485	270	75
Netherlands	37	31 2.2	2.5%	3,300	250	5	50.0	2,700	93	32	240	115	90
Greece	38	29 2.9	6.2%	1,900	490	18	27.2	4,150	118	50	300	340	78
Romania	39	1,587 69.0	9.4%	4,600	500	15	34.2	4,280	117	59	350	235	101
Belgium	40	16 1.6	1.5%	2,100	110	6	18.3	2,005	55	22	144	111	84
Bulgaria	41	173 19.2	6.1%	1,800	270	13	20.8	2,700	100	89	265	210	187
Hungary	42	75 6.8	2.9%	2,100	200	6	33.3	3,135	64	45	160	150	145
Finland	43	4 0.9	2.3%	1,100	101	4	23.5	1,200	84	3	42	137	17
Austria	50	11 1.5	2.5%	1,600	172	12	14.4	637	271	5	32	149	25
Portugal	55	22 2.2	1.7%	1,950	112	6	18.7	300	373	17	85	135	75
Denmark	56	0 0.0	3.7%	1,100	143	5	25.5	950	150	29	116	48	178
Norway	57	152 37.2	10.7%	800	228	5	45.5	600	380	32	130	75	158
Albania	79	25 8.9	3.2%	750	50	2	25.0	200	250	9	100	54	58
Ireland	81	0 0.0	1.6%	700	51	3	15.4	134	380	1	15	23	21
Cyprus (Greek)	84	3 6.0	8.6%	80	40	1	17.2	70	564	0	0	2	40
Cyprus (Turkish)	93	0 0.0	10.0%	40	20	1	20.0	50	400	0	0	0	0
Luxembourg	115	1 1.4	0.7%	80	2	0	19.0	5	380	0	0	0	0
Malta	128	3 3.9	1.2%	80	3	0	12.5	0	0	0	0	8	13
Iceland	143	? 0.0	0.5%	50	1	0	10.0	0	0	0	0	0	0

NATIONS OF THE WORLD: EUROPEAN NATIONS

Country	Rnk	Navy Profile Type	Navy Profile Mbl Men	Cmbt Ships	Other Ships	Men/ Ship	Tons	Tons/ Ship	Men/ Shp/T	Manpower Mbl Men	% Incr	% Army	% AF	% Navy
Averages & Totals			3,387	3,256	6,493	347	18,125	1,859	5.35	57,323	200%	82%	10%	6%
Russia	1	S	800.0	845	940	448	845	474	1.06	7,600	100%	75%	14%	11%
Germany, West	5	R	58.4	81	118	293	247	1,243	4.24	798	61%	68%	25%	7%
France	7	S	55.0	83	52	407	581	4,305	10.57	762	55%	77%	16%	7%
Sweden	8	C	35.0	50	74	282	100	808	2.86	1,264	0%	92%	4%	5%
Britain	11	S	76.8	99	200	257	1,079	3,609	14.05	411	28%	58%	24%	19%
Switzerland	12	R	0.0	0	0	0	0	0	0.00	1,124	0%	94%	6%	0%
Turkey	16	R	115.0	50	175	511	238	1,060	2.07	1,410	148%	83%	9%	8%
Italy	20	R	55.0	41	81	451	219	1,798	3.99	610	64%	73%	18%	9%
Poland	22	L	30.0	18	102	250	46	379	1.52	896	163%	79%	17%	3%
Germany, East	23	L	39.0	35	102	285	80	585	2.06	552	231%	81%	12%	7%
Yugoslavia	24	L	30.0	27	81	278	49	452	1.63	2,795	1066%	97%	2%	1%
Spain	25	R	100.0	42	71	885	222	1,963	2.22	1,000	188%	85%	5%	10%
Czechoslovakia	30	-	0.0	0	0	0	0	0	0.00	405	98%	86%	14%	0%
Netherlands	37	R	35.0	27	66	376	142	1,526	4.05	317	208%	79%	10%	11%
Greece	38	R	48.0	47	170	221	157	723	3.27	588	218%	83%	9%	8%
Romania	39	C	19.5	3	125	152	71	552	3.63	579	205%	86%	10%	3%
Belgium	40	C	4.6	4	54	79	9	157	1.98	136	43%	81%	16%	3%
Bulgaria	41	C	14.5	12	43	264	36	660	2.50	373	129%	72%	24%	4%
Hungary	42	P	1.2	0	10	120	1	100	0.83	246	134%	81%	18%	0%
Finland	43	P	2.5	12	23	71	15	429	6.00	107	164%	95%	3%	2%
Austria	50	P	0.1	0	12	8	0	8	1.00	177	254%	97%	3%	0%
Portugal	55	L	15.0	20	20	375	57	1,415	3.77	144	126%	78%	11%	10%
Denmark	56	C	14.8	29	25	274	43	804	2.93	187	409%	76%	16%	8%
Norway	57	C	24.9	64	35	252	52	521	2.07	285	560%	80%	11%	9%
Albania	79	C	4.5	3	83	52	11	122	2.33	64	57%	79%	14%	7%
Ireland	81	P	1.3	5	3	163	10	1,200	7.38	53	249%	96%	2%	2%
Cyprus (Greek)	84	P	0.5	0	12	42	1	42	1.00	40	301%	99%	0%	1%
Cyprus (Turkish)	93	-	0.0	0	0	0	0	0	0.00	20	344%	100%	0%	0%
Luxembourg	115	P	0.0	0	0	0	0	0	0.00	2	171%	100%	0%	0%
Malta	128	P	0.3	0	9	33	1	67	2.00	3	190%	86%	3%	10%
Iceland	143	P	0.2	0	6	33	7	1,083	32.50	1	1100%	83%	0%	17%

NATIONS OF THE WORLD: EUROPEAN NATIONS

Averages & Totals		2.9	2.8	2.3	1.7	1.8	3.1
Country		Force Multipliers					
	Rnk	Ldrs	Eqp	Exp	Spt	Mob	Trad
Russia	1	4	6	4	6	9	7
Germany, West	5	8	8	3	8	8	9
France	7	7	7	3	7	6	7
Sweden	8	4	5	2	5	2	5
Britain	11	8	7	4	6	7	8
Switzerland	12	4	5	2	3	1	6
Turkey	16	5	3	2	3	2	9
Italy	20	5	4	2	5	7	5
Poland	22	5	4	2	3	6	5
Germany, East	23	6	6	3	3	7	8
Yugoslavia	24	5	3	4	3	3	5
Spain	25	3	3	2	3	6	6
Czechoslovakia	30	4	4	1	3	5	3
Netherlands	37	4	7	1	4	6	5
Greece	38	3	4	2	3	4	4
Romania	39	3	3	1	2	4	5
Belgium	40	4	4	2	5	5	5
Bulgaria	41	3	3	2	2	3	5
Hungary	42	4	3	2	3	3	5
Finland	43	7	5	3	3	3	9
Austria	50	4	5	2	4	3	7
Portugal	55	3	3	5	2	3	5
Denmark	56	4	6	2	5	5	5
Norway	57	3	6	2	5	6	4
Albania	79	2	1	0	1	2	4
Ireland	81	3	3	1	1	2	5
Cyprus (Greek)	84	3	2	5	1	1	3
Cyprus (Turkish)	93	3	3	6	0	0	6
Luxembourg	115	2	6	1	3	3	4
Malta	128	1	2	0	1	1	5
Iceland	143	2	5	1	1	1	1

NATIONS OF THE WORLD: AMERICAN NATIONS

Country	Rnk	National Summary			War Pwr	Atck Pwr	Long War	Tot Qual	Nukes	% Off	Geographic Profile				
		War State	Allies	Gov Stab							Area 1000 KmSq	Agr	Grz	For	Othr
Averages & Totals		1.7	5.9	5.8	6,083	3,255	7,337	6.8	2.4	23%	132,278	21	16	27	33
United States	2	2	9	9	820	656	724	38	9	80%	9,363	20	26	32	22
Canada	29	1	9	9	28	14	75	34	5	50%	9,976	4	2	47	50
Brazil	31	2	7	9	23	4	58	8	4	16%	8,512	4	13	60	25
Cuba	32	6	2	6	23	5	49	15	2	20%	115	35	30	15	20
Argentina	34	1	6	7	22	5	56	14	6	25%	2,767	57	46	25	18
Chile	53	1	7	6	8	3	33	8	3	40%	757	9	15	29	47
Peru	59	2	6	6	5	2	23	4	3	30%	1,285	2	14	55	29
Nicaragua	61	4	3	7	5	2	23	11	1	35%	130	5	7	50	36
Colombia	62	3	7	7	4	1	21	6	2	20%	1,139	5	35	50	10
Mexico	64	1	6	8	3	1	19	3	4	30%	1,973	12	40	22	26
El Salvador	74	7	8	4	2	0	14	8	1	30%	21	32	26	12	30
Venezuela	75	1	6	8	2	1	14	4	3	30%	912	4	18	21	57
Uruguay	87	1	6	6	1	0	8	2	2	30%	178	10	75	5	10
Bolivia	89	1	7	4	1	0	7	1	1	20%	1,099	2	11	40	47
Ecuador	92	1	6	6	0	0	7	2	2	20%	283	11	8	55	26
Paraguay	96	1	6	5	0	0	6	2	1	60%	407	2	24	52	22
Honduras	98	3	6	6	0	0	5	2	1	20%	112	7	30	27	36
Costa Rica	99	1	6	8	0	0	5	3	1	20%	51	8	22	60	10
Guatemala	100	3	6	6	0	0	4	1	1	20%	109	14	10	57	19
Dominican Rep.	103	1	7	7	0	0	4	1	1	20%	49	28	17	45	20
Jamaica	113	1	8	7	0	0	2	2	1	10%	11	21	23	19	37
Guyana	123	1	6	6	0	0	2	0	1	10%	215	1	11	66	22
Panama	124	1	8	7	0	0	2	1	1	10%	77	13	11	20	56
Haiti	131	2	7	2	0	0	1	0	1	0%	28	31	18	7	44
Trinidad	132	1	6	7	0	0	0	1	1	10%	5	26	2	11	4
Belize	137	1	5	7	0	0	1	1	1	0%	23	38	?	46	16
Suriname	145	1	4	2	0	0	0	0	1	0%	163	8	0	76	16

NATIONS OF THE WORLD: AMERICAN NATIONS

Country	Rnk	Trans Net	MEI	Pop SqKm	Pop Tot	% Lit	% Urban	Ind	GDP	% Frgn Trade	% Soc Exp	Per Cap	Qual Life
Averages & Totals		3.8	5.4	35	4,674	54	42	3.3	12,375	26	4.9	2.6	3.6
United States	2	9	3	25	234	99	74	9	$3,400.0	12.4	14.5	$14.5	9
Canada	29	3	5	3	25	99	75	9	$293.9	24.2	13.0	$11.8	9
Brazil	31	2	5	15	131	83	61	6	$288.1	8.1	1.4	$2.2	4
Cuba	32	6	7	87	10	96	60	5	$16.0	33.1	8.0	$1.6	3
Argentina	34	5	7	10	29	85	81	6	$57.0	16.0	5.6	$2.0	4
Chile	53	5	7	16	12	92	79	6	$26.0	15.1	5.0	$2.2	4
Peru	59	2	4	15	19	45	63	4	$20.1	15.9	3.2	$1.1	3
Nicaragua	61	3	4	22	2.8	52	50	3	$2.7	19.5	3.5	$1.0	3
Colombia	62	3	3	25	28	75	65	5	$37.3	7.8	3.2	$1.3	3
Mexico	64	4	5	38	75	65	64	5	$239.6	8.1	3.3	$3.2	4
El Salvador	74	5	7	234	4.9	50	42	3	$3.7	21.4	4.7	$0.8	2
Venezuela	75	6	6	18	16	75	75	3	$69.5	28.9	7.4	$4.3	5
Uruguay	87	6	4	17	3.1	90	83	5	$11.6	10.3	6.0	$3.7	6
Bolivia	89	2	3	5	5.8	38	39	3	$7.4	12.7	5.3	$1.3	3
Ecuador	92	3	5	30	8.6	57	42	3	$12.3	20.3	3.9	$1.4	3
Paraguay	96	2	6	8	3.1	40	40	2	$5.5	5.6	1.9	$1.8	2
Honduras	98	4	3	37	4.2	47	31	2	$2.8	28.8	4.6	$0.7	2
Costa Rica	99	4	4	49	2.5	90	41	4	$4.8	20.8	7.5	$1.9	3
Guatemala	100	4	4	70	7.6	30	36	3	$9.9	11.8	2.0	$1.3	3
Dominican Rep.	103	4	5	123	.6	70	47	4	$7.2	10.7	3.0	$1.2	3
Jamaica	113	5	8	209	2.3	45	41	3	$2.8	25.4	9.1	$1.2	4
Guyana	123	2	4	4	0.9	86	40	0	$0.5	64.8	10.3	$0.6	2
Panama	124	4	7	27	2.1	82	54	3	$2.2	14.3	6.0	$1.0	4
Haiti	131	1	5	220	6.1	10	24	1	$1.5	12.3	2.2	$0.2	1
Trinidad	132	6	8	235	1.2	95	50	5	$6.9	46.4	6.0	$5.8	5
Belize	137	2	5	7	0.16	75	50	0	$0.1	79.2	4.0	$0.8	2
Suriname	145	1	4	2	0.4	80	60	1	$0.7	73.4	6.0	$1.8	3

NATIONS OF THE WORLD: AMERICAN NATIONS

Country	Rnk	Military Capability		Mil Bud	% GDP	Bud Man	Bang per $	Bang M/Pop.	Bang T$/GDP	Reserves	Men p/mil	% Act
		Act Men	% Cadre							Men		
Averages & Totals		28,636	68	757,734	6.1%	26	8.0	1.3	492	28,687	6.1	22
United States	2	2,136	100	$255,000	7.5%	$119	3.2	3.51	241	1,074	4.6	73
Canada	29	83	100	$6,430	2.2%	$78	4.3	1.11	95	32	1.3	100
Brazil	31	277	52	$1,838	0.6%	$7	12.7	0.18	81	688	5.3	35
Cuba	32	153	38	$1,271	7.9%	$8	18.0	2.29	1,431	188	18.8	100
Argentina	34	153	29	$3,279	5.8%	$21	6.7	0.75	383	331	11.4	30
Chile	53	96	66	$2,103	8.1%	$22	3.8	0.67	310	191	15.9	0
Peru	59	136	48	$716	3.6%	$5	7.6	0.29	270	185	9.7	0
Nicaragua	61	49	49	$125	4.6%	$3	41.2	1.84	1,909	27	9.7	100
Colombia	62	70	59	$420	1.1%	$6	10.0	0.15	113	71	2.5	0
Mexico	64	120	100	$695	0.3%	$6	4.8	0.04	14	279	3.7	100
El Salvador	74	25	?	$158	4.3%	$6	12.2	0.39	521	18	3.6	100
Venezuela	75	41	75	$1,142	1.6%	$28	1.6	0.11	26	50	3.1	0
Uruguay	87	30	100	$386	3.3%	$13	1.6	0.19	52	127	41.1	0
Bolivia	89	28	35	$186	2.5%	$7	3.0	0.10	75	60	10.3	0
Ecuador	92	37	76	$177	1.4%	$5	2.5	0.05	36	29	3.4	0
Paraguay	96	16	32	$88	1.6%	$5	3.7	0.10	59	19	6.1	100
Honduras	98	15	33	$60	2.1%	$4	3.5	0.10	76	17	4.1	0
Costa Rica	99	7	100	$14	0.3%	$2	15.1	0.08	44	17	0.0	0
Guatemala	100	22	40	$92	0.9%	$4	1.9	0.02	17	13	1.7	0
Dominican Rep.	103	23	100	$103	1.4%	$4	1.3	0.02	19	0	0.0	0
Jamaica	113	3	100	$35	1.3%	$11	1.6	0.03	21	0	.0	0
Guyana	123	7	100	$25	5.0%	$4	1.1	0.03	56	0	0.0	0
Panama	124	2	100	$40	1.8%	$20	0.6	0.01	11	0	0.0	0
Haiti	131	7	100	$15	1.0%	$2	0.9	.00	9	0	0.0	0
Trinidad	132	1	100	$7	0.1%	$5	1.6	0.01	2	0.5	0.4	100
Belize	137	1	100	$1	0.8%	$1	7.9	0.05	61	0	0.0	?
Suriname	145	1	100	$7	1.0%	$7	0.3	0.01	3	0	0.0	0

NATIONS OF THE WORLD: AMERICAN NATIONS

Rnk	Country	Paramilitary Profile			Army Profile				AFV	Men/ AFV	Air Force Profile			
		Tot	p/mil	%Pop Srv	Ult Men	Mbl Men	Eqtd Divs	Men Div			Mbl Men	Cmbt A/C	Other A/C	Men/ A/C
	Averages & Totals	43,502	9.3	2.2%	779,530	47,146	1,681	28.0	360,972	131	5,782	46,848	39,835	67
2	United States	237	1.0	1.5%	50,000	1,600	44	36.4	31,000	52	1,100	8,700	12,400	52
29	Canada	8	0.3	0.5%	5,900	53	2	26.5	1,586	33	38	200	300	77
31	Brazil	185	1.4	0.9%	22,100	820	20	41.0	1,750	469	75	200	500	107
32	Cuba	720	72.0	10.6%	1,700	275	25	11.0	1,350	204	38	290	220	75
34	Argentina	21	0.7	1.7%	6,000	365	12	30.4	1,100	332	40	216	350	71
53	Chile	27	2.3	2.6%	2,300	240	8	32.0	1,000	240	17	90	255	48
59	Peru	32	1.7	1.9%	3,100	235	15	15.7	1,000	235	50	135	180	159
61	Nicaragua	40	14.3	4.1%	380	75	6	12.5	100	750	5	10	12	27
62	Colombia	52	1.9	0.7%	5,000	132	4	33.0	350	377	5	40	220	19
64	Mexico	145	1.9	0.7%	14,000	378	12	30.7	253	1,494	6	95	242	17
74	El Salvador	80	16.3	2.5%	700	40	4	9.9	60	658	2	60	46	23
75	Venezuela	40	2.5	0.8%	3,300	82	4	20.6	350	235	5	200	160	13
87	Uruguay	19	6.0	5.7%	550	150	9	50.0	120	1,250	3	32	110	24
89	Bolivia	5	0.0	1.6%	900	80	9	8.9	103	777	5	22	114	34
92	Ecuador	0	0.0	0.8%	1,400	58	6	9.6	305	189	4	54	71	34
96	Paraguay	2	0.5	1.2%	700	28	3	9.3	21	1,333	3	20	94	22
98	Honduras	5	1.1	0.9%	600	31	1	23.5	28	1,089	2	26	57	18
99	Costa Rica	0	0.0	0.3%	470	7	0	21.7	0	0	0	0	14	14
100	Guatemala	312	41.0	4.6%	1,200	33	3	11.9	61	546	1	20	128	8
103	Dominican Rep.	10	1.7	0.6%	875	15	1	12.5	46	326	4	19	50	58
113	Jamaica	6	2.6	0.4%	400	3	0	15.0	10	300	0	0	12	8
123	Guyana	5	5.6	1.3%	170	7	0	21.7	25	260	0	0	16	13
124	Panama	8	3.6	0.5%	360	2	0	15.0	16	94	0	0	47	4
131	Haiti	15	2.4	0.4%	700	6	0	21.0	11	573	0	8	27	6
132	Trinidad	0	0.1	0.2%	240	1	0	6.5	0	0	0	0	5	10
137	Belize	?	0.0	0.6%	25	1	0	5.1	15	34	0	0	4	13
145	Suriname	0	0.0	0.3%	40	1	0	8.0	12	67	0	0	0	0

NATIONS OF THE WORLD: AMERICAN NATIONS

Country	Rnk	Navy Profile Type	Navy Profile Mbl Men	Cmbt Ships	Other Ships	Men/ Ship	Tons	Tons/ Ship	Men/ Shp/T	Manpower Mbl Men	Manpower Distribution Incr	% Army	% AF	% Navy
Averages & Totals			3,387	3,256	6,493	347	18,125	1,859	5.35	57,323	200%	82%	10%	6%
United States	2	S	510.0	429	412	606	9,496	11,292	18.62	3,210	50%	50%	34%	16%
Canada	29	R	23.0	25	48	315	217	2,968	9.42	114	38%	46%	34%	20%
Brazil	31	R	70.0	25	75	700	178	1,784	2.55	965	248%	85%	8%	7%
Cuba	32	C	28.0	30	85	243	24	208	0.85	341	123%	81%	11%	8%
Argentina	34	R	79.0	30	44	1068	183	2,472	2.32	484	216%	75%	8%	16%
Chile	53	R	30.0	14	46	500	167	2,785	5.57	287	198%	84%	6%	10%
Peru	59	L	35.0	32	44	461	230	3,026	6.57	320	136%	73%	16%	11%
Nicaragua	61	P	0.3	0	15	20	0	27	1.33	76	56%	99%	1%	0%
Colombia	62	L	4.0	8	19	148	32	1,178	7.95	141	101%	94%	4%	3%
Mexico	64	L	15.0	21	68	169	87	981	5.82	399	232%	95%	1%	4%
El Salvador	74	P	0.3	0	10	30	1	100	3.33	42	71%	94%	6%	1%
Venezuela	75	L	4.0	14	50	63	49	766	12.25	91	124%	91%	5%	4%
Uruguay	87	C	4.0	3	9	333	11	917	2.75	157	425%	95%	2%	3%
Bolivia	89	C	3.0	0	44	68	10	236	3.47	88	217%	91%	5%	3%
Ecuador	92	C	4.5	16	18	118	24	709	6.03	66	79%	87%	7%	6%
Paraguay	96	L	0.6	0	17	265	5	265	1.00	35	117%	80%	7%	13%
Honduras	98	P	0.3	0	11	35	1	29	0.83	33	114%	94%	5%	2%
Costa Rica	99	P	0.2	0	11	27	0	55	2.00	7	0%	93%	3%	4%
Guatemala	100	P	0.2	0	8	25	0	50	2.00	35	61%	75%	3%	1%
Dominican Rep.	103	C	1.0	20	20	25	16	395	15.80	23	0%	75%	20%	5%
Jamaica	113	P	0.2	0	4	50	0	75	1.50	3	3%	91%	3%	6%
Guyana	123	P	0.3	0	11	27	1	55	2.00	7	3%	93%	3%	4%
Panama	124	C	0.3	0	14	21	4	250	11.67	7	0%	75%	10%	15%
Haiti	131	P	0.3	0	15	20	2	127	6.33	2	0%	93%	3%	4%
Trinidad	132	P	0.4	0	14	29	2	107	3.75	2	35%	74%	3%	23%
Belize	137	P	0.1	0	2	25	0	15	0.60	1	0%	84%	8%	8%
Suriname	145	P	0.2	0	10	20	1	70	3.50	1	0%	76%	5%	19%

NATIONS OF THE WORLD: AMERICAN NATIONS

Averages & Totals		2.9	2.8	2.3	1.7	1.8	3.1
Country		Force Multipliers					
	Rnk	Ldrs	Eqp	Exp	Spt	Mob	Trad
United States	2	6	6	5	8	7	6
Canada	29	6	7	3	5	6	7
Brazil	31	3	3	1	3	5	2
Cuba	32	4	4	6	2	2	3
Argentina	34	3	4	5	3	5	4
Chile	53	3	4	1	3	4	2
Peru	59	2	2	2	1	2	3
Nicaragua	61	4	2	6	1	1	2
Colombia	62	3	2	2	1	2	3
Mexico	64	2	2	1	2	2	0
El Salvador	74	3	3	7	1	1	1
Venezuela	75	2	4	1	2	3	1
Uruguay	87	2	2	0	2	1	0
Bolivia	89	2	2	0	1	1	1
Ecuador	92	2	1	0	1	1	0
Paraguay	96	2	2	0	1	1	1
Honduras	98	1	1	2	1	1	2
Costa Rica	99	3	1	1	1	1	1
Guatemala	100	1	1	1	1	1	0
Dominican Rep.	103	1	1	0	1	1	0
Jamaica	113	1	2	2	1	1	3
Guyana	123	1	1	0	0	1	0
Panama	124	2	2	0	1	0	0
Haiti	131	1	1	0	0	0	0
Trinidad	132	1	1	1	1	0	1
Belize	137	4	1	0	0	0	0
Suriname	145	1	1	0	0	0	0

NATIONS OF THE WORLD: AFRICAN NATIONS

Country	Rnk	National Summary									Geographic Profile			
		War State	Allies	Gov Stab	War Pwr	Atck Pwr	Long War	Tot Qual	Nukes	% Off	Area 1000 KmSq	Agr	Grz	For	Othr
Averages & Totals		1.7	5.9	5.8	6,083	3,255	7,337	6.8	2.4	23%	132,278	21	16	27	33
South Africa	26	4	7	8	35	16	86	42	6	45%	1,221	12	?	2	86
Ethiopia	35	3	3	3	20	3	45	8	2	16%	1,222	10	55	6	29
Nigeria	36	2	6	5	20	11	45	15	2	55%	924	25	?	35	40
Angola	60	5	4	4	5	1	23	6	1	16%	1,247	6	22	44	33
Zimbabwe	71	3	5	4	2	1	16	6	1	23%	391	6	60	34	33
Tanzania	77	1	5	5	1	0	12	4	1	20%	942	15	31	48	?
Somalia	80	2	6	6	1	0	11	2	2	20%	638	13	32	14	6
Kenya	83	1	6	5	1	0	10	6	1	20%	583	12	65	20	41
Senegambia	91	1	6	5	0	0	7	3	1	10%	209	14	10	12	3
Ghana	94	4	6	5	0	0	6	5	1	10%	239	19	?	60	76
Mozambique	95	4	3	4	0	0	6	3	1	10%	787	30	?	56	21
Uganda	97	3	6	1	0	0	5	1	1	0%	236	20	10	50	14
Chad	101	5	6	3	0	0	4	2	1	10%	1,284	17	35	45	20
Zaire	102	2	7	5	0	0	4	1	1	10%	2,345	17	20	50	46
Cameroon	104	2	6	5	0	0	4	2	1	10%	475	5	18	21	35
Madagascar	105	1	6	5	0	0	4	2	1	0%	587	1	58	75	15
Gabon	109	1	7	6	0	0	3	4	1	10%	268	?	15	40	16
Guinea-Bisseau	110	1	6	6	0	0	3	1	1	10%	35	8	?	40	9
Ivory Coast	111	1	6	5	0	0	2	2	1	10%	323	25	45	20	7
Mali	114	1	8	4	0	0	2	1	1	10%	1,240	33	?	30	75
Liberia	116	1	6	5	0	0	2	1	1	10%	111	25	20	63	40
Rwanda	117	1	6	4	0	0	2	1	1	0%	26	65	33	13	14
Guinea	118	1	5	5	0	0	2	0	1	0%	246	10	40	62	10
Niger	119	1	6	4	0	0	2	2	1	10%	1,267	6	40	10	77
Congo	120	1	4	3	0	0	2	0	1	0%	342	33	20	35	4
Sierra Leone	121	1	6	5	0	0	2	1	1	0%	72	65	27	19	8
Zambia	122	2	6	3	0	0	2	0	1	0%	753	10	71	25	6
Botswana	125	1	7	7	0	0	2	1	1	0%	600	6	10	75	94
Djibouti	126	1	6	6	0	0	1	1	1	0%	23	?	1	5	90
Burundi	127	1	6	4	0	0	1	0	1	0%	28	28	10	10	10
Mauretania	129	1	6	3	0	0	1	0	1	10%	1,031	1	9	62	90
Upper Volta	130	1	6	2	0	0	1	0	1	0%	274	30	50	10	10
Togo	133	1	6	5	0	0	1	0	1	0%	57	15	40	35	10
Equatorial Guinea	134	1	4	5	0	0	1	0	1	0%	28	15	?	90	5
Malawi	135	1	6	2	0	0	1	0	1	0%	119	31	6	25	38
Benin	138	1	7	5	0	0	1	0	1	0%	113	80	?	19	1
Lesotho	139	2	6	7	0	0	0	0	1	0%	30	15	?	?	85
Central Afr. Rep.	140	1	6	2	0	0	0	0	1	0%	623	10	75	75	10
Swaziland	141	1	6	6	0	0	0	0	1	0%	17	80	?	5	20
Cape Verde Is.	144	1	6	6	0	0	0	0	1	0%	4	35	20	10	35
Comoro Is.	147	1	6	2	0	0	0	0	1	0%	2	48	7	15	30
Seychelle Is	146	1	6	6	0	0	0	0	1	0%	0.03	55	?	17	28
Sao Tome & Princ.	149	1	6	6	0	0	0	0	1	0%	1	1	?	?	?

NATIONS OF THE WORLD: AFRICAN NATIONS

Country	Rnk	Trans Net	MEI	Population Profile				Economic Profile					
				Pop SqKm	Pop Tot	% Lit	% Urban	Ind	GDP	% Frgn Trade	% Soc Exp	Per Cap	Qual Life
Averages & Totals		3.8	5.4	35	4,674	54	42	3.3	12,375	26	4.9	2.6	3.6
South Africa	26	4	5	24	29	64	48	7	$49.4	35.6	4.5	$1.7	4
Ethiopia	35	2	4	29	35	20	15	2	$4.5	8.3	4.5	$0.1	1
Nigeria	36	2	3	92	85	25	23	1	$55.3	30.0	2.9	$0.7	2
Angola	60	2	4		6.5	12	21	1	$3.3	51.5	?	$0.5	2
Zimbabwe	71	3	4	19	7.3	28	20	3	$6.2	15.1	2.0	$0.8	2
Tanzania	77	1	3	19	18	61	7	3	$6.1	9.2	5.6	$0.3	1
Somalia	80	5	5	8		8	7	0	$1.8	6.2	5.0	$0.4	1
Kenya	83	3	6	31	18	27	10	3	$6.0	17.2	7.1	$0.3	1
Senegambia	91	3	6	32	6.6	9	33	3	$2.4	19.1	5.0	$0.4	1
Ghana	94	1	3	55	13	25	31	3	$10.7	10.2	4.0	$0.8	2
Mozambique	95	3	4	13	10	15	8	1	$2.8	13.8	?	$0.3	1
Uganda	97	3	4	59	14	30	7	0	$0.8	53.3	2.0	$0.1	1
Chad	101	1	6	4	4.9	8	14	0	$0.6	10.7	3.0	$0.2	1
Zaire	102	1	2	13	31	5	30	2	$5.3	12.5	4.3	$0.8	1
Cameroon	104	2	3	19	9	25	25	1	$6.8	16.2	3.5	$0.3	1
Madagascar	105	2	5	15	9	45	14	2	$2.7	12.6	9.0	$0.3	3
Gabon	109	2	5	3	0.7	30	32	0	$3.5	62.0	4.5	$5.0	1
Guinea-Bissau	110	1	4	23	0.8	2	?	3	$0.2	30.0	?	$0.3	1
Ivory Coast	111	3	4	27	8.8	65	32	3	$10.8	23.1	8.0	$1.2	3
Mali	114	2	5	6	7.2	5	17	0	$1.2	14.7	5.5	$0.2	1
Liberia	116	1	5	19	2.1	24	28	2	$0.8	75.0	7.0	$0.4	1
Rwanda	117	2	7	205	5.4	25	9	0	$1.3	5.5	3.0	$0.2	1
Guinea	118	2	5	23	5.6	8	9	1	$1.6	21.4	5.5	$0.3	1
Niger	119	1	4	5	6	8	6	0	$2.9	15.8	5.0	$0.5	1
Congo	120	2	4	5	1.7	20	40	1	$1.4	13.2	9.0	$0.8	1
Sierra Leone	121	2	5	50	3.6	10	18	1	$1.1	17.3	5.0	$0.3	1
Zambia	122	2	5	7	5.6	28	43	1	$3.5	28.6	6.0	$0.6	1
Botswana	125	6	6	1	0.76	32	12	3	$0.9	56.0	8.0	$1.2	2
Djibouti	126	5	7	13	0.3	5	65	0	$0.4	5.0	3.5	$1.3	3
Burundi	127	2	4	169	4.7	15	5	0	$1.1	5.9	6.0	$0.2	1
Mauretania	129	1	5	2	1.7	10	23	1	$0.7	27.7	6.0	$0.4	1
Upper Volta	130	3	7	24	6.5	55	11	0	$1.3	5.8	7.8	$0.2	1
Togo	133	3	7	48	2.7	20	15	1	$1.2	18.3	?	$0.4	1
Equatorial Guinea	134	1	2	11	0.3	20	15	0	$0.1	16.0	3.2	$0.3	1
Malawi	135	4	6	48	5.7	15	10	0	$1.5	19.5	6.0	$0.5	1
Benin	138	3	6	32	3.6	20	14	0	$1.3	13.1	6.1	$0.4	1
Lesotho	139	3	9	43	1.3	40	6	0	$1.4	2.9	5.0	$1.1	1
Central Afr. Rep.	140	1	7	4	2.5	8	20	0	$0.6	13.4	7.3	$0.8	1
Swaziland	141	2	7	29	0.5	25	15	1	$0.4	83.1	2.0	$0.2	1
Cape Verde Is.	144	2	8	75	0.3	37	20	1	$0.1	7.0	8.0	$0.3	1
Comoro Is.	147	2	8	200	0.36	15	37	0	$0.1	15.0	6.0	$0.3	1
Seychelle Is	146	2	8	2,333	0.07	60	?	0	$0.1	18.0	?	$1.4	3
Sao Tome & Princ.	149	2	5	104	0.1	?	?	0	$0.1	45.0	?	$0.6	1

NATIONS OF THE WORLD: AFRICAN NATIONS

Country	Rnk	Military Capability Act Men	% Cadre	Mil Bud	% GDP	Bud Man	Bang per $	Bang M/Pop.	Bang T$/GDP	Reserves Men	p/mil	% Act
Averages & Totals		28,636	68	757,734	6.1%	26	8.0	1.3	492	28,687	6.1	22
South Africa	26	82	36	$2,769	5.6%	$34	12.5	1.19	701	160	5.5	49
Ethiopia	35	251	10	$378	8.4%	$2	53.0	0.57	4,453	206	5.9	0
Nigeria	36	133	100	$1,800	3.3%	$14	11.1	0.23	360	2		0
Angola	60	88	20	$1,000	30.3%	$11	5.4	0.83	1,632	10	1.5	0
Zimbabwe	71	41	100	$337	5.4%	$8	7.4	0.34	400	30	4.1	0
Tanzania	77	40	100	$316	5.2%	$8	4.6	0.08	238	50	2.8	0
Somalia	80	62	100	$127	7.1%	$2	9.8	0.25	692	30	6.1	0
Kenya	83	16	10	$220	3.7%	$14	4.4	0.05	160	2	0.1	0
Senegambia	91	10	40	$55	2.3%	$5	8.9	0.07	204	7	1.0	0
Ghana	94	13	100	$155	1.4%	$12	2.3	0.03	33	5	0.4	0
Mozambique	95	28	10	$200	7.1%	$7	1.7	0.03	120	9	0.9	0
Uganda	97	15	?	$94	11.8%	$6	3.2	0.02	375	20	1.4	0
Chad	101	4	30	$52	8.6%	$12	3.2	0.03	280	7	1.4	0
Zaire	102	26	100	$150	2.8%	$6	1.0	0.01	29	22	0.7	0
Cameroon	104	7	100	$79	1.2%	$11	1.7	0.01	19	5	0.6	0
Madagascar	105	21	35	$79	2.9%	$4	1.6	0.01	47	1	0.1	0
Gabon	109	2	100	$89	2.5%	$40	1.0	0.13	26	3	4.0	0
Guinea-Bisseau	110	6	100	$8	4.1%	$1	10.5	0.11	427	0	0.0	0
Ivory Coast	111	5	100	$92	0.9%	$18	0.7	0.01	6	3	0.3	0
Mali	114	5	100	$40	3.3%	$8	1.3	0.01	42	5	0.7	0
Liberia	116	6	100	$51	6.4%	$9	0.9	0.02	56	13	6.1	0
Rwanda	117	5	100	$24	1.9%	$5	1.7	0.01	32	1	0.2	0
Guinea	118	10	100	$80	5.0%	$8	0.5	0.01	25	2	0.4	0
Niger	119	2	100	$19	0.7%	$9	1.8	0.01	12	3	0.4	0
Congo	120	9	100	$150	10.7%	$17	0.2	0.02	25	3	.0	0
Sierra Leone	121	3	100	$22	2.0%	$7	1.4	0.01	28	1	0.2	0
Zambia	122	14	100	$105	3.0%	$7	0.3	0.01	8	0	0.2	0
Botswana	125	3	100	$27	0.7%	$9	0.9	0.03	27	0	0.0	0
Djibouti	126	3	100	$3	0.7%	$1	7.4	0.07	54	2	7.1	0
Burundi	127	5	100	$40	3.6%	$8	0.5	.00	19	1	0.3	0
Mauretania	129	9	100	$6	0.9%	$1	2.7	0.01	24	6	3.5	?
Upper Volta	130	4	100	$32	2.5%	$8	0.5	.00	12	0	0.0	0
Togo	133	5	30	$21	1.8%	$4	0.5	.00	9	0	.0	0
Equatorial Guinea	134	2	20	$3	2.5%	$2	3.8	0.03	96	0	0.0	?
Malawi	135	5	100	$20	1.3%	$4	0.5	.00	6	3	0.6	0
Benin	138	3	100	$24	1.8%	$7	0.3	.00	5	1	0.3	0
Lesotho	139	1	100	$2	0.2%	$2	2.9	.00	4	0	0.0	?
Central Afr. Rep.	140	2	100	$20	3.3%	$9	0.2	.00	8	2	0.6	?
Swaziland	141	1	100	$1	0.3%	$1	4.0	0.01	10	1	2.0	?
Cape Verde Is.	144	1	100	$4	3.5%	$3	0.6	0.01	22	0	.0	?
Comoro Is.	147	1	100	$1	1.0%	$1	2.0	0.01	20	0.1	0.1	?
Seychelle Is	146	1	100	$1	8.0%	$8	0.3	0.03	20	1	14.3	?
Sao Tome & Princ.	149	0.20	100	$1	1.7%	$5	0.4	.00	7	1	8.0	?

NATIONS OF THE WORLD: AFRICAN NATIONS

Country	Rnk	Paramilitary Profile			Army Profile						Air Force Profile			
		Tot	p/mil	%Pop Srv	Ult Men	Mbl Men	Eqtd Divs	Men Div	AFV	Men/AFV	Mbl Men	Cmbt A/C	Other A/C	Men/A/C
Averages & Totals		43,502	9.3	2.2%	779,530	47,146	1,681	28.0	360,972	131	5,782	46,848	39,835	67
South Africa	26	145	5.0	1.3%	3,700	200	3	66.7	3,350	60	35	325	388	49
Ethiopia	35	180	5.1	1.8%	3,800	450	25	18.0	1,750	257	4	130	150	13
Nigeria	36	.	.	0.2%	10,500	120	4	27.9	326	368	9	48	179	40
Angola	60	510	78.5	9.4%	850	96	7	13.1	725	132	2	67	127	8
Zimbabwe	71	45	6.2	1.6%	1,100	70	4	18.4	91	769	1	30	78	12
Tanzania	77	52	2.9	0.8%	2,500	89	2	44.3	166	533	1	29	40	14
Somalia	80	30	6.0	2.5%	700	90	7	12.9	750	120	2	64	41	19
Kenya	83	2	0.1	0.1%	2,300	15	1	14.8	240	62	3	28	55	30
Senegambia	91	7	1.0	0.4%	800	16	1	19.6	100	157	1	2	27	17
Ghana	94	150	11.5	1.3%	1,600	15	1	18.8	200	75	1	12	35	30
Mozambique	95	100	10.0	1.4%	1,700	36	4	8.9	430	83	1	35	26	16
Uganda	97	2	0.1	0.3%	1,600	35	2	17.5	200	175	?	0	49	4
Chad	101	6	1.2	0.4%	600	11	1	22.0	26	423	3	0	100	24
Zaire	102	22	0.7	0.2%	3,500	44	6	7.3	300	147	0	19	27	10
Cameroon	104	8	0.6	0.2%	1,000	12	1	11.6	100	116	1	14	27	13
Madagascar	105	5	0.9	0.3%	1,275	21	1	35.0	25	840	0	12	35	12
Gabon	109	5	4.0	1.1%	110	4	0	14.3	55	78	1	8	7	14
Guinea-Bisseau	110	3	6.3	1.4%	110	7	0	14.3	50	114	1	0	33	16
Ivory Coast	111	3	0.3	0.1%	1,120	7	0	17.5	47	149	0	5	18	13
Mali	114	3	0.7	0.2%	820	10	1	19.2	106	91	1	5	16	19
Liberia	116	8	3.7	1.2%	250	18	1	22.1	12	1,475	0	5	9	18
Rwanda	117	1	0.2	0.1%	600	6	1	20.7	20	310	0	0	28	24
Guinea	118	9	1.6	0.4%	600	11	1	15.7	115	91	1	2	17	6
Niger	119	1	0.4	0.1%	600	5	0	15.0	54	87	0	6	27	10
Congo	120	3	1.8	0.7%	190	8	0	26.7	75	107	1	21	?	0
Sierra Leone	121	1	0.2	0.1%	440	4	1	19.0	200	19	1	0	88	13
Zambia	122	1	0.2	0.3%	700	14	0	13.7	177	77	2	51	10	10
Botswana	125	2	1.6	0.6%	100	3	0	28.5	50	57	0	5	6	17
Djibouti	126	2	7.0	2.3%	400	5	1	23.5	34	138	0	3	8	9
Burundi	127	6	0.3	0.2%	540	6	0	21.3	55	116	0	7	9	13
Mauretania	129	1	3.5	1.2%	170	14	1	23.3	106	132	1	0	13	8
Upper Volta	130	1	0.1	0.1%	900	4	0	12.3	80	46	0	11	16	11
Togo	133	2	0.3	0.2%	300	5	0	16.0	98	49	0	0	6	6
Equatorial Guinea	134	2	6.7	1.2%	30		0	14.0	20	70	1	11	16	6
Malawi	135	1	0.2	0.2%	710	8	1	25.7	70	133	0	0	15	7
Benin	138	1	0.3	0.1%	400	4	0	13.3	10	770	0	0	0	0
Lesotho	139	5	3.8	0.5%	180	2	0	17.5	30	0	0	0	0	0
Central Afr. Rep.	140	2	0.6	0.2%	290	4	0	20.0	20	175	0	0	32	9
Swaziland	141	?	0.0	0.4%	80	2	0	20.0	0	0	0	0	2	0
Cape Verde Is.	144	0	0.0	0.4%	50	1	0	10.0	8	125	0	0		15
Comoro Is.	147	?	0.0	0.3%	60	1	0	10.0	1	170	0	0	2	0
Seychelle Is	146	1	12.9	4.1%	10	2	0	17.0	10	0	0	0	6	17
Sao Tome & Princ.	149	?	0.0	1.0%	15	1	0	10.0	0	0	0	0		0

NATIONS OF THE WORLD: AFRICAN NATIONS

Country	Rnk	Navy Profile Type	Navy Profile Mbl Men	Cmbt Ships	Other Ships	Men/ Ship	Tons	Tons/ Ship	Men/ Shp/T	Manpower Distribution Mbl Men	% Incr	% Army	% AF	% Navy
Averages & Totals			3,387	3,256	6,493	347	18,125	1,859	5.35	57,323	200%	82%	10%	6%
South Africa	26	R	7.0	15	53	103	39	572	5.56	242	194%	83%	14%	3%
Ethiopia	35	C	2.5	8	16	104	8	325	3.12	456	82%	99%	1%	1%
Nigeria	36	L	6.0	12	125	44	39	284	6.48	135	2%	89%	7%	4%
Angola	60	P	1.0	2	29	32	6	203	6.30	98	11%	97%	2%	1%
Zimbabwe	71	-	1.0	0	0	0	0	0	0.00	71	73%	98%	2%	0%
Tanzania	77	C	1.0	0	28	36	2	75	2.10	91	124%	98%	1%	1%
Somalia	80	C	0.6	2	18	30	3	155	5.17	93	49%	97%	2%	1%
Kenya	83	C	0.7	5	3	88	1	138	1.57	18	13%	82%	14%	4%
Senegambia	91	P	0.8	0	10	80	2	150	1.88	17	67%	92%	3%	5%
Ghana	94	P	1.2	0	10	120	3	260	2.17	18	40%	85%	8%	7%
Mozambique	95	P	0.7	0	15	47	3	133	2.86	37	33%	95%	3%	2%
Uganda	97	?	?	0	0	0	0	0	0.00	35	133%	100%	0%	0%
Chad	101	-	0.0	0	0	0	0	0	0.00	11	167%	98%	2%	0%
Zaire	102	P	0.9	0	42	21	1	26	1.22	48	84%	92%	6%	2%
Cameroon	104	P	0.4	2	6	50	2	300	5.20	12	70%	94%	3%	3%
Madagascar	105	P	0.5	1	8	56	3	289	5.20	22	4%	95%	3%	2%
Gabon	109	P	0.2	1	5	33	1	100	3.00	5	127%	86%	10%	4%
Guinea-Bisseau	110	P	0.5	0	3	100	0	33	0.33	6	0%	93%	2%	5%
Ivory Coast	111	C	0.5	2	3	100	2	420	4.20	8	59%	86%	7%	6%
Mali	114	-	0.1	0	3	17	0	27	1.60	10	99%	96%	3%	1%
Liberia	116	P	0.4	0	5	80	2	400	5.00	18	229%	96%	2%	2%
Rwanda	117	-	0.0	0	0	0	0	0	0.00	6	23%	97%	3%	0%
Guinea	118	P	0.6	0	12	50	3	208	4.17	12	20%	88%	7%	5%
Niger	119	-	0.0	0	0	0	0	0	0.00	5	118%	98%	2%	0%
Congo	120	P	0.2	0	7	29	1	129	4.50	9	0%	92%	6%	2%
Sierra Leone	121	P	0.1	0	4	25	1	125	5.00	4	27%	97%	1%	3%
Zambia	122	-	0.0	0	0	0	0	0	0.00	16	8%	88%	12%	0%
Botswana	125	-	0.0	0	0	0	0	0	0.00	3	0%	95%	5%	0%
Djibouti	126	P	0.0	0	3	7	0	33	5.00	5	79%	97%	2%	0%
Burundi	127	-	0.1	0	3	33	0	27	0.80	7	27%	98%	2%	2%
Mauretania	129	P	0.3	0	7	43	0	129	3.00	15	71%	97%	1%	2%
Upper Volta	130	-	0.0	0	0	0	0	0	0.00	4	0%	97%	3%	0%
Togo	133	P	0.1	0	2	50	0	100	2.00	5	2%	92%	6%	2%
Equatorial Guinea	134	P	0.1	0	2	50	0	100	2.00	2	0%	90%	3%	6%
Malawi	135	P	0.2	0	4	50	0	25	0.50	8	70%	96%	1%	3%
Benin	138	P	0.1	0	8	13	0	38	3.00	4	31%	95%	2%	2%
Lesotho	139	-	0.0	0	0	0	0	0	0.00	1	0%	100%	0%	0%
Central Afr. Rep.	140	-	0.0	0	0	0	0	0	0.00	4	65%	92%	8%	0%
Swaziland	141	-	0.0	0	0	0	0	0	0.00	2	100%	100%	0%	0%
Cape Verde Is.	144	P	0.1	0	5	16	1	120	7.50	1	1%	90%	3%	7%
Comoro Is.	147	P	0.1	0	1	50	1	50	20.00	1	5%	95%	5%	5%
Seychelle Is	146	P	0.1	0	4	50	2	400	8.00	2	100%	85%	5%	0%
Sao Tome & Princ.	149	P	0.2	0	0	0	0	0	0.00	1	400%	100%	0%	10%

NATIONS OF THE WORLD: AFRICAN NATIONS

Averages & Totals		2.9	2.8	2.3	1.7	1.8	3.1
Country	Rnk	Force Multipliers					
		Ldrs	Eqp	Exp	Spt	Mob	Trad
African Nations							
South Africa	26	7	6	7	4	6	7
Ethiopia	35	4	1	4	1	1	3
Nigeria	36	4	3	6	1	2	5
Angola	60	3	1	5	1	0	2
Zimbabwe	71	3	1	4	1	1	3
Tanzania	77	3	1	3	0	0	2
Somalia	80	2	1	2	0	1	1
Kenya	83	3	3	2	1	1	3
Senegambia	91	3	2	2	1	0	3
Ghana	94	2	1	2	1	0	3
Mozambique	95	1	1	3	0	1	1
Uganda	97	2	1	4	0	0	0
Chad	101	2	2	5	0	1	2
Zaire	102	1	1	1	1	0	0
Cameroon	104	3	1	0	0	0	2
Madagascar	105	1	1	0	0	0	2
Gabon	109	3	4	0	1	0	2
Guinea-Bisseau	110	1	1	4	0	0	2
Ivory Coast	111	1	3	0	1	0	2
Mali	114	1	1	0	1	0	3
Liberia	116	1	3	0	1	0	0
Rwanda	117	1	1	1	0	0	2
Guinea	118	1	1	1	0	0	0
Niger	119	2	2	0	0	0	2
Congo	120	1	2	0	0	0	0
Sierra Leone	121	1	1	0	0	0	4
Zambia	122	1	1	0	0	0	0
Botswana	125	1	2	1	1	0	0
Djibouti	126	1	1	1	0	0	2
Burundi	127	1	1	0	0	0	1
Mauretania	129	1	1	0	0	0	0
Upper Volta	130	1	1	1	0	0	0
Togo	133	1	1	0	0	0	0
Equatorial Guinea	134	1	1	0	0	0	2
Malawi	135	1	1	0	0	0	0
Benin	138	1	1	0	0	0	0
Lesotho	139	1	1	0	0	0	2
Central Afr. Rep.	140	1	1	0	0	0	0
Swaziland	141	1	1	0	0	0	1
Cape Verde Is.	144	1	1	0	0	0	0
Comoro Is.	147	1	1	0	0	0	0
Seychelle Is	146	1	1	0	0	0	0
Sao Tome & Princ.	149	1	1	0	0	0	0

Averages & Totals—Shown for each column as appropriate. They give you a sense of proportion for all values for each nation.

Country—An independent nation. In addition, the top left of the chart shows summaries by political alignment.

Western Bloc—All nations with a 7, 8, or 9 in the Allies column.
Eastern Bloc—All nations with a 1, 2, or 3 in the Allies column.

Neutrals—All nations with a 4, 5, or 6 in the Allies column.
NATO—All members
NATO (w/o US)—NATO nations without North American members (United States and Canada).
Warsaw Pact—All members
Russia—All by itself, for comparison purposes.
On Russian Border—All hostile nations on the Russian border. By Russian reckoning, this includes everyone except those nations with Russian armed forces present, namely the East European countries, Mongolia, and North Korea. Note that despite Russia's superior combat power, it is still outnumbered by its immediate neighbors. This is the basis of Russia's seemingly paranoid and aggressive stance toward the rest of the world. But wait, it gets worse.
Russian Enemies—To the neighbors add those traditional enemies that border the European satellites (particularly West Germany). At this point Russia is outnumbered three to one. And this does not consider the United States or many other Western nations.
United States—Included for comparison purposes only. The United States has no significant local enemies and is protected by two rather large oceans and the world's largest, and probably most effective, fleet.
Pacific Allies—A quarter of United States strength plus United States allies in the western Pacific. This demonstrates the basis for the hostile Chinese and Russian attitudes in this part of the world. Russia deploys about 30 percent of its combat strength here. Most of it is facing Chinese ground forces.
Rnk—Rank of each nation according to whatever criterion was being applied for that profile.
Percentage Analysis—Below the summaries for blocs and regions there is a Percentage Analysis. This shows each item's percentage of the world total or difference from the world average, whichever is appropriate. This analysis quickly summarizes the differences among the world's regions and armed groups.

National Summary

Allies—Indicates the nation's political and diplomatic orientation. A 1 shows Eastern (Russian) leanings, while a 9 indicates Western (pro-United States) leanings. A 5 would be as neutral as one could get. This is a simplistic way to tackle the subject of alliances. The alternative is to consider the thicket of local likes and dislikes, which often cause nations to switch sides rather rapidly. An obvious example is the Middle East, where Israel and many Arab states are United States allies. Although Israel and many Arab nations do not get along, their mutual alliance with the United States does lessen the potential for violence.

Gov Stab—Government Stability (1–9), an indication of the ability of the government to act without fear of being overthrown. A 9 shows great stability; a 1 is a very shaky regime.

War State—Shows the current state of involvement in war. A 1 indicates relative peace. A 2 or a 3 indicates low levels of terrorism or armed resistance. Values of 4 through 6 indicate involvement of that nation's forces is organized conflict. A 7 through 9 indicates a major war.

War Pwr—War Power, our rating of a nation's overall war-making power at the present time. The two primary components of this value are active military manpower (that which can be mobilized within 24 hours) and the Total Quality-per-man value (see below). The War Power values do not pretend to be a foolproof prediction of whose armed forces are going to prevail in a war. The system we used to derive these values consisted of compiling a great many real (more or less, given military security) data on military forces. We made judgments based on historical experience for the less tangible values (military experience and the like), then applied the same formula to all nations. Using these results, we sorted all nations and kept tinkering with the simple formula until the results made sense with historical experience and current perceptions. Use these values with caution.

Atck Pwr—Attack (Offensive) Power, a variation on the War Power shown above. It gives you an idea of how much combat power a nation can bring to bear beyond its own borders. This value is often substantially less than the country's War Power, which essentially measures defensive capability. Attack Power requires more depth in logistical and technical support.

Long War—The ability to sustain a long war. After the first few months to a year, many nations rapidly run out of war-making resources. This value includes reserves as well as the country's ability to provide long-term industrial, logistical, and technical support.

Tot Qual—Total Quality, the value for the per-man combat ability of the nation. It is derived from several Force Multipliers. These multipliers, found toward the end of the chart, include human factors such as military tradition, practical experience, and general efficiency. The most critical factor, however, is military leadership. Strangely enough, this is one subject many nations talk a lot about but do little. It's hardly a dirty little secret that military leadership in most armies is deplorable. Why this is so could fill another book. The most concise explanation is that the military is generally an unattractive career choice. You hardly ever actually do what you are trained for, and thus there is generally no reliable way to determine who is doing his job well, much less who will perform adequately once the shooting starts. Some nations manage to develop superior military leadership, which is demonstrated whenever they are involved in a war. In peacetime that superior leadership continues. This column in the chart shows where we feel each nation stands in regard to military leadership and overall military efficiency.

Nukes—The nation's capability of manufacturing nuclear weapons. An 8 indicates manufacture and possession, a 9 means full deployment. A 7 shows the ability to manufacture (if not already being done in secret). Numbers 1 through 6 indicate varying potentials to make nuclear weapons.

% Off—Percentage Offensive Capability, the degree of War Power that can be used outside the nation's borders. In most cases this measures the ability to attack a neighbor. The superpower nations (with large fleets and a considerable portion of their GDP devoted to foreign trade) can project their military power many thousands of miles from their home countries.

Geographic Profile

Area (1,000s KmSq)—Surface area in thousands of square kilometers.

Agr—Agricultural, percentage of area devoted to agriculture.

Grz—Grazing, percentage of area devoted to livestock.

For—Forested, percentage of area covered by forest or jungle.

Othr—Percentage of area consisting of mountains, swamps, deserts, inland waters, and cities.

Trans Net—Transportation Net, efficiency of internal transportation system on a scale of 0, none, to 9, highly developed rail, highway, and river systems.

MEI—Military Environment Index, suitability of the country for military operations, on a scale of 0, highly unfavorable, to 9, highly favorable—essentially an analysis of the country's terrain. A combination of country size, terrain, climate patterns, border length, and location, plus the accessibility of vital civil, economic, and military resources to conventional external attack.

Population Profile

Pop SqKm—Population density per square kilometer.

Pop Tot—Population total, in millions.

% Lit—Percentage literate, indicates portion of the population technically able to read and write (often means merely the ability to sign one's name).

% Urban—Percentage of the population living in cities and towns.
Economic Profile

Ind—Industrialization Index, shows the degree of mechanization and flexibility in the production of goods and services on a scale of 0, no industrial capability, to 9, a highly developed and flexible industrial plant.

GDP—Gross Domestic Product, in billions of dollars for the most recent year available. GDP is the total value of goods and services produced for internal consumption, or how much wealth the nation produces in a year.

% Frgn Trade—Percentage of GDP is Foreign Trade, represents total value of goods and services exported, expressed as a percentage of the GDP. This indicates how self-sufficient a nation is and how vulnerable it would be to a blockade or unfriendly naval activity.

% Soc Exp—Percentage of GDP spent for social welfare (education and medical care). Expressed as a percentage of the GDP to indicate a nation's priorities (compare with percentage of GDP spent on defense).

Per Cap—Per-Capita GDP, value in thousands of dollars. This

value is a common measure of individual well-being from nation to nation.

Qual Life—Quality of Life, an indication of relative standard of living on a scale of 1, virtual subsistence level, to 9, that of the United States or better. (For some, a matter of taste, but considering the number of people trying to get into the United States, a reasonable measure of living standard.)

Military Capability

Act Men—Active Manpower, number of men and women on active service in the armed forces, expressed in thousands. Exceptions have been made in the case of Israel, Sweden, and Switzerland, which can raise a considerable number of effective troops within 24 hours; in these cases, shown are the number of troops available after 24 hours of mobilization.

% Cadre—Percentage of active personnel who are volunteers as opposed to conscripts. A good indicator of the force's professionalism, although in highly literate industrialized nations, conscripts are equal, if not often superior, to regulars

Mil Bud—Military Budget, annual expenditures on defense in millions of dollars. Expressing this value is a tricky business, as few nations agree on what is a defense expenditure and what is not. Most nations underestimate these expenses by not including certain overhead costs, such as transportation expenses on the nationalized railroads or use of government facilities. The Chinese go so far as officially to omit pay and maintenance for the troops. In most cases we have made some adjustments to make these numbers meaningful.

% GDP—Defense expenditures as a percentage of the GDP. Compare this figure with % Soc Exp above for an indication of the country's priorities.

Bud Man—Budget per Man, defense expenditures per person on active duty. It indicates how much the nation depends on people, or machines, to do their fighting. You can have a very effective "low-tech" armed force, as each additional dollar spent on the more expensive weapons provides a lesser amount of increased effectiveness.

Bang per $—Bang per Dollar, the nation's War Power value (times 1,000) divided by its annual defense expenditures (in millions of dollars). In other words, it means the "Bang per Buck" in terms of how much each unit of combat value costs. It is readily apparent that the cost of military power increases enormously as a nation approaches superpower status. This is partly a result of inefficient peacetime military establishments and partly created by the additional costs a super-power has to bear for nuclear weapons, space programs, worldwide communications, and intercontinental air- and sealifts. Added to these expenses are the costs of supporting one's allies. These items are often hidden in defense budgets by selling arms and equipment to real or prospective allies at artificially low prices.

Bang M/Pop—Shows how much Attack Power is produced per million population. This is a more reliable guide to a nation's warmaking efficiency. Money is important, but often not as important as the people.

Bang T$/GDP—Shows how much Attack Power is produced per trillion dollars of GDP. Money does not always buy security.

Reserves

Men—Reserve forces available in thousands. In many cases a nation declares that all who have served in the military (or everyone in general) are reserves until a certain age. In the latter cases we have counted only those who have left the service within five years.

p/mil—Reservists in thousands per million population. An indicator of how heavily the population is armed and trained for war.

% Act—Percentage of reservists receiving regular refresher training, an important indicator of the quality of reserves. Regular training often brings these troops up to the same effectiveness level as the regulars.

Paramilitary Profile

Tot—Paramilitary forces available in thousands, includes barracks police, part-time militia, coast guards, and volunteer defense workers. This last category can be quite large, and even if they are lightly armed this does not eliminate their effectiveness in the long run as guerrillas, etc.

p/mil—Paramilitary forces in thousands-per-million population, another indicator of how heavily militarized the population is. In many nations this shows how much force is required to keep the peace or maintain the government's power.

% Pop Srv—Total percentage of population on active duty, in reserves or in paramilitary forces. This number varies considerably from nation to nation, and again shows how militarized a country really is.

Ult Men—Ultimate Manpower that is militarily useful, available in thousands, which should be nearly doubled if women are utilized.

Army Profile

Mbl Men—Total ground combat force personnel upon mobilization, including air and naval forces, marines, and air defense.

Eqtd Div—Number of divisions available, assuming organized forces are grouped according to standard tables of organization. The division is the standard ground combat unit.

Men Div—Average manpower per division, including noncombat personnel for supply, maintenance, and so forth. Ideas on how divisions should be manned and organized differ within nations; this value demonstrates the differences. Larger divisions usually indicate more reliance on technology (more technicians are needed).

AFV—Armored Fighting Vehicles, total number of tanks, infantry combat vehicles, scout cars, armored assault guns, and amphibious assault vehicles. It is a good indicator of how well equipped a nation is for land warfare.

Men/AFV—Manpower available per AFV, shows how mechanized the land forces are.

Air Forces Profile

Mbl Men—Mobilized Manpower, total personnel available to support air operations, including air force or ground and naval forces.

Cmbt A/C—Combat aircraft, total number of combat-capable airplanes and helicopters.

Other A/C—Total number of noncombatant (training and transportation) airplanes and helicopters. Note that many could be modified for limited combat roles.

Men/A/C—Average number of personnel available per aircraft. Aircraft must be supported, and skilled people provide the support. Between 30 and 60 is a reasonable number. There are vast differences among air forces, particularly in quality (check Israel and Bulgaria).

Navy Profile

Type—Mission capability (what the navy's job is): P = maritime police force; C = coast-defense navy; L = local combat force (no more than 500-mile radius); R = regional combat capacity (1,500-mile radius); S = strategic capability (global range).

Mbl Men—Mobilized Manpower, total personnel available to support naval operations.

Cmbt Ships—Major warships of 1,000 standard-displacement tons or greater, plus submarines and smaller vessels equipped with antiship missiles

Other Ships—All other (smaller) warships, plus amphibious vessels, logistical support ships, and seagoing naval auxiliaries.

Men/Ship—Average number of personnel available per ship. This includes the crew and support personnel ashore.

Tons—Total tonnage of combatant and other ships in thousands of standard displacement tons, a more accurate indicator of a navy's size than number of ships. The more technically complex ships are larger and heavier.

Tons/Ship—Average displacement tonnage per ship, the higher this figure, the greater the seakeeping capacity of the average ship in the fleet.

Men/Ship/T—Average ship tonnage per man, indicates how much is invested in hardware per sailor; in other words, how heavily equipped the navy is.

Manpower Distribution

Mbl Men—Net Mobilized Manpower, total organized personnel who can be mobilized into the armed forces.

% Incr—The percentage increase of mobilized manpower over normal peacetime active manpower.

% Army—Percentage of mobilized forces in the army.

% AF—Percentage of mobilized manpower in the air forces.

% Navy—Percentage of mobilized forces in the navy.

Force Multipliers—Factors modifying raw data to produce the Total Quality on a scale of 0, none, to 9, excellent.

Ldrs—Leadership, officers and noncommissioned officers (sergeants and so forth, indicates quantity, quality, and training. Overall effectiveness of leadership from the lowest level to the highest.

Eqp—Equipment, quality and quantity of equipment available per man.

Exp—Experience, quality of recent military experience; a 5 indicates sound, lengthy peacetime operations only. A politically active military is rated lower. An armed force with recent combat experience is rated higher.

Spt—Support, quality of logistical apparatus, maintenance capacity, and general ability to sustain combat operations. Includes civilian resources also.

Mob—Mobilization Index, ability to expand forces rapidly beyond Mobilized Manpower. This rating depends upon the unused portion of the country's Ultimate Manpower, the availability of equipment, and what technical and managerial skills are available in the population. Thus a high Industrialization Index would yield a higher Mobilization Index, as would a large population, even if it is only poorly armed.

Trad—Tradition, quality of psychological factors such as culture, military history, and tradition, a vital and often underrated factor in combat performance.

USING THE "NATIONS OF THE WORLD" CHART

To demonstrate how useful all these data can be, let's walk through the information on three countries, Russia, West Germany, and Israel. All three are among the top ten military powers in the world for quite different reasons. Russia is simply huge in all respects. Germany has more conventional strengths; it does well with what it's got. Israel is unusual. Small and surrounded by many enemies, Israel is also highly educated and industrial in a region where these are not common. This combination has produced one of the most efficient, powerful armed forces in the world. Moreover, Israel maintains this force with part-time soldiers. These troops take advantage of the small size of their country; when the alarm goes off, they simply run down the road and join their units.

Complete explanations of each column in the chart are found on pages 000–000. Here we will highlight the relationships of the various bits of data and what they say about the nations.

The **Averages & Totals** line invites comparisons with the world averages and totals for each item.

Country	Rnk	War State	Allies	National Summary Gov Stab	War Pwr	Atck Pwr	Long War	Tot Qual	Nukes	% Off
Averages & Totals		1.7	5.9	5.8	6,083	3,255	7,337	6.8	2.4	23%
Russia	1	4	1	7	1000	800	699	26	9	80%
Germany, West	5	1	9	9	285	200	466	58	6	70%
Israel	6	4	8	9	235	165	154	48	7	70%

The nations are ranked (**Rnk**) according to war power (**War Pwr**). **War State** indicates the degree of the nation's current participation in active warfare. A 1 is the peaceful end of the scale; a 9 is nuclear war. In terms of **Allies** (political alignment), Russia is at one end of the spectrum with a 1; West Germany and Israel are at the other end, aligning themselves with the Western powers. **War Pwr**, the general combat power of the peacetime forces, is derived from multiplying active manpower (**Act Men**) and total quality (**Tot Qual**) and dividing by 100. Active manpower is a statistic we often see; total quality is rarely mentioned, as it reflects **Force Multipliers**, which most nations are not anxious to examine too closely. These values are covered in more detail at the end of the chart.

Atck Pwr combines **War Pwr** and **% Off** (the percentage of the nation's war power that can be sent across its borders). **Long War** capability adds in the effects of the reserves and the ability to provide logistical and mobilization support for a long war. Despite Russia's substantial military advantage, the prospects of Russia taking on either Germany or Israel in a one-on-one war are remote. Russia's vast military superiority is misleading; it is inadequate to Russian defense requirements.

All these combat values are based on nonnuclear warfare. The **Nukes** value shows how well-armed a nation is with nuclear weapons. Russia has them, Israel may have them, and West Germany could have them if it wanted to. Using nuclear weapons would give Russia an absolute military advantage over any opponent not so armed. This is one reason many nations ally themselves with one of the two nuclear superpowers.

Russia's **Off %** is a high 90 percent. Russia holds that the best way to deal with a potential threat is to attack it. Ask the Afghans, among many others, about this.

Averages & Totals			132,278	21	16	27	33
Country		Geographic Profile					
	Rnk	Area 1000 KmSq	Agr	Grz	For	Othr	
Russia	1	22,401	10	17	35	38	
Germany, West	5	249	33	23	29	15	
Israel	6	20	20	40	4	36	

The **Geographic Profile** begins to demonstrate Russia's precarious military position. Its territory is vast, especially in comparison with its military forces. Germany's and Israel's troops are much more concentrated. Note that only 10 percent of Russia's territory is devoted to agriculture. Forest and waste cover much larger areas.

Russia's Transportation Net (**Trans Net**—roads, railways, waterways) is less developed than Germany's or Israel's. The number of

Country	Rnk Trans Net	MEI	Population Profile				Ind	Economic Profile				
			Pop SqKm	Pop Tot	% Lit	% Urban		GDP	% Frgn Trade	% Soc Exp	Per Cap	Qual Life
Averages & Totals	3.8	5.4	35	4,674	54	42	3.3	12,375	26	4.9	2.6	3.6
Russia	1	4	12	272	98	62	7	$1,450.0	4.6	6.9	$5.3	4
Germany, West	5	6	249	62	99	86	9	$659.2	26.8	7.0	$10.6	9
Israel	6	9	188	4	72	86	7	$20.6	27.2	8.1	$5.4	7

people living in built-up areas (% **Urban**) is lower for Russia because the country is spread out. This factor and the **MEI** (it is low, indicating a difficult nation to fight in) give Russia a defense advantage. They also make it difficult for Russia to concentrate its far-flung military forces. This vast nation contains numerous independent military forces.

Economically, Russia is much weaker than Germany and Israel, which accounts for the frequently poor performance of Russian weapons. They look great and there are many of them, but a relatively underdeveloped economy cannot produce consistently efficient and technically superior weapons.

Russian foreign trade (% **Frgn Trade**) as a percentage of GDP shows its self-sufficiency. It is a military advantage to be less vulnerable when trade is disrupted by war. Per-capita GDP (**Per Cap**) does not show the full extent of Russia's poverty. This can be seen more readily by looking at the portion of Russia's GDP that is devoted to military expenditures (% **GDP**).

		Military Capability							
Averages & Totals	28,636		68	757,734	6.1%	26	8.0	1.3	492
Country	Rnk	Act Men	% Cadre	Mil Bud	% GDP	Bud Man	Bang per $	Bang M/Pop.	Bang T$/GDP
Russia	1	3,800	22	$214,000	14.8%	$56	4.7	3.68	690
Germany, West	5	495	52	$18,934	2.9%	$38	15.1	4.60	433
Israel	6	488	30	$6,461	31.4%	$13	36.4	61.85	11,409

The percentage of active peacetime troops (**Act Men**) is high for the Russians, but the percentage of full-time soldiers (**Cadre**) is low. The Russian armed forces are not pleasant to be in. Most of the troops are draftees. Western nations, particularly those which, like Israel, live with an ever-present military threat, get more performance out of their draftees.

The budget expenditures per man (**Bud Man**) are quite high for Russia, as they usually are for superpowers. They reflect the high cost of strategic nuclear weapons and the inefficiencies of large armed forces. The Bang-per-Buck value (**Bang per $**) is a telling statistic. It shows how much combat power each nation gets for its annual defense expenditures. Larger armed forces tend to be less efficient. Israel is an exception, as it must be efficient or perish.

Averages & Totals		28,687	6.1	22	43,502	9.3	2.2%	779,530

Country		Reserves			Paramilitary Profile			
	Rnk			%			%Pop	Ult
		Men	p/mil	Act	Tot	p/mil	Srv	Men
Russia	1	3,800	14.0	5	5,600	20.6	4.9%	54,800
Germany, West	5	303	4.9	100	20	0.3	1.3%	13,750
Israel	6	9	2.4	29	100	26.3	15.7%	670

The **Paramilitary Profile** shows an element that most nations in the world, except the United States, must contend with. Large internal-security forces, particularly as they form part of the population (**p/mil**), advertise a need to maintain internal order. This is particularly true of Russia. The percentage of the population in the armed forces (% **Pop Serv**) also indicates the degree to which the nation is militarized. This value is high partly as a result of fear, partly because sufficient wealth is there to support it.

	47,146	1,681	28.0	360,972	131

Army Profile				
Mbl	Eqtd	Men		Men/
Men	Divs	Div	AFV	AFV
5,700	220	25.9	115,000	50
540	18	30.0	11,890	45
450	18	24.6	11,600	39

The **Army Profile** shows the composition of the ground forces. Mobilized men (**Mbl Men**) indicates how many will be under arms when the under-strength peacetime divisions (**Eqtd Divs**) are brought up to strength by adding former soldiers (who usually are in the reserves). The number of men per AFV (armored fighting vehicle) shows how well equipped the ground forces are. Industrial nations tend to go more for equipment than simply masses of troops.

The **Air Force** and **Navy** profiles work the same way, although they place emphasis on aircraft and ships.

The most critical value in the navy is not the number of combat ships (**Cmbt Ships**), but total tonnage of ships. The tons of ship per man (**Men/Shp/T**) value shows the navy's efficiency, how well the sailors handle their ships.

Averages & Totals		5,782	46,848	39,835	67		3,387	3,256	6,493	347	18,125	1,859	5.35
Country		Air Force Profile				Navy Profile							
	Rnk	Mbl Men	Cmbt A/C	Other A/C	Men/ A/C	Type	Mbl Men	Cmbt Ships	Other Ships	Men/ Ship	Tons	Tons/ Ship	Men/ Shp/T
Russia	1	1,100	11,500	3,500	73	S	800.0	845	940	448	845	474	1.06
Germany, West	5	200	1,127	441	128	R	58.4	81	118	293	247	1,243	4.24
Israel	6	37	675	365	36	L	10.0	28	75	97	21	203	2.09

Averages & Totals		57,323	200%	82%	10%	6%
Country		Manpower Distribution				
	Rnk	Mbl Men	% Incr	% Army	% AF	% Navy
Russia	1	7,600	100%	75%	14%	11%
Germany, West	5	798	61%	68%	25%	7%
Israel	6	497	2%	91%	7%	2%

The **Manpower Distribution** indicates total mobilized manpower (**Mbl Men**) and the increase of this mobilized number over peacetime strength. A high percentage indicates that the armed forces will go to war with a lot of civilians who were once in the military but no longer consider themselves professional warriors. The only way around this problem is to keep reserves in training. Russia, along with many less than affluent nations, is unwilling to accept this expense and thus has a lot of problems when untrained reserves are put back into uniform. Israel has the most active and extensive training program for its reserves.

The percentage distribution shows a nation's military priorities. In Russia the emphasis is on paramilitary forces to control its own and the newly conquered peoples. Russia also uses extensive paramilitary force to keep its own troops in line.

Averages & Totals		2.9	2.8	2.3	1.7	1.8	3.1
Country		Force Multipliers					
	Rnk	Ldrs	Eqp	Exp	Spt	Mob	Trad
Russia	1	4	6	4	6	9	7
Germany, West	5	8	8	3	8	8	9
Israel	6	9	8	9	2	1	8

The **Force Multipliers** are the key to understanding true combat power. The quality of leadership (**Ldrs**) is most important. This value applies to leaders ranging from tank commander to heads of divisions and ships and beyond. Equipment (**Eqp**), experience (**Exp**), material support (**Spt**), mobilization capability (**Mob**), and military tradition (**Trad**) are important but less so.

TOP 15 MILITARY SPENDERS

Ranked by Total Military Spending

Shows how throwing a lot of money at peacetime soldiers does not usually have the desired effect.

RANK BY MILITARY BUDGET

Country	Rnk	Mil Bud	% GDP	Bud Man	Bang per $	Bang M/Pop.
Averages & Totals		757,734	6.1%	26	8.0	1.3
United States	1	$255,000	7.5%	$119	3.2	3.51
Russia	2	$214,000	14.8%	$56	4.7	3.68
Britain	3	$25,168	5.3%	$79	6.5	2.93
China	4	$22,800	6.3%	$6	28.0	0.60
Saudi Arabia	5	$21,952	14.4%	$287	0.4	0.92
France	6	$21,381	4.0%	$43	9.7	3.83
Germany, West	7	$18,934	2.9%	$38	15.1	4.60
Iran	8	$15,000	14.7%	$18	12.2	4.36
Japan	9	$10,360	1.0%	$43	8.7	0.75
Italy	10	$9,788	2.8%	$26	8.1	1.41
Iraq	11	$7,722	21.7%	$16	15.2	9.00
Germany, East	12	$7,700	7.7%	$46	7.0	3.18
Israel	13	$6,461	31.4%	$13	36.4	61.85
Canada	14	$6,430	2.2%	$78	4.3	1.11
Poland	15	$6,254	5.2%	$18	10.9	1.84

TOP 15 SPENDERS AS PERCENTAGE OF GDP

Ranked According to Percentage of GDP Spent on Defense

Spending over 10 percent of the GDP on nonproductive defense items has a long-lasting debilitating effect on the economy.

RANK BY PERCENTAGE OF GDP SPENT ON DEFENSE

Country	Rnk	Qual Life	Military Capability Act Men	% Cadre	Mil Bud	% GDP	Bud Man
Averages & Totals		3.6	28,636	68	757,734	6.1%	26
Israel	1	7	488	30	$6,461	31.4%	$13
United Arab Emir.	2	7	49	100	$2,915	30.4%	$59
Angola	3	1	88	20	$1,000	30.3%	$11
Syria	4	2	330	37	$2,548	28.6%	$8
Oman	5	4	24	100	$1,772	28.6%	$75
Iraq	6	3	480	15	$7,722	21.7%	$16
Mongolia	7	3	25	20	$244	20.3%	$10
Vietnam	8	2	900	10	$2,200	20.0%	$2
Yemen, North	9	1	22	60	$527	18.8%	$24
Jordan	10	3	73	90	$465	17.9%	$6
Lebanon	11	3	35	20	$576	16.5%	$16
Yemen, South	12	1	26	30	$159	15.9%	$6
Russia	13	4	3,800	22	$214,000	14.8%	$56
Iran	14	3	850	7	$15,000	14.7%	$18
Saudi Arabia	15	6	77	100	$21,952	14.4%	$287

TOP 15 IN PERCENTAGE OF POPULATION ARMED

Ranked According to Percentage of Population Under Arms

You don't have to be wealthy to be armed.

RANK BY PERCENTAGE OF POPULATION ARMED

Averages & Totals		28,687	6.1	22	43,502	9.3	2.2%	779,530
Country		Reserves			Paramilitary		Profile	
	Rnk			%			%Pop	Ult
		Men	p/mil	Act	Tot	p/mil	Srv	Men
Yugoslavia	1	2,555	111.1	100	4,000	173.9	29.5%	4,800
Korea, South	2	1,558	38.0	10	9,520	232.2	28.5%	7,700
Switzerland	3	0	0.0	0	500	76.9	25.0%	1,450
Qatar	4	20	100.0	0	20	100.0	23.0%	60
Sweden	5	0	0.0	0	500	60.2	21.3%	1,800
Israel	6	9	2.4	29	100	26.3	15.7%	670
Korea, North	7	369	19.4	0	1,800	94.7	15.5%	2,700
Taiwan	8	1,668	92.7	50	25	1.4	12.0%	3,900
Singapore	9	181	72.2	100	40	16.0	11.0%	580
Norway	10	242	59.0	40	152	37.2	10.7%	800
Cuba	11	188	18.8	100	720	72.0	10.6%	1,700
Cyprus (Turkish)	12	16	77.5	36	0	0.0	10.0%	40
Romania	13	389	16.9	5	1,587	69.0	9.4%	4,600
Angola	14	10	1.5	0	510	78.5	9.4%	850
Iraq	15	275	21.2	100	450	34.6	9.3%	1,900

TOP 15 IN QUALITY OF MILITARY FORCES

Ranked According to Overall Quality of Forces

These are the nations which for one reason or another have superior force quality.

RANK BY QUALITY OF ARMED FORCES

Averages & Totals		5.8	6,083	3,255	7,337	6.8	2.4	23%
Country	Rnk	Gov Stab	War Pwr	Atck Pwr	Long War	Tot Qual	Nukes	% Off
Germany, West	1	9	285	200	466	58	6	70%
Britain	2	9	164	131	220	51	9	80%
Israel	3	9	235	165	154	48	7	70%
France	4	9	207	124	294	42	9	60%
South Africa	5	8	35	16	86	42	6	45%
United States	6	9	820	656	724	38	9	80%
Japan	7	9	90	36	186	37	6	40%
Canada	8	9	28	14	75	34	5	50%
Germany, East	9	8	54	24	94	32	4	45%
Finland	10	9	13	2	40	32	4	15%
Australia	11	9	23	16	81	31	4	70%
India	12	6	301	90	200	27	8	30%
Russia	13	7	1000	800	699	26	9	80%
Iraq	14	5	117	59	119	24	4	50%
New Zealand	15	9	3	2	23	24	3	70%

TOP 15 IN WARMAKING POWER

Ranked According to Overall War-Making Power

RANK BY WARMAKING POWER

Averages & Totals		6,083	3,255	7,337	6.8	2.4	23%	132,278
Country								Geographic Pr
	Rnk	War Pwr	Atck Pwr	Long War	Tot Qual	Nukes	% Off	Area 1000 KmSq
Russia	1	1000	800	699	26	9	80%	22,401
United States	2	820	656	724	38	9	80%	9,363
China	3	638	191	300	16	9	30%	9,597
India	4	301	90	200	27	8	30%	3,288
Germany, West	5	285	200	466	58	6	70%	249
Israel	6	235	165	154	48	7	70%	20
France	7	207	124	294	42	9	60%	547
Sweden	8	192	38	155	15	5	20%	450
Vietnam	9	186	93	139	21	3	50%	333
Iran	10	183	73	137	22	4	40%	1,647
Britain	11	164	131	220	51	9	80%	244
Switzerland	12	153	31	125	14	5	20%	41
Korea, South	13	137	82	194	22	5	60%	99
Iraq	14	117	59	119	24	4	50%	432
Korea, North	15	115	52	111	15	3	45%	121

Data and Sources

Analysts have to be better than their data. The authors and their researcher, Al Nofi, found five different 1981 GDPs for Zaire. That's all right—Zaire probably doesn't know what its 1981 GDP was. We used an averaged figure. In December 1983 we found published aggregate foreign-debt estimates for the Philippines that ranged from $17 billion to over $25 billion. That's a difference of more than 40 percent. The figures are suspect, but both indicate that the Philippines has a severe debt problem.

Many of the numbers have gone through the wash and come out scrubbed. They are not, however, squeaky clean. They are colored by the authors' interpretation. We have no doubt made some mistakes in interpretation, but the intent was always to try to penetrate the statistics. Governments, especially dictatorships, purposely lie to their people and the world. That is part of their survival strategy. Even governments in open societies regularly mislead their people. This is called politics or public relations.

Our sources of information are many. There are the obvious ones: *International Defense Review, Janes Defence Weekly, Aviation Week & Space Technology, International Security, Time* magazine, *U.S. News and World Report, The New York Times, The Washington Post, The Wall Street Journal, The Christian Science Monitor, The Economist, Oil and Gas Journal, Le Monde, Die Zeit, Stern,* and a half dozen others.

Some sources are not so obvious: *Focus, The Jerusalem Post, The Week in Germany,* and many other newsletters or international reports. We did not use a scrap of classified evidence or data, though no doubt censors would scream if they found out what a good library can provide. We have also used information provided by Afghan resistance groups, transcripts from *The MacNeil/Lehrer Report,* sources provided by dissidents, propaganda provided by governments. We made use of the U.S. State Department's *Background Notes* series, *Facts on File,* and *Fiche du Monde Arabe.*

Strategy and Tactics magazine, which Jim Dunnigan used to edit, has been a valuable resource, especially for the chapters covering the Middle East and Central America. Our South African chapter relied on Brad Hessel's article which appeared in *S & T*'s June 1977 issue. The Afghanistan chapter was taken in large part from a 1980 research paper by Austin Bay. As noted, our invasion timetable drew heavily on Anthony Arnold's *Afghanistan: The Soviet Invasion in Perspective.*

The real sources of this book lie in what we'll call "deep background." Machiavelli's *The Prince* and Von Clausewitz's *On War* are vital to any adequate understanding of power politics. Both theorists have aged well. Their books are utilized by today's power politicians.

Other useful references include Hyams's *Soil and Civilization,* Tuchman's *A Distant Mirror,* Newbigin's *Geographical Aspects of Balkan Problems* (a work of genius and apparently out of print since 1915), Liddell Hart's *Strategy,* Thucydides's *The Peloponnesian War,* Fuller's *The Foundations of the Science of War,* White's *Metahistory,* Chomsky's *Language and Responsibility,* Said's *Orientalism,* and Fall's *Street Without Joy.* An elemental work was Orwell's *Homage to Catalonia,* the story of the sellout of the Spanish workers' revolution.

Index

Note: This is a nontraditional index. You will find here not only names and places, but also key phrases and buzz words that play an important role in this book and in the rhetoric of international politics and the vocabulary of grand strategy and tactics.

In most cases, page references are to the start of a discussion of the topic of some length, sometimes of many pages, not to a peripheral mention of the name, place, word, or subject.